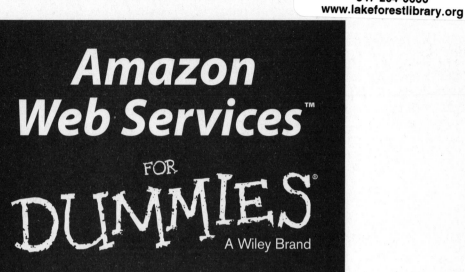

Amazon Web Services™

FOR DUMMIES®

A Wiley Brand

by Bernard Golden

FOR DUMMIES®

A Wiley Brand

Amazon Web Services™ For Dummies®

Published by: **John Wiley & Sons, Inc.,** 111 River Street, Hoboken, NJ 07030-5774, www.wiley.com

Copyright © 2013 by John Wiley & Sons, Inc., Hoboken, New Jersey

Published simultaneously in Canada

No part of this publication may be reproduced, stored in a retrieval system or transmitted in any form or by any means, electronic, mechanical, photocopying, recording, scanning or otherwise, except as permitted under Sections 107 or 108 of the 1976 United States Copyright Act, without the prior written permission of the Publisher. Requests to the Publisher for permission should be addressed to the Permissions Department, John Wiley & Sons, Inc., 111 River Street, Hoboken, NJ 07030, (201) 748-6011, fax (201) 748-6008, or online at http://www.wiley.com/go/permissions.

Trademarks: Wiley, For Dummies, the Dummies Man logo, Dummies.com, Making Everything Easier, and related trade dress are trademarks or registered trademarks of John Wiley & Sons, Inc. and may not be used without written permission. Amazon Web Services is a trademark of Amazon Technologies, Inc. All other trademarks are the property of their respective owners. John Wiley & Sons, Inc. is not associated with any product or vendor mentioned in this book.

For general information on our other products and services, please contact our Customer Care Department within the U.S. at 877-762-2974, outside the U.S. at 317-572-3993, or fax 317-572-4002. For technical support, please visit www.wiley.com/techsupport.

Wiley publishes in a variety of print and electronic formats and by print-on-demand. Some material included with standard print versions of this book may not be included in e-books or in print-on-demand. If this book refers to media such as a CD or DVD that is not included in the version you purchased, you may download this material at http://booksupport.wiley.com. For more information about Wiley products, visit www.wiley.com.

Library of Congress Control Number: 2013942773

ISBN 978-1-118-57183-5 (pbk); ISBN 978-1-118-65198-8 (ebk); ISBN 978-1-118-65226-8 (ebk)

Manufactured in the United States of America

10 9 8 7 6 5 4 3 2 1

Praise for Amazon Web Services For Dummies

This is a great resource for anyone considering the jump into cloud computing. Golden accurately explores the roster of AWS services while clearly illustrating ways for developers to make applications easier to build and manage. He manages to address both business requirements and technical content in a way that will appeal to almost any audience.

> — Jeff Barr, Sr. Technology Evangelist,
> Amazon Web Services

One of the challenges Bitnami users face is understanding the breadth and power of AWS. *Amazon Web Services For Dummies* helps our users build a great foundation of AWS skills. Anyone who is new to AWS and wants to be successful should start with this book.

> — Erica Brescia, COO and co-founder of Bitnami

Netflix is all-in on AWS. We believe it is the richest, most scalable, most innovative cloud platform in the industry. Building AWS skills is critical for careers today — and *Amazon Web Services For Dummies* is the best resource I know of to learn AWS from the ground up. Buy this book to learn what your future will look like.

> — Adrian Cockcroft, Netflix Cloud Architect

Contents at a Glance

Table of Contents

Introduction

● ●

*T*his book is designed with one purpose in mind: to make it easy for you, the reader, to understand and begin using Amazon Web Services (AWS) — an emerging technology platform that is profoundly disrupting the technology industry and enabling hundreds of thousands of individuals, businesses, and nonprofit organizations to gain easy access to on-demand computing resources.

About This Book

In a sense, this book is an extension of my earlier book *Virtualization For Dummies* (Wiley Publishing), which has a chapter describing "The Future of Virtualization." In my research to identify which direction virtualization would take, I came across Amazon Web Services, a then-new offering was referred to by Amazon employees as *Infrastructure as a Service.* To indicate how briefly this new type of computing has been available, the term *cloud computing* was still more than a year away when *Virtualization For Dummies* was published.

As I spoke to Amazon representatives about the company's new offering, I experienced the same reaction I had when first exposed to open source software — a visceral response that made me ask out loud: "If this service is available to users, who will stick with the old way of doing things?"

Nothing in the subsequent years has changed my mind — in fact, that experience strengthens my conviction that cloud computing in general, and Amazon Web Services in particular, will transform the way applications are designed and built. I've worked with people from many companies who have resigned themselves to the length of the usual IT resource provisioning process — taking six weeks or more to obtain a virtual machine. When I demonstrate the ability of AWS to provision an instance (Amazon's term for a virtual machine) in ten minutes or less, these people regard what they're seeing with disbelief, staggered that the conventional (lengthy) provisioning process isn't somehow set in stone.

Amazon continues to challenge the incumbent community of technology vendors, releasing new services and cutting prices at an unrelenting pace.

I fully expect that a decade from now, AWS will be one of the top two or three global technology vendors, and that a number of today's giants will be gone, driven out of business, or into forced mergers by their inability to compete on Amazon's terms.

But (there's always a *but,* isn't there?) how to get started is a challenge that many people face when they consider using AWS. AWS documentation is quite thorough, but you won't find there a general guide for beginners to start from scratch and develop new skills.

For this reason, I proposed this book to the publisher. I've heard from many people who are excited about using AWS but frustrated about how to learn about and use AWS. The Powers That Be at Wiley and I agreed that an introductory book about AWS that helps newbies begin using it productively would be extremely useful — and so we set to work to create the book that you now hold in your hands. I hope that you'll find it a useful and helpful roadmap for your AWS journey.

Using This Book

This book contains a mix of text, URLs, and terminal commands that you can execute. Please note these stylistic tidbits:

- ✔ Text that you type just as it appears in the book is in **bold**. The exception is when you're working through a step list: Because each step is bold, the text to type is not in bold.

- ✔ Web addresses and programming code appear in `monofont` type. If you're reading a digital version of this book on a device connected to the Internet, you can click the web address to visit that website, such as this one: `www.dummies.com`.

Foolish Assumptions

This book is designed to address a range of readers. Part I is an overview of AWS and an introduction to how the service works. It's appropriate for executives, project managers, and IT managers wanting to gain a basic understanding of the service so that they have a context for the benefits their organization can realize by using AWS. No particular technical background is assumed or necessary in Part I.

If you plan to work with AWS in a hands-on manner, Parts II and III provide a comprehensive review of all AWS offerings. I devote a full chapter to the use of the AWS technology, with a set of exercises that begin with a simple example and progressively build into a more complex application that leverages a number of AWS products. A technical background is necessary to comprehend Parts II and III; however, none of the information or exercises is particularly difficult from a technology perspective.

Icons Used in This Book

The Tip icon marks tips (duh!) and shortcuts that you can use to make using Amazon Web Services easier.

Remember icons mark information that's especially important to know. To siphon off the most important information in each chapter, just skim these icons.

The Technical Stuff icon marks information of a highly technical nature that you can normally skip over.

The Warning icon tells you to watch out! It marks important information that may save you headaches.

Beyond the Book

The technology industry continues to invent and evolve rapidly — and that goes double for cloud computing. It's important to have up-to-the-minute information on important new technology trends, and we're committed to providing new information as AWS evolves over time.

Here are three places you can look for information and help outside of this book:

✔ **Cheat Sheet:** You can find the Cheat Sheet for this book at www. dummies.com/cheatsheet/amazonwebservices. It describes the family of AWS services and provides guidelines for using them. Given how complex AWS is turning out to be, a general set of recommendations is useful indeed!

✔ **Dummies.com online articles:** Be sure to check out www.dummies.com/extras/amazonwebservices for additional online content dealing with AWS. Not everything I wanted to say could fit within the pages of this book, so I parceled out some content for the World Wide Web.

✔ **Updates:** Amazon Web Services continues to evolve rapidly. Amazon rolls out new services extremely quickly. I'll post updates about new AWS services at www.bernardgolden.com. Look there to learn the latest about AWS.

Unlike a novel, which requires you to begin at the beginning and carry on methodically throughout the book, *Amazon Web Services For Dummies* is designed to support what I like to call "random access" — if you hear about a particular AWS product and want to find out more, well, dig right in to that section of the book. If you want to understand the phenomenon of AWS, read the first part and then pick and choose among other areas that seem intriguing. This book supports your learning pattern and imposes no "official" reading approach. Dive in anywhere that makes sense to you.

Part I

Getting Started with AWS

In this part . . .

- ✔ See how Amazon designed Amazon Web Services from the beginning to be extremely scalable, modular in design, and highly robust.

- ✔ Find out how AWS reflects Amazon's unique approach to operating its business.

- ✔ Get an introduction to AWS, its business and technology underpinnings, and even get a small taste of hands-on use.

- ✔ Visit www.dummies.com for great Dummies content online.

Chapter 1

Amazon Web Services Philosophy and Design

● ●

In This Chapter

▶ Figuring out the cloud

▶ Watching Amazon grow from retailer to the world's first cloud provider

▶ Understanding the foundation of Amazon Web Services

▶ Introducing the Amazon Web Services ecosystem

▶ Seeing how the network effect helps you

▶ Comparing Amazon Web Services to other cloud computing providers

● ●

*Y*ou may be forgiven if you're puzzled about how Amazon, which started out as an online bookstore, has become *the* leading cloud computing provider. This chapter solves that mystery by discussing the circumstances that led Amazon into the cloud computing services arena and why Amazon Web Services, far from being an oddly different offering from a retailer, is a logical outgrowth of Amazon's business.

This chapter also compares Amazon's cloud offering to other competitors in the market and explains how its approach differs. As part of this comparison, I present some statistics on the size and growth of Amazon's offering, while describing why it's difficult to get a handle on its exact size.

The chapter concludes with a brief discussion about the Amazon Web Services ecosystem and why it is far richer than what Amazon itself provides — and why it offers more value for users of Amazon's cloud service.

But before I reveal all the answers to the Amazon mystery, I answer an even more fundamental question: What *is* all this cloud computing stuff, anyway?

Cloud Computing Defined

I believe that skill is built on a foundation of knowledge. Anyone who wants to work with Amazon Web Services (AWS, from now on) should have a firm understanding of cloud computing — what it is and what it provides.

IaaS, PaaS, SaaS

As a general overview, cloud computing refers to the delivery of computing services from a remote location over a network. The National Institute of Standards and Technology (NIST), a U.S. government agency, has a definition of cloud computing that is generally considered the gold standard. Rather than trying to create my own definition, I always defer to NIST's definition. The following information is drawn directly from it.

> Cloud computing is a model for enabling ubiquitous, convenient, on-demand network access to a shared pool of configurable computing resources (e.g., networks, servers, storage, applications, and services) that can be rapidly provisioned and released with minimal management effort or service provider interaction.

This cloud model is composed of five essential characteristics:

- **On-demand self-service:** A consumer can unilaterally provision computing capabilities, such as server time and network storage, automatically as needed without requiring human interaction with each service provider.

- **Broad network access:** Capabilities are available over the network and accessed via standard mechanisms that promote use by heterogeneous thin or thick client platforms (such as mobile phones, tablets, laptops, and workstations).

- **Resource pooling:** The provider's computing resources are pooled to serve multiple consumers using a multi-tenant model, with different physical and virtual resources dynamically assigned and reassigned according to consumer demand. There's a sense of so-called *location independence,* in that the customer generally has no control or knowledge over the exact location of the provided resources but may be able to specify location at a higher level of abstraction (by country, state, or data center, for example). Examples of resources are storage, processing, memory, and network bandwidth.

- **Rapid elasticity:** Capabilities can be elastically provisioned and released, in some cases automatically, to scale rapidly outward and inward commensurate with demand. To the consumer, the capabilities available for provisioning often appear to be unlimited and can be appropriated in any quantity at any time.

✔ **Measured service:** Cloud systems automatically control and optimize resource use by leveraging a metering capability at a level of abstraction that's appropriate to the type of service (storage, processing, bandwidth, or active user accounts, for example). Resource usage can be monitored, controlled, and reported, providing transparency for both the provider and consumer of the utilized service.

Cloud computing is commonly characterized as providing three types of functionality, referred to *IaaS, PaaS,* and *SaaS,* where *aaS* is shorthand for "as a service" and *service* implies that the functionality isn't local to the user but rather originates elsewhere (a location in a remote location accessed via a network). The letters *I, P,* and *S* in the acronyms refer to different types of functionality, as the following list makes clear:

✔ **Infrastructure as a Service (Iaas):** Offers users the basic building blocks of computing: processing, network connectivity, and storage. (Of course, you also need other capabilities in order to fully support IaaS functionality — such as user accounts, usage tracking, and security.) You would use an IaaS cloud provider if you want to build an application from scratch and need access to fairly low-level functionality within the operating system.

✔ **Platform as a Service (PaaS):** Instead of offering low-level functions within the operating system, offers higher-level programming frameworks that a developer interacts with to obtain computing services. For example, rather than open a file and write a collection of bits to it, in a PaaS environment the developer simply calls a function and then provides the function with the collection of bits. The PaaS framework then handles the grunt work, such as opening a file, writing the bits to it, and ensuring that the bits have been successfully received by the file system. The PaaS framework provider takes care of backing up the data and managing the collection of backups, for example, thus relieving the user of having to complete further burdensome administrative tasks.

✔ **Software as a Service (SaaS):** Has clambered to an even higher rung on the evolutionary ladder than PaaS. With SaaS, all application functionality is delivered over a network in a pretty package. The user need do nothing more than use the application; the SaaS provider deals with the hassle associated with creating and operating the application, segregating user data, providing security for each user as well as the overall SaaS environment, and handling a myriad of other details.

As with every model, this division into *I, P,* and *S* provides a certain explanatory leverage and seeks to make neat and clean an element that in real life can be rather complicated. In the case of IPS, the model is presented as though the types are cleanly defined though they no longer are. Many cloud providers offer services of more than one type. Amazon, in particular, has begun to provide many platform-like services as it has built out its offerings, and has even ventured into a few full-blown application services that you'd associate with SaaS. You could say that Amazon provides all three types of cloud computing.

Private-versus-public cloud computing

If you find the mix of *I*, *P*, and *S* in the preceding section confusing, wait 'til you hear about the whole private-versus-public cloud computing distinction. Note the sequence of events:

1. Amazon, as the first cloud computing provider, offers *public cloud computing* — anyone can use it.

2. Many IT organizations, when contemplating this new Amazon Web Services creature, asked why they couldn't create and offer a service like AWS to their own users, hosted in their own data centers. This on-premise version became known as *private cloud computing.*

3. Continuing the trend, several hosting providers thought they could offer their IT customers a segregated part of their data centers and let customers build clouds there. This concept can also be considered private cloud computing because it's dedicated to one user. On the other hand, because the data to and from this private cloud runs over a shared network, is the cloud truly private?

4. Finally, after one bright bulb noted that companies may not choose only public or private, the term *hybrid* was coined to refer to companies using both private and public cloud environments.

As you go further on your journey in the cloud, you'll likely witness vociferous discussions devoted to which of these particular cloud environments is the better option. My own position is that no matter where you stand on the private/public/hybrid issue, public cloud computing will undoubtedly become a significant part of every company's IT environment. Moreover, Amazon will almost certainly be the largest provider of public cloud computing, so it makes sense to plan for a future that includes AWS. (Reading this book is part of that planning effort, so you get a gold star for already being well on your way!)

If you want to drill down further into cloud computing definitions, check out NIST's full description at `http://csrc.nist.gov/publications/nist pubs/800-145/SP800-145.pdf`. The U.S. federal government has been an early adopter of, and hard charger in, cloud adoption, and NIST has been assigned to create this (excellent) government-wide cloud computing resource.

Understanding the Amazon Business Philosophy

Amazon Web Services was officially revealed to the world on March 13, 2006. On that day, AWS offered the Simple Storage Service, its first service. (As you may imagine, Simple Storage Services was soon shortened to S3.) The idea behind S3 was simple: It could offer the concept of object storage over the web, a setup where anyone could put an object — essentially, any bunch of bytes — into S3. Those bytes may comprise a digital photo or a file backup or a software package or a video or audio recording or a spreadsheet file or — well, you get the idea.

S3 was relatively limited when it first started out. Though objects could, admittedly, be written or read from anywhere, they could be stored in only one region: the United States. Moreover, objects could be no larger than 5 gigabytes — not tiny by any means, but certainly smaller than many files that people may want to store in S3. The actions available for objects were also quite limited: You could write, read, and delete them, and that was it.

In its first six years, S3 has grown in all dimensions. The service is now offered throughout the world in a number of different regions. Objects can now be as large as 5 terabytes. S3 can also offer many more capabilities regarding objects. An object can now have a termination date, for example: You can set a date and time after which an object is no longer available for access. (This capability may be useful if you want to make a video available for viewing for only a certain period, such as the next two weeks.) S3 can now also be used to host websites — in other words, individual pages can be stored as objects, and your domain name (say, www.example.com) can point to S3, which serves up the pages.

S3 did not remain the lone AWS example for long. Just a few months after it was launched, Amazon began offering Simple Queue Service (SQS), which provides a way to pass messages between different programs. SQS can accept or deliver messages within the AWS environment or outside the environment to other programs (your web browser, for example) and can be used to build highly scalable distributed applications.

Later in 2006 came Elastic Compute Cloud (known affectionately as EC2). As the AWS computing service, EC2 offers computing capacity on demand, with immediate availability and no set commitment to length of use.

Don't worry if this description of AWS seems overwhelming at first — in the rest of this book, you can find out all about the various pieces of AWS, how they work, and how you can use them to address your computing requirements. This chapter provides a framework in which to understand the genesis of AWS, with details to follow. The important thing for you to understand is how AWS got started, how big of a change it represents in the way computing is done, and why it's important to your future.

The overall pattern of AWS has been to add additional services steadily, and then quickly improve each service over time. AWS is now composed of more than 25 different services, many offered with different capabilities via different configurations or formats. This rich set of services can be mixed and matched to create interesting and unique applications, limited only by your imagination or needs.

So, from one simple service (S3) to more than 25 in just over six years, and throughout the world — and growing and improving all the time! You're probably impressed by how fast all of this has happened. You're not alone. Within the industry, Amazon is regarded with a mixture of awe and envy because of how rapidly it delivers new AWS functionality. If you're interested, you can keep up with changes to AWS via its What's New web page on the AWS site, at

```
http://aws.amazon.com/about-aws/whats-new
```

This torrid pace of improvement is great news for you because it means that AWS continually presents new things you can do — things you probably couldn't do in the past because the AWS functionality would be too difficult to implement or too expensive to afford even if you could implement it.

Measuring the scale of AWS

Amazon is the pioneer of cloud computing and, because you'd have to have been living under a rock not to have heard about "the cloud," being the pioneer in this area is a big deal. The obvious question is this: If AWS is the big dog in the market and if cloud computing is the hottest thing since sliced bread, how big are we talking about?

That's an interesting question because Amazon reveals little about the extent of its business. Rather than break out AWS revenues, the company lumps them into an Other category in its financial reports.

Nevertheless, we have some clues to its size, based on information from the company itself and on informed speculation by industry pundits.

Amazon itself provides a proxy for the growth of the AWS service. Every so often, it announces how many objects are stored in the S3 service. Take a peek at Figure 1-1, which shows how the number of objects stored in S3 has increased at an enormous pace, jumping from 2.9 billion at the end of 2006 to over 2 trillion objects by the end of the second quarter of 2012. Given that pace of growth, it's obvious that the business of AWS is booming.

Other estimates of the size of the AWS service exist as well. A very clever consultant named Huan Liu examined AWS IP addresses and projected the total number of server racks held by AWS, based on an estimate of how many servers reside in a rack. Table 1-1 breaks down the numbers by region.

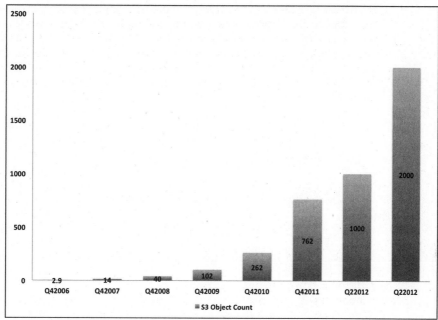

Figure 1-1:
Counting S3
objects over
the years.

Table 1-1	Total AWS Servers	
AWS Region	*Number of Server Racks*	*Number of Servers*
US East	5,030	321,920
US West (Oregon)	41	2,624
US West (California)	630	40,320
EU West (Ireland)	814	52,096
AP Northeast (Japan)	314	20,096
AP Southeast (Singapore)	246	15,744
SA East (Brazil)	25	1,600
Total	**7,100**	**454,400**

That's a lot of servers. (To see the original document outlining Liu's estimates, along with his methodology, go to http://huanliu.wordpress.com/2012/03/13/amazon-data-center-size). If you consider that each server can support a number of virtual machines (the number would vary, of course, according to the size of the virtual machines), AWS could support several million running virtual machines.

Amazon publishes a list of public IP addresses; as of May 2013, there are over four million available in AWS. This number is not inconsistent with Liu's estimated number of physical servers; it's also a convenient place to look to track how much AWS is growing. If you're interested, you can look at the AWS numbers at `https://forums.aws.amazon.com/ann.jspa?annID=1701`.

If you're not familiar with the term virtual machines, don't worry: I describe AWS technology in depth in Chapter 4. For an even more detailed discussion of virtual machines and virtualization proper, check out *Virtualization For Dummies,* by yours truly (published by John Wiley & Sons, Inc.).

Checking the bottom line

Though Amazon doesn't announce how many dollars AWS pulls in, that hasn't stopped others from making their own estimates of the size of AWS business — and their estimates make it clear that AWS is a very large business indeed.

Early in 2012, several analysts from Morgan Stanley analyzed the AWS business and judged that the service pulled in $1.19 billion in 2011. (You gotta love the precision that these pundits come up with, eh?) Other analysts from JP Morgan Chase and UBS have calculated that AWS will achieve 2015 revenues of around $2.5 billion.

The bottom line: AWS is big and getting bigger (and better) every day. It really is no exaggeration to say that AWS represents a revolution in computing. People are doing amazing things with it, and this book shows you how you can take advantage of it.

The AWS Infrastructure

If what Amazon is doing with AWS represents a revolution, as I describe in the previous section, how is the company bringing it about? In other words, how is it delivering this amazing service? Throughout this book, I go into the specifics of how the service operates, but for now I outline the general approach that Amazon has taken in building AWS.

First and foremost, Amazon has approached the job in a unique fashion, befitting a company that changed the face of retail. Amazon specializes in a low-margin approach to business, and it carries that perspective into AWS. Unlike almost every other player in the cloud computing market, Amazon has focused on creating a low-margin, highly efficient offering, and that offering starts with the way Amazon has built out its infrastructure.

Making hard hardware decisions

Unlike most of its competitors, Amazon builds its hardware infrastructure from commodity components. *Commodity,* in this case, refers to using equipment from lesser-known manufacturers who charge less than their brand-name competitors. For components for which commodity offerings aren't available, Amazon (known as a ferocious negotiator) gets rock-bottom prices.

On the hardware side of the AWS offering, Amazon's approach is clear: Buy equipment as cheaply as possible. But wait, you may say, won't the commodity approach result in a less reliable infrastructure? After all, the brand-name hardware providers assert that one benefit of paying premium prices is that you get higher-quality gear. Well . . . yes and no. It may be true that premium-priced equipment (traditionally called enterprise equipment because of the assumption that large enterprises require more reliability and are willing to pay extra to obtain it) is more reliable in an apples-to-apples comparison. That is, an enterprise-grade server lasts longer and suffers fewer outages than its commodity-class counterpart.

The issue, from Amazon's perspective, is how much more reliable the enterprise gear is than the commodity version, and how much that improved reliability is worth. In other words, it needs to know the cost-benefit ratio of enterprise-versus-commodity.

Making this evaluation more challenging is a fundamental fact: At the scale on which an Amazon operates (remember that it has nearly half a million servers running in its AWS service), equipment — no matter *who* provides it — is breaking all the time.

If you're a cloud provider with an infrastructure the size of Amazon's, you have to assume, for every type of hardware you use, an endless round of crashed disk drives, fried motherboards, packet-dropping network switches, and on and on.

Therefore, even if you buy the highest-quality, most expensive gear available, you'll still end up (if you're fortunate enough to grow into a very large cloud computing provider like, say, Amazon) with an unreliable infrastructure. Put another way, at a very large scale, even highly reliable individual components still result in an unreliable overall infrastructure because of the failure of components, as rare as the failure of a specific piece of equipment may be.

The scale at which Amazon operates affects other aspects of its hardware infrastructure as well. Besides components such as servers, networks, and storage, data centers also have power supplies, cooling, generators, and backup batteries. Depending on the specific component, Amazon may have to use custom-designed equipment to operate at the scale required.

Think of AWS hardware infrastructure this way: If you had to design and operate data centers to deal with massive scale and in a way that aligns with a corporate mandate to operate inexpensively, you'd probably end up with a solution much like Amazon's. You'd use commodity computing equipment whenever possible, jawbone prices down when you couldn't obtain commodity offerings, and custom-design equipment to manage your unusually large-scale operation.

For more detail on Amazon's data center approach, check out James Hamilton's blog at `http://perspectives.mvdirona.com`. (He's one of Amazon's premier data center architects.) The blog includes links to videos of his extremely interesting and educational presentations on how Amazon has approached its hardware environment.

Examining Amazon's software infrastructure strategy

Because of Amazon's low-margin, highly scaled requirements, you'd probably expect it to have a unique approach to the cloud computing software infrastructure running on top of its hardware environment, right?

You'd be correct.

Amazon has created a unique, highly specialized software environment in order to provide its cloud computing services. I stress the word unique because, at first glance, people often find AWS different and confusing — it is unlike any other computing environment they've previously encountered.

After users understand how AWS operates, however, they generally find that its design makes sense and that it's appropriate for what it delivers — and, more important, for how people use the service.

Though Amazon has an unusual approach to its hardware environment, it's in the software infrastructure that its uniqueness truly stands out. Let me give you a quick overview of its features. The software infrastructure is

> ✔ **Based on virtualization:** Virtualization — a technology that abstracts software components from dependence on their underlying hardware — lies at the heart of AWS. Being able to create virtual machines, start them, terminate them, and restart them quickly makes the AWS service possible.
>
> As you might expect, Amazon has approached virtualization in a unique fashion. Naturally, it wanted a low-cost way to use virtualization, so it chose the open source Xen Hypervisor as its software foundation. Then

it made significant changes to the "vanilla" Xen product so that it could fulfill the requirements of AWS.

The result is that Amazon leverages virtualization, but the virtualization solution it came up with is extended in ways that support vast scale and a plethora of services built atop it.

✔ **Operated as a service:** I know what you're going to say: "Of course it's operated as a service — that's why it's called Amazon Web Services!"

That's true, but Amazon had to create a tremendous software infrastructure in order to be able to offer its computing capability as a service.

For example, Amazon had to create a way for users to operate their AWS resources from a distance and with no requirement for local hands-on interaction. And it had to segregate a user's resources from everyone else's resources in a way that ensures security, because no one wants other users to be able to see, access, or change his resources.

Amazon had to provide a set of interfaces — an Application Programming Interface (API) — to allow users to manage every aspect of AWS. (I cover the AWS API in Chapter 5.)

✔ **Designed for flexibility:** Amazon designed AWS to address users like itself — users that need rich computing services available at a moment's notice to support their application needs and constantly changing business conditions.

In other words, just as Amazon can't predict what its computing requirements will be in a year or two, neither can the market for which Amazon built AWS.

In that situation, it makes sense to implement few constraints on the service. Consequently, rather than offer a tightly integrated set of services that provides only a few ways to use them, Amazon provides a highly granular set of services that can be "mixed and matched" by the user to create an application that meets its exact needs.

By designing the service in a highly flexible fashion, Amazon enables its customers to be creative, thereby supporting innovation. Throughout the book, I'll offer examples of some of the interesting things companies are doing with AWS.

Not only are the computing services themselves highly flexible, the conditions of use of AWS are flexible as well. You need nothing more to get started than an e-mail address and a credit card.

✔ **Highly resilient:** If you took the message from earlier in the chapter about the inherent unreliability of hardware to heart, you now recognize that there is no way to implement resiliency via hardware. The obvious alternative is with software, and that is the path Amazon has chosen.

Amazon makes AWS highly resilient by implementing resource redundancy — essentially using multiple copies of a resource to ensure that failure of a single resource does not cause the service to fail. For example, if you were to store just one copy of each of your objects within its S3 service, that object may sometimes be unavailable because the disk drive on which it resides has broken down. Instead, AWS keeps multiple copies of an object, ensuring that even if one — or two! — objects become unavailable because of hardware failure, users can still access the object, thereby improving S3 reliability and durability.

In summary, Amazon has implemented a rich software infrastructure to allow users access to large quantities of computing resources at rock-bottom prices. And if you take another look at Figure 1-1 (the one outlining the number of objects stored in S3), you'd have to draw the conclusion that a large number of users are increasingly benefiting from AWS.

The AWS Ecosystem

Thus far, I haven't delved too deeply into the various pieces of the AWS puzzle, but it should be clear (if you're reading this chapter from start to finish) that Amazon offers a number of services to its users. However, AWS hosts a far richer set of services than only the ones it provides. In fact, users can find nearly everything they need within the confines of AWS to create almost any application they may want to implement. These services are available via the *AWS ecosystem* — the offerings of Amazon partners and third parties that host their offerings on AWS.

So, in addition to the 25+ services AWS itself offers, users can find services that

✔ Offer preconfigured virtual machines with software components already installed and configured, to enable quick use

✔ Manipulate images

✔ Transmit or stream video

✔ Integrate applications with one another

✔ Monitor application performance

✔ Ensure application security

✔ Operate billing and subscriptions

✔ Manage healthcare claims

✔ Offer real estate for sale

✔ Analyze genomic data

✔ Host websites

✔ Provide customer support

And really, this list barely scratches the surface of what's available within AWS. In a way, AWS is a modern-day bazaar, providing an incredibly rich set of computing capabilities *from* anyone who chooses to set up shop *to* anyone who chooses to purchase what's being offered.

On closer inspection, you can see that the AWS ecosystem is made up of three distinct subsystems:

✔ **AWS computing services provided by Amazon:** As noted earlier, Amazon currently provides more than 25 AWS services and is launching more all the time. AWS provides a large range of cloud computing services — you'll be introduced to many of them over the course of this book.

✔ **Computing services provided by third parties that operate on AWS:** These services tend to offer functionality that enables you to build applications of a type that AWS doesn't strictly offer. For example, AWS offers some billing capability to enable users to build applications and charge people to use them, but the AWS service doesn't support many billing use cases — user-specific discounts based on the size of the company, for example. Many companies (and even individuals) offer services complementary to AWS that then allow users to build richer applications more quickly. (If you carry out the AWS exercises I set out for you later in this book, you'll use one such service offered by Bitnami.)

✔ **Complete applications offered by third parties that run on AWS:** You can use these services, often referred to as SaaS (Software as a Service), over a network without having to install them on your own hardware. (Check out the "IaaS, Paas, SaaS" section, earlier in this chapter, for more on SaaS.) Many, many companies host their applications on AWS, drawn to it for the same reasons that end users are drawn to it: low cost, easy access, and high scalability. An interesting trend within AWS is the increasing move by traditional software vendors to migrate their applications to AWS and provide them as SaaS offerings rather than as applications that users install from a CD or DVD on their own machines.

As you go forward with using AWS, be careful to recognize the differences between these three offerings within the AWS ecosystem, especially Amazon's role (or lack thereof) in all three. Though third-party services or SaaS applications can be incredibly valuable to your computing efforts, Amazon, quite reasonably, offers no support or guarantee about their functionality or performance. It's up to you to decide whether a given non-AWS service is fit for your needs.

Amazon, always working to make it ever easier to locate and integrate third-party services into your application, has created the Amazon Marketplace as your go-to place for finding AWS-enabled applications. Moreover, being part of the Marketplace implies an endorsement by AWS, which will make you more confident about using a Marketplace application. You can read more about the Marketplace at

```
https://aws.amazon.com/marketplace
```

Counting Up the Network Effects Benefit

The reason the AWS ecosystem has become *the* computing marketplace for all and sundry can be captured in the phrase *network effect,* which can be thought of as the value derived from a network because other network participants are part of the network. The classic case of a network effect is the telephone: The more people who use telephones, the more value there is to someone getting a telephone — because the larger the number of telephones being used, the easier it is to communicate with a large number of people. Conversely, if you're the only person in town with a telephone, well, you're going to be pretty lonely — and not very talkative! Said another way, for a service with network effects, the more people who use it, the more attractive it is to potential users, and the more value they receive when they use the service.

From the AWS perspective, the network effect means that, if you're providing a new cloud-based service, it makes sense to offer it where lots of other cloud users are located — someplace like AWS, for example. This network effect benefits AWS greatly, simply because many people, when they start to think about doing something with cloud computing, naturally gravitate to AWS because it's a brand name that they recognize.

However, with respect to AWS, there's an even greater network effect than the fact that lots of people are using it: The technical aspects of AWS play a part as well.

When one service talks to another over the Internet, a certain amount of time passes when the communication between the services travels over the Internet network — even at the speed of light, information traveling long distances takes a certain amount of time. Also, while information is traveling across the Internet, it's constantly being shunted through routers to ensure that it's being sent in the right direction. This combination of network length and device interaction is called *latency,* a measure of how much of a delay is imposed by network traffic distance.

In concrete terms, if you use a web browser to access data from a website hosted within 50 miles of you, it will likely respond faster than if the same website were hosted 7,000 miles away.

To continue this concept, using a service that's located nearby makes your application run faster — always a good thing. So if your service runs on AWS, you'd like any services you depend on to also run on AWS — because the latency affecting your application is much lower than if those services originated somewhere else.

Folks who build services tend to be smart, so they'll notice that their potential customers like the idea of having services nearby. If you're setting up a new service, you'll be attracted to AWS because lots of other services are already located there. And if you're considering using a cloud service, you're likely to choose AWS because the number of services there will make it easier to build your application, from the perspective of service availability *and* low-latency performance.

The network effects associated with AWS give you a rich set of services to leverage as you create applications to run on Amazon's cloud offering. They can work to reduce your workload and speed your application development delivery by relieving you of much of the burden traditionally associated with integrating external software components and services into your application.

Here are some benefits of being able to leverage the network effects of the AWS ecosystem in your application:

- ✔ **The service is already up and running within AWS.** You don't have to obtain the software, install it, configure it, test it, and then integrate it into your application. Because it's already operational in the AWS environment, you can skip directly to the last step — perform the technical integration.

- ✔ **The services have a cloud-friendly licensing model.** Vendors have already figured out how to offer their software and charge for it in the AWS environment. Vendors often align with the AWS billing methodology, charging per hour of use or offering a subscription for monthly access. But one thing you don't have to do is approach a vendor that has a large, upfront license fee and negotiate to operate in the AWS environment — it's already taken care of.

- ✔ **Support is available for the service.** You don't have to figure out why a software component you want to use doesn't work properly in the AWS environment — the vendor takes responsibility for it. In the parlance of the world of support, you have, as the technology industry rather indelicately puts it, a throat to choke.

✔ **Performance improves.** Because the service operates in the same environment that your application runs in, it provides low latency and helps your application perform better.

Before you start thinking about finding a packaged software application to integrate into your application, or about writing your own software component to provide certain functionality, search the Marketplace to see whether one or more applications already provide the necessary functionality.

AWS versus Other Cloud Providers

Nature abhors a vacuum, and markets abhor monopoly providers, so it stands to reason that competitors always enter an attractive market. Cloud computing is no different: There are a plethora of cloud computing providers. Naturally, you'll want to get the lowdown on how AWS measures up.

The most important difference between AWS and almost all other cloud providers revolves around what market they target. To understand that aspect, you must understand the basis of the service they offer.

Now, AWS grew out of the capabilities that Amazon developed to enable its developers to rapidly create and deploy applications. The service is focused on making developers more productive and, in a word, happier.

By contrast, most other cloud providers have a hosting heritage: Their backgrounds involve supporting infrastructure for IT operations groups responsible for maintaining system uptime. A significant part of the value proposition for hosting providers has traditionally been the high quality of their infrastructures — in other words, the enterprise nature of their servers, networks, storage, and so on.

This heritage carries several implications about enterprise cloud providers:

✔ **The focus is on the concerns of IT operations rather than on the concerns of developers.** Often, this concern translates as, "The service is not easy to use." For example, an enterprise cloud provider may require a discussion with a sales representative before granting access to the service and then impose a back-and-forth manual process as part of the account setup. By contrast, AWS allows anyone with an e-mail address and a credit card access to the service within ten minutes.

✔ **The service itself reflects its hosting heritage, with its functionality and use model mirroring how physical servers operate.** Often, the only storage an enterprise cloud service provider offers is associated with individual virtual machines — no object storage, such as S3, is offered, because it isn't part of a typical hosting environment.

✔ **Enterprise cloud service providers often require a multiyear commitment to resource use with a specific level of computing capacity.** Though this strategy makes it easier for a cloud service provider to plan its business, it's much less convenient for users — *and* it imposes some of the same issues that they're trying to escape from!

✔ **The use of enterprise equipment often means higher prices when compared to AWS.** I have seen enterprise cloud service providers charge 800 percent more than AWS. Depending on organization requirements and the nature of the application, users may be willing to pay a premium for these providers; on the other hand, higher prices and the long-term commitment that often accompanies the use of an AWS competitor may strike many users as unattractive or even unacceptable.

The rise of shadow IT

Frustration at being unable to get hold of server resources in a timely fashion has led to the phenomenon of *shadow IT:* developers bypassing IT proper and obtaining resources themselves. This phenomenon is powerful and growing — at one conference, I heard a CIO state that he had examined the expense reports submitted to him for reimbursement and found more than 50 different AWS accounts being used by his development staff!

Here's something to consider: Shadow IT is a pejorative term, implying stealth and a definite whiff of illicit behavior. On the other hand, someone engaging in shadow IT might, reasonably enough, think of it as "getting the job done" in the face of existing processes that can stretch out to several months the length of time required to obtain resources.

This conflict is unlikely to subside in the near future. Developers relish the freedom and flexibility that AWS provides, though many IT groups are engaged in a fruitless struggle to go back to "the good old days," where they set the rules.

The conflict will ultimately be resolved in favor of developers. The reason is simple: The application is the way businesses gain value from IT, and applications are often directly tied to revenue-generating offerings (say, a mobile phone app that enables users to order goods or services online). Infrastructure, the province of mainstream IT, is then seen as a necessary evil — the plumbing that supports applications.

The advantage held by developers can be seen in cloud computing market share. One technology analyst told me that, by his estimate, AWS represents 75 percent of the market for cloud service providers. I expect pressure to build on enterprise cloud providers to rapidly improve their offerings to include more developer-friendly services. Amazon's six-year head start may make it too elusive to overtake.

If you analyze how well Amazon matches up against the NIST definition of cloud computing (discussed at the beginning if this chapter) when compared with its competitors, AWS usually emerges victorious. In part, that's because AWS was the pioneer, and because the first entrant into a market typically gets to define it. There's more to it than that, though.

Amazon's stroke of genius was to put together an innovative offering addressing a market poorly served by traditional IT practices. Though hosting companies typically serve IT operations groups well, the emphasis on enterprise equipment and high uptime availability frustrates developers trying to get access to resources. Stories of waiting weeks or months for servers to be provisioned are rife within the industry. As you might imagine, developers (and the application managers and executives they work for) longed for a different way of doing things — and that's what AWS offers.

Getting Ready for the 21st Century

This chapter provides an overview of Amazon Web Services. It lets you see how AWS has grown from Amazon's own computing needs and infrastructure to now represent Amazon's response to this simple hypothesis: If *we* need a flexible, cost-effective, and highly scalable infrastructure, *a lot of other organizations* could probably use one as well."

From that initial insight, Amazon created the computing platform of the 21st century. Targeted at developers, and provided throughout the world, AWS is undergoing explosive growth as more and more people explore how it can enable them to solve problems that were unsolvable by the traditional methods of managing infrastructure.

I hope that you can't wait to jump in to exploring AWS. This book aims to provide you with knowledge you need so that you, too, can leverage the amazing AWS cloud computing offering.

Chapter 2

Introducing the AWS API

- -

- -

The AWS environment acts as an integrated collection of hardware and software services designed to enable the easy, quick, and inexpensive use of computing resources. (Chapter 1 gives all the details, if you're curious.) Now, sitting atop this integrated collection is the AWS application programming interface (API, for short): In essence, an *API* represents a way to communicate with a computing resource. (I tell you more about this topic later in this chapter.) With respect to AWS, nothing gets done without using the AWS API. The AWS API is the sole way that external users interact with AWS resources, and there's literally no way to use AWS resources without the API being involved. In fact, if you access AWS through the AWS Management Console or the command line tools, you are actually using tools that make calls to the AWS API.

In this chapter, I start by offering an introduction to the world of APIs and an explanation of why they've become increasingly important in the world of computing. I then discuss the AWS API and outline how it's used. Along the way, I discuss other, third-party services that you may want to use and tell you how they interact with the AWS API. Finally, I describe the AWS API security model, which is critical to understanding how Amazon ensures that only the right people perform acceptable actions within the AWS environment.

APIs: Understanding the Basics

You may consider yourself the kind of person who'd never, ever have to use an API. You'd be wrong. APIs have been important, they are important now, and they'll become even more important. More likely than not, you've been using APIs for years without even knowing it.

With respect to Amazon, the API is the sole external interface to computing resources and services. Without API calls being made, nothing gets done.

API is short for application programming interface, as I mention elsewhere. A good way to describe an API is to say that it represents a way for one program to interact with another via a defined *interface* — in other words, a mechanism by which any other program that communicates with the program can be assured that it will fulfill its role. The idea is that if a calling program provides the right information within the correct syntax, the program with the API will respond in the requested manner.

Understanding APIs

The term *API* traditionally referred to the programming interface offered by one or more routines that were bundled into a library of functions. Someone would supply a library that, say, performs date-and-time manipulation functions. A software engineer would bundle that library into a program and could then call those functions via the API that the library offers.

The API represents the "contract" that the library offers. The API defines the functional interface, the format of any information supplied to the functions (commonly called *arguments* or *parameters)* within the library, the operation to be performed, and the output that each function would return to the calling program.

One benefit of this "contractual" approach is that it offers *encapsulation* within the library — the actual code that implements the contract is hidden from the calling function. The library code can then be modified, updated, or even replaced entirely with another set of code, all without disturbing the calling function — as long as the new library code fulfills the old contract. Encapsulation allows much more flexibility in software environments, because different parts of the overall environment evolve at different rates; changing one part of the environment

doesn't require changing everything. As long as the contract is adhered to, every other part of the environment can remain undisturbed.

The meaning of the term *API* has been extended: Rather than be used solely to discuss libraries that are directly attached to other programs, it's now used to refer to software environments in which the different software programs run on different servers and communicate across a network. Furthermore, that network may be contained within a single data center or, quite commonly, extend across the Internet. This network-based API approach is often referred to as a *web services environment* — notice how Amazon's cloud computing offering is named Amazon Web Services? It's no accident.

One critical factor that web services require, but traditional API libraries don't, is the whole notion of security. If two programs are communicating across the Internet, the one calling the service must be able to provide information regarding who it is (its identity), and the called service must be able to validate that whoever is doing the calling is allowed (authorized) to access the service it has requested. I discuss Amazon's approach to its web services security later in this chapter.

Benefiting from Web Services

I've heard people say that we're now living in a web services world, which, on the face of it, seems like an odd thing to say — after all, you may be able to go about much of your life today just as you did a decade ago without giving a moment's thought to something called "web services." However, even though you may not notice the fact, your everyday life is surrounded by web services.

As more aspects of our lives move to the Internet — banking, shopping, paying our taxes, collaborating at work, our social lives — people naturally want to be able to combine two or more of them into a new creation. It's the technological equivalent of the musical mash-up that's all the rage these days — a combination of two elements to create a new one that reflects parts of both. An early example of this phenomenon was an Internet application that combined Google Maps with craigslist apartment listings to create a map identifying the location of every available apartment. All the application did was combine (mash up) two basic services, but from that union came an extremely useful result — a guide to apartments in a particular area, making the process of selecting some to view and getting driving directions to them much more efficient.

The huge growth of mobile computing — the brave new world of smart-phones and tablets — has worked to fuel the growth of APIs as well as mash-up applications. The "app culture" of mobile computing is a natural place to combine services, especially those tied to location. The apartment map application I just described is even more useful when it can be accessed while you're out and about. Finished looking at one apartment? Pull up the app and let it show you where the next nearest apartment for rent is located.

The next great frontier for web services is the so-called "Internet of Things," a term that refers to computing devices used not by humans, but by each other — interacting to complete useful tasks (smart electric meters that com-municate with power company billing systems, for example). Soon, however, you'll be surrounded by all manner of devices that constantly interact with cloud-based applications. How big will the Internet of Things become? One senior Cisco executive predicts that *1 trillion* devices will soon be interacting over the Internet.

As more proof (if more proof were needed) that today's world is a web services world, companies, government agencies, and nonprofit organiza-tions are feverishly making their resources available as online services acces-sible via APIs. Engineers are combining online web services to create new applications that combine individual services and provide unique and useful capabilities.

This web services revolution that I describe makes possible a number of interesting benefits:

- ✔ **Innovation:** Just as musical mash-ups let people combine musical resources into new creations, so, too, do web services foster innovation. Though I may not be able to see the value in a combination of, say, vehicle gas mileage ratings, local gas prices, and state park reviews, someone else may conclude that an application allowing someone to enter the make and model of her automobile to find out which parks she can visit for less than $25 in gas costs would be just the ticket — and a whole lot of people may agree. (In fact, I may put that app on my to-do list!)

- ✔ **Niche market support:** In a non-web-services world, the only people who can develop applications are those working for organizations. Only they have access to the computing resources or data — so the only applications that are developed are ones that the company deems useful. However, once those resources and data are made available via web services, anyone can create an application, which allows the development of applications targeted at niche markets. For example, someone can combine Google Maps with a municipal bus schedule in a mobile app to allow users to see when and where the next bus will be available nearby.

- ✔ **New sources of revenue:** Companies can provide a web services interface into their business transaction systems and allow outside entities to sell their goods. For example, the large retailer Sears has made it possible for mobile app developers and bloggers to sell Sears goods via a Sears web service. These developers and bloggers reach audiences that Sears may not be able to reach — but Sears can prosper without having to be involved. As another example, Netflix has made its web services interface to its video offerings available, and many device and game manufacturers have used the interface to incorporate Netflix into their products. Netflix can gain new revenues every time someone buys a Wii or an Xbox and decides that it would be cool to use his new toy to access online movies and television.

These examples should give you an understanding of why many people (and I include myself in that number) regard the rise of web services as a true technology revolution.

This revolution is nowhere near the end, either. Mobile computing is still growing extremely rapidly, and it's just getting going in emerging economies. The journey of the Internet of Things has barely begun. But I hope that you recognize just how important web services are to you — even if you're unaware of their presence.

The myth of excess capacity

This is probably as good a place as any to address a persistent myth about AWS. Many people think that the AWS service represents Amazon's effort to rent its excess computing capacity during periods of low demand throughout the year. They believe that because Amazon has to have a lot of capacity on hand to address the heavy load of retail shopping during the Christmas season, it created AWS to encourage people to use its infrastructure the rest of the year.

There's only one problem with that theory — many AWS customers also have Christmas seasonality, so if Amazon is selling its excess capacity the rest of the year, what does it do in December when those AWS customers want access to computing capacity and Amazon doesn't have much excess capacity available?

The truth is that AWS doesn't rely on excess Amazon retail capacity. AWS has its own capacity, thank you very much — and it's a good thing, given that Amazon retail's entire web server functionality now runs on AWS. If AWS depended on excess Amazon retail computing capacity but Amazon retail now runs on

AWS . . . well, trying to understand that scenario is like trying to figure out an Escher drawing!

The bottom line: AWS has its own computing capacity, and it is growing dramatically. Early in 2010, I heard Werner Vogels, Amazon's chief technology officer (CTO), say that, because of customer demand, AWS installs, each and every day, as much computing capacity as all of Amazon ran on in 2000, when it was a $2.7 billion company.

Vogels updated his statement in late 2012, saying that, again because of customer demand, AWS now installs as much computing capacity daily as all of Amazon ran on in the year 2003, when it was a $5.2 billion company.

So the next time you hear someone say that AWS is primarily a way for Amazon to rent its off-season excess capacity, you'll know better, and you can @— if you dare! — set that person straight. AWS is its own, significant business, it has its own, significant computing infrastructure, and it is experiencing, by all evidence, very rapid expansion.

An Overview of the AWS API

I've said it before and I'll say it again: The only way you can interact with AWS is via its API. Every service you can ever use is called (and returns data) via its API, so using the API is critical to working with AWS. However, don't worry about having to know the details of a low-level programming interface — you'll likely never have to interact directly with the API. Nevertheless, you *must* understand at least the broad outline of how the AWS API functions, so that's what I describe in this section.

Web services: SOAP or REST?

You can choose from a couple of different schools of thought for how web services should be delivered. The older approach, SOAP (short for Simple Object Access Protocol), had widespread industry support, complete with a comprehensive set of standards. Those standards were too comprehensive, unfortunately. The people designing SOAP set it up to be extremely flexible — it can communicate across the web, e-mail, and private networks. To ensure security and manageability, a number of supporting standards that integrate with SOAP were also defined.

SOAP is based on a document encoding standard known as Extensible Markup Language (XML, for short), and the SOAP service is defined in such a way that users can then leverage XML no matter what the underlying communication network is. For this system to work, though, the data transferred by SOAP (commonly referred to as the *payload*) also needs to be in XML format. Notice a pattern here? The push to be comprehensive and flexible (or, to be all things to all people) plus the XML payload requirement meant that SOAP ended up being quite complex, making it a lot of work to use properly. As you might guess, many IT people found SOAP daunting and, consequently, resisted using it.

About a decade ago, a doctoral student defined another web services approach as part of his thesis: REST, or Representational State Transfer. (Frankly, I think he coined the term REST first, because it sounded easier and more relaxing than SOAP, and then configured the name to fit the acronym.)

REST, which is far less comprehensive than SOAP, aspires to solve fewer problems. It doesn't address some aspects of SOAP that seemed important but that, in retrospect, made it more complex to use — security, for example.

The most important aspect of REST is that it's designed to integrate with standard web protocols so that REST services can be called with standard web verbs and URLs. For example, a valid REST call looks like this:

```
http://search.examplecompany.com/CompanyDirectory/Employee
       Info?empname=BernardGolden
```

That's all it takes to make a query to the REST service of `examplecompany` to see my personnel information. The HTTP verb that accompanies this request is GET, asking for information to be returned. To delete information, you use the verb DELETE. To insert my information, you use the verb POST. To update my information, you use the verb PUT.

For the POST and PUT actions, additional information would accompany the `empname` and be separated by an ampersand (`&`) to indicate another argument to be used by the service.

REST imposes no particular formatting requirements on the service payloads; in this respect, it differs from SOAP, which requires XML. For simple interactions, a string of bytes is all you need for the payload; for more complex interactions (say, in addition to returning my employee information, I want to place a request for the employee information of all employees whose names start with G), the encoding convention JSON is used. (JSON, if you're curious, stands for Javascript Object Notation.)

As you might expect, REST's simpler use model, its alignment with standard web protocols and verbs, and its less restrictive payload formatting made it catch on with developers like a house on fire.

AWS originally launched with SOAP support for interactions with its API, but it has steadily *deprecated* (reduced its support for, in other words) its SOAP interface in favor of REST. My recommendation for any use of the AWS API is that you focus on using REST. That way, you won't end up with programs that someday stop working — long after you've forgotten the details of the interaction mechanisms. Unfortunately, I've experienced — many times — the unpleasant task of having to go back into a system and attempt to reconstruct my actions from months or years earlier. There's no sense in tempting fate with AWS — if you want to interact with the AWS API, use REST, which is Amazon's long-term direction.

The AWS API

As you might imagine, given the comprehensiveness of AWS services and the way Amazon has been improving and extending them, the AWS API is one large puppy — the AWS S3 API reference manual is 269 pages. (Think that's a lot of pages? The AWS EC2 API reference manual is *561 pages.*)

However, if you take a quick look at the following example of an API call, you'll quickly see that it closely resembles the (quite simple) REST example in the preceding section:

```
https://ec2.amazonaws.com/?Action=RunInstances
&ImageId=ami-60a54009
&MaxCount=3
&MinCount=1
&Placement.AvailabilityZone=us-east-1b
&Monitoring.Enabled=true
&AUTHPARAMS
```

The call, which is straightforward, instructs AWS to run between one and three instances based on an Amazon machine image of ami-60a54009 and to place them in the us-east-1b availability zone. AWS provides monitoring capabilities, and this call instructs AWS to enable this monitoring. The AUTHPARAMS part is a stand-in for the information that AWS uses to implement security in its API. I discuss this topic later in this chapter, so just accept for now that this call has the appropriate security mechanisms in place to ensure its execution. (For more on instances and availability zones, check out Chapter 4.)

The AWS API in real-world use

That's it. That's all there is to the AWS API. Easy, right? Well, even though the concept is easily understood, in practice it can be extremely challenging to use the AWS API properly — as you would expect, given the hundreds of pages devoted to the reference guide.

At this point, you might not feel confident about your ability to successfully use AWS. Understandably, you might feel that interacting with AWS is too complicated and difficult for even the old college try.

Never fear. Though the down-and-dirty details of using the AWS API are quite challenging, they're unlikely to become stumbling blocks to achieving success with AWS.

That's because many clever people have recognized that the API is difficult to use and have created tools to make AWS simpler to use. In Figure 2-1, you can see the four major categories of AWS interaction mechanisms that spare you from the burden of interacting with the AWS API directly.

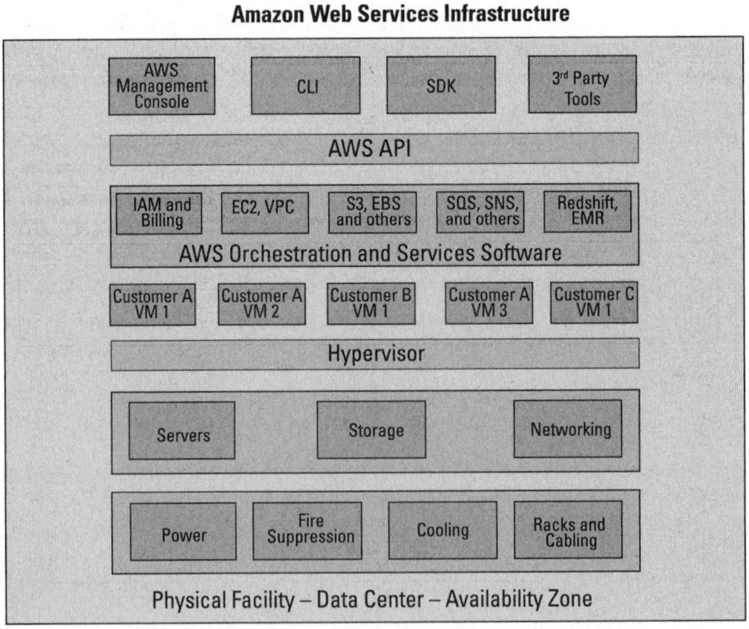

Amazon Web Services Infrastructure

Figure 2-1:
The AWS interface tools.

✔ **AWS management console:** Amazon offers a graphical web interface that allows you to interact with service (and your own) computing resources. For many people, the AWS management console is the primary mechanism they use to operate AWS. Even people who use the other two mechanisms to interact with AWS also make heavy use of the management console. I use the management console to explain the examples in this book, and I even focus a complete chapter on it to help you get started with AWS.

✔ **CLI/SDK:** Many software engineers write applications that need to interact with AWS services directly. Now, calling the web services API directly is complicated and error-prone. *Plumbing* is a common way to refer to this sort of underlying functionality, like the AWS API — just as most of us wouldn't want to have to install a whole new set of pipes only to fill a teapot, most software engineers would prefer not to have to deal with the details of the AWS API. To help them, Amazon and other companies have created language libraries (commonly called SDKs, standing for *S*oftware *D*evelopment *K*its) and a command line interface (commonly called a CLI), which allows commands to be entered in a terminal connected to AWS. The idea here is to offer a simpler programmatic interface to the set of functions that do the heavy lifting of interacting with the AWS API. A software engineer can more easily incorporate library routines into an application, making it easier and faster to build AWS-based applications.

✔ **Third-party tools:** Many companies build tools that incorporate AWS. Some of these tools extend or simplify AWS itself, similar to what the language libraries do for software engineers. Other tools are products that offer separate functionality or even entire applications. For example, my company provides cloud management software that offers additional functionality not offered by the AWS management console. Other examples include programming environments from companies like Heroku and Engine Yard, data warehousing technology from Informatica and JasperSoft, and load-testing services from SOASTA. What these tools have in common is that they provide functionality to shield users from interacting with the AWS API, making AWS easier and faster to use.

All four of these AWS API interaction mechanisms act as *proxies* on your behalf — under the covers they make the necessary calls to the AWS API to use the AWS functionality for actions you want to perform.

Netflix runs on AWS

If you live in the United States (or, increasingly, in many places throughout the world), there's a good chance that you subscribe to the online video streaming service known as Netflix. If you're a Netflix subscriber, you also use AWS — because the Netflix service runs on AWS.

Yes, that's right: Every time you log on to Netflix, browse its selections, read your personalized recommendations, view your queue, or select a video to watch, it's all running on AWS. And Netflix uses AWS for much more than these functions. All the *transcoding* that Netflix must perform (the process of converting one digital format to another, or several others, because Netflix must create separate versions for different mobile phones, tablets, TVs, and gaming devices) is done using AWS.

All use of AWS by Netflix is via the AWS API. Netflix runs tens of thousands of AWS EC2 instances, and trying to track and manage that number of resources via the AWS Management Console would be unworkable. So Netflix created its own AWS management tools to manage any of its applications running in AWS. Netflix even offers the tools under open source licenses so that other AWS users can take advantage of its work. You can learn more about Netflix and its open source efforts

at `www.slideshare.net/adrianco/ netflix-and-open-source`.

How broadly does Netflix use AWS? Well, consider this: Netflix has over 29 million subscribers. At peak viewing times (evenings, when hardworking people generally "kick back" by watching videos), Netflix accounts for a staggering *30 percent* of total Internet traffic. Of all Internetconnected TVs, 40 percent are used to access Netflix shows. And Netflix is growing — fast.

In fact, this level of growth is the reason that Netflix has chosen to rely on AWS as its infrastructure environment. Netflix realizes that it doesn't excel at building and operating data centers (its core business is media and video streaming, in case you didn't notice), so offloading the infrastructure work to AWS allows Netflix to focus on its core business.

Many people find this decision strange. Doesn't the Amazon video streaming service compete with Netflix? Yes, but Netflix has concluded that AWS is now *the* most advanced cloud provider and that Netflix support by AWS won't be tainted by the parent company's own video offering. If another cloud provider comes along and offers the scale and functionality of AWS, Netflix might reevaluate its commitment to AWS, but for now, if you use Netflix, you use AWS.

AWS API Security

Here's an obvious question when dealing with third-party proxies: If these tools act on your behalf, how does AWS know that the person on whose behalf they're acting is in fact *you?* In other words, how can AWS authenticate your identity to ensure that the commands it receives are from you? In fact, the same question is valid even if you interact with the AWS API directly. How can AWS validate your identity to ensure that it executes commands only for you?

One way, of course, is for you to include your account username and password in the API calls. Though some cloud providers take this approach, Amazon does not. Rather than rely on a username and password, it relies on two other identifiers to authenticate its API service calls: the access key and the secret access key. It uses these keys in service calls to implement security in a way that's much more secure than using only your username and password.

So how does it work? When you sign up for an account with AWS, you have the opportunity to create an access key and to have a secret access key sent to you. Each one is a lengthy string of random characters, and the secret access key is the longer of the two. When you download the secret access key, you should store it somewhere very secure because it is the key (sorry — bad pun) to implementing secure service calls. After you do this, both you and Amazon have a copy of the access key and the secret access key. Retaining a copy of the secret access key is crucial because it's used to encrypt information sent back and forth between you and AWS, and if you don't have the Secret Access Key, you can't execute any service calls on AWS.

The way the two keys are used is conceptually simple, although somewhat challenging in detail.

Essentially, for every service call you want carried out, you (or a tool operating on your behalf) do the following:

1. Create the service call payload.

   This is the data you need to send to AWS. It may be an object you want to store in S3 or the image identifier of an image you want to launch. (You'll also attach other pieces of information to the payload, but because they vary according to the specifics of the service call, I don't list them here. One piece of data is the current time.)

2. Encrypt the payload using the secret access key.

   Doing so ensures that no one can examine the payload and discover what's in it.

3. Digitally sign the encrypted payload by adding the secret access key to the encrypted payload and performing a digital signature process using the secret access key.

   Secret access keys are longer and more random than typical user passwords; the lengthy secret access key makes the encryption performed with it more secure than it would be if it were performed with a typical user password.

4. Send the total encrypted payload, along with your access key, to AWS via a service call.

   Amazon uses the access key to look up your secret access key, which it uses to decrypt the payload. If the decrypted payload represents readable text that can be executed, AWS executes the service call. Otherwise, it concludes that something is wrong with the service call (perhaps that it was called by a malevolent actor) and doesn't execute the service call.

In addition to the encryption just described, AWS has two other methods it uses to ensure the legitimacy of the service call:

✔ The first is based on the date information included with the service call payload, which it uses to determine whether the time associated with the making of the service call is appropriate; if the date in the service call is much different from what it should be (much earlier or later than the current time, in other words), AWS concludes that it isn't a legitimate service call and discards it.

✔ The second additional security measure involves a checksum you calculate for the payload. (A *checksum* is a number that represents the content of a message.) AWS computes a checksum for the payload; if its checksum doesn't agree with yours, it disallows the service call and doesn't execute it. This checksum approach ensures that no one tampers with the contents of a message and prevents a malevolent actor from intercepting a legitimate service call and changing it to perform an unacceptable action. If someone tampers with the message, when AWS calculates a checksum, that checksum no longer matches the one included in the message, and AWS refuses to execute the service call.

If, like most AWS users, you use a proxy method to interact with AWS — the AWS management console, a language library, or a third-party tool — you need to provide your access key and secret access key to the proxy. When the proxy executes AWS service calls on your behalf, it includes the access key in the call and use the secret access key to perform payload encryption.

Because of the critical role that these keys fulfill in AWS, you should share them *only* with entities you trust. If you want to try out a new third-party tool and you don't know much about the company, set up an AWS test account for the trial instead of using your production AWS account credentials. That way, if you decide not to go forward with the tool, you can drop it, terminate the test AWS account, and move forward, unconcerned about potential security vulnerabilities in your main production accounts. Of course, you can always create new access keys and secret access keys, but using your production keys for tests and then changing the keys creates a lot of work, because you need to update every place that makes reference to your existing keys. If you're like many other AWS users, you'll use a number of tools and libraries, and going back to them to update your keys is a pain. You're better off using nonproduction accounts to test new tools.

AWS offers a service to make managing keys/secret access keys easier. It's called IAM and is covered in Chapter 8. IAM allows you to assign keys and secret access keys to individuals or to applications, making it much easier to avoid wholesale changes when one person leaves an organization; it's also a great help when you need to give each application access to the AWS services and resources that it needs.

Chapter 3

Introducing the AWS Management Console

*O*kay, so you're ready to start working with Amazon Web Services (AWS) and cloud computing. But how? Well, it turns out that the *services* part of Amazon Web Services refers to the fact that all interaction with Amazon's cloud computing service is performed with the help of numerous Application Programming Interface (API) calls over the Internet. These calls are accomplished by either SOAP or REST interfaces carrying data in XML or JSON formats.

Whew! Sounds complicated.

Never fear. Amazon offers its own, web-based interface to enable users to work with AWS. This interface, the *AWS Management Console,* hides all the complex details of interacting with the AWS API. You interact with the console, and Amazon's program deals with all the complexity under the hood.

In fact, many people never interact with AWS except through the Console — it's that powerful. This chapter introduces you to the Console, steps you through setting up your very own AWS account, and even provides your first taste of cloud computing. You get to interact with AWS's S3 storage service, upload a picture of your choice, and then connect to it over the Internet and display it in your browser. How fun is that?

I provide screen shots of the various screens you see during your introduction to the Console so that you know exactly what you should see and do.

By the end of this chapter, you'll be ready to interact with AWS and, more importantly, to learn all about AWS's great computing services.

Amazon updates the Management Console screens fairly frequently, so the screenshots in this book may look different than what you see displayed on your terminal. Fortunately, it's usually pretty easy to map functionality from one screen version to another, but I wanted to provide a heads-up before you get worried about seeing a display that looks different from what's in the book. The Management Console display changes are a side effect of the rapid evolution and innovation within AWS.

Setting Up Your Amazon Web Services Account

The first thing to do is to create your very own AWS account. In this multi-step process, you sign up for the service, provide your billing information, and then confirm your agreement with AWS to create your account. Ready? Let's jump right in:

1. **Point your favorite web browser to the main Amazon Web Services page at** `http://aws.amazon.com.`

   You should see a screen that looks something like Figure 3-1.

2. **Click the Sign Up button.**

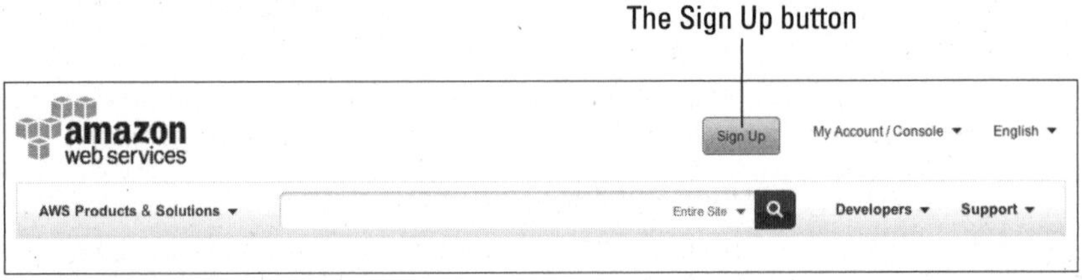

The Sign Up button

Figure 3-1:
The main
AWS land-
ing page.

On the next screen (see Figure 3-2), you're given the opportunity to sign in with an existing AWS account or set up a new account. You're setting up a new account.

Technically, you can also use your existing Amazon retail account if you have one, although I don't recommend that. Think about it — if you share your AWS account and use a retail identifier for it, down the line someone you're sharing your AWS with may end up buying a nice big flatscreen TV on your dime. So my recommendation is that you set up a new AWS account.

3. **Make sure that the I Am a New User radio button is selected, fill in an appropriate e-mail address in the given field, and then click the Sign In Using Our Secure Server button.**

Enter an e-mail address

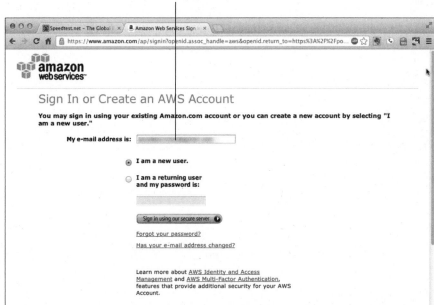

Figure 3-2:
The initial account-creation page.

AWS takes you to a new page (see Figure 3-3), where you're asked to enter your login credentials.

4. **Enter a username, your e-mail address (twice, just to be sure), and the password you want to use (again, twice, just to be sure).**

5. **Click Continue button.**

Doing so brings up the Account Information screen, asking for your address and phone number information, as shown in Figure 3-4. You're asked to select the box confirming that you agree to the terms of the AWS customer agreement.

6. **Enter the required personal information, confirm your acceptance of the customer agreement, and then click the Create Account and Continue button.**

The next page (see Figure 3-5) asks you for a credit card number and your billing address information. Amazon has to be sure to get paid, right?

7. **Enter the required payment information in the appropriate fields and then Click Continue.**

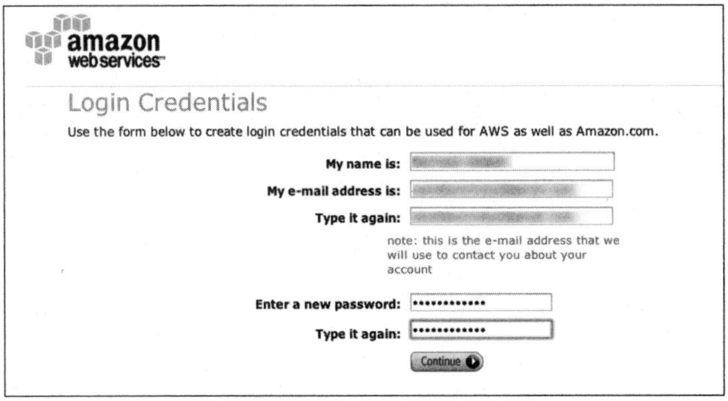

Figure 3-3:
Creating
your login
credentials.

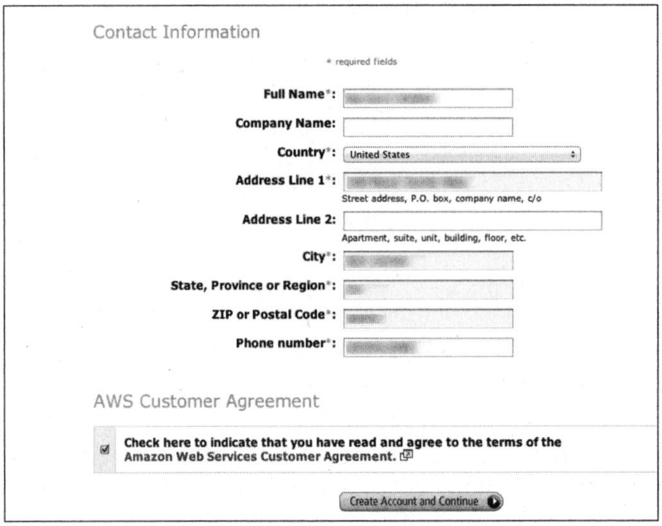

Figure 3-4:
The contact
informa-
tion and
customer
agreement
page.

The next page you see is a bit curious-looking. Amazon wants to confirm your identity, so it asks for a phone number it can use to call you.

8. **Enter your telephone number in the appropriate field and click the Call Me Now button, as shown in Figure 3-6.**

AWS displays a pin code on the screen and then calls you on the phone number you supplied.

9. **Answer the phone and enter the displayed PIN code on the telephone keypad.**

   The AWS screen updates to look like Figure 3-7.

10. **Click the Continue button.**

    You're asked to wait a bit to have your account set up by AWS, but, in my experience, this is no more than two or three minutes. You'll then be sent an e-mail confirming your account setup; you have to click on a link in that e-mail to complete the account signup process.

    After setup is complete, you should see a screen that lists all the services you're already signed up for automatically, just by creating your account. Quite an impressive list, eh?

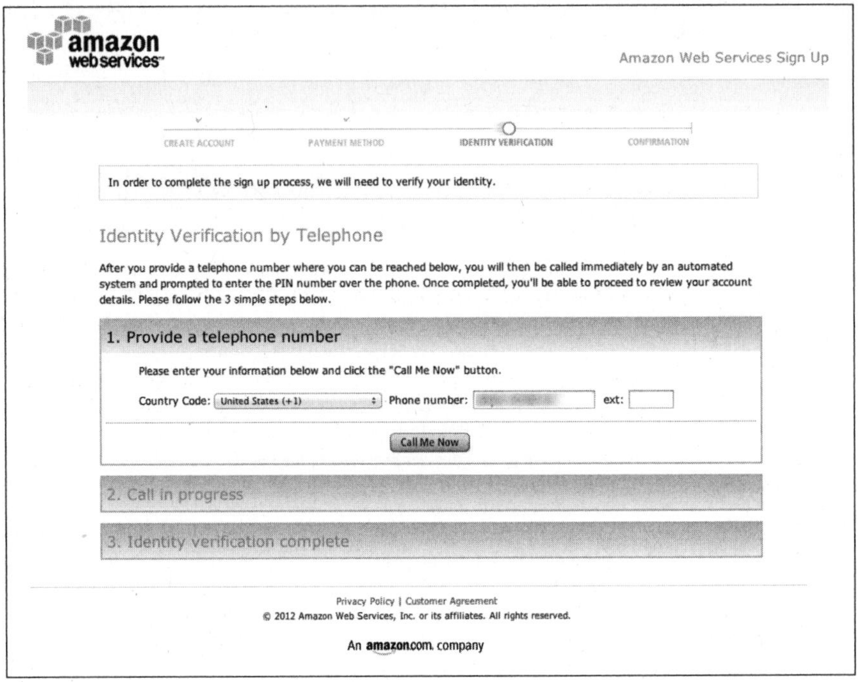

Figure 3-6:
Verifying
your identity
using the
telephone.

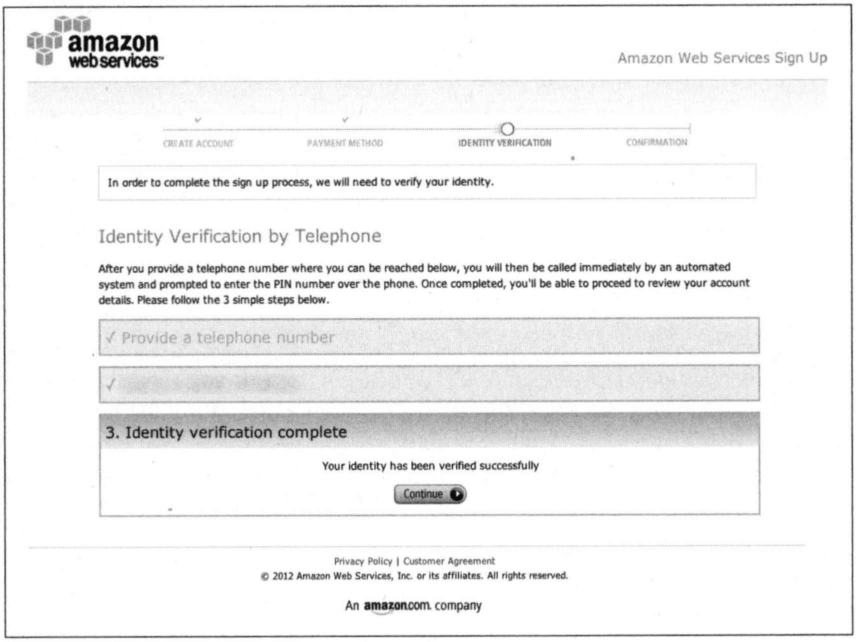

Figure 3-7:
Identity
verification
complete.

Here are two important points to take away from this initial account setup:

- ✔ **Your account is now set up as a general AWS account.** You can use AWS resources anywhere in the AWS system — the US East or either of the two US West regions, Asia Pacific (Tokyo, Singapore, or Australia), South America (Brazil), and Europe (Ireland). Put another way, your account is scoped over the entirety of AWS, but resources are located within a specific region.

- ✔ **You have given AWS a credit card number to pay for the resources you use.** In effect, you have an open tab with AWS, so *be careful* about how much computing resource you consume. For the purposes of this book, you don't have to worry much about costs — your initial sign-up provides a free level of service for a year that should be sufficient for you to perform the steps in this book as well as experiment on your own without breaking your piggy bank.

If you're concerned about overspending on AWS, Amazon's got your back. You can set a billing alert with a specified amount you don't want to go over; if your AWS total use for a month approaches that number, Amazon will send you an alert. You can enable billing alerts by clicking My Account in the Management Console landing page and then clicking on Account Activity on the subsequent page.

That's it. You're all set up in AWS and ready to begin cloud computing. If you're anything like me, you're eager to go for a bit of a spin, just to see how AWS works. So get ready to do one small task with AWS — store and retrieve a photo from the AWS object storage service knows as S3.

You start by going to the AWS home page and placing the cursor over the My Account/Console button in the upper-right corner of the screen. (Refer to Figure 3-1.) You should see a menu displayed underneath the cursor. Click the top item listed: AWS Management Console. You then see a page that provides access to all the services you're signed up for (see Figure 3-8), including S3. (You may have to enter your password again to access the Management Console from the pull-down menu).

The pull-down menu on the left side of the page allows you to define your AWS Management Console start page. (It's right there under the *Set Start Page* heading.) The default is the general landing page, although you can choose any one of the specific pages associated with a particular AWS service. For now, leave your start page as is.

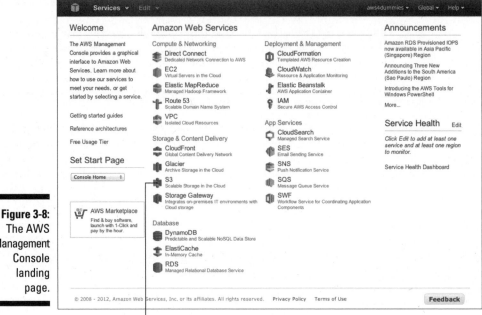

Figure 3-8:
The AWS
Management
Console
landing
page.

Your link to the S3 page

The Silicon Valley Education Foundation runs on AWS

Do you have to be a huge company, like Netflix or Amazon, to take advantage of AWS?

Not at all. Let me share a case study I was personally involved in: the Silicon Valley Education Foundation (SVEF). Unlike Amazon.com or Netflix, SVEF is a tiny organization — it has fewer than 30 employees. And, unlike Amazon.com or Netflix, SVEF isn't a sophisticated technology user; though its mission focuses on helping students with vital science, technology, engineering, and math (STEM) skills, its staff isn't strong on IT skills.

SVEF engaged the technology consulting firm I ran at the time to evaluate one of its most critical applications, designed to let teachers contribute, share, and improve lesson plans for their classes. SVEF had engaged an outside firm to design and build the application; it evaluated whether the infrastructure on which the application was running was robust enough to avoid downtime and could support large growth in traffic, which SVEF expected as more teachers adopted the application.

That the entire application was hosted on a single server in a colocation facility made the answer obvious: The application wasn't protected against hardware failure, had no redundancy, and would face significant challenges if application use scaled significantly.

We performed a study comparing three options: Install additional hardware to implement redundancy; implement virtualization to abstract the application from specific hardware and make it easy to migrate to new hardware in case of failure; and use Amazon Web Services.

Our conclusion, based on both economics and the shortage of IT skills within the SVEF organization, was that SVEF should move its application to AWS. SVEF would *save* money running

on AWS, compared to its ongoing hosting fee. It would also suffer no more than ten minutes of downtime if the AWS hardware were to fail. And, finally, if the application required more resources as a result of heavy use, it would be trivially easy to shut down one application instance and start another, larger one.

Based on this recommendation, SVEF moved its application to AWS, where it has run happily ever since and with little downtime. Inspired by the success of moving this application to AWS, SVEF evaluated all the applications it was running, and within six months migrated all of them to cloud environments.

So even if your organization isn't a giant of technology, you can still use AWS and benefit from it.

Accessing Your First AWS Service

After you're the proud owner of an AWS account, it's time to do something useful. Start by checking out your S3 resources. To do so, click the S3 link on your AWS Management Console start page. (Refer to Figure 3-8.)

You're taken to a page that lets you manage your S3 resources. (See Figure 3-9.) If you have sharp eyes, you'll quickly notice that there's nothing listed on the page. So the first thing you have to do is create a storage resource where you can place your first object.

Before I walk you through the step-by-step process of creating a storage resource, though, I want to talk a bit about terminology. You'll notice on the left side of the S3 screen is a button labeled *Create Buckets.* Now, you may wonder why something that sounds like you'd buy it at a hardware store is prominently displayed in AWS. The answer is simple: AWS refers to all top-level identifiers within S3 as *buckets,* signifying, you may presume, a place to put stuff to store. (The term *bucket* is, perhaps, your first exposure to AWS's curious nomenclature, but I assure you it won't be the last!)

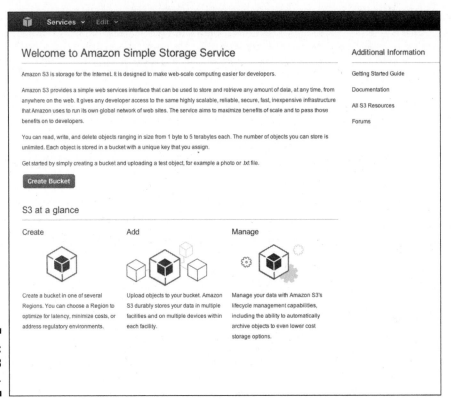

The first thing to do, therefore, is to create a bucket. Before you run out and do so, however, keep a few AWS conditions in mind:

- **Bucket names must be unique within the entire AWS system.** The names must be *unique across all user accounts.* So if I have a pet named Star and decide to name one of my buckets Star in his honor, and somebody else has already named one of her buckets Star, well, I'm out of luck. This isn't terribly convenient, but that's the way it is.

- **Although bucket names are global (unique across the entire AWS system, in other words), buckets themselves are located in a particular region.** Let's say you want a bucket to reflect your company's name — Corpname, for example. If you use Corpname to create a bucket, you'll isolate that name to a single region, even if you want to place objects throughout the world in a bucket associated with your company's name. So, a better strategy is to use a common identifier with region-specific information as part of the bucket name; for example, you can use Corpname-US-East for a bucket in the eastern US region and Corpname-US-West-Oregon for a bucket in the region associated with Oregon.

- **Use all lowercase letters in creating a bucket.** Even though the official S3 naming rules let you use uppercase letters, the S3 Management

Console doesn't allow them for buckets created in most AWS regions. If you try to include uppercase letters in the bucket name, the Console returns an error message. Keep in mind that, although AWS is a wonderful service, it does have its quirks. You can always find a way around them, but don't be surprised when you run into things that don't work just the way AWS says they will.

Enough about terminology and naming conventions — it's time to create your first bucket:

1. **On the S3 home page (refer to Figure 3-9), click the Create Bucket button.**

   Doing so brings up a screen similar to the one you see in Figure 3-10.

2. **Enter a name for your bucket in the Bucket Name field.**

   Because this is just an experiment, feel free to choose any name you like — and don't worry — if it's a bucket name that's already in use, AWS lets you know.

3. **Choose a region from the Region pull-down menu.**

   Choose the "Oregon" item.

4. **Click the Create button.**

   AWS creates your new bucket and returns you to the S3 page for managing your resources. There, you see something like Figure 3-11, which now lists the bucket you just created.

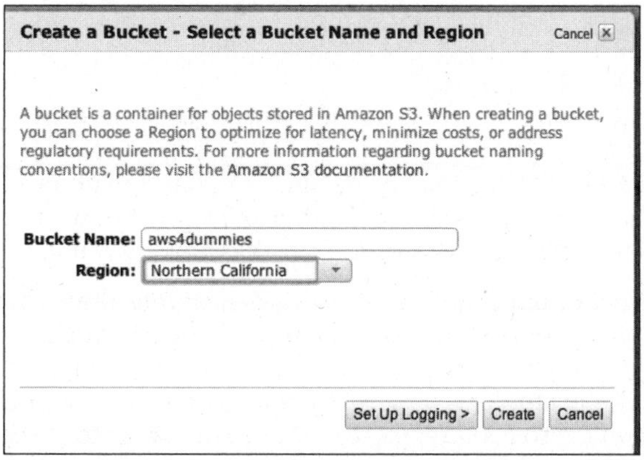

Create a Bucket - Select a Bucket Name and Region Cancel ☒

A bucket is a container for objects stored in Amazon S3. When creating a bucket, you can choose a Region to optimize for latency, minimize costs, or address regulatory requirements. For more information regarding bucket naming conventions, please visit the Amazon S3 documentation.

Bucket Name: aws4dummies
Region: Northern California ▾

Set Up Logging > | Create | Cancel

Figure 3-10: Name your bucket.

Congratulations! You've now done your first bit of cloud computing. Of course, it's not useful yet — your bucket just sits there, like an empty filing cabinet, so put something into it so that you can see how it all hangs together.

Your first bucket

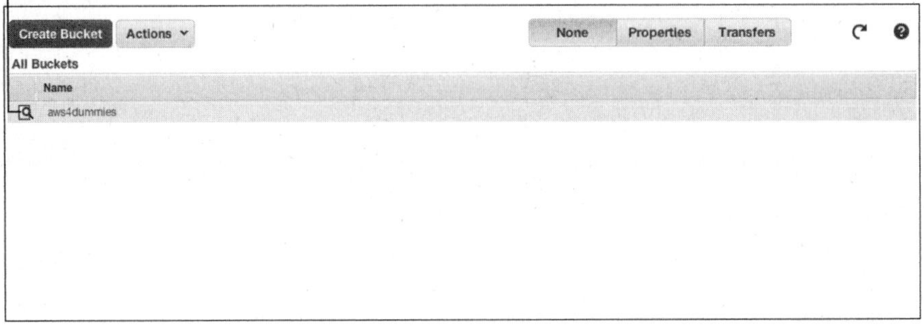

Figure 3-11:
The S3
management
page, with
your first
bucket now
listed.

| Create Bucket | Actions ∨ | | None | Properties | Transfers | C | @ |

All Buckets

Name

aws4dummies

Loading Data into S3 Buckets

I suggest that for your first S3 experiment, you upload a picture that you can then retrieve and see displayed in your browser.

You start out on the S3 page for managing your resources. (Refer to Figure 3-11.) Look for the bucket you just created. Found it? Good!

1. **Click to select the bucket you created.**

   Doing so opens the bucket, and the right side of the screen lists a number of actions you can take within the bucket.

2. **Click the Upload button.**

   The Upload-Select Files dialog box appears, as shown in Figure 3-12.

3. **Click the Add Files button.**

4. **Using the file selector widget that appears, browse your local file system, select a file to upload, and then click Open at the bottom of the widget.**

   You return to the Upload-Select Files dialog box.

5. **Click the Start Upload button in the bottom-right corner of the dialog box.**

   After a few seconds, your bucket lists the file you just uploaded.

   If you click on the Properties button on the upper right, you'll see information on the file, as shown in Figure 3-13.

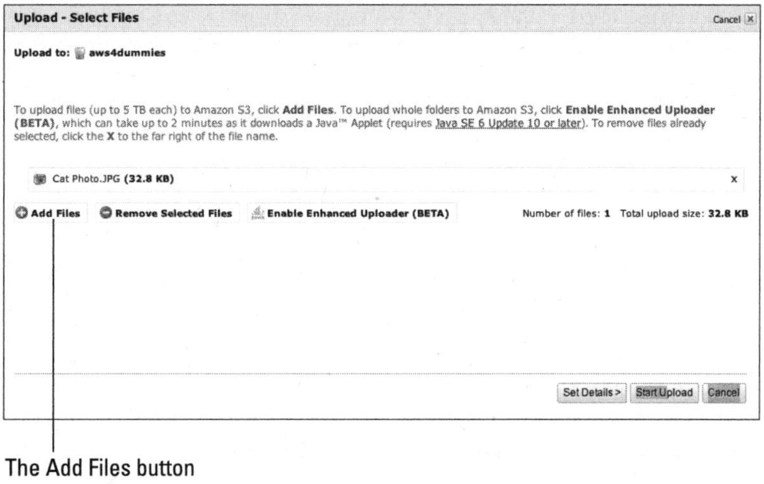

Figure 3-12:
The Upload
Files dialog
box.

The Add Files button

Your uploaded file

Figure 3-13:
Your bucket
now shows
the file
you just
uploaded.

Uploading the file is half the battle. Now all you have to do, via a browser, is access the picture you just uploaded. Before you can do that, however, you need to set permissions on the object to make it available over the Internet to someone other than the owner (that's you, by the way). To do that, follow these steps:

1. **In the listing of uploaded files (refer to Figure 3-12), click to select the file you just uploaded.**

2. **Click the Properties button in the upper-right corner of the screen.**

   Doing so brings up a pane filled with all kinds of information about the selected object.

   You can also access a file's Properties information by right-clicking a selected file and choosing Properties from the menu that appears.

3. **Click the arrow next to *Permissions*.**

   The Permissions section expands to show the Permissions information. You should see only yourself listed next to Grantee as someone able to access the file. You need to add a permission so that others can access the file as well.

4. **Click the Add More Permissions link.**

   An additional drop-down menu (labeled Grantee as well) appears below the first menu, as shown in Figure 3-14.

Figure 3-14:
Adding
permissions
to an S3
object.

5. **Choose Everyone from this second drop-down menu, select the associated Open/Download check box (refer to Figure 3-13), and then click Save.**

   The file is now accessible to everyone. To access it, you only have to track down the URL you want to use.

6. **Go back to the Properties screen.**

   Here you will see a panel of information on the object, including its URL.

7. **Copy the URL listed in the Link section, create a new tab in your browser, enter the URL you just copied into the address line, and hit Enter.**

   You should see your picture appear in the browser, just like magic! (See Figure 3-15 for proof.)

Your S3 URL

https://s3-us-west-1.amazonaws.com/aws4dummies/Cat+Photo.JPG

Figure 3-15: A picture of our cat Star, snoozing in a chair, straight from S3.

S3 URL Naming Conventions

If you take a closer look at the URL in Figure 3-14, you see that it follows an unusual naming convention. The domain is amazonaws.com, but to the left of the domain is s3-us-west-1. You can probably figure out that it represents the region in which you chose to create your bucket. AWS prepends regional information to its domain in order to direct requests to access the object. DNS can then efficiently and reliably locate the overall resource storing an S3 object.

To the right of the domain is the name of the bucket you created. (In Figure 3-15, that name is aws4dummies.) The bucket name is part of every request to S3 and is included in the URL. Following the bucket name in the URL is the filename of the actual object. In the case of my example, it's the not-very-clever name Cat Photo. (Note that S3 replaces spaces in a filename with plus signs.)

A bucket can contain only files. It's possible to create folders within a bucket to allow better organization of files. In fact, folders can contain folders themselves, thus allowing S3 to mimic the conventions of computer file systems. AWS presents the organization of S3 as a set of buckets containing objects or folders, which can contain other folders or objects.

Things are not what they seem

Keep in mind that although the S3 Management Console presents files in a nice, neat folder structure, there is in fact no hierarchical organization of objects within S3 buckets. It's just a collection of objects spread throughout S3, with arbitrarily complex resource names that contain conventions, like the slash (/), as part of the resource name. S3 is referred to as a *flat storage* system, which means that all objects reside at the top level, with those resource names appearing to reflect hierarchy, but in fact being nothing but an S3 naming convention. It's hard to wrap your head around this concept, but it provides AWS with enormous flexibility and scalability.

Because no hierarchical organization is truly present, AWS can add storage capacity to a nearly infinite degree and add it without disrupting what's already in the S3 system. This clever arrangement takes some getting used to, given how most people are familiar with file systems reflecting hierarchical organization.

Last Words on the AWS Management Console

You've accomplished a lot in this chapter: You've become acquainted with the AWS Management Console, set up your own AWS account, and even chalked up your first AWS experience by experimenting with the S3 storage service.

I hope that this information has helped you understand how easy it is to get started with AWS. If you followed the step-by-step instructions in this chapter, you probably spent no more than 30 minutes on them, from typing aws. amazon.com in a browser address window to accessing your first cloud computing resource. I also hope this first taste of AWS has whetted your appetite to learn more about it, because I dive next into the full panoply of AWS services.

Part II
Diving into AWS Offerings

Check out the article "Amazon.com Runs on AWS" (and more) online at www.dummies.com/extras/amazonwebservices.

In this part . . .

- ✔ Explore the universe of AWS offerings — and a large universe it is!

- ✔ Find out how AWS differs from its competition.

- ✔ See how AWS offerings work in combination to enable developers to build powerful, scalable, and robust applications easily.

- ✔ Check out the article "Amazon.com Runs on AWS" (and more) online at www.dummies.com/extras/amazonweb services.

Chapter 4

Setting Up AWS Storage

Though Chapter 3 is all about AWS Management Console, this chapter helps you tackle an entirely different task: diving in to the individual AWS offerings — a bunch of them!

Every journey has a beginning. I strongly recommend that you start your journey through AWS by taking a long, hard look at storage, for several reasons:

✓ **Storage is an increasingly important topic to IT because of the recent staggering increase in the amount of data that businesses use in their day-to-day operations.** Though traditional structured data (the database) is growing quite rapidly, the use of digital media (video) by businesses is exploding. IT organizations are using more and more storage, and they often look to communication service providers (CSPs) such as Amazon to provide storage. Another driver of storage consumption is the recent rise of *big data,* which refers to analyzing very large datasets.

Companies are drowning in data, and many are finding it nearly impossible to keep up with managing their own, on-premises storage systems.

✓ **Storage is the first AWS offering that Amazon offered.** Storage therefore holds a significant place in the AWS ecosystem, including some extremely innovative uses of its storage services by AWS customers over the years.

✓ **A number of AWS offerings rely on AWS storage, especially Simple Storage Service (S3).** Understanding AWS storage services helps you better understand the operation of the AWS offerings that rely on AWS storage.

✔ **AWS continues to innovate and deliver new storage services.** Glacier, for example, provides a fresh twist on addressing a historic IT issue: archival storage. Glacier is discussed later in this chapter as well (in case you need something to look forward to).

The term *Amazon's storage service* (which may be the largest in the industry) is a misnomer: The company offers four different storage services within AWS. The scale of the overall storage service that subsumes all four specific services is enormous. Chapter 1 presents information on the number of objects stored in the AWS Simple Storage Service (known as *S3)*; in just more than six years, S3 has grown so rapidly that it now contains more than 2 trillion objects. To put the staggering growth of S3 into perspective, the service spent six years reaching 1 trillion objects, and less than ten months growing from 1 to 2 trillion objects.

Despite the rock star status of S3, this chapter still covers all four AWS storage services (drumroll, please):

✔ **Simple Storage Service (S3):** Provides highly scalable object storage in the form of unstructured collections of bits

✔ **Elastic Block Storage (EBS):** Provides highly available and reliable data volumes that can be attached to a virtual machine (VM), detached, and then reattached to another VM

✔ **Glacier:** A data archiving solution; provides low-cost, highly robust archival data storage and retrieval

✔ **DynamoDB:** Key-value storage; provides highly scalable, high-performance storage based on tables indexed by data values referred to as *keys*

AWS also offers a managed database service called Relational Database Service, or RDS. I talk more about RDS in Chapter 8.

This list presents the basics, but as you may expect, there's more to this topic. Let's get down to business and examine the storage offerings from Amazon.

Differentiating the Amazon Storage Options

You may be forgiven for asking the obvious question: Why does Amazon offer four different AWS storage services? This interesting question, which strikes at the heart of Amazon's unique cloud computing offering, addresses how well it's responding to the data deluge I mention earlier in this chapter.

Put simply, the enormous growth of storage makes traditional approaches (local storage, network-attached storage, storage-area networks, and the like) no longer appropriate, for these three reasons:

- ✔ **Scaling:** Traditional methods simply can't scale large enough to handle the volume of data that companies now generate. The amounts of data that companies must manage outstrip the capabilities of almost all storage solutions.

- ✔ **Speed:** They can't move data fast enough to respond to the demands that companies are placing on their storage solutions. To be blunt, most corporate networks cannot handle the level of traffic required to shunt around all the bits that companies store.

- ✔ **Cost:** Given the volumes of data being addressed, the established solutions aren't economically viable — they're unaffordable at the scale that companies now require.

For these reasons, the issue of storage has long since moved beyond local storage (for example, disk drives located within the server using the data). Over the past couple decades, two other forms of traditional storage have entered the market — network-attached storage (NAS) and storage-area networks (SAN) — which move storage from the local server to within the network on which the server sits. When the server requires data, rather than search a local disk for it, it seeks it out over the network.

The two types of network-based storage differ significantly (notwithstanding the similarity of their acronyms). NAS, which operates as an extension of the server's local file system, is used like local files: Reads and writes operate the same as though the file were located on the server itself. In other words, NAS makes storage look like it's part of the local server. SANs operate quite differently. They offer remote storage that is separate from the local server; that storage doesn't appear as local to the server. Instead, the server must operate a special protocol to communicate with the SAN device; you can say that the SAN device offers detached storage that the server must make special arrangements to use.

Both types of storage continue to be widely used, but the much larger volumes of data make neither NAS nor SAN storage able to support requirements. Consequently, newer storage types have come to the fore that provide better functionality.

In particular, two new storage types are now available:

- ✔ **Object:** Reliably stores and retrieves unstructured digital objects
- ✔ **Key-value:** Manages structured data

The next couple sections unpack the meanings behind a few terms, such as *unstructured digital object, structured data,* and *key-value storage,"* so don't worry if the vocabulary seems daunting.

Object storage

Object storage provides the ability to store, well, objects — which are essentially collections of digital bits. Those bits may represent a digital photo, an MRI scan, a structured document such as an XML file — or the video of your cousin's embarrassing attempt to ride a skateboard down the steps at the public library (the one you premiered at his wedding).

Object storage offers the reliable (and highly scalable) storage of collections of bits, but imposes no structure on the bits. The structure is chosen by the user, who needs to know, for example, whether an object is a photo (which can be edited), or an MRI scan (which requires a special application for viewing it). The user has to know both the format as well as the manipulation methods of the object. The object storage service simply provides reliable storage of the bits.

Object storage differs from file storage, which you may be more familiar with from using a PC. File storage offers *update functionality,* and object storage does not. For example, suppose you are storing logging output from a program. The program constantly adds new logging entries as events occur; creating a new object each time an additional log record is created would be incredibly inconvenient. By contrast, using file storage allows you to continuously update the file by *appending* new information to it — in other words, you update the file as the program creates new log records.

Object storage offers no such update ability. You can insert or retrieve an object, but you can't change it. Instead, you update the object in the local application and then insert the object into the object store. To let the new version retain the same name as the old version, delete the original object before inserting the new object with the same name. The difference may seem minor, but it requires different approaches to managing stored objects.

Distributed key-value storage

Distributed key-value storage, in contrast to object storage, provides structured storage that is somewhat akin to a database but different in important ways in order to provide additional scalability and performance.

Perhaps you've already used a *relational database management system* — a storage product that's commonly referred to as *RDBMS*. Its rows of data have one or more keys (hence the name *key-value storage*) that support manipulation of the data. Though RDBMS systems are fantastically useful, they typically face challenges in scaling beyond a single server. Newer distributed key-value storage products are designed from the get-go to support huge amounts of data by spreading across multiple (perhaps *thousands* of) servers.

Key-value storage systems often make use of redundancy within hardware resources to prevent outages; this concept is important when you're running thousands of servers, because they're bound to suffer hardware breakdowns. Without redundancy, the entire storage system can be knocked out of commission by a single server; the use of redundancy makes the key-value system always available — and, more importantly, your data is always available because it's protected from hardware outages.

Literally dozens of key-value storage products are available. Many of them were first developed by so-called webscale companies, such as Facebook and LinkedIn, to ensure that they can handle massive amounts of traffic. Those companies then turned around and released the products under open source licenses, so now you (or anyone else) can use them in other environments.

Though key-value storage systems vary in different ways, they have these common characteristics:

- ✔ **Data is structured with a single key that's used to identify the record in which all remaining data resides.** The key is almost always unique — such as a user number, a unique username (title_1795456, for example), or a part number. This ensures that each record has a unique key, which helps facilitate scale and performance.

- ✔ **Retrieval is restricted to the key value.** For example, to find all records with a common address (where the address is not the key), every record has to be examined.

- ✔ **No support exists for performing searches across multiple datasets with common data elements.** RDBMS systems allow *joins:* For a given username in a dataset, find all records in a second dataset that have the username in individual records. For example, to find all books that a library patron has checked out, perform a join of the user table (where the user's last name is used to identify her library ID) and the book checkout table (where each book is listed along with the library IDs of everyone who has checked it out). You can use the join functionality of an RDBMS system to execute this query; by contrast, because key-value systems don't support joins, the two tables would have to be matched at the application level rather than by the storage systems. Using this concept, commonly described as "The intelligence resides in the application," executing joins requires application "smarts" and lots of additional coding.

Key-value storage represents a trade-off between ease of use and scalability, and the trade-off is biased toward scalability (and less ease of use).

This proliferation of storage types gives users a much richer set of options to manage the data associated with their applications. Though they gain much more flexibility and can match the storage solution with functional requirements, they also face a challenge: A broader set of skills is required in order to manage a larger number of storage solutions. Moreover, using a key-value solution requires them to manage hundreds or thousands of servers.

Fortunately, Amazon recognizes that all these storage solutions are important, even with the management challenges that they bring, and offers four types of storage solutions. A user can select one that's appropriate to her requirements — rather than be forced to shoehorn into her application a solution that doesn't support the required functionality.

The need for storage flexibility is why Amazon offers four types of storage. You may not need all four — many users manage with only one or two. You should understand *all* options that AWS offers, because you may then choose to pursue a new one rather than rely on the existing one.

Storing Items in the Simple Storage Service (S3) Bucket

Simple Storage Service (fondly known as S3) is one of the richest, most flexible, and, certainly, most widely used AWS offerings. It's no exaggeration to call S3 "the filing cabinet of the Internet." Its object storage is used in an enormous variety of applications by individuals and businesses, such as

- ✔ **Dropbox:** This file storage and syncing service uses S3 to store all of the documents it stores on behalf of its users.
- ✔ **Netflix:** This popular online consumer video service uses S3 to store videos before they go out to its Content Delivery Network. In fact, Netflix operates almost 100 percent on AWS, making it somewhat of a poster child for the service.
- ✔ **Medcommons:** This company stores customers' health records online in S3 — and, by the way, it complies with the strict requirements of the Health Insurance Portability and Accountability Act (HIPAA).

Thousands of companies large and small (and individuals) use S3 to store the information that's used within their businesses.

The richness and flexibility of S3 are limited only by your imagination. The variety of ways in which it's used is mind-boggling. And Amazon continually improves S3, adding functionality to make it even more useful.

S3 has evolved into a highly functional, widely used storage service. How widely used? Cedexis, a company that analyzed a large sample set of enterprise applications, found that *25 percent* of them had accessed S3. The reason is simple: S3 is so useful, so easy to use, *and* so inexpensive that it almost seductively infiltrates applications.

S3 storage basics

Let me get down to brass tacks and talk about how S3 works. S3 objects are treated as *web objects* — that is, they're accessed via Internet protocols using a URL identifier.

> ✓ **Every S3 object has a unique URL, in this format:**
> ```
> http://s3.amazonaws.com/bucket/key
> ```
> ✓ **An actual S3 object using this format looks like this:**
> ```
> http://s3-us-west-1.amazonaws.com/aws4dummies/Cat+
>         Photo.JPG
> ```

Now, you may ask, what are the *bucket* and *key,* listed in the first example?

A *bucket* in AWS is a group of objects. The bucket's name is associated with an account — for example, the bucket named aws4dummies is associated with my aws4dummies account. The bucket name doesn't need to be the same as the account name; it can be anything. However, the bucket namespace is completely *flat:* Every bucket name must be unique among all users of AWS. If you try to create a bucket name of test within your account, you'll see an error message because you can bet your bottom dollar that someone else has already claimed that name. (Just so you know, an account is limited to 100 buckets.)

Bucket names have a number of restrictions, as described at

```
http://docs.amazonwebservices.com/AmazonS3/latest/dev/
        BucketRestrictions.html
```

My recommendation: Stick with simple names that are easily understood, to simplify using S3 and avoid problems.

A *key* in AWS is the name of an object, and it acts as an identifier to locate the data associated with the key. In AWS, a key can be either an object name (as in Cat+Photo.JPG) or a more complex arrangement that imposes some structure on the organization of objects within a bucket (as in bucketname/photos/catphotos/Cat+Photo.JPG, where /photos/catphotos is part of the object name). This convenient arrangement provides a familiar directory-like or URL-like format for object names; however, it doesn't represent the actual structure of the S3 storage system — it's merely a comfortable and memorable method of naming objects, making it easy for humans to keep track. Even though many tools present S3 storage as though it's in a familiar file folder organization (including the AWS Management Console itself), they imply nothing about how the objects are stored within S3.

S3 object management

An S3 object isn't a complicated creature — it's simply a collection of bytes. The service imposes no restrictions on the object format — it's up to you. The only limitation is on object size: An S3 object is limited to 5TB. (That's *large.*)

Managing objects in S3

Like all AWS offerings, S3 is accessed via an application programming interface, or API, and it supports both SOAP and REST interfaces. (For more information on the details of these interfaces, see Chapter 2.)

Of course, you probably won't use the (not particularly user-friendly) API to post (create), get (retrieve), or delete S3 objects. You may access them via a programming library that encapsulates the API calls and offers higher-level S3 functions that are easier to use. More likely, however, you'll use an even higher-level tool or application that provides a graphical interface to manage S3 objects. You can be sure, however, that somewhere down in the depths of the library or higher-level tool, are calls to the S3 API.

In addition to the most obvious and useful actions for objects (such as post, get, and delete), S3 offers a wide range of object management actions — for example, an API call to get the version number of an object. Earlier in this chapter, I mention that object storage disallows updating an object (unlike a file residing within a file system). S3 works around this issue by allowing versioning of S3 objects — you can modify version 2 of an S3 object, for example, and store the modified version as version 3. This gets around the process to update objects outlined earlier: Retrieve old object, modify object in application, delete old object from S3, and then insert modified object with original object name.

S3 bucket and object security

AWS offers *fine-grained* access controls to implement S3 security: You can use these controls to explicitly control who-can-do-what with your S3 objects. The mechanism by which this access control is enforced is, naturally enough, the Access Control List (ACL).

These four types of people can access S3 objects:

- ✔ **Owner:** The person who created the object; he can also read or delete the object.

- ✔ **Specific users or groups:** Particular users, or groups of users, within AWS. (Access may be restricted to other members of the owner's company.)

- ✔ **Authenticated users:** People who have accounts within AWS and have been successfully authenticated.

- ✔ **Everyone:** Anyone on the Internet (as you may expect).

S3 provides a rich set of actions in the S3 API. Several functions, for example, allow the manipulation of object versions to retrieve a certain version of an object. And, of course, I mention elsewhere the expiration capability that was added early in 2012 — it's in the API as well.

The access controls specify who, and the actions specify what — who has the right to do what with a given object. The interaction between the S3 access controls and the object actions gives S3 its fine-grained object management functionality.

S3 uses, large and small

Making specific recommendations about what you should do with S3 is difficult because it's extremely flexible and capable. Individual (rather than corporate) users tend to use S3 as secure, location-independent storage of digital media. Another common personal use for S3 is to back up local files, via either the AWS Management Console or one of the many consumer-oriented backup services.

Companies use S3 for the same reasons as individuals, and for many more use cases. For example, companies store content files used by their partners in S3. Most consumer electronics and appliance manufacturers now offer their user manuals in digital format; many of them store those files in S3. Many companies place images and videos used in their corporate websites in S3, which reduces their storage management headaches — and ensures that in conditions of heavy web traffic, website performance isn't hindered by inadequate network bandwidth.

The most common S3 actions revolve, naturally enough, around creating, retrieving, and deleting objects. Here's the common lifecycle of an S3 object: Create the object in preparation to use it; set permissions to control access to the object; allow applications and people to retrieve the object as part of an application's functionality; and delete the object when the application that uses the object no longer requires it. Of course, many objects are never removed, because they're *evergreen:* They have ongoing purpose over a long time span.

As you get more familiar with S3, you'll undoubtedly start exploring additional S3 functionality. S3 offers encryption of objects stored in the service, securing your data from anyone attempting to access it inappropriately. You can log requests made against S3 objects to audit when objects are accessed and by whom. S3 can even be used to host *static* websites: They don't dynamically assemble data to create the pages served up as part of the website — removing the need to run a web server.

Many online computing services that you use (or will use) as part of your personal or business life make use of S3; it is increasingly being used as part of the solutions delivered by both large and small technology companies. The filing cabinet of the Internet, indeed!

S3 scope and availability

S3 functionality, and how you use it to access objects, is only a piece of the puzzle; you also need to consider the overall organization of S3.

AWS as a whole is organized into regions, each of which contains one or more availability zones, or AZs. Although S3 locates buckets within regions, keep in mind that S3 bucket names are unique across *all* S3 regions, even though buckets themselves reside in particular regions. For example, if you create a bucket named after your company, you have to choose in which region to locate the bucket.

In the cat photo example I mention earlier in this chapter

```
http://s3-us-west-1.amazonaws.com/aws4dummies/Cat+
            Photo.JPG
```

you see that the bucket aws4dummies is located in the US West region. (Note the s3-us-west-1 section of the URL.) All objects in the aws4dummies bucket have to reside in US West. No big deal, right?

Well, it depends. When an AWS virtual machine (VM) needs to access an S3 object, and the VM and the object reside in the same AWS region, Amazon imposes no charge for the network traffic that carries the object from S3 to EC2. If the VM and the object are in different regions, however (the traffic is carried over the Internet), AWS charges a few cents per gigabyte — which can be costly for very large objects or heavy use.

One way around this problem is to locate multiple buckets with duplicate objects in each region and tweak the bucket names to avoid conflicts — for example, by renaming my aws4dummies to aws4dummies_us_west and creating similarly named buckets in all other regions. I can then create duplicate objects in each of the similarly named buckets, to eliminate network traffic charges no matter where I run an EC2 instance (albeit at somewhat greater complexity and somewhat higher charges to pay for storing all the duplicate objects).

Don't worry about this need for duplicate objects and nearly identical buckets. AWS has another, much easier solution: *CloudFront* (described in Chapter 9) lets you store only one copy of an object and have Amazon make it available in every region.

Given S3's importance to many applications, an obvious question is how reliable is the service? The answer: It's reliable. In fact, because AWS designed the service for 99.99-percent availability, it should only be unavailable for approximately 53 minutes per year. A complementary issue to availability is durability — how reliable is S3 at never losing your object? The answer to this question is even more exact — 99.999999999 percent.

How does AWS achieve this high level of availability and durability? In a word, redundancy. Within each region, AWS stores multiple copies of every S3 object, to prevent a hardware failure from making it impossible to access an object, or, even worse, from destroying the only copy of it. Even if one copy is unavailable because of hardware failure, another is always available for access. If a hardware failure deletes a copy or makes it unavailable, AWS automatically creates a new, third copy to ensure that the object remains available and durable.

An S3 example

The nuts-and-bolts of how to set up an S3 bucket and upload and download S3 objects are covered in Chapter 3. (If you want to see how it happens, head on over there.) In this section, however, I walk you through a typical action that would occur after you have an AWS account and have created an S3 bucket. Of course, you're likely to use S3 from applications, so I show you an example of the S3 API.

If you want to insert an object, the API call should look similar to this example:

```
PUT /my-image.jpg HTTP/1.1
Host: myBucket.s3.amazonaws.com
Date: Wed, 12 Oct 2009 17:50:00 GMT
Authorization: AWS AKIAIOSFODNN7EXAMPLE:xQE0diMbLRepdf3YB+
          FIEXAMPLE=
Content-Type: text/plain
Content-Length: 11434
Expect: 100-continue
[11434 bytes of object data]
```

Of course, you may want a higher-level abstraction within your code. AWS provides SDKs for several languages, including PHP. To perform the same insert operation in PHP, follow this example:

```
require_once 'sdk.class.php';
$s3 = new AmazonS3();

$bucket = '*** Provide bucket name ***';
$keyname1 = '*** Provide object key ***';
$filepath = '*** Provide file name to upload ***';

$response = $s3->create_object(
$bucket,
$keyname1,
array(
'fileUpload' => $filepath,
'contentType' => 'text/plain',
),
```

These actions are common to both code examples:

- ✔ **Provide credentials to authorize actions:** You can see this directly in the API call in the line that begins with `Authorization`. In the PHP program, you put the access key and secret access key in environment variables that the SDK retrieves when it assembles the API call it will perform on your behalf.

- ✔ **Define the action:** In the API, it's the line beginning with `PUT`; in the PHP SDK, it's the `create_object` call.

- ✔ **Identify the bucket:** This step identifies where to insert the object. In the API call, the bucket is identified in the host as `myBucket.s3.amazonaws.com`. In the PHP example it's `$bucket`, which would be loaded with the bucket name.

- ✔ **Identify the object key name:** The object is identified by this index within the bucket. In the API, it's `my-image.jpg`; in the PHP example, it's `$keyname1`, which would have been set to the index name you chose at the top of the code example.

- ✔ **Identify the object:** It's the "thing" to be stored in the S3 bucket. The API example has a placeholder labeled `[11434 bytes of object data]`. In a real-life API call, the actual bytes comprising the object would have followed. In the PHP example, the code points to a file to be uploaded, and the path to it is stored in `$filepath`.

- ✔ **Identify the content type:** It specifies the kind of data AWS is dealing with in the bucket and uses an appropriate program to manage any interaction with the object. (Note that my examples here use test/plain.)

To understand the authentication mechanisms within the AWS API, see Chapter 2.

S3 cost

S3 has a simple cost structure: You pay per gigabyte of storage used by your objects. You're also charged for API calls to S3, which don't vary by volume. Finally, you pay for the network traffic caused by the delivery of S3 objects.

Storage costs start at $.095 per gigabyte per month for the first terabyte, and they trend downward as total storage increases to $.055 per gigabyte per month for more than 5000 terabytes of storage.

The API call costs vary from $.01 per 1,000 requests (for PUT, COPY, POST, or LIST calls) to $.01 per 10,000 requests (for GET and all other requests). DELETE requests are free.

Data transfer pricing — for transfers into or out of an AWS region — varies (as you can surmise) by volume. Transferring data in is a gift — there's no charge for inbound network traffic placing data into S3 storage. For outbound traffic, there's no charge for the first gigabyte of traffic. Then the charge becomes $.12 per gigabyte up to 10TB, with pricing lowered based on scale. The price is reduced to $.05 per gigabyte for traffic between 150TB and 500TB.

Amazon also offers *reduced redundancy* for S3 storage, which retains fewer copies of your data — and trades reliability for cost. Reduced redundancy storage starts at $.076 per gigabyte of storage and decreases to $.037 per gigabyte at volumes higher than 5,000TB.

If S3 prices don't seem low enough for you, well, just wait a bit. Amazon has lowered prices on S3 storage consistently since launching the service, and it continues to do so. The last price change before this book was published in late 2012, when S3 prices dropped, on average, 25 percent.

If S3 prices don't seem low enough for you, well, just wait a bit. Amazon has lowered prices on S3 storage consistently since launching the service, and it continues to do so. The last price change before this book was published was in late 2012, when S3 prices dropped, on average, 25 percent. For up-to-date pricing on S3, see `http://aws.amazon.com/s3/pricing/`.

Managing Volumes of Information with Elastic Block Storage (EBS)

Elastic Block Storage (EBS) is volume-based storage that isn't associated with any particular instance; rather, it's attached to *instances* to provide additional storage. A different way to say this is that an EBS volume is independent and has a lifespan separate from EC2 instances. It can be attached to any instance to provide storage for that instance, but is detached from the instance when it terminates. (If you've ever worked with SAN storage, you're familiar with the concept. If you haven't worked with SAN storage, don't worry — EBS is simple to understand.) In any case, you'll almost certainly work with EBS, because it's extremely useful and it addresses some significant limitations in AWS.

The network-based EBS storage service is delivered in *volumes,* which can be attached to an EC2 instance and used just like a disk drive. Because a volume can become unformatted, it must have a file system installed (formatted) on it before it can be used. For example, if you want to attach an EBS volume to a Linux machine, you must first format the volume in one of the many Linux file system formats and then mount it to the instance file system, which allows the operating system to access the EBS volume and to read and write to the volume.

Because an EBS volume is network-based, it can be longer-lived than any specific instance. Consequently, an EBS volume offers persistent storage that's safe from being lost when an instance is terminated or crashes. The most common (though certainly not only) EBS use case is the file system for a database server. The database storage is placed on the EBS volume, which must be attached to an instance that is running the database software so that the software can read and write to the EBS-based database storage. This process is a bit more complicated than using the instance's own storage, but it has a great virtue: By using EBS, the application owner can ensure that data isn't subject to loss caused by instance interruption. Even if the instance crashes, the EBS volume is safe from data loss. A new instance can be started, the EBS volume can be attached to it, and the instance can begin database operations again.

The size of an EBS volume can be configured by the user and can range from 1GB to 1TB. Volumes are associated with accounts and limited by default to 20 per account.

AWS commonly places default limits on different types of resources; it makes sense to prevent users from reserving resources and then not using them. In the case of EBS, Amazon avoids letting a customer claim 1,000 volumes and never using 995 of them. AWS, though extremely large, isn't infinite, and rationing resources is one way that Amazon can provide its service to large numbers of customers. However, should you need additional resources (of any type, not just EBS), you can contact Amazon and tell it why you need more resources. Typically, Amazon is very supportive of people who truly need additional resources and is responsive to requests for them.

What if your very large database needs more than 1TB of storage? You can attach multiple EBS volumes to the instance and stripe your file system across the volumes. (*Stripe* here refers to placing portions of a file system onto multiple volumes to increase overall read and write speed, increasing performance because all the reads and writes are spread across multiple hard drives.)

EBS reliability

EBS *can* make your applications more reliable, because the storage is separate from any specific instance (as mentioned in the previous section). No matter what happens to an instance, your data stays nice and safe.

But how reliable is EBS itself? After all, why protect yourself against instance failure if the EBS service itself is unreliable?

With EBS, Amazon has again used redundancy to increase reliability. Though Amazon divulges few details about its service, it states that multiple copies of every EBS volume are available at all times to protect against data loss from hardware failure. If a disk drive containing an EBS volume goes bad, Amazon makes a new drive available and copies the EBS volume data to the new drive to ensure that it maintains appropriate redundancy.

Though EBS is highly reliable, AWS has suffered several major outages, and the culprit at least a couple times has turned out to be EBS. What's up with that?

The storage aspect of the EBS service isn't at fault. Instead, the EBS management layer (or control plane, a geeky term that means . . . EBS management layer) has malfunctioned. The control plane is part of the intelligent AWS infrastructure software (discussed in Chapter 2), and, unfortunately, problems can crop up.

Not to minimize the problems associated with the outages, but try to see them as the inevitable by-products of the innovation that AWS represents. (EBS has been around only since 2008, and, believe it or not, AWS is only a couple years older.) In any new and different product, failure inevitably occurs. If you're concerned about outages, compare AWS reliability with that of your own data center. This comparison usually helps put AWS outages into perspective and portrays them as less alarming.

EBS scope

AWS as a whole is organized into regions, each of which contains one or more availability zones (AZs). With EBS, volumes reside in a single AZ within a particular region. When you create an EBS volume, you define which AZ to locate (only) within a given region.

These statements imply, of course, that any EC2 instance that needs to mount and use this EBS volume must be located within the same AZ.

Such a setup clearly presents a challenge. Even though Amazon retains multiple copies of the EBS volume, they're all located within the same AZ. So doesn't that conflict with the general advice to make applications more robust by letting them operate in (or be able to operate in) multiple AZs, or even across AWS regions?

The short answer is yes. If your application uses EBS volumes (and, frankly, most do), it's more difficult to follow AWS best practices and operate your applications across multiple AZs. Fortunately, there's a relatively straightforward way to address this issue — by using EBS snapshots. (I tell you more on that topic later in this chapter — for now, take it on faith that the restriction that EBS volumes reside in a single AZ isn't insurmountable.)

EBS use

To use EBS, you simply create the volume with the help of the AWS API or (more likely) by using either the AWS Management Console or a third-party tool. As mentioned earlier in this chapter, before you can begin using the volume, you must attach it to an appropriate operating system device on a running EC2 instance and then format it with a file system that's appropriate for the operating system. The volume is then ready for use. It's already attached to a running EC2 instance as part of your prep work, and you can start using it immediately.

When you decide to terminate the EC2 instance to which you've attached the volume, you simply detach the volume (again, via the AWS API or Management Console or a third-party tool you're using). The EBS volume moves into a quiescent state, ready to be attached to a new EC2 instance whenever you choose. Actually, it's even easier than that — AWS detaches the volume for you when you terminate an EC2 instance, although best practices suggest not relying on the automatic detachment.

Many people avoid the manual attachment/detachment effort altogether and implement an automated approach instead, by configuring the EC2 AMI launch process to automate the EBS attachment process. (*AMI* refers to *Amazon Machine Image*, which is the format EC2 stores instances in when they are not actively running.) Alternatively, many tools (from Amazon or from third parties) do this work and avoid the need to implement it within the AMI. These tools start an AMI and then execute the API commands to attach the volume.

EBS performance

Obviously, if EBS volumes are used for important application resources, such as databases, you may wonder whether their performance is critical. How do they rank?

Typical EBS performance is around 100 IOPS (I/O operations per second) — that's what EBS is designed for. The question is, what is the real-world performance of EBS?

Well, it depends. (You may not like that answer, but it's true. Here's why.) As I note earlier in this chapter, EBS is *network-based* storage: It's remote from the instance that attaches to it. Therefore, all data reads and writes to the volume must pass across the AWS network — and this is where things get tricky.

Any time data must pass across a shared resource like a network, it's subject to delays and interruptions caused by traffic from other applications. (This is true, by the way, of all data center environments, not just AWS.) The traditional way to deal with this issue is to create a dedicated storage network (thus the term storage-area network, or SAN).

Amazon, true to its roots as a low-cost company, did not implement a dedicated network for its EBS service, leading to the major complaint about EBS — spotty performance. Overall, EBS performance wasn't that great, but even worse, it tended to be extremely inconsistent because of the issue of network congestion caused by other applications.

AWS addressed this shortcoming by extending the EBS service in mid-2012 with Provisioned IOPS for EBS — designed to provide fast, predictable EBS performance.

Provisioned IOPS delivers between 500 IOPS and 4000 IOPS of guaranteed throughput to EBS volumes. It requires the use of EBS-optimized instances, which provide dedicated throughput, presumably via the use of a storage-dedicated network. The same strategy of volume striping across multiple EBS volumes can be used with Provisioned IOPS volumes to increase performance well beyond the 4000 Mbps limit.

In keeping with AWS pricing, there's an increased cost for Provisioned IOPS use, which I describe later, in the section "EBS pricing." You'll need to determine whether the higher, more consistent EBS performance associated with Provisioned IOPS is necessary and therefore worth paying for. The cost of Provisioned IOPS isn't *that* high, but you can always hold off for a while and then move to Provisioned IOPS later, if necessary.

EBS snapshots

You may recall that EBS volumes are always associated with a single availability zone (AZ), which can present a challenge if a major goal is being able to create highly available applications. You may also recall that I hinted at a way to work around the challenge. I'll let the other shoe drop here and tell you all about the workaround.

In addition to EBS's persistent storage, AWS offers *another* function within EBS: the *snapshot*. It's a point-in-time backup of the data within an EBS volume. The snapshot is stored in S3 in the same region in which the EBS volume resides.

After an initial snapshot of an EBS volume is created, subsequent snapshots store only the modified bits of the volume. So if you have a 10GB volume and create an initial snapshot, all of the data on the volume is in the snapshot. Snapshots of the volume that are created later only store bits that have changed since the previous snapshot. In this way, an EBS snapshot is a highly efficient way to ensure the durability of EBS data, even if the EBS volume itself were to somehow be lost or damaged.

A snapshot can be used to create a new volume, so instead of starting with an empty volume, you create a new volume via a snapshot, and when it's attached to a running instance, all of the data in the original volume is available to you.

The EBS snapshot provides the method by which you can ensure a higher level of application availability even in the event of an outage in the entire availability zone. You can create ongoing snapshots of the EBS volume that reside in S3, which is scoped at the regional level. If the original availability zone becomes unavailable, you can launch a new instance from the AMI (which also is scoped at the regional level, and can therefore be launched in another availability zone). When you create in the availability zone a new EBS volume containing the newly launched instance and then attach the volume to the new instance, the EBS volume data becomes available, ready to be used by your application. Snapshots can also be transferred between AWS regions so that you can easily create a new volume in an entirely different region, attach it to an instance running in an availability zone within that region, and run your application in a location completely different from the original one.

By using EBS volumes and snapshots, you can make highly persistent data available throughout the entire AWS environment.

A snapshot is, in effect, a picture of the EBS volume at a given time. The snapshot can be used to re-create an EBS volume. EBS snapshots aren't backups of the data residing on the volume. You must understand the difference between snapshots and backups for dealing with databases (the most common uses of EBS volumes). When an EBS volume is re-created, it reflects the bits that were residing on it. A database backup, on the other hand, is a file dump of the data residing in the database; the backup can be used to re-create the database on AWS, but also on another cloud service or even in your own data center.

EBS snapshots are useful if you want to re-create storage in AWS; database backups are useful if you want to restore a database either in AWS or somewhere else.

A further twist on this topic is your restore time (or, if you need to re-create a database, how long *that* takes). Creating a new database from a backup can cost you an hour or more. (The process typically takes several hours because the entire backup has to be read into the database before it's ready.) The EBS approach provides restoration more quickly. After you tell AWS to create a new volume from a snapshot, it returns almost immediately with the volume ID, which you can attach to an instance. The data is then loaded into the volume in the background, and you can request data from anywhere in the volume after it's mounted. If the data isn't yet available, AWS requests the necessary blocks; when they're available, it returns from the request. Though extremely convenient, this process can negatively impact performance until all the data is available on the volume.

So what can you do if you want high availability and you don't want to endure poor performance while you wait for a volume to be re-created? The most common way to address this issue is to run databases on EBS volumes in multiple AZs — a master database in one AZ and a slave database in another AZ, with replication from the master to the slave so that the latter gets updated bits when a change is made to the master database. The replication offers good performance because (as mentioned earlier) AWS has dedicated, high-performance connections between AZs within a region. The application can be configured so that read requests from the database can originate from either the master or the slave. And if an AZ becomes unavailable, all database traffic can be sent to the database that's running in the other AZ.

EBS pricing

EBS pricing follows the standard AWS practice of paying for what you use and is relatively straightforward, although you should understand the "what you use" part of the equation.

Keep in mind that new AWS accounts get a certain amount of EBS use at no charge, making it easy (and cheap!) to get started. Also keep in mind that you'll encounter minor EBS pricing variations depending on which region the EBS volume resides in. The variation is around 10 percent, so keep it in mind when making plans. The prices described in this section reflect the AWS US East region.

EBS storage is priced at \$.10 per gigabyte per month. (By way of comparison, in the Singapore region, the charge is \$11 per GB per month, which gives you a concrete example of the pricing variations associated with regional volume location.)

AWS also charges for I/O requests to EBS volumes — \$.10 per million I/O requests.

Provisioned IOPS is a bit trickier. You pay a slightly higher rate for storage — \$.0125 per gigabyte per month (in the AWS US Eastern region). In addition, you pay \$.10 per IOPS month. Provisioned IOPS can measure as much as 4000 IOPS per volume. So if you use 1000 Provisioned IOPS for a full month, you pay \$.10 times 1000, or \$100.

A snapshot costs \$.095 per gigabyte per month. However, understanding exactly how much storage a volume snapshot will require isn't a straightforward calculation. AWS compresses snapshots, so a snapshot of a 10GB EBS volume doesn't fill 10GB. Moreover, subsequent snapshots of the volume store only copies of the blocks that have changed in the volume since the previous snapshot was taken, which further reduces the amount that's stored, and therefore how much you pay for that subsequent snapshot. So the first snapshot of a 10GB EBS volume may (with compression) take only, say, 5GB. If 10 percent (1GB) of the volume is changed before the next snapshot is taken, that snapshot will contain 1GB (or less, in fact, because compression would be applied to this snapshot.)

As you can see, it's not a simple matter to predict the exact cost of using an EBS volume. On the other hand, it's inexpensive per gigabyte. The bigger issue for most organizations occurs when they start using a lot of AWS resources. Even though the per-gigabyte cost of EBS isn't too expensive, if you use a lot of resources, it can add up — particularly if your personnel create a bunch of volumes that aren't used. You pay for the storage whether it's in use or not.

Amazon offers a certain amount of free EBS use for one year for new AWS accounts — a useful benefit. The free level of EBS is as much as 30GB of storage, 1GB of snapshot storage, and 2 million IOs per month.

Obviously, this amount isn't enough storage to run a company's production applications. It is, however, plenty for an individual developer to get started with AWS and experiment with its services. The amount is even enough to prototype an application or two.

An EBS example

To continue the practice of delving into the nuts-and-bolts of *using* AWS, check out the steps to create an EBS volume with the help of the Management Console:

1. **Starting from your AWS account's home page, click the EC2 link, as shown in Figure 4-1.**

   Doing so opens the EC2 Management Console.

   Despite EBS being a storage offering, all your management tasks take place within EC2.

The EC2 link

Figure 4-1:
The AWS
main land-
ing page.

2. **In the Navigation pane on the left, click the Elastic Block Store Volumes heading, highlighted in Figure 4-2.**

   Though this account has no volumes now, it will have some in a minute.

3. **Click the Create Volume button.**

   The Create Volume Wizard launches, as shown in Figure 4-3.

4. **In the wizard, choose Standard from the Volume Type drop-down menu, set the Size at 2GB, choose US East 1a from the Availability Zone drop-down menu, and specify No Snapshot in the Snapshot drop-down menu.**

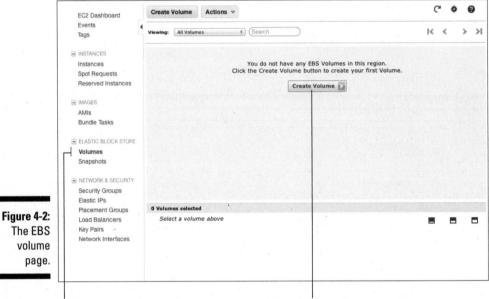

Figure 4-2:
The EBS volume page.

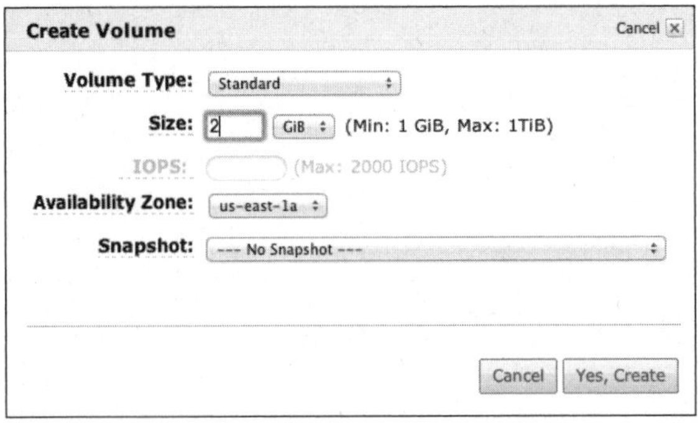

The Volumes link   The Create Volume button

Figure 4-3:
The Create Volume Wizard.

You can create this volume from an existing snapshot, but for this example, start afresh.

5. Click the Yes, Create button.

The volume is created, sporting a new volume ID. (In Figure 4-4, it's vol-e1da4892.)

Now, if you want to interact with the volume via the API, here's an example of a call you can use to create a snapshot:

```
https://ec2.amazonaws.com/
?Action=CreateSnapshot
&VolumeId=volume-id
&AUTHPARAMS
```

Note that this call follows the general pattern: a REST call with the "Create Snapshot" action, along with a volume ID and a set of authentication parameters.

The Volume ID

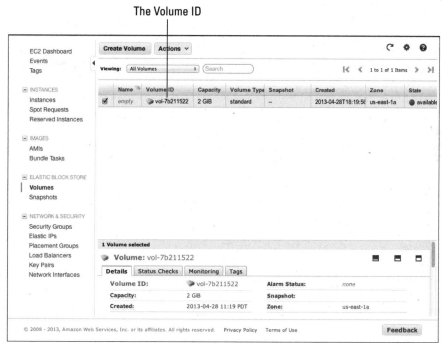

Figure 4-4:
The created
volume.

Managing Archive Material with the Glacier Storage Service

Glacier, released in August 2012, is a storage service targeted at a critical (yet often poorly managed) IT requirement: archival storage.

Simply stated, *archival storage* is backup data of any sort. The best-known use of archival storage involves server backups — complete dumps of all data on the server's drive. Today, of course, with the rise of NAS and SAN technology, backups also include dumps of storage device data.

Glacier is designed to address the shortcomings of a number of traditional archive solutions, none of which is completely satisfactory, as you'll soon find out.

The tape archive is the oldest solution for archive storage. Data is written out to a device that stores the data on magnetic tapes, which are then sent off-site to ensure that no on-premise disaster can wipe out all of a company's data, both live and archived. Tape archiving is burdened by these issues:

- ✔ **It's expensive:** You usually have to use a commercial, off-site storage facility, and it costs a lot — companies sometimes even trim the amount of data they archive. That strategy is tempting, but it can become a big problem if worse comes to worst and your on-premise data disappears.

- ✔ **It's inconvenient:** You have to move the tapes to the off-site storage location, and if you need to recover information from the archive, you have to physically return tapes and restore from the tape.

- ✔ **It's slow:** Obviously, sending and retrieving physical tapes is slow because you have to transport them. A secondary aspect of slowness — writing and reading tapes — is a very slow process. Removing data from a tape can take hours (or even days, if your archive tapes are disorganized and you need to pick through a number of tapes to find the data you want).

- ✔ **It's insecure:** Your tapes are located off-site. Somebody can obtain them and read the data from the tape, putting your data security and privacy at risk.

- ✔ **It may not work:** Tape archives are notorious for not working properly, and the original write of the data to the tape can eventually deteriorate in storage.

A newer form of archiving in the past few years is based on the ever-decreasing cost of disk drives: In *disk archiving*, backups are written from live disk storage to another set of disk-based storage. Disk archiving solves some of the problems associated with tape issues, like speed, but it has its own set of (familiar) issues:

- ✔ **Expense:** Though tape archiving can be expensive, disk archiving is even more expensive. If you have a lot of data, backing it up to other disks can represent a huge cost, especially because an awful lot of archive storage is redundant — you backed up this file yesterday, and you're backing it up today. Keeping multiple copies of files on an expensive medium like disk can make costs skyrocket. Fortunately, solutions have come along in the form of de-duplication, which uses clever software and data layout to track which parts of files change so that you archive only the changed bits. This approach can reduce the amount of storage required to archive data by up to 90 percent.

- ✔ **Speed:** Though disks operate much quicker than tape, moving the archived data across the network to the remote archive location can be a problem when you encounter slow Internet network speeds and (potentially) a high level of network latency.

- ✔ **Reliability:** It may not work — disks can fail, just like tapes do. Typically, the remote disk backup is isolated to a single set of disks, and if one of those disks fails, well . . . there goes your archive.

Glacier leverages the AWS infrastructure to provide archival storage that addresses the shortcomings of both tape and disk solutions:

- ✔ **It's inexpensive:** Glacier costs start at less than $.02 per gigabyte of archival storage. That's significantly less expensive than disk archive, and even less expensive than tape archive, the previous low-cost archive solution.

- ✔ **It's durable:** Glacier uses the S3 infrastructure, which means it can offer the same 99.999999999-percent durability as the S3 service. That's a lot more reliable than the previous archive solutions.

- ✔ **It's convenient:** You just send and retrieve archive files over the Internet, making it simple to extend your current backup solution to Glacier. Many of today's newer, commercial backup solutions provide deduplication functionality, so if you use one of those, you can be sure that it will soon have an Archive to Glacier option.

- ✔ **It's highly scalable:** An archive file can be as large as 40TB, which should be big — enough for anyone.

- ✔ **It's secure:** Data is transmitted to and from Glacier over SSL encryption, and the archives themselves are encrypted as well while in storage.

- ✔ **It's fast:** Data can be pulled from Glacier in as little as five hours, making it significantly faster than tape archive solutions, which require schlepping out to the archive storage facility. And while Glacier confronts the same issue as disk archive of having to send data over the Internet, AWS has a couple solutions to this issue:

- AWS Import/Export is a service that allows lets you to send Amazon physical disk drives with your data on them. At the Amazon end, an Amazon employee downloads the data from the drive and adds it into AWS.

- AWS Direct Connect is a service offered by Amazon in partnership with network service providers that place a high bandwidth connection between their facilities (or, indeed, your own data center) and AWS. The connection can be 1 Gbps or 10 Gbps, making it possible to transmit or receive very large volumes of data quickly.

Glacier in action

Glacier is straightforward, conceptually. The idea is for you to create Glacier vaults within your AWS account and then store archives in those vaults. The conceptual similarity between this arrangement and S3 buckets and objects is obvious.

Each AWS account can have 1,000 vaults, and each vault can contain an unlimited number of archives. As previously noted, an archive can be as large as 40TB.

Two ways exist to create an archive:

- ✔ **Archive S3 objects into Glacier by setting S3 retention policies for the object.** You may, for example, set a retention period of 90 days; after 90 days were up, S3 would migrate the object into Glacier. To retrieve the object, execute an S3 Restore command, and a few hours later the object is back in S3, ready to be accessed. S3 maintains a mapping between S3 object IDs and Glacier archive IDs and takes care of all archiving management. In fact, you can't even access S3-managed objects from Glacier via the API.

- ✔ **Use the Glacier API to manage the creation and retrieval of archives, and let Glacier takes care of storing it securely and robustly.** If you need to retrieve an archive, you issue a command (again via the API), specifying the file location you want the retrieved archive placed in, and five hours or so later, the archive is available on the server on which the file location exists. The server can be located in EC2 or in some another non-AWS data center. You can set AWS to notify you when the archive is available by using the Simple Notification Service (SNS), which is discussed in Chapter 9.

One potential sticking point for this second method of using Glacier is the fact that a very large archive may not fit on the file system of the server on which the archive is to be retrieved — if you have a 40TB archive and are trying to download a 40TB archive to a small EC2 instance, for example, there aren't enough file systems on the entire server to store the archive. How would you handle this situation? The answer takes advantage of Glacier's ability to retrieve a portion of an archive — so you would either retrieve the archive in pieces, or limit your retrieval to a specified portion of the archive.

In the case of non-S3 managed archives, each archive has an AWS-assigned identifier, which is a *very* long alphanumeric string. When you want to perform an activity on an archive, you must supply the archive identifier; therefore, it's imperative that you keep track of archives, with a cross-reference between your backup identifier (that is, backup_01_17_2013) and the AWS archive identifier. AWS DynamoDB (described a bit further on later in this chapter) would be an ideal way to store these mappings.

However (and it's a big however), at the time of this writing, actually using Glacier in non-S3 managed use is a bit complicated, because it isn't fully integrated into the AWS Management Console. The Management Console only supports creating or deleting vaults; all other interaction with Glacier must be done via the Glacier API or one of the two Glacier libraries, (one Java-based and one .NET-based). I expect to see Glacier fully integrated into the Management Console in the near future, and it may very well be the case that, by the time you read this book, Amazon may have already implemented this integration.

Nevertheless, Glacier is such a useful service that I believe people will use the libraries to create Glacier interfaces and applications. Some of these interfaces may be released under open source licenses so that anyone (and by anyone, I mean you!) can leverage them to use Glacier.

Glacier scoping

Glacier vaults, the repositories for all your archives, are scoped by region. You can, of course, create vaults in multiple regions, but each single vault is located in (and thus limited to) a single region, and all archives within that vault reside within the region as well.

At the time of this writing, Glacier is available in all three U.S. regions, in the Asia Pacific region (Tokyo), and in the EU region; however, you can expect to see Glacier extended to other regions.

Glacier pricing

Glacier storage pricing varies according to which region contains the vault. Vaults in the US Eastern region cost $.01 per gigabyte per month; in the Asia Pacific region (Tokyo), the cost is $.012 per gigabyte per month.

You pay a modest charge also for upload and retrieval requests: $.05 to $.06 per 1,000 requests. You may not immediately see how this price can add up to much, even for a large company over the course of a year, but it's there.

There's no charge for transferring data into Glacier, whether the data comes from an EC2 instance or from outside AWS altogether. The cost for retrieving data is a bit more complicated — there's no charge for

- ✔ **The first gigabyte of data retrieval, whether the data is retrieved into an EC2 instance or an outside data center.**
- ✔ **Retrieval of S3-managed objects from Glacier.**
- ✔ **Archives retrieved into EC2 instances within the same region in which the archive is located.**

For archives retrieved into other AWS regions or into non-AWS data centers, there's a charge based on total gigabytes of traffic. The charge per transferred gigabyte decreases as total traffic increases. The calculation of total traffic is based on all outbound network traffic across all AWS offerings, so the traffic fee associated with an archive retrieval may be different based on how much total traffic the customer has incurred over the course of a month.

Glacier represents a typical Amazon AWS offering:

1. Find a well-established technology market.
2. Calculate how to make the service far more efficient and less expensive.
3. Enable self-service.
4. Avoid imposing complex pricing, and require negotiation before using the service.
5. Become the dominant player in the field, in typical Amazon fashion.

I predict that the new AWS offering named Glacier will become a popular one, based on personal experience dealing with the hassles of off-site tape archiving — and its far simpler ease of use.

A Glacier example

In my Glacier example, you'll use the Management Console to create a new Glacier archive. As you can see from Figure 4-5, Glacier is listed under the Storage and Content Delivery heading on the Management Console home page. From this starting point, it's really not complicated:

1. **Click the Glacier link.**

   Doing so brings you to the Glacier main page. Notice that you don't (yet) have Glacier vaults in the account.

2. **Click the Create Vault button, as shown in Figure 4-6.**

   This step brings up the Create Vault Wizard, as shown in Figure 4-7.

3. **Enter a name for the new vault in the Vault Name field.**

   For now, type **Trial Vault**.

4. **Click the Create Vault Now button.**

   Glacier goes off to do its magic.

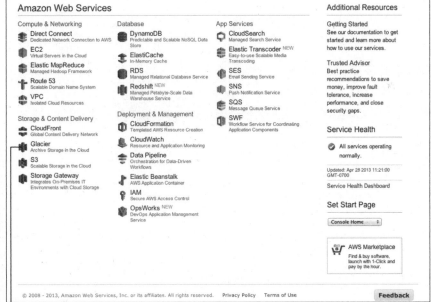

Figure 4-5: The Management Console home page, with Glacier highlighted

The Glacier link

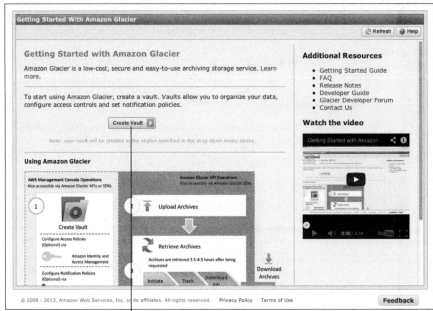

© 2008 - 2013, Amazon Web Services, Inc. or its affiliates. All rights reserved.   Privacy Policy   Terms of Use

Figure 4-6:
Creating
the Glacier
vault.

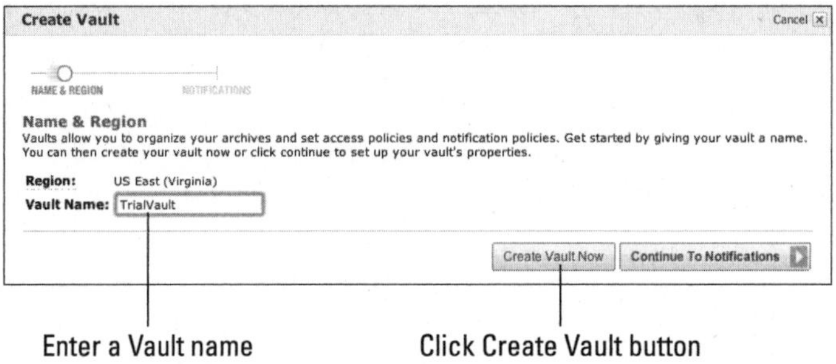

The Create Vault button

Figure 4-7:
The Glacier
Vault
Creation
Wizard.

Enter a Vault name   Click Create Vault button

After a few minutes, the new vault is ready, as shown in Figure 4-8.
You can see that the new vault has an Amazon Resource Name
(ARN): `arn:aws:glacier:us-east-1:204956053165:vaults/`
`TrialVault`.

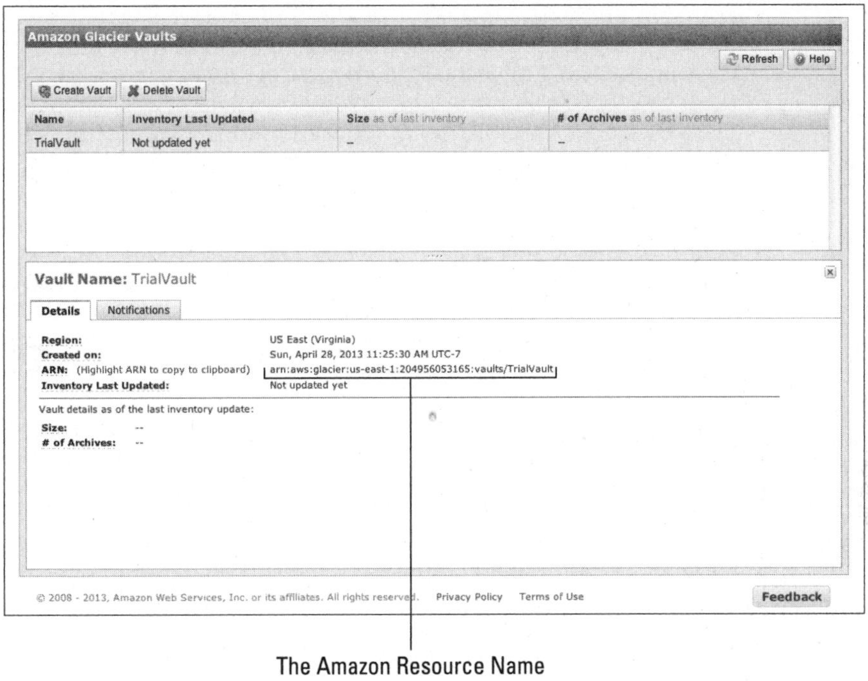

Figure 4-8:
The Glacier
Vault, at the
ready.

The Amazon Resource Name

If you were to use the API to upload an archive to the new vault, here's the command you'd use:

```
POST /AccountId/vaults/VaultName/archives
Host: glacier.Region.amazonaws.com
x-amz-glacier-version: 2012-06-01
Date: Date
Authorization: SignatureValue
x-amz-archive-description: Description
x-amz-sha256-tree-hash: SHA256 tree hash
x-amz-content-sha256: SHA256 linear hash
Content-Length: Length
<Request body.>
```

Scaling Key-Value Data with DynamoDB

DynamoDB is Amazon's latest AWS storage offering. This key-value storage service is designed to provide very high scalability and performance for the most demanding applications. The genius of DynamoDB is that even though it's quite challenging to deploy and operate a very large key-value environment that may span (literally) hundreds (if not thousands) of servers, Amazon has made DynamoDB extremely easy to use. In other words, Amazon takes on all the heavy lifting of running the service, and you can focus on using the service to make your application work better.

The concept of *key-value storage* should be familiar to anyone who has ever created a Microsoft Word table — say, a table containing information about people. A person's last name is used to organize the overall table — as the *key* term — and other information about the person (first name, address, or perhaps a favorite TV show) is strung out to the right of the last name. Conceptually, that's how DynamoDB operates. Naturally, it's a bit more complex as AWS implements it, and it has much richer functionality, but from the perspective of how to think about it, just think "Word tables."

Key-value storage creates a hash (essentially, a random assignment of the key into the storage pool), which makes data lookups extremely efficient because data records are spread throughout the pool, thereby reducing the likelihood that reads or writes will be concentrated on a single server and reduce performance caused by resource contention. When you call DynamoDB to insert a row of data, it hashes the *index value* (the data item used to organize the table, such as the customer's last name, used as the index for the customer table) and places the row randomly throughout the storage pool. When you request that row, DynamoDB again hashes the index value, goes to the location that the hash identifies, retrieves the data, and gives it back to you.

Key-value versus relational databases

Key-value storage can manage much larger data pools and operate with much higher performance than traditional relational databases because it can span larger number of servers to store its data. You face some trade-offs from using it, however, because it doesn't support the following features:

- ✔ **Range retrieval:** Using this feature, you can say, "Give me all records from the customer table where the customer last name equals **Jones**." Relational databases excel at these kinds of queries.

- ✔ **Joined queries:** This type of query lets you say, "Give me a customer name from the customer table and a corresponding address from the address table where the customer name equals **Jones** and the address city equals **Los Angeles**." Joins can be extremely useful in applications, but they harm database performance, particularly when overall storage is very large.

Both key-value and relational databases have their uses, and in fact it's not uncommon for applications to use both, with each applied to the portions of the application for which it's best suited.

DynamoDB characteristics

Amazon has designed DynamoDB to be high-performance, extremely flexible, and with high availability, all based on these characteristics:

- ✔ **The total amount of storage can be increased (or decreased) at any time.** You're not forced to forecast how much storage is required for an application. For many of the webscale applications that would have a natural affinity for DynamoDB-type storage, this is a strong selling point. Such applications are unpredictable in terms of how much storage they will ultimately require, so the flexible scalability of DynamoDB can be a real benefit.

- ✔ **No downtime is required in order to resize a DynamoDB table.** AWS automatically adds additional servers to a DynamoDB table pool and redistributes the table data across the pool. This task is performed in the background and requires no application downtime, making it possible to continue running applications, even while resizing the underlying DynamoDB table pool to support necessary throughput.

- ✔ **The schema is flexible.** Relational databases require you to define the items you'll manage, and their types (string or integer, for example) and sizes, all before using the system; this definition is referred to as the *database schema.* What happens if you need to store additional information in your database? You have to alter the original database schema, which, if a large amount of data is already in the database, can take (literally) days to execute. DynamoDB, by contrast, has a flexible schema — you can add items to a record at any time without requiring an Alter operation. Moreover, if you add, say, a second address to an individual customer's record, no other customer's record needs to be changed, and no additional storage needs to be allocated for all those other customers' potential second addresses. This makes DynamoDB very easy to use, extremely flexible in the type of data that can be stored, and highly efficient in its use of storage.

- ✔ **Solid-state drives are used instead of disk drives.** DynamoDB avoids the dreaded latency of data lookups that require seeks across spinning disks by using solid-state drives that incorporate flash storage, to increase data throughput and increase DynamoDB performance.

- ✔ **Performance levels can be changed dynamically while in operation.** If you realize that you need more (or less) performance capability from your DynamoDB database, you can adjust it on the fly, without needing to take DynamoDB down. This allows you to dynamically tune your database performance while your application is still in production.

- ✔ **Storage is redundant to ensure high availability.** DynamoDB stores multiple copies of each record, thereby avoiding outages caused by hardware failure.

> ✔ **Storage is dispersed across multiple availability zones.** By dispersing DynamoDB tables across multiple availability zones, AWS ensures that even a large-scale outage, such as the loss of an entire data center, doesn't affect the availability of DynamoDB.

Using DynamoDB

You can easily create a DynamoDB table via the AWS Management Console, by following this process (in broad terms):

1. Define the table name.

   Note: When you name a table, your character pool is limited to a–z, A–Z, 0–9, and the underscore, hyphen, and period; no other characters are allowed.

2. Name and define the *primary key* — the index for the table.

   You can choose the type of data you'll use as index: string, number, or binary. (The Technical Stuff paragraph in this section further defines the primary key.)

3. Define how much read and write capacity you want for your DynamoDB table.

   The amount of capacity affects your DynamoDB table performance, so your choices here are important to overall application performance. You can have up to ten read capacity units and five write capacity units for free each month. (Read and write units are a measurement of performance and represent throughput in these operations — see the DynamoDB cost section below for details.) Don't worry if you're unsure about how much you'll ultimately need — you can dynamically adjust these figures; DynamoDB supports performance levels from tens to hundreds of thousands of capacity units per table.

4. Decide whether to have throughput alarms sent to you.

   A *throughput alarm* indicates whether your table's request rate is consistently above a certain level for an hour. (The default level is 80 percent.) It's the mechanism that tells you when to increase your table's read and write capacity.

5. Press the Create button to create the DynamoDB table.

A couple minutes later, your DynamoDB table is ready. Easy, eh? It's easy, especially in comparison with provisioning your own instances, loading a key-value product onto each of them, arranging for redundancy, and so on. DynamoDB hasn't been around long, but I predict that it will be a huge hit as more and more highly scaled webscale Internet sites adopt it as a more attractive alternative to "rolling their own."

In addition to the REST/SOAP API interface, Amazon has made available four client-side Software Development Kit (SDK) libraries: Java, .NET, Python and PHP. It is also possible to access a DynamoDB table from the Management Console, although that ability is more development- and testing-focused rather than to be used as production functionality.

I expect that Amazon will eventually extend richer DynamoDB support to the Management Console. I also expect that someone will release a commercial or open source product that offers graphical interaction with DynamoDB.

Here's a deeper dive in to the "why and what" of DynamoDB indexes. First, and vitally important, it's crucial to use an appropriate index for key-value storage. A key-value product performs a hash on the index value to determine where in the storage pool to place the data associated with the index.

The hash implements an algorithm to create unique values for different indexes, which places the data randomly throughout the storage pool. For example, an index value of 1234 may go to machine 7, and 1235 may go to machine 12.

It's this randomness that provides the high-performance capability of key-value storage; by randomly distributing the data around the resource pool, the storage spreads reads and writes among all servers in the pool, thus avoiding hammering a single server, which would reduce performance.

The key (excuse the pun) issue with an index is to define it with a highly variable index. For example, if you have millions of customers, it's a bad idea to index them by zip code, because the amount of duplication would choke performance. When creating a DynamoDB table, be sure to choose your index carefully.

Amazon has also made interesting changes to DynamoDB indexes. In addition to the standard hash index value I just mentioned, Amazon lets you define the index as hash-and-range so that you can, so to speak, create a secondary index associated with the table. The range can be used to retrieve data that you might like to select by a list of some sort. For example, you may create a customer table with the last name (or, even more hash-appropriate, a sequential customer number) as the index. However, if you're, say, an online marketing company, you may want to be able to select customers located in certain zip code areas (that is, all customers located in zip codes 30000 to 40000). You can create a customer table index using sequential customer numbers with an associated range of zip code. That way, DynamoDB would use the highly variable customer number to spread the data randomly across the entire table resource pool but keep pointers to the zip code values that it can use in queries on that range. With hash-and-range, users can gain the full benefit of key-value storage along with a limited amount of the benefit available to relational database storage.

DynamoDB read consistency

One common drawback to using key-value storage that's spread out across many servers is read consistency: When a write to key-value storage is made, the data must be written to multiple servers (because data is stored redundantly). A bit of time elapses before the write is copied out to all necessary servers. A read that closely follows a write may get a copy of the data that reflects the old value, not the new.

Many developers face challenges when working with key-value storage because of this issue of *eventual consistency.* More experienced with relational databases, which implement immediate consistency, these developers struggle to design applications that can operate with uncertain consistency.

Amazon takes a different tack: Provide two types of reads — consistent and eventually consistent. The former performs a read only after DynamoDB is certain that it reflects the latest version of data, and the latter returns data immediately with no guarantee that it reflects the latest-and-greatest version. This choice offers a trade-off: The consistent method is simpler but may provide lower performance, whereas the eventually consistent option is less certain but offers the highest possible level of performance.

DynamoDB scope and availability

DynamoDB tables are AWS region-scoped. The servers that make up the table resource pool are spread among availability zones within the region in which the table lives.

Amazon publishes no projection of the expected level of DynamoDB availability. Given its use of redundancy, you should expect extremely high availability from DynamoDB.

DynamoDB cost

DynamoDB has three separate and distinct cost variables:

- ✔ **The size of the server pool, defined as read and write capacity:** As you'd expect, larger read and write capacity requires spreading the table across larger numbers of servers, with an accompanying increase in cost. The first 10 units of read capacity and the first 5 units of write capacity per month are free. Above that level, however, the cost is $.01 per hour for every 10 units of write capacity, and $.01 per hour for every 50 units of read capacity. 1 unit of write capacity enables you to perform 1 write per second for items as large as 1KB. Similarly, 1 unit of read capacity enables you to perform one strongly consistent read per second (or two eventually consistent reads per second) of items as large as 1KB.

✔ **The storage associated with the DynamoDB table:** You get 100MB of storage for free every month; above that level, storage is priced at $.25 per gigabyte. The total amount of storage within DynamoDB is a little larger than the size of the data being stored; DynamoDB adds 100 bytes of indexing information to each item stored in DynamoDB, which is added to the total storage in DynamoDB.

✔ **Data transfer, which is the same price and conditions as for all AWS offerings:** The first gigabyte of transfer per month is free, and above that the cost of data transfer varies between $.12 and $.05 per gigabyte, depending on total traffic.

A DynamoDB example

When it's time for some hands-on DynamoDB-ing, follow these steps:

1. **Make your way to the Management Console main page, as shown in Figure 4-9.**

The DynamoDB link

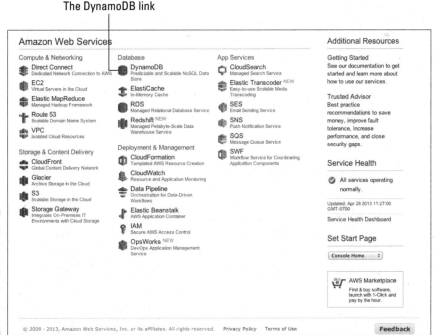

Figure 4-9:
The AWS Management Console landing page.

Note that DynamoDB is (no surprise here) listed under the Database heading.

2. **Click the DynamoDB link.**

   Doing so takes you to the DynamoDB administration page. Your account doesn't have a DynamoDB yet, so the page invites you (as shown in Figure 4-10) to create one.

3. **Accept the invitation by clicking the Create Table button.**

   This step brings up the Create DynamoDB Wizard.

4. **Enter a name for the table in the Table Name field, set the Primary Key, as shown in Figure 4-11, select the Hash option, and then click Continue.**

   Type **DynamoTrial** for the name, and use a simple hash string for the key (**"CustomerID"**).

The Create Table button

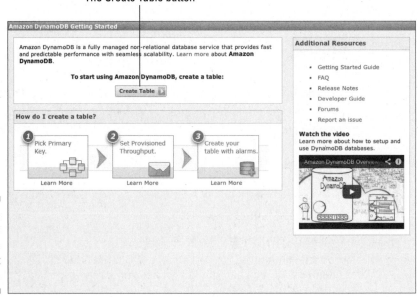

Figure 4-10:
An invita-
tion to
createthefirst
DynamoDB.

Enter a Table name

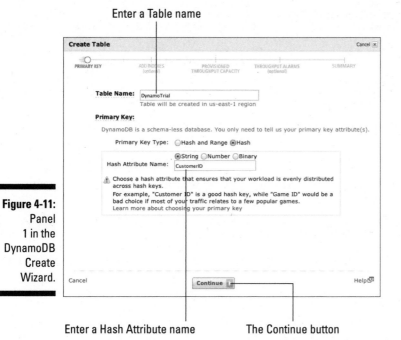

Figure 4-11:
Panel
1 in the
DynamoDB
Create
Wizard.

Enter a Hash Attribute name   The Continue button

Doing so takes you to the next page of the wizard, as shown in Figure 4-12, where you set the read and write capacities.

5. **Enter a request of ten units for read capacity as well as ten units for write capacity, and then click Continue.**

6. **In the new page of the wizard that appears, select the Use Basic Alarms check box (as shown in Figure 4-13), enter the e-mail address where you want these notifications sent, and then click Continue.**

   This will take you to a review screen.

7. **After reviewing your setup, click Create.**

   After a few minutes, the new DynamoDB table is ready, as shown in Figure 4-14. You can now begin inserting, retrieving, and deleting records, which will be indexed by CustomerID.

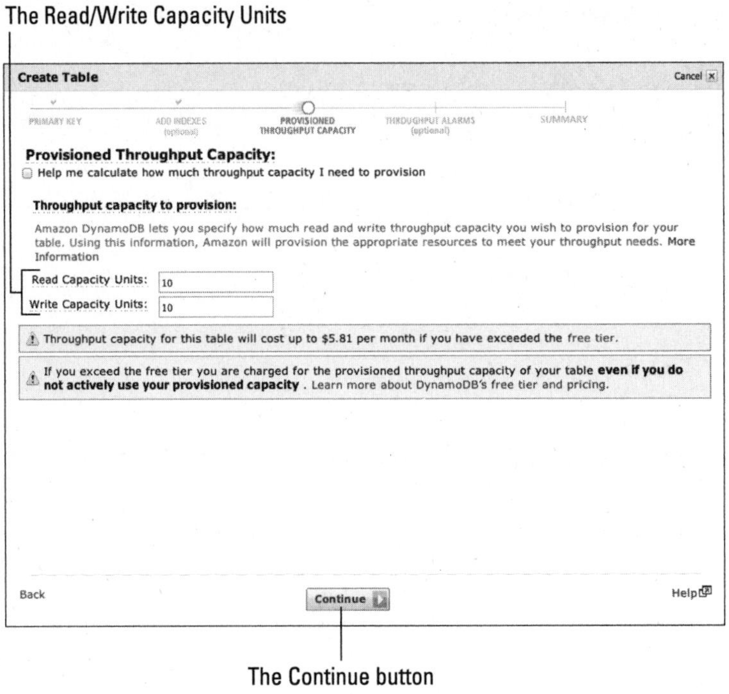

The Read/Write Capacity Units

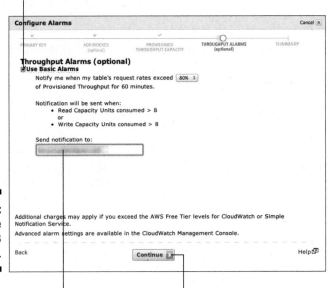

Figure 4-12:
Defining the
DynamoDB
read and
write units.

The Continue button

Use Basic Alarms

Figure 4-13:
Creating the
DynamoDB
table.

Enter an e-mail address   The Continue button

Your new DynamoDB table

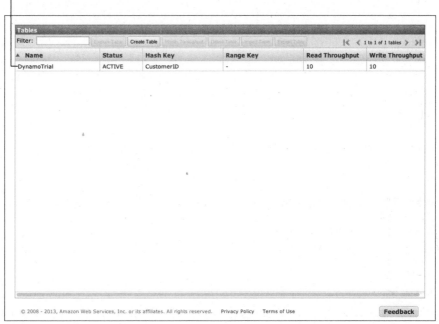

Figure 4-14:
The
DynamoDB
table is
ready.

After the DynamoDB table is ready for use, you'll probably interact with it
within a program. Assuming that data is already in the table, here's an example of the kind of PHP code you use to retrieve data:

```php
$dynamodb = new AmazonDynamoDB();
$get_response = $dynamodb->get_item(array(
'TableName' => 'DynamoTrial',
'Key' => array(
'HashKeyElement' => array( AmazonDynamoDB::CustomerID =>
         '104' )
)
));
```

This example retrieves the data for Customer 104 from DynamoTrial and
adds it to the $get_response variable, where other parts of the application
can then use the retrieved data.

Backupify runs on AWS

Backupify is, well, a data backup service. It offers a secure storage service to consumers and businesses, with a strong focus on backing up data from popular consumer and Software as a Service (SaaS) providers, such as Facebook, Flickr, Gmail, and Salesforce. With over 200,000 customers, Backupify is a very large business, with enormous storage requirements (multi-petabytes), as you might imagine.

Backupify is totally AWS-based. For indexing and tracking user data objects, the company runs a 21-node Cassandra cluster. For storage, Backupify originally relied on S3; however, with the release of Glacier, the company has moved large parts of its storage to the lower-cost archive storage service. Because Backupify can rely on the AWS infrastructure, it hasn't needed operations staff. Instead, its developers manage all aspects of running the application, including deploying code, monitoring availability, and managing scale up and scale down. By using AWS, Backupify can direct investment that would have been used for operations personnel into additional user functionality and the growth of its business.

Backupify represents one of the interesting phenomenon made possible by AWS:

Entrepreneurs create new businesses based on the easy availability of unlimited, cheap infrastructure. For a company like Backupify to have been created pre-AWS, it would have had to invest hundreds of thousands of dollars to create its own infrastructure just to test the level of demand for a service like the one it planned to offer.

Instead, Backupify launched for only a few thousand dollars; moreover, it was able to get started almost immediately, instead of having to order, install, and configure racks of servers, network switches, and storage.

Backupify was able to validate demand for its service quickly and scale it rapidly, using the resources of AWS. Because of Amazon's pay-as-you-go pricing, the company was able to bootstrap-fund itself until it had grown a significant business, whereupon it took on outside financing.

Backupify illustrates how Amazon is enabling entrepreneurs to create new types of businesses, leveraging the AWS technology to develop innovative offerings that can be created and validated with low investment and then easily scaled up when the offering takes off in the marketplace.

Selecting an AWS Storage Service

AWS presents an embarrassment of riches to its users for deciding which storage service to use as part of their applications. With such a broad range of offerings and functionality, it may seem hard to know where to begin as you choose whether to use these items:

 ✔ **S3, the highly scalable object store:** S3's URL object addressing allows data to be accessed from within AWS as well as externally from the Internet. Though S3 objects are regionally scoped, you can access them from anywhere.

- ✔ **EBS, the volume storage offering:** EBS allows highly persistent volumes to be attached (and detached) from running EC instances, but keep in mind that EBS volumes are accessible only within the availability zone in which they're created — and you can access them only by the EC2 instance to which they're attached.

- ✔ **DynamoDB, the highly scalable key-value service:** DynamoDB provides flexible, high-performance, and robust storage for webscale applications.

- ✔ **Glacier, the inexpensive and highly durable archiving service:** Glacier's job is to ensure that critical data is never lost, and it does its job well.

In the time-honored (and infuriating!) words associated with most IT topics, the question "which service should I use?" typically requires a response of "It depends." Many technology folks get familiar with a given technology, and become comfortable using it, and then seek to apply it to nearly every situation — even ones to which the technology isn't well suited. It's the classic story: If you only have a hammer, every problem looks like a nail.

You can certainly use more than one AWS storage service to address the same need. For example, you can store objects in an EBS volume, using a bucket/object scheme based on file system layout; you can also use S3 to store objects.

You can also use more than one AWS storage service in an application, so don't feel that you have to choose one or limit your options. In fact, one key Amazon strategy is to offer a rich set of complementary services that support and reinforce one another, all with the goal of making it easier to develop and deploy applications on AWS. Therefore, you can be sure that using one AWS offering doesn't preclude using another; and, of course, the more services you use, the more money AWS makes!

When you choose among the AWS storage services, keep these guidelines in mind:

- ✔ **Become knowledgeable about all services.** Develop a good understanding of each service's characteristics, strengths, and weaknesses. You'll stand in good stead during all your AWS work.

- ✔ **Leverage service strengths so that AWS does the "heavy lifting" and you avoid unnecessary work.** Then you can avoid the typically repetitive, boring, mistake-prone work — and focus on the high-value portions of the application — the business functionality. For example, if you'll use object storage in the application, it makes sense to use S3 rather than roll your own on an EBS volume. You don't have to develop object management and storage functionality; you don't have to worry about running out of storage space; and you don't have to worry about backing up the storage.

✔ **Choose services that are appropriate and necessary for application requirements.** I recommend an approach that's driven by application functionality to evaluating AWS storage choices. By understanding the functionality an application delivers, you can make wise choices about which AWS storage service to use.

✔ **Use the what-if approach to make service choices driven by functionality.** Imagine which services you may use in these situations:

- Your application grows a user population ten times larger than you envision.

- You experience the "Facebook effect," in which the application gets recommended and you suddenly attract 100 times the traffic you expect.

- Your company decides to add new functionality, and you need to extend the application to another type of storage. This guideline addresses application design as well as AWS storage service choice, but remember that cloud computing, in general, presents application developers with a much less predictable environment and roadmap than did previous generation IT platforms.

✔ **Be prepared to mix and match storage services.** AWS instance operation makes EBS nearly mandatory for applications, so you almost always need to use EBS within an application. For many applications, S3 is an excellent complement to manage objects. (In fact, in Chapter 8, you can read more about why S3 is a good complement to many applications because of its S3-based CloudFront content distribution network functionality). As DynamoDB becomes more widely understood, many more applications will undoubtedly incorporate it for high-performance functionality, whereas EBS-based databases will be used more for the transactional functionality that's necessary to capture financial interactions.

✔ **Prepare for new storage offerings from Amazon.** Amazon has filled out the storage side of the AWS offering over the past few years, and it should deliver new offerings over the next few years. Each new offering will bring new capabilities — you should learn enough about them to understand how they fit into the overall AWS storage picture and how the application functionality may be better served by choosing a new offering rather than an existing service.

In fact, my recommendation to choose appropriate AWS storage services according to what the application requires is generally good advice regarding *all* AWS offerings — so many of them exist that it makes more sense to figure out what the application needs and then map *that* need to what's available. Many people are unaware of the rich set of AWS offerings, but knowing about them increases the overall application design flexibility — and makes it faster and easier to develop applications.

I hope that you'll develop a good foundation for understanding how to manage the AWS application's storage and, more importantly, resolve to fully explore how to leverage these services. People commonly use previously accepted limitations to inform future decisions, despite the removal of the constraints of the previous available solutions; in other words, if it has always been difficult to obtain sufficient volumes of storage, people typically constrain their application design decisions based on those previous limitations. True effort is required in order to remove these mental limitations and consider what is possible with a much more expansive capability, but it can pay real dividends in better applications and more satisfied users.

Because Amazon offers a managed object service and a managed key-value service, you may wonder where to find a managed relational database service. Never fear: the managed RDBMS service does exist, and I talk about it in Chapter 8. You'll see that my recommendation about the AWS Relational Database Service (RDS) service is the same as the one regarding AWS storage — leverage it to reduce low-value repetitive work in order to free up time to focus on customer-facing, high-value functionality.

Chapter 5

Stretching Out with Elastic Compute Cloud

. . . .

In This Chapter

▶ Introducing EC2, the AWS cloud computing component

▶ Understanding images and instances

▶ Exploring EC2's infinite varieties

▶ Addressing key issues with EC2 instances

▶ Deciding which computing type is right for your application

. . . .

*T*his chapter discusses EC2 — the Elastic Compute Cloud, which is the most widely used AWS service. Even the term "cloud computing" emphasizes computing — and its computing that EC2 delivers, at scale, in wide varieties of types, and at ridiculously low prices. By the time this chapter ends, you'll have a knowledge foundation about EC2 and why it represents a true revolution in information technology.

Introducing EC2

EC2 is the most revolutionary of the AWS services because it has transformed a fundamental part of IT: the use of provisioning servers. EC2 provides virtual servers in a matter of minutes, all via self-service. It's difficult to overstate the shift that this strategy represents compared to how things used to be done.

In earlier days when you needed a server, you had to scare up enough money to buy one, complete the purchase process, and then have the server delivered, installed, and connected to the network. Finally (finally!), you gained access to your server. It wasn't uncommon for this process to take from three to six months!

"But wait," you may say, "what about virtualization? Didn't that trim the workload and reduce the time it takes to provision a (virtual) server?" As the author of *Virtualization For Dummies* (John Wiley & Sons, Inc.), I'm perfectly willing to sing the praises of *virtualization* (the systemic use of virtual machines that act like real computers, with an operating system and everything). But virtualization isn't the solution to all your problems. It's true that using virtualization may negate the need to order hardware, but many IT organizations hedge their bets by choosing to maintain established manual processes regarding provisioning. In other words, even though the provisioning process can be streamlined when in virtualization mode, it often isn't done. So instead of three to six months, the timeframe for obtaining a virtual machine may be three to six *weeks* — better, but still not great.

Amazon, as is its wont, reevaluated the entire provisioning process and realized that an enormous improvement was possible by automating the process. Rather than continue the manual-gatekeeper approach, where requests for virtual resources were still handled by living, breathing (and accident-prone) humans, Amazon overlaid its virtualization layer with a sophisticated software layer designed to obviate the need for human intervention in the provisioning process.

With this innovation from Amazon, the perspective of the entire IT industry shifted. Users now understand what is truly possible, and they've come to expect resource availability to meet the benchmark achieved by Amazon with its AWS offering. This perspective has certainly presented a challenge to chief information officers (CIOs), who manage IT organizations that are still geared to the rhythms and timeframes of the past. (But it has certainly helped Amazon's prospects!)

In addition to this accelerated provisioning capability, EC2 requires no time commitment to use its resources. The total commitment a user has to make is one hour — the minimum billing period for an EC2 instance.

The accelerated provisioning access and the lack of required commitment has driven wholesale EC2 adoption by all types of companies and organizations, ranging from individuals to some of the largest institutions in the world. This adoption reflects just how attractive the EC2 value proposition is — and, after you've seen EC2 in action, how unattractive the traditional approach to resource provisioning is.

That's not to say that it's all rainbows and ponies with regard to EC2. EC2 is a unique beast; its operation is dictated by the design approach taken by Amazon while creating the service, and that design carries far-reaching implications for how EC2 applications should be architected and managed. The difference between success and failure with EC2 is dictated by how well you understand the service's characteristics and how well you align your applications with those characteristics. I tell you more about that topic in later sections of this chapter.

Seeing EC2's Unique Nature

EC2 is based on *virtualization* — the process of using software to create virtual machines that then carry out all the tasks you'd associate with a "real" computer using a "real" operating system. If you have any experience with virtualization, you'll understand the foundation of EC2.

The foundation isn't everything to everyone, though. There are significant differences between EC2 and traditional virtualization, typified by products such as VMware ESX and Citrix XenServer — differences that you'll recognize quickly enough when you begin to use EC2. In a standard virtualization product, a virtual machine is either running or *quiescent* (a fancy way of saying "not running"). EC2 has come up with its own terminology: When a virtual machine is running in EC2, it's referred to as an *instance;* when an instance isn't running in EC2, it's referred to as an *image.* Likewise, in virtualization, a virtual machine is *started,* and in EC2 an instance is *launched.*

Terminology aside, a more significant difference between virtualization and EC2 lies in how a nonrunning virtual machine/instance is stored when it isn't running. A virtualization product stores the entire virtual machine on disk; the only difference in storage between a running virtual machine and a quiescent virtual machine is that the running machine is brought into the virtual machine manager and made operational — the disk storage requirements are exactly the same.

The implication is that you may have wasted disk storage. If you have, say, a virtual machine with 1.7GB of disk space but the virtual machine operating system and application software require only 300MB of disk space — you have 1.4GB of unused storage and by extension, 1.4GB of wasted disk space. EC2, by contrast, stores only the actual data necessary to provide the virtual machine and operating system, so only 300MB is stored on disk when the instance is not running — and, crucially, you don't pay for the 1.4GB of unused disk space that otherwise would sit empty. This arrangement reduces your EC2 cost when your instances are not running.

I've presented only a simplified version of what really happens. AWS actually has two types of Amazon Machine Images (AMIs). I've just described what happens when EC2 handles images that are stored in the Amazon Simple Storage Service (known as S3). These S3-backed images are given the standard treatment — a full file system while running as an instance but a stripped-down image when not running. The other type of image, referred to as an *EBS-backed* image (because of its links to the AWS product Elastic Block Storage), operates more like traditional virtualization, with full storage of the entire instance file system, even if much of it has no data. (I describe the two types of images in more detail later in this chapter.)

S3-backed instances don't store changes made to the file system when the instance is shut down *(terminated)*. The next time the image is launched, the running instance reflects the layout of the image as originally created. It's similar to a *gold image* or a *LiveCD* (in case you've used a CD-based Linux system).

Understanding the transient nature of the file system for S3-backed instances is critical. No changes made to an instance are persistent post-termination — unlike in any operating system you've ever used (except for LiveCD). If your instance will process and save data, you must find a way to save the data outside of the instance. Simply put, S3-backed images don't make data persistent. This issue is so important that I mention it many times during this book, just to hammer it home.

Understanding images

An *image* is the collection of bits needed to create a running instance. This collection includes the elements described in this list:

✔ **At minimum, the operating system that will run on the instance:** That means it can be Windows or Linux.

✔ **Any software packages you've chosen to install:** The package can be software that you've written or a package from a third-party provider (assuming, of course, that the software license supports this type of use). For example, you may include the Apache web server along with the load balancer HAProxy — both are open source products that can be freely included in your image.

✔ **Any configuration information needed for the instance to operate properly:** For example, in an image containing Linux, Apache, and HAProxy, you may include configuration information for HAProxy to communicate with the Apache server located on the same instance. Adding this information to the image prevents having to configure the packages every time you launch the image.

An image carries *access rights:* Someone owns it, and the owner can control who may launch (or even see) the image. The following list describes the image-ownership categories, which are listed on the drop-down menu (see Figure 5-1):

✔ **Owned by me:** Images created by your account, whether you are its sole user or you share it with others; may include both public and private images

✔ **Amazon images:** Images created by Amazon and made available to anyone who wants to use them

✔ **Public images:** Images owned by other accounts but made available to anyone who wants to use them

✔ **Private images:** Images owned by you and made available only to you or to other accounts you specify

✔ **EBS images:** Images that use Elastic Block Storage (EBS) as the storage for the AMI

✔ **Instance-store images:** Images that are stored in Simple Storage Service (S3)

✔ **32-bit:** Images built on 32-bit operating systems (can be either instance- or EBS-backed)

✔ **64-bit:** Images built on 64-bit operating systems (can be either instance- or EBS-backed)

✔ **AWS Marketplace:** Images, created by third parties, that are available for a fee

Commercial software companies that offer images containing their software commonly make this type available. Marketplace images address the issue of commercial software licensing: If you're a user, you don't want to pay a full perpetual license fee for an instance that you may run for only a few hours or days; on the other hand, the software creator wants to be paid for the value its software offers. Marketplace images allow software companies to offer their software on a pay-per-use basis, allowing both vendor and user a payment mode that aligns with the overall AWS approach.

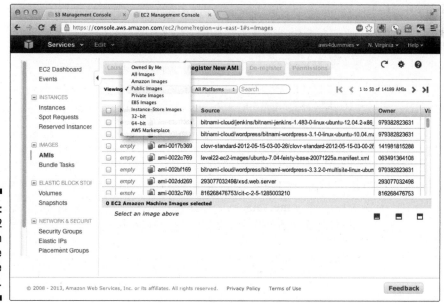

Figure 5-1:
The EC2
Amazon
Machine
Image
panel.

Be extremely careful about which AMIs you use. When you launch an instance from a public image, you're launching whatever software packages the creator placed on the image. It doesn't take much imagination to envision the kinds of malicious software that can end up on an AMI. For any task beyond prototyping, use images only from sources you trust. Even better, create your own images so that you know exactly what's on the AMI.

A closer look at Figure 5-1 reveals a cornucopia of other AMI information:

- ✔ **AMI ID:** Peeking out from the AMI Type drop-down menu to identify every AMI, this AWS-assigned number is unique for every AMI.

- ✔ **Source:** The description of the AMI typically includes information about the AMI creator's name, the operating system, and the software components installed on the AMI.

- ✔ **Owner:** This long number is the image owner's AWS account number.

The following image information isn't visible in the screenshot in Figure 5-1, but if you scroll to the right, you can see it:

- ✔ **Visibility:** Tells you who can see the AMI

- ✔ **Platform:** Points out which operating system is installed on the AMI

- ✔ **Root device:** Indicates whether the image is an S3-backed instance or an EBS-backed instance

- ✔ **Virtualization:** Specifies how the instance interacts with the virtualization hypervisor in EC2 (information that you generally don't need to be concerned about or, indeed, have control of)

S3-backed images

S3 images are stored as multiple 10MB files, along with a special XML file called a manifest. The *manifest file* is similar to the assembly instructions in an Ikea flat-pack piece of furniture — it gives AWS the information it needs to construct a running instance from the collection of 10MB S3 objects.

When you give AWS the command to launch an S3-backed image, the system reads the manifest file and uses it to construct and launch the instance by downloading it to the instance's local drive. It then becomes an operational instance and, depending on what was in the image when it was created, starts executing the software that was part of the image.

S3-backed images come with limitations, and you should fully understand what they are. The following list spells them out for you:

- ✔ **Root device limitations:** It's crucial to understand precisely what's stored in the image proper. With S3-backed images, all you have is the root device — the part of the system containing system files (including the operating system) — plus, any other software that was installed when the image was created.

  An S3-backed image is limited to 10GB in the root device. All other parts of the file system are constructed at the time of launch; for example, in a small instance with 170GB of disk space, 160GB of the instance storage is created at launch-time, and only 10GB is persistent. If you want to include a lot of software packages or data in the root device, you may exceed this 10GB limit.

- ✔ **Long launch times:** Because the instance has to be created from the various 10MB files making up a collection, it takes a while to assemble them, which extends the launch times.

  Removing an S3-backed instance from production requires terminating it — no ifs, ands, or buts: Doing so discards all data written to its file system since the launch.

- ✔ **The AWS management console doesn't support the creation of a new image from an S3-backed instance.** If you want to create a new image from an S3-backed instance, first install AWS AMI tools on the instance, and then run scripts to create the image. Though this task is perfectly possible, it's not a trivial matter, so it's a definite limitation.

In summary, S3-backed images are widely used, but they carry operational implications that you should be aware of if you plan to use them.

EBS-backed images

EBS-backed images have been available since late 2009. The primary difference between an EBS-backed image and an S3-backed image is that the former uses a persistent EBS volume for instance storage — instances can now be stopped and started after launch, in addition to being terminated.

Practically speaking, therefore, an EBS-backed image, when launched, can create an instance that can then retain changes when it's not running. For example, if an EBS-backed image is launched and the resulting instance is added to a pool of instances in an application, if the instance is no longer required as part of the instance pool, it can be stopped and put into a quiescent mode. If the application pool later requires additional resources, rather than launch a new instance from the EBS-backed image, the first instance can be started up and added to the pool.

Starting a stopped instance is not only faster than a full launch, but any changes made to the instance also persist across stops and starts — even multiple stops and starts. Not bad.

In addition to the luxury of instance stops and starts and data persistence across the stop/start cycle, EBS-backed images offer a number of advantages versus S3-backed images:

- ✔ **EBS-backed images allow for much larger root volumes than S3-backed images.** Instead of the mere 10GB root volumes found in S3-backed images, EBS-backed images can have root volumes as large as 1TB, which allows more room for additional software packages or data storage on the image.

- ✔ **If an EBS-backed instance is stopped, you incur no EC2 charges:** Concern yourself only with the image storage costs on EBS, similar to the storage cost you pay to store an S3 image in S3.

- ✔ **If something goes wrong with an EBS-backed image, its root volume can be mounted on another instance.** You can then examine or even repair it.

- ✔ **If you need to adjust the instance size of an EBS-backed instance, stop it and then restart it at the new size.** This method is a lot more flexible and faster than S3-backed instances. (Don't forget that the data in the EBS-backed instance is persistent across that stop/start cycle.)

- ✔ **Only an EBS-backed type supports the EC2 Micro instance type.** The Micro type is useful for testing and for certain use cases of low-volume processing, and, crucially, it's part of the Free Usage Tier that Amazon makes available. If you want to work with EC2 at no charge, you must use EBS-backed images.

Though Amazon continues to support both S3- and EBS-backed images, the AWS user community has a clear — but not universal — preference for EBS-backed images. The primary reservation appears to be related to the EBS proper — namely, concerns about inconsistent EBS throughput performance associated with network contention. This issue can be addressed by launching an EBS-backed instance with *Provisioned IOPS*, the relatively recent EBS service extension that provides guaranteed levels of throughput. It doesn't necessarily satisfy critics of EBS-backed instances (they point out the additional cost it imposes), but then there's no making some people happy, is there? (For more on these concerns — and more on EBS in general and Provisioned IOPS in particular — see Chapter 4.)

Though EBS-backed images let you stop and start instances, with data persistence across the stop/start cycle, they do not — I repeat, do *not* — persist data in the event of a termination. Any data that isn't present on the image is discarded when an EBS-backed instance terminates. For that reason, you should follow the same practice with EBS-backed instances that you follow with S3-backed instances: Place all data that requires persistence on separate EBS volumes that persist even if the instance they're attached to terminates.

EC2 instance types

Image types are just one side of the EC2 coin. You also have to consider instance types — the types of virtual machines you can run in AWS.

Instances vary by the amount of three types of compute resources:

- **Processing power:** Every instance has a certain number of *EC2 compute units* (ECU), which is a benchmarked amount of processing power (the equivalent of the CPU capacity of a 1.0-1.2 GHz 2007 Opteron or 2007 Xeon processor). For example, the small instance in AWS has 1 EC2 compute unit, or 1 ECU.

- **Memory:** Every instance contains a given amount of memory, measured in gigabytes. A small instance has 1.7GB of memory.

- **Storage:** Every instance has a certain amount of disk storage. A small instance has 170GB of disk storage.

  Depending on the instance type, some of the disk storage associated with an instance may be provided in unformatted form — before it can be used, it must be formatted with a file system that's usable by the operating system of the instance.

- **Network connectivity:** Every instance comes supplied with one virtual network interface card (NIC), which it uses to communicate with other devices or services. Every instance is given two IP addresses: one private address that's used solely within AWS and one public address that's used for Internet access to the instance. (For more on AWS network connectivity, see Chapter 7.)

  Not all instance types get only one NIC. Instances within the AWS Virtual Private Cloud (VPC) can have more than one NIC. I discuss the VPC in Chapter 8.

A few years ago, choosing which instance to use for an application was a straightforward affair. AWS provided a few instance types that varied in a primarily linear fashion; that is, if you wanted more processing power, you selected an instance type that contained more ECUs, and it came supplied with larger amounts of memory and storage — a cakewalk.

It's much more difficult now to decide which instance type to use, because Amazon has launched (excuse the pun) several families of instances designed to help you optimize for a certain type of functionality. For example, what if your application is memory intensive, as certain analytics applications are? You used to have to use an instance from the family of standard instance types, and you had to use instances with large amounts of memory that carried high numbers of ECUs, even if your application didn't require much processing power. That's just the way it was.

Obviously, on one hand, this is a positive dilemma because you may find one family that's well-tuned for your application's use profile; on the other hand (and there's *always* an other hand), you have to use due diligence in deciding which instance family is most congenial to your application (which requires understanding your application's operating characteristics in detail).

In the EC2 documentation, Amazon describes the offerings of EC2 instances (High-CPU, for example) as *families,* and the different sizes of instances (M1, where M stands for medium, for example), as *types.* In my experience, nearly everyone else (including AWS employees whom I have heard speak) refers to a *family* from the AWS documentation as a *type* ("That's a High-CPU type instance," for example) and to *type* from the AWS documentation as *size* ("That's an M1 Large Size instance," for example). In this discussion, I use the more common approach because it's the way you hear it discussed by nearly everyone, but also because I think it's more logical.

With that, let me jump in to a description of the instance types:

- ✔ **Micro:** Very, very small; provides a limited amount of both CPU and memory, although Micro instance types can burst to 2 ECU for short periods. Use this type for lower-throughput applications and low-traffic websites. The Micro type is also available as part of the AWS Free Usage Tier, which is useful for learning and experimentation.

- ✔ **Standard:** The "average" type and by far the most widely used; offers a balance of CU, memory, and disk that's suitable for mainstream applications.

- ✔ **High CPU:** Goes for higher CUs rather than memory and is well suited for processing-heavy applications. A number-crunching application is the canonical use case for high-CPU instances.

- ✔ **High Memory:** Bumps up memory rather than CPU. This type is well suited for database apps, analytics apps, and apps that rely on memory caching. If you run a caching tier product like memcached, this instance type is a good choice.

- ✔ **High I/O:** Provides high-throughput (input + output — I/O, in other words) and is well suited for applications that move a lot of data. It's a good choice for running your own key-value storage service, like Cassandra or MongoDB, rather than using AWS's DynamoDB service. High-I/O instances have high throughput connections (10 Gbps) and use solid-state drives to provide high disk performance.

- ✔ **Cluster Compute:** Provides a large number of ECUs along with high-performance networking (10 Gbps). This instance type, which is well suited for high-performance computing tasks (very large applications for specialized number crunching, like oil field seismic analysis), runs on specialized hardware, with custom AMIs that use a different, more efficient type of virtualization as well as closely connected machines for better network performance.

✔ **Cluster GPU:** Analogous to Cluster Compute instances, but uses graphical processing units (think of the processor inside the graphics card on your PC, if you're a gamer) that are better suited for certain types of applications, including certain variants of high-performance computing (HPC) network analysis. Cluster GPU instances operate similarly to Cluster Compute instances, albeit with different CPU chips in the servers these instances run on.

EC2 image sizes

If you think that the variety of instance types makes it difficult to decide what to do, the variety of image sizes will make your mind reel. Suffice it to say that AWS provides a wide range of image sizes, which should make it possible for you to meet your application performance needs by tuning the EC2 infrastructure it runs on.

The original instance type (Standard) aims for a good mixture of resources to meet the requirements of, well, standard applications. The other instance types contain a larger amount of one type of resource in terms of the other resource types of the instance; one particular instance type can then better support a particular set of application requirements than another.

Table 5-1 illustrates the range of resources available across the instance types, just to give you an idea of the flexibility you have in choosing them for your application.

Table 5-1	Size Range of AWS Instance Resources	
Resource	*Minimum*	*Maximum*
Compute unit	1 (Standard M1.Small)	88 (Cluster Compute cc2.8 x Large)
Virtual core	1 (Micro, M1.Small, M1.Medium)	16 (2 x Intel Zeon 8 core Sandy Bridge architecture)
Memory	615MB (Micro)	68.4GB (High-Memory Quadruple Extra Large)
Instance store volume	None (Micro)	3360GB (Cluster Compute Eight Extra Large)
Network I/O	Low (Micro)	10 Gbps (High I/O Quadruple Extra Large, Cluster Compute Quadruple Extra Large, Cluster Compute Eight Extra Large, Cluster GPU Quadruple Extra Large)

Amazon documentation lists 18 instance sizes, spread across the 7 instance types. That doesn't mean each type has two sizes, however. There are 4 standard instance types, though several of the more exotic types (Cluster GPU, for example) come in a single very large size. For exotic types with a single size, Amazon's thinking is that the type of computing you're likely to do with them requires such high resource capacity that they'll go ahead and provide the largest possible numbers of resources within its overall infrastructure constraints. Another way to say it is that the users who are likely to use these exotic instance types are so demanding of resources that they will want only the largest possible type that can be delivered, so Amazon hasn't bothered creating smaller sizes of these instance types. If you find all of this mind-boggling, there is an excellent third-party website that lists and compares all the different instance types and sizes. You can find it at `http://ec2 instances.info`.

AWS defaults to delivering the M1.small version if you fail to explicitly choose an instance type and size. The most common use case for most users is the Standard instance types, but they end up moving to the Large instance sizes after first beginning with sizes lower on the scale.

EC2 scope

EC2 images and instances contained within AWS regions, which can create a challenge if you want your instances to be able to run in multiple regions. Now, why would you want your instances to run in multiple regions? I'm glad you asked:

- ✔ **As protection against failure in an AWS availability zone (AZ) or region:** If AWS suffered an outage in one portion of its service area, you can continue to operate your application in another availability zone or region.

- ✔ **To reduce latency when serving users located in specific geographic regions:** By placing instances in, say, the Australia-based Asia Pacific region, you would reduce overall network transit time to users located nearby.

- ✔ **So that you can operate a multiregion application to ensure the best possible performance to a user base spread throughout the world:** In addition to the need to manage images in multiple locations, you may take advantage of two other AWS services:

    Route 53: Amazon's distributed DNS service

    CloudFront: Amazon's S3-based content delivery network

    Both services are discussed in greater detail in Chapter 8.

✔ **To comply with national requirements for data privacy:** Some countries impose restrictions on the locations where data related to their
citizens or businesses resides. You may choose to run your application
in multiple regions to comply with these restrictions.

EBS-backed images can be launched in any availability zone within the region
where the image resides; this is different from the general EBS scoping limitation (as discussed in Chapter 5), which restricts the use of an EBS volume to
the availability zone in which it's located.

EC2 pricing and deployment options

In addition to the different types and sizes of the EC2 offerings, EC2 offers
three deployment options. To say it another way, you can pay a different
hourly rate for the same type and size instance, depending on how you
choose to deploy it. Each deployment option affects pricing:

✔ **On-demand:** You start these instances when you choose. Here, you pay
the standard rate for every hour they run.

✔ **Reserved:** You pay an upfront fee for these instances and in return
receive a reduced rate for every hour they run. There are a few variations of reserved deployment options, which I discuss later in this
chapter.

✔ **Spot:** You offer a bid price for these instances — a price you're willing
to pay for every hour they run. Amazon runs a reverse auction for spare
EC2 capacity and runs every spot instance for which bids have been
received that meet or exceed the spot instance "clearing" price.

In the following three sections, I dig in to each type so that you can understand the differences.

On-demand instances

The *on-demand* instance is the most straightforward deployment option: You
choose when you want the instance to run, and AWS guarantees to run it at a
standard, documented rate per hour.

It's important to understand what on-demand instances represent. As a cloud
service provider, Amazon asserts that it's ready to offer computing resources
whenever a customer requests them; in effect, the store is always open for
business. The default limitation is 20 instances per account, but the company
provides an easy way to request additional instances and, to my knowledge,
has never failed to offer more, if requested.

The implications of this offer are quite important: Amazon *must* have capacity available in every region whenever customers may request instances.

As you probably recognize, this offer for on-demand instances and requiring capacity to support customer demand isn't limited to instances: Amazon must have capacity available for all its services when someone requests them. Whenever the company rolls out a new service or extends a service to a new region, it must therefore be confident that it can respond to whatever demand may arise. It's obviously a significant challenge — how to provide enough capacity to support potential demand, but not to overprovision capacity and have idle hardware. I maintain that capacity planning is extremely difficult in an on-demand world, where demand is quite hard to forecast; for Amazon, which has to perform this capacity planning in an environment in which it's growing torridly, the challenge is doubly difficult.

Another element of note for on-demand pricing is that AWS must make this capacity available while imposing no commitment whatsoever. The moment that you decide you no longer want to use AWS resources, you terminate them and walk away. This is in stark contrast, by the way, to almost all other providers, who, as part of the agreement to provide you with resources at a certain price, expect you to make a commitment (typically, three years). These providers can then manage capacity at the cost of imposing a financial burden on you.

On-demand pricing varies according to instance type, size, and region. Micro instances, as I describe earlier in this chapter, are available for free to a certain usage level: for the first year of a new account, users receive 750 hours of Linux/Unix and 750 hours of Windows Micro instance use per month. After that, Micro instances cost $.02 to $.027 per hour, depending on which region the instance runs in.

Other instance types and sizes range from M1.small, which runs from $.065 per hour (in the US East region) to $.115 per hour (South America São Paulo) to High I/O, Quadruple Extra Large, which ranges from $3.10 per hour (US East region) to $3.40 per hour (EU Ireland).

As you look at the more exotic (larger or more hardware-dependent) instance types, you see restrictions on region availability. Amazon commonly rolls out new services in the US East region first, and then, over the course of a few months, makes them available in other regions. Keep this point in mind as you make your AWS plans, because using a service that's bound to a single region (or only a few regions) will impose data-transfer and network-latency costs on your application.

As with many of its services, Amazon has steadily reduced the prices of its on-demand instances. A couple years ago, an M1.Small (US East region) was $.085 per hour; today, it's $.065 per hour, a drop of 23 percent.

AWS pricing across regions

When you're considering EC2, this obvious question crops up: Why do prices for its on-demand instances vary across AWS regions? Shouldn't Amazon have consistent pricing?

In one sense, it may be more convenient to charge the same price everywhere — it would simplify your cost calculations, for sure. Amazon's philosophy, however, is to provide the most cost-effective computing possible, and part of that philosophy is to reduce prices in line with its costs. Amazon experiences differing costs by region and aligns its prices to its costs.

Which brings up the second question: Why do AWS prices vary across regions? Amazon has provided no official reason, but I'll offer my opinion: In the United States, Amazon owns its own data centers, though in other regions it rents space from data center providers, like Equinix. Amazon probably cannot obtain pricing from outside providers as low as it can from its own data centers, so it passes those higher costs along to users in the form of higher regional pricing. In addition, Amazon's operating costs vary throughout the world based on electricity prices, real estate costs, employee salaries, and so on. All of these factors affect Amazon's data center costs, and therefore the prices Amazon charges for AWS services.

To understand the reason behind the pricing differential across regions, you can look at it as either paying higher prices in some regions or getting an even better deal in regions in which Amazon owns its own facilities. As you can probably guess, I'm in the latter camp, which perhaps makes me someone who sees the glass as half-full rather than half-empty.

Reserved instances

Another instance-pricing option that Amazon provides is *reserved instances.* In essence, in exchange for a customer making an upfront financial payment, Amazon offers a lower hourly rate for instances. The term for reserved instance pricing can run either one or three years, with, as you may expect, a larger up-front payment for the three-year term.

To see how this strategy works in practice, consider the M1.Small instance type. On-demand instances cost (using US East region pricing) $.065 per hour. For M1.Small reserved instances with a 1-year term, you pay $69 up front, and the hourly rate is $.039, a 39-percent savings. For a 3-year term, you pay $106.30 up front, and the hourly rate is $.031 per hour, a 53-percent discount. AWS clearly isn't a marketing-driven company, because an upfront payment of $106.30 is strange — why tack on 30 cents?

The overall discount you receive depends on how many hours you run the instance, because you have to amortize the upfront payment across all the hours that you run the reserved instance at the lower price.

When reserved instances were first announced, the general wisdom was that the tipping point at which using a reserved instance was less expensive than using an on-demand instance was around 30 percent. In other words, if you ran an instance more than eight hours a day, it was worthwhile to use a reserved instance.

Choosing an instance type has become more complicated since then, as Amazon has further refined its reserved instance pricing and introduced two additional reserved instance-pricing levels. In addition to the original reserved instance pricing (now called *light utilization* reserved instances), Amazon now offers medium utilization and heavy utilization reserved instances. For larger upfront payments, these reserved instance types offer even deeper discounts. So if you expect to run your instance 24 (rather than 8) hours per day, you're better off using heavy utilization reserved instances, where you pay $195 up front and then pay $.016 per instance-hour (rather than $69 for a 1-year discount to $.039 per hour).

These new reserved instance options give you more flexibility in trading off your likely level of instance use versus the total cost of operation (TCO) for your instances.

Another benefit of reserved instances is that Amazon assures its customers that capacity will be available to run their reserved instances. By contrast, Amazon makes no such guarantees for on-demand instances, so it is possible you can attempt to launch an on-demand instance and find that Amazon has no capacity available. In return for your upfront payment for a reserved instance, Amazon promises that it will always have capacity available for you. Think of it as your VIP status!

Most companies don't take advantage of reserved instances as much as they should. Usage analyses indicate that a large proportion of AWS users can save money if they used reserved instances. Certainly, for the baseline resources used in an application that's required 24 hours per day (a company's website, for example), reserved instances are appropriate. Companies may be reluctant to use reserved instances for several reasons, if they decide to

> ✔ **Stop running the application and then worry that they'll waste the money they've spent on the upfront payment.** Though this concern may be valid, companies should look at the application characteristics and decide how likely it is to be taken down. A company's website is an unlikely candidate for termination, and using reserved instances for baseline resources that are never shut down is a reasonably safe investment. Moreover, if a reserved instance is no longer needed, you can sell it within Amazon's Reserved Instance Marketplace.

✔ **Move the application using the reserved instances to another cloud service provider to avoid being locked in to AWS:** That's a fair consideration, but a reserved instance (even at the lowest level of reservation) needs to run 24/7 for only three or four months to break even. I don't know about your company, but the management of most companies couldn't decide to move an application and then execute the move in a similar timeframe — so the company would likely still save money using reserved instances.

✔ **Move to an instance of a different size, resulting in losing the money they invested in buying a reserved instance:** It's a valid concern. If, after a few weeks, you decide that you need to use an instance of a different size and you terminate the original instance, you have a stranded investment. Fortunately, Amazon has created an exchange where you can sell your reservation to another person or company that wants a reserved instance the same size as your choice who then takes on your reserved instance.

For more information on AWS utilization and cost management, see Chapter 12.

Spot-priced instances

Amazon also offers a deployment option called *spot-priced* instances, which allows AWS users to bid on unused AWS capacity to run their applications.

An AWS user interested in using spot-pricing places a bid that represents the amount the user is willing to pay to have the application run. For example, though the on-demand price for an M1.small may be $.065 per hour, you may bid $.02 per hour to run the application.

If the current price for spot-priced instances of the type and size you want is at or below the current spot-price, AWS launches the instance you want to run and runs it as long as you request it or until the spot-price increases beyond your bid.

If the spot-price is below the amount you've bid, don't worry: You pay only the current spot-price. If the current spot-price for M1.Small is only $.01 per hour, for example, you pay that rate, not your $.02 bid.

Know the maximum price you're willing to pay to run your spot-price instance, and bid only that price. During the holiday season in 2011, a time of high demand and low spot-price availability, a number of users who had thoughtlessly placed maximum bids of $99 per hour were blindsided when the spot-price matched their bids. Needless to say, most of them were unhappy because their applications weren't critical at that price. Be sure to only bid the maximum amount you're willing to pay for a spot instance.

When the spot-price increases beyond your bid, your instance is terminated immediately, which raises some obvious flags:

✔ **Your application may be in the middle of performing work, even a transaction.**

✔ **If your spot-price instance is S3-backed, any data in the file system is lost upon termination.**

✔ **If your spot-price instance is EBS-backed, it still loses any data that's placed in the file system post-launch.** Put another way, EBS-backed spot instances are terminated, not stopped, and are launched, not started.

✔ **Even if your application is architected to manage this kind of possible interruption, it still needs to be the kind of application that can handle having instances terminated at any time.** Don't run your company's website running on spot-price instances.

On the other hand, according to Amazon, only about 4 percent of all spot-price instances are ever terminated unexpectedly, so the odds of your application running into problems because of termination are fairly low.

There are some powerful arguments in favor of using spot-price instances:

✔ **They can be quite cost effective.** They're typically offered at 50-percent to 66-percent discounts from the associated on-demand instance cost.

✔ **For applications that don't need to be always running, using them can be a good approach.** For example, if your application needs to process images sometime during the next seven days, using spot-price instances would be a cost-effective approach with little downside.

✔ **They can make a great deal of sense when combined with other instance payment options.** You may want to have a certain amount of image processing capacity at all times (which is a good use case for reserved instances) but occasionally use additional capacity to work through any possible backlog (which is a good use case for spot-price instances).

Spot-price instances are undoubtedly the least-often-used of the three instance deployment options, but this option provides real benefits because it offers the financial savings associated with reserved instances, matched by the lack of commitment associated with on-demand instances.

Pinterest: Leveraging spot-price instances

Pinterest, the wildly popular sharing service, runs entirely on Amazon. One challenge in using free applications is finding ways to keep costs down, given that no revenue is associated with the use of the application.

Pinterest leverages spot-price instances heavily and has saved a ton of money by doing so. When it was using on-demand instances to support its services, it was paying $1,200 per day for AWS resources. By judiciously using reserved and spot-price instances, Amazon has reduced its daily cost to $440 — a 63-percent savings.

As you can see from this example, it pays to pay attention to your AWS use and to think about whether the alternatives to on-demand prices make sense for your application.

Why AWS has three deployment options

You may be curious about why Amazon offers three deployment options, especially when two of the three options provide discounts on the already low on-demand pricing that Amazon offers.

After all, AWS pricing is already lower than most users can achieve by other means. For example, I've compared AWS pricing with other cloud providers and found that AWS pricing can be as low as 12 percent of the amount that other providers charge for a similar service. If you're already 88-percent less expensive than the alternatives, why provide ways to save even more money? Is that just "leaving money on the table," so to speak?

I believe there are two answers to this question — one AWS-focused and one user-focused.

The AWS-focused answer has to do with what Amazon is selling: computing capacity. The cost structure of computing capacity is largely fixed cost, with very small amounts of variable cost. In other words, Amazon spends a lot of money building data centers and funding the smart software it has created to provide automated computing services in those data centers, but it doesn't spend much to run those services. Most of its costs are fixed, whether or not any user work is going on within AWS.

In common with other industries that share these characteristics, the key to maximum profitability is to drive the maximum use of capacity. This may entail selling part of the capacity at a lower price than it may otherwise be sold for.

An easy analogy to help in understanding this concept is the airline industry. It costs a lot to buy an airplane, fuel it, and staff it to fly to destinations. The cost associated with placing an additional passenger on an airplane is quite low — perhaps a couple sodas or a low-cost meal on an international flight. Selling a seat that would otherwise remain unoccupied provides almost pure additional profit, assuming that the fixed cost of flying the airplane has been covered. And even if it hasn't, it's better to gain some revenue to apply against the fixed cost than to suffer the loss associated with flying the air-plane without that additional revenue.

Airline pricing is a curious case, however: Rather than sell unused capacity at a low price near departure time to induce people to purchase an otherwise unoccupied seat, airlines typically charge very high prices. The reason is presumably that they believe they're selling a last-minute ticket to someone for whom the ability to go to the intended destination is highly valuable — a businessperson for whom reaching that destination is quite important. This situation is different from cruise ships, which typically sell last-minute capac-ity quite cheaply in an effort to fill the vessel.

Amazon clearly considers itself more like the cruise industry than the airline industry, in that it doesn't attempt to sell excess capacity at a premium. In some ways, it makes sense. After all, there's commonly little time pressure to run a job at a certain point, so it would be difficult to charge a premium. In fact, in some ways, AWS is clearly like the cruise industry. Just as there is little demand for cruises during certain months of the year (for example, the Christmas holiday period, when people are engaged in family activities), sometimes AWS experiences low use volumes — for example, during the middle of the night, when few people are using applications that require AWS resources, but clearly not during the Christmas holiday period, when AWS customers probably experience very high usage because many of them are e-commerce sites.

From the Amazon perspective, offering a mix of instance purchase options is a way to drive capacity utilization upward, leading to the highest possible revenue stream.

The question remains, though: Why is Amazon doing this for customers, many of whom, presumably, would use on-demand instances in place of the lower-cost options? Netflix and Pinterest, after all, aren't likely to stop using AWS, even if it were to cost more. Because AWS is much cheaper than the alternatives, whether in a company's own data center or in another cloud provider's capacity, these customers are captives to some degree and, would presumably pay the full on-demand price.

So why should Amazon go out of its way to provide even lower-cost alterna-tives? The answer, I feel, has to do with Amazon's general approach to busi-ness. It believes that if it provides great value to customers, even if it fails to derive a maximum margin in the short term, it will prosper in the long term. By offering a way to achieve lower-cost computing during times of low demand, it reinforces its position of offering the best possible computing prices and increases its long-term customer loyalty. Amazon's approach in all elements of its business is to offer the best possible value to customers, with the belief that this approach will provide long-term dividends to the company.

By the way, an added benefit of Amazon's options for instance pricing may not be obvious to you if you haven't worked much with cloud computing: transparency in pricing. Amazon lists on-demand and reserved instance pricing on its website and lets customers easily find current and historic spot-instance pricing. Customers then know immediately how much an application costs to run or how much it's likely to cost if it's run on spot-price instances.

This strategy is in stark contrast to most other cloud providers, who require you to talk with a salesperson to find out service prices. That method costs you time — you have to schedule the discussion, describe your use, estimate how much capacity you'll require, and specify the time commitment you're willing to make. And then, of course, you have to negotiate the price and negotiate the terms of a contract. All of this is extremely annoying. It's as inconvenient as buying a car — and as painful as visiting a dentist. That Amazon posts its prices publicly is much more revolutionary than it may seem — and it's a true benefit of using the service.

Creating new EC2 images

Until this point in the chapter, I've explained your options for managing images that already exist. But what about creating your own images? Though it's certainly possible to use images that have been created by Amazon or other third parties, you may at some point want to create your own images, for two reasons:

- ✔ You have used an Amazon image, or another third-party image, and you have extended it by installing your own software components, and now you want to use the extended image as your baseline image going forward rather than endure the launch image/install software cycle for every instance you launch.
- ✔ You want to use your own system as the basis for the images you use because of a general preference or a concern about the security of the image.

Creating EBS-backed images

The image creation process varies based on whether you're creating an EBS- or an S3-backed image, and whether you're creating a Linux- or Windows-based image.

The EBS-backed image creation process is significantly simpler, though it's accompanied by limitations. Typically, you start with an already existing EBS-backed instance that you have modified. However, it's possible to create an EBS-backed image from an S3-backed instance — though it's possible only if the instance is Linux-based. Creating an EBS-backed Windows image from an S3-backed Windows instance isn't possible.

You can easily create an EBS-backed image from the AWS management console by right-clicking the target instance in the instance listing. One item on the contextual menu that appears is Create Image (EBS AMI). The AWS management console handles everything from there. During the image creation process, AWS stops the instance from which you're creating the image in order to have a stable instance. If you have additional EBS volumes attached to the instance, AWS creates (and attaches) fresh volumes to the new image; however, there's no data on those volumes. (For more on the AWS management console, see Chapter 3.)

You can also use a set of AWS API tools to create an EBS-backed image. You install the tools on the instance from which you want to create a new image and then execute the `ec2-create-image` command. This is possible only in Linux-based instances; Windows-based EBS-backed images can be created only via the AWS management console. This command requires that the access key and secret access key be available to confirm your right to create the image. (For more on the role of the access key and secret access key, see Chapter 3, where I discuss the AWS API.)

Creating S3-backed images

The process of creating S3-backed images can be more complex than creating EBS-backed images, depending on whether you're creating a Windows-based or Linux-based image.

For Windows-based images, you follow a process similar to the one outlined in the preceding section for Windows-based EBS-backed images. You start with an S3-backed Windows instance, extend it by installing additional software components, and then right-click the instance in the AWS management console and select Bundle Instance (Instance Store AMI) from the menu that appears. S3-backed images (Amazon refers to them as *instance-stored* images) require a separate bucket — in fact, it can be a top-level, uniquely named bucket in your account or a folder within a top-level bucket — in your S3 account in which to store the Windows AMI, so you must create that bucket before beginning the image creation process. After you select Bundle Instance (Instance Store AMI) from the contextual menu, the AWS management console completes the bundling process.

What's with this "bundle instance" stuff, eh? Though it sounds more like something you do with a baby, not with cloud computing, it's one of those quirks of AWS that you have to live with. Because an S3-backed instance is made up of a number of 10MB files along with an XML manifest file, you can think of the totality of the files as a "bundle" of files, which is where the term *bundle* comes from.

After you upload the new image bundle into S3, you need to register the new image with EC2 so that it appears in a listing of your images. (For EBS-backed images, AWS takes care of this registration step.)

To register a new S3-backed image, start out in the AWS management console and find the new AMI entry in the listing of your images. Now right-click the entry and enter the path to the bucket in which the AMI manifest resides (which should also be the bucket in which the collection of 10MB files that make up the image reside). The S3-backed image is now registered!

Creating S3-backed Linux images is significantly more complicated than the process I just outlined for S3-backed Windows images. The AWS management console offers no support for the image creation process, so you have to use AWS AMI tools on the instance from which you'll create the new image.

The process (generally speaking) goes like this:

1. Launch an S3-backed Linux instance.

2. Modify the instance by adding software components.

3. Install the AWS AMI tools.

4. Copy your X.509 certificate and private key to the instance.

   Note: These items should be placed in a nonroot area of the file system so that AWS doesn't include them in the resulting AMI. They're included so that AWS can store them and use them in the AMI launch process, but you don't want to include the certificate and private key in an area of the resulting AMI where someone can find them, which would compromise your account security.

5. Run the `ec2-bundle-vol` command to create the collection of 10MB files and the XML manifest file that describes the AMI.

6. Upload the bundle to S3 using the `ec2-upload-bundle` command.

7. Register the new AMI in EC2.

The AMI registration process requires that you type the entire path to the bucket holding the manifest file into the Image Registration dialog box; there's no file system wizard to point-and-click to the bucket, so you have to type the entire path correctly. Otherwise, you see the Bucket Not Found error message — one more reason for using easy-to-remember bucket names.

I've simplified the preceding step list because each of the AMI tool commands is a long, complicated function with a number of arguments that must be typed perfectly. Overall, however, dealing with S3-backed AMIs is much more complex than dealing with EBS-backed AMIs, another likely reason that Amazon recommends using EBS-backed images.

The final step is deciding who can use the AMI. Still in the AWS management console, right-click the AMI entry; a pop-up window appears, offering the Edit Permissions choice. Selecting that menu item brings up a screen where you can set controls regarding who may access your AMI. You can choose to leave the image with public availability, which is the default choice. If you don't want to enable everyone to access your image, you can change the AMI availability to

- **Private:** Enables only your account to access it
- **Private with Access:** Available to specific accounts you identify in the Edit Permissions screen

You can also make your AMI available publicly and charge for using it. AWS provides two payment methods associated with the commercial use of AMIs: DevPay and the AWS Marketplace. I don't delve in to the details of creating commercial AMIs, because they're typically specialized offerings from software companies. Suffice it to say that setting up the AMI structure and making payment arrangements with Amazon is fairly complicated, although, if you have a popular AMI, it can also provide a revenue stream for your applications.

Working with an EC2 Example

To end this chapter on a more concrete note, let me walk you through an example of launching an actual EC2 instance, from beginning to end:

1. **Go to** `aws.amazon.com` **and click on My Account/Console in the upper right-hand corner of the page.**

2. **From the pull-down menu that appears, select AWS Management Console.**

3. **(Optional) If you are not logged in to AWS, enter your login credentials on the login page and click Continue to access the EC2 dashboard, shown in Figure 5-2.**

   NOTE: You must be in the US East region to access the AMI for this exercise. Once you enter the EC2 dashboard, look at the upper right-hand part of the page, where a region will be displayed. Click on the pull-down menu and select US East (N. Virginia).

   Note that you have quite a number of options running down the left side of the dashboard. Note also that, under the Resources heading near the top-center area of the screen, I have one key pair and 14 security groups. You see them addressed in this example.

4. **Under the Images heading on the left side of the dashboard, click the AMIs link.**

   A new screen appears, listing all available Amazon machine images.

© 2008 - 2013, Amazon Web Services, Inc. or its affiliates. All rights reserved.   Privacy Policy   Terms of Use

Figure 5-2:
The EC2
dashboard.

5. **Choose Public Images from the Filter menu near the top of the new screen, and then enter the word** getting **in to the Search field.**

   The screen refreshes to show a screen similar to the one you see in Figure 5-3.

   To keep things simple, I use an Amazon-supplied AMI — a Public Image, in other words — that is extremely simple: All it does is launch and run a stripped-down web page.

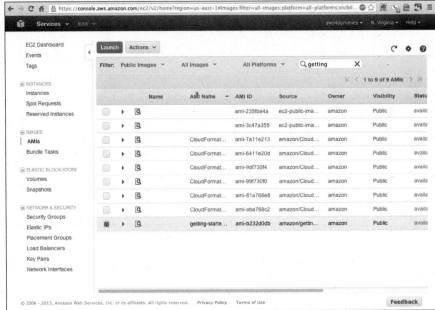

Figure 5-3:
The AMI
selection
screen.

6. **Select the check box next to Getting Started with EBS Boot — the last AMI listed.**

   Doing so enables the Launch button near the upper-left corner of the screen.

7. **Click the Launch button.**

   The first screen of the Request Instances Wizard appears, as shown in Figure 5-4. You use the wizard to select values for items that will control the type, size, and location of the instance you launch.

8. **On the wizard screen that appears, leave the Number of Instances and the Instance Type options set to their defaults (1 and T1 Micro, respectively).**

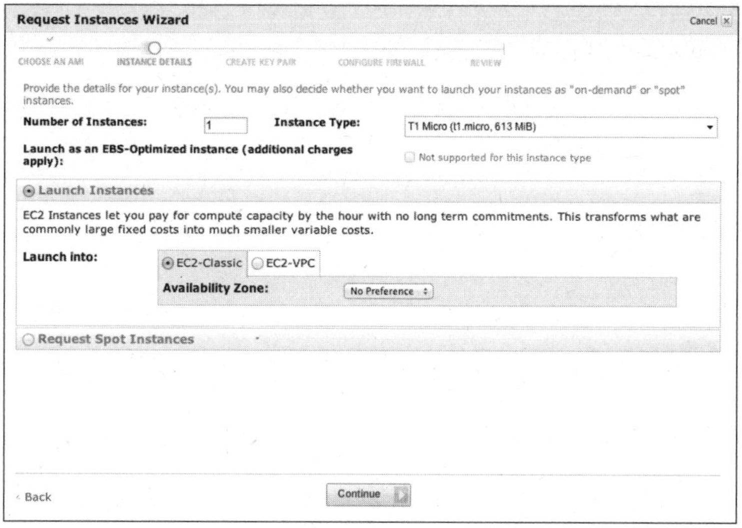

Request Instances Wizard   Cancel ✕

CHOOSE AN AMI   INSTANCE DETAILS   CREATE KEY PAIR   CONFIGURE FIREWALL   REVIEW

Provide the details for your instance(s). You may also decide whether you want to launch your instances as "on-demand" or "spot" instances.

Number of Instances: [1]   **Instance Type:**   [T1 Micro (t1.micro, 613 MiB)   ▾]

Launch as an EBS-Optimized instance (additional charges apply):   ☐ Not supported for this instance type

⊙ **Launch Instances**

EC2 Instances let you pay for compute capacity by the hour with no long term commitments. This transforms what are commonly large fixed costs into much smaller variable costs.

Launch into: ⊙ EC2-Classic   ○ EC2-VPC
                          Availability Zone: [No Preference ⬍]

○ **Request Spot Instances**

‹ Back   [Continue ▷]

Figure 5-4:
The Request
Instances
Wizard
details
screen.

7. **Make sure that the Launch Instances radio button is selected and leave the EC2-Classic radio button selected.**

   The VPC part of the EC2-VPC option stands for *V*irtual *P*rivate *C*loud, which is a more secure AWS environment. I discuss VPC in Chapter 7, which focuses on security, so don't worry — you'll know all about VPC shortly!

8. **Leave the Availability Zone option set to the default.**

   Notice a pattern here? No Preference means that you let AWS choose which availability zone (AZ) to use when launching the instance.

9. **Click Continue.**

   The Launch Wizard now takes you to the next screen, as shown in Figure 5-5, which allows you to fine-tune the instance you'll launch. You can use the Kernel ID and RAM Disk ID fields to modify the operating system code, or you can use the User Data section to enter information that will be passed to the instance when it's booting. You don't want to do any of these things for this exercise, so you change nothing on this panel and . . .

10. **Click Continue to move forward with the instance launch.**

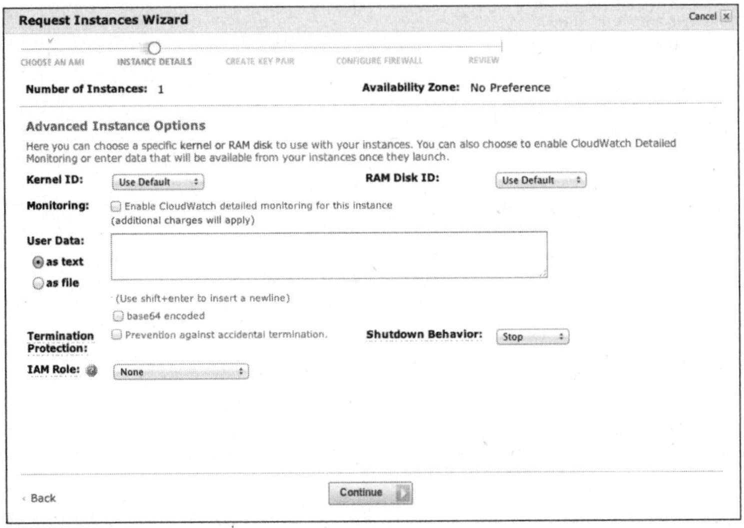

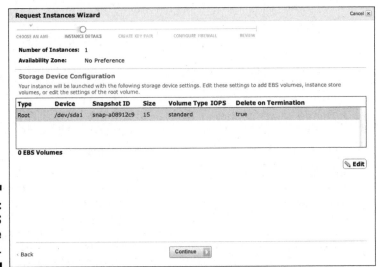

Figure 5-5:
The
advanced
instance
options.

The wizard now moves on to another instance definition panel, this one focused on storage devices — more specifically, how many EBS volumes you want to attach to this instance. As you can see in Figure 5-6, you already have one volume associated with this instance — the volume the AMI resides on.

For purposes of this example, the single AMI volume will suffice.

11. **Click Continue.**

Figure 5-6:
The EBS
volume
screen.

The wizard now displays a new screen, as shown in Figure 5-7, that lets you define tags to be associated with the running instance. Tags can be useful if you're running a large number of instances and you want a convenient method to identify a subset of the instances; for example, if you want to find all instances running on behalf of the sales department, you would place `sales` as an instance tag to facilitate searching.

In this example, tags aren't necessary, so don't enter anything on this screen.

12. Click Continue.

A (very important) new screen appears, as shown in Figure 5-8. Here's where you identify which of your key pairs you want to use when the new instance is launched. *Key pair* refers to two secure shell (ssh) keys — one private and one public — which are used to enable secure administrative access to the running instance. If you refer to Figure 5-2, you'll notice that one key pair — `aws4dummies` — is listed. It's the default key pair shown in Figure 5-8, and you'll want to stick with the default, so . . .

13. Click Continue to move forward to the next panel in the Launch Wizard.

NOTE: If this is your first use of AWS, you won't have an existing keypair, and AWS will put up a screen inviting you to create one. While you won't use the key for this exercise, it's not a bad idea to create one. However, and this is really important, when AWS creates a keypair, you must download and store the private key — store it somewhere you can find it, because if you launch an instance with a keypair for which you can't find the private key portion, you won't be able to access the instance, which is a big problem! So download and store the private key somewhere you easily find it.

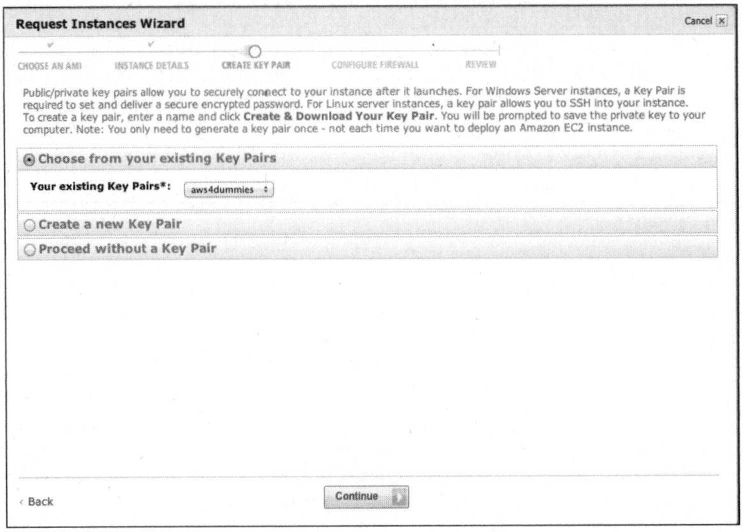

Figure 5-8:
The Key Pair
screen.

Doing so brings up yet another screen where you're asked to select a security group to be associated with this instance, as shown in Figure 5-9. Security groups control network access to running instances and are very important. You should use the default Security Group for this example (and, unlike the screenshot from my account, you'll probably only have the default security group). AWS has already selected the default as the suggested choice, and you should follow that suggestion.

14. Click Continue.

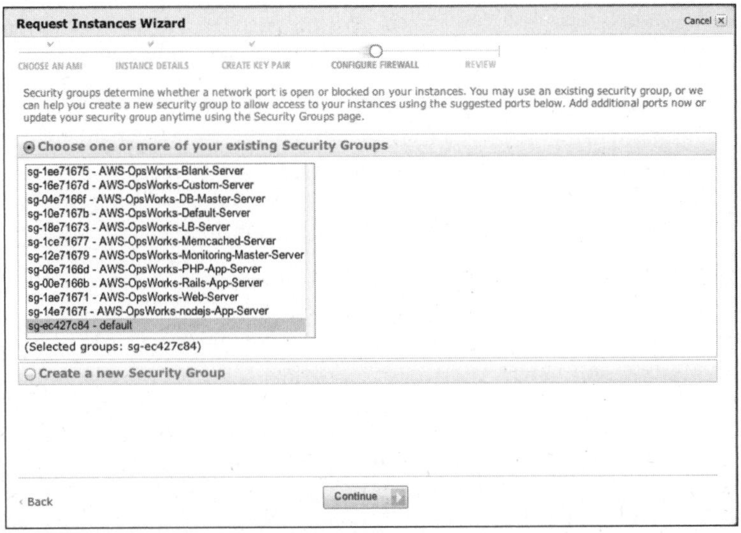

Figure 5-9:
The Security
Groups
screen.

You're now nearing the end of the launch setup process. AWS puts up a summary screen, as shown in Figure 5-10, that displays all the information you've selected throughout the wizard. You can take one last look at the instance information before launch and decide whether everything is good to go.

15. After reviewing the posted information, click the Launch button.

AWS now starts the launch, and a panel notes that the launch process is under way, as shown in Figure 5-11. As you can see in the figure, you're told that the instance is launching and the instance ID is displayed — yours will be different than the screenshot, since all instance IDs are unique.

16. Click the Close button.

It's time to move on to the next stage.

When you close the final panel of the Launch Wizard, AWS automatically takes you to the Instance section of the EC2 interface. As you can see in Figure 5-12, the instance is already up and running. Note the information on the bottom half of the screen. There, you'll find the instance ID (which is the same as on the final screen of the Launch Wizard) as well as the DNS name of the instance: `ec2-54-234-60-116.compute-1.amazonaws.com`; again, yours will be different because instance IDs are unique.

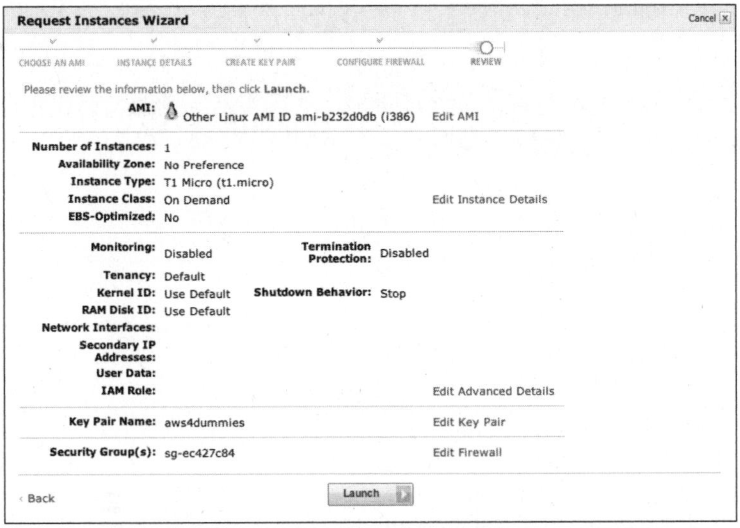

Figure 5-10:
The
Summary
screen.

Figure 5-11:
The
Conclusion
screen.

Below the DNS name is further information about this instance, including the AMI name, the key pair that this instance holds, and the availability zone it's running in.

Out of view in Figure 5-12 is more information about the private DNS name and private IP address associated with this instance. Every instance has both a public IP address, for access from outside AWS, and a private IP address, which can be used for access within AWS. These are also shown on the instance information panel. (For more on IP addresses as they relate to AWS networking, see Chapter 6.)

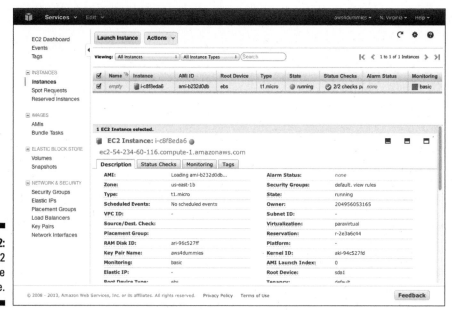

Figure 5-12:
The EC2
instance
page.

Of course, the AWS management console isn't the only way to interact with EC2. Here's an API example of how to launch an EBS-backed server:

```
https://ec2.amazonaws.com/?Action=RunInstances
&ImageId=ami-60a54009
&MaxCount=3
&MinCount=1
&Placement.AvailabilityZone=us-east-1b
&Monitoring.Enabled=true
&AUTHPARAMS
```

This API example identifies an AMI that should be launched, and it instructs AWS to launch up to three instances (set with the `MaxCount` parameter). Note that this command also instructs AWS to launch the instance in the `us-east-1b` availability zone, with monitoring enabled. A large number of parameter options exist to control the characteristics of the launched instance, including the ones you set using the Launch Wizard — which security group(s) to use, which key pair, and so on.

There you go! You've successfully launched your first EC2 instance and are now cloud computing. After basking in your glory, you'll want to terminate this instance, since it's generally a bad practice to leave unneeded AWS resources in operation, and you will be charged for it if your usage exceeds that provided by the Free Usage Tier

To terminate the instance, click on the check box to the left of your instance ID, and then click on the Instance Actions buttons above the instance list. As shown in Figure 5-13, the pull-down menu has a Terminate option. Click on that, and AWS will terminate your instance.

Figure 5-13:
The
Terminate
option.

Chapter 6

AWS Networking

*N*etworking is a big deal in the AWS scheme of things. Without it, none of your AWS instances would be able to send and receive network traffic. However, in networking, as in all other pieces of the AWS design, Amazon has implemented a solution that's clearly ingenious — but just as clearly different from the traditional solutions that are familiar to most people. And AWS has taken the path less traveled, for the same reasons it broke ground in other aspects of its design: to increase scale and foster automation.

When Amazon set out to develop its AWS offering, it thought "big" — really big. Actually, Amazon's vision has *always* been focused on a future much more expansive than it is now. Though it started out as an online bookseller, it has always set its sights on becoming a general (and enormously profitable) online retailer. Its bookselling effort worked well because it was a convenient category that encountered relatively little consumer resistance in using the (the then still unfamiliar) medium of Internet commerce. This strategy of thinking ahead allowed the AWS designers to create an offering that could scale way beyond anything then existing in the industry.

It may surprise you that networking emerged as a major stumbling block in executing the Amazon plan. It shouldn't surprise you, though, that Amazon developed a unique approach to networking in a cloud computing environment that sidestepped that stumbling block quite handily.

In this chapter, I help you work through a few basic principles of networking so that you can better understand the reasons Amazon came up with its networking design. With the fundamentals out of the way, you can then find out how EC2 instances interact with the network. Finally, I introduce you to a typically clever AWS solution to some problems that arise when you try to use the basic networking scheme to address the need for persistent IP addresses.

Brushing Up on Networking Basics

When computers talk to one another, they do so over a network. For the vast majority of computing done throughout the world, this talking activity takes place on a TCP/IP network. The *TCP/IP* network standard uses the concept of layers to illustrate how communication takes place. In this model, the layers are numbered 1, 2, and 3:

- ✔ **The physical layer (Layer 1):** Is associated with the cables that sit in your office or how your wireless access point talks to the wireless card in your computer.

- ✔ **The data-link layer (Layer 2):** Controls the flow of data between network entities (Hosts, Domain Names, Subnets, whatever) residing on the *same* network; this *local-area network (LAN)* is dedicated to a single organization. These entities typically have a network interface card (NIC), each of which carries a unique identifier — its Media Access Control (MAC) address. Layer 2 specifies how two entities with MAC addresses can send data to one another. (Note that this data is sent with the help of a NIC, a handy piece of hardware that's kept on a server.)

- ✔ **The network layer (Layer 3):** Controls the flow of data between network entities residing on different networks. In this wide-area network (WAN), users communicate across multiple LANS and cannot count on being connected on the same local physical layer. Layer 3 most commonly works by using the Internet Protocol (IP), which uses a logical addressing scheme (called, logically enough, IP addresses) to communicate. IP addresses most commonly have four digits — say, 10.1.2.3 — where each digit is represented by eight bit sets of data.

The display uses periods to separate 8-bit segments, and the collection of all four segments is supposed to represent a hierarchy; that is, the 10.1 part of the address is supposed to contain a collection of network devices that reside below the 10.1 portion of the address. For example, your ISP has a large range of addresses available to it because it may control the set of addresses starting with, say, the number 16. Two special cases, the high-level numbers 10 and 192, do not represent publicly addressable IP addresses but are used for private addresses. (They cannot be routed over the public Internet.) Multiple entities can therefore use these high-level numbers within their own data centers as sort of a set of private identifiers.

There are other, higher layers in a TCP/IP network, but the important ones in a cloud-computing network are Layers 2 and 3, where the challenges of being a cloud-computing provider present themselves.

You may ask, "How do virtual machines send and receive network traffic?" After all, they're virtual and have no hardware NIC. The answer, naturally enough, is that they have a *virtual* NIC (sometimes referred to as a VNIC) — a software construct through which the virtual machine sends and receives network traffic. The virtualization hypervisor manages the job of mapping these packets to and from the physical NIC that connects to (and communicates with) the physical network in the data center.

Virtual LANS — keeping data private

In a shared networking environment (and don't forget that that's precisely what a cloud-computing provider, at its core, is offering), how can you assure one user that his or her data is not accessible to another user? Obviously, one way is to create separate physical networks and let each user account have its own local-area network; however, that would be a logistical nightmare (and an extremely expensive one). Moreover, this method would require that each user have his or her own router to the outside world to communicate all its Layer 3 traffic to other, outside users.

Routers have been upgraded to provide virtual LANs (VLANs) that essentially cordon off sections of larger, shared networks to specific users. Within that VLAN, traffic flows via Layer 2; any traffic to other parts of the shared network, or out on the Internet, flows via Layer 3.

What's the big deal about traffic flowing over Layer 2 or Layer 3? Why would anyone care about which layer is doing the communicating? Well, for many years, traffic at Layer 2 would run faster because the network switches handling the traffic didn't need to look at the packet to determine where to send it; it could broadcast the initial packet to all devices on the LAN, note which one responded and its MAC address, and thereafter directly route traffic to that MAC address.

Layer 3, by contrast, required looking at the packet to determine which IP address the packet was aimed at, looking up the address in an IP address/ MAC mapping table, and then sending the packet to that MAC address. The lookup impaired network performance.

Switches are now robust enough that the overhead of the IP/MAC lookup is trivial — not enough to truly address performance, in other words. Consequently, the reason to have VLANs in a cloud environment is so that you can separate user traffic, not improve performance.

Most hosting companies use VLAN technology to assign a VLAN to every customer so that its computers are segregated from other customers' computers. This strategy, which provides a secure networking solution to customers, communicates to them that their network traffic is immune from interception.

Generally speaking, most hosting companies do all the work associated with assigning and configuring VLANs manually, during account setup. A network administrator accesses the provider's router and configures a VLAN for the new customer. The customer's computers are then placed on the newly configured VLAN, and network traffic to them flows over it.

As hosting companies have moved in to cloud computing, they have almost universally continued this practice of creating a VLAN for every new customer, with new virtual machines assigned into the address space of the VLAN. This VLAN may be manually or automatically configured, depending on the provider's cloud infrastructure.

The continued use of VLANs within these environments makes sense, particularly because many providers offer both hosting and cloud computing from the same facility; using a consistent VLAN approach enables the sharing of resources and simplicity of infrastructure.

However (isn't there always a *however?*), this use of VLANs for cloud computing carries some drawbacks:

- ✔ **A delay in the account setup:** Cloud computing providers that continue to create and configure VLANs manually impose a delay on the initial customer account setup. Many customers find this delay inconvenient; others consider it a barrier to using that cloud computing provider.

- ✔ **A limit on the number of VLANs that a router can manage:** Though this limitation can be addressed via the use of multiple routers, it imposes complexity on the provider's infrastructure.

- ✔ **A limit on the number of computers that can be attached to a specific VLAN:** Though many customers are unaffected, this limit is an unacceptable problem for webscale applications that can require hundreds (if not thousands) of computers.

Criticisms (fair and unfair) of VLANS and AWS security

You may have read articles about AWS where IT people express their concern about AWS security as well as skepticism that Amazon can assure customers that their network traffic is safe from access by other users. Usually, these articles end with the IT folks saying that they prefer to use another, "enterprise," provider. Given that the other providers use VLAN technology, which, by definition, uses shared network devices, you may wonder why the IT folks feel secure with these providers, but not with Amazon? I can't really answer this question, especially in light of a Microsoft study stating that the most common error made in a data center is misconfiguring VLANs. At bottom, I believe that these "concerns" about AWS reflect little more than prejudice — an (unfounded) belief that Amazon somehow isn't as capable as other providers. In my opinion, if you're leveraging a shared environment because of efficiency or cost-effectiveness, you have to recognize and acknowledge that you're sharing an environment, which presents risk. Your choices: Accept that risk, along with the benefits of leveraging the environment, or conclude that the risk is too significant, even though maintaining your own, dedicated environment is more expensive and less convenient.

The Amazon alternative to VLANs

Because Amazon wants to avoid the scaling limitations of VLAN technology in its cloud service, the VLAN approach is obviously unacceptable, for these reasons:

- ✔ **The limitation on the number of VLANs would limit the number of customers Amazon could support with its AWS service.** When Amazon first sketched out its plans for AWS, it expected hundreds of thousands of different customers to eventually use AWS, so this limitation was too constrictive.

- ✔ **The limitation on the number of computers a customer could have within a single VLAN would limit the number of instances that could be used in its applications.** Amazon itself had experience with its applications spanning hundreds, if not thousands, of instances, so it expected that its customers would, too. A solution that constrains the number of computers used by individual customers is clearly unacceptable.

Consequently, Amazon designed its network quite differently from conventional approaches, and it implemented a networking design with these features:

✔ **The use of Layer 3 technology throughout the infrastructure:** All traffic is directed based on the IP address, with no reliance on Layer 2 MAC addressing.

✔ **The requirements that every instance is assigned an IP address and all traffic to that instance must be directed by IP address:** This is true whether the traffic originates within AWS or externally — no exceptions.

✔ **No use or support of VLAN technology:** Within every region, Amazon has one or more ranges of IP addresses, and customer instances are assigned IP addresses randomly within those address ranges. A corollary to this approach is that all AWS IP addresses are Amazon's, not the customer's. So if a customer decides to move its website from its own data center to AWS, the website will have a new IP address.

AWS networking is often described as being *completely flat* — all traffic is iPad-address-based, and no hierarchy is implied by the IP address assigned to an instance. Undoubtedly, managing a completely flat network imposes challenges and complexity on Amazon, but it simplifies customer network use.

Because customers have no specific VLAN created or configured for them, the account setup process is immensely simplified — so much so that the entire process can be automated to a much greater extent than can other, more traditional, cloud computing providers. Moreover, because customers aren't segregated into assigned VLANs, growing and shrinking the number of instances a customer uses are much simpler — customers can simply request additional instances, and Amazon can launch a new instance, assign it an IP address from Amazon's much larger overall IP address pool, and return the instance's IP address to the customer. The IP address may be quite different from the others assigned to the customer, but because all traffic is directed based on IP address, the discontinuity in address range causes no issues.

Many experienced network administrators, familiar with networking practices typically used by IT organizations and hosting providers, find Amazon's approach disquieting. They have commonly devoted intense effort to designing and tuning network configurations to obtain maximum throughput, and they feel that Amazon's design, as clever as it is for achieving scale, must suffer performance penalties.

AWS Network IP Addressing

Unlike other cloud-computing providers, which assign a fixed range of addresses to virtual machines hosted within a customer's assigned VLANs, AWS dynamically assigns IP addresses from within its own IP address range.

No IP address is persistently assigned to a customer account, and a server launched from a given image may be assigned one IP address today and a different IP address tomorrow.

This shifting about of IP addresses can seem confusing, so let me dive a bit further into describing how AWS organizes its IP addressing.

To start off, every instance on the network has its own virtual network interface card, or VNIC — a software construct that mimics the functionality of a hardware NIC. The Xen hypervisor within AWS maps traffic between each instance's VNIC and the actual hardware NIC on the physical server on which the Xen hypervisor runs.

AWS assigns two IP addresses to an instance's VNIC: a public IP address and a private IP address. The latter is within the `10.X.X.X` address range — a range designed to be unroutable over the public Internet and to serve to enable private traffic within data centers. Figure 6-1 illustrates this division by showing the public DNS and private IP address for a single instance. The public IP address is contained in the AWS public DNS entry — `54.234.60.116`, in this case.

Figure 6-1:
The public DNS and private IP address for a single instance.

Private IP address

Public DNS addresses

Having two IP addresses means that each instance can send and receive traffic from outside AWS on a public IP address that anyone can reach.

Within AWS, instances can communicate with one another using the private IP address they've been assigned. In other words, if I have two servers, one of which AWS has assigned 10.1.2.3 and one of which it has assigned 10.1.2.4, those servers can send traffic to one another via the 10.X.X.X addresses rather than via the public IP address that AWS assigned. That traffic isn't routed by the public Internet; instead, it's confined within AWS.

Figure 6-2 illustrates the IP addressing scheme and how traffic flows over the public and private IP addresses.

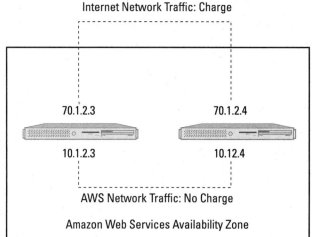

Figure 6-2:
AWS IP
addresses
and network
traffic.

This division between private and public IP addresses may seem like an academic distinction — after all, if the traffic contains TCP packets, who cares what address they're sent to, as long as the instance receives them?

The difference between the two IP addresses is quite important, however, for your AWS bill because traffic within the local AWS network (the 10.X.X.X addresses, in other words) is at a much lower cost than traffic sent to public IP addresses. To illustrate the difference, traffic between two availability zones within the same region costs $.01 per GB, while traffic between two availability zones that is sent to a public IP address (and thereby travels by the public Internet) costs $.12 per GB — 12 times as much!

The key aspect of this concept relates to network traffic *sent* by an instance — all inbound traffic (traffic that an instance *receives)* is free whether it comes from inside AWS or via the public Internet. Outbound traffic (traffic that an instance sends), on the other hand, is low cost if its destination resides within the same AWS region and incurs a high network charge if the network address resides outside AWS.

In Figure 6-2, you can see that the lower network path (traffic between 10.1.2.3 (Instance 1) and 10.1.2.4 (Instance 2) is considered internal to AWS and is low cost, whereas traffic between 70.1.2.3 and 70.1.2.4 travels outside AWS and incurs a higher fee for traffic that one instance sends to the other. This is true even though the instances referenced by these addresses are the same in both cases — it's all a matter of how the traffic is sent.

A corollary to this economic rule is a throughput rule: For performance reasons, traffic should, if possible, be sent between private IP addresses. The reason is that traffic between private IP addresses, whether it's an intra-availability zone or an inter-availability zone (within a single region) flows across high-performance, Amazon-dedicated network connections, whereas traffic that flows between public IP addresses flows across lower-performance, public Internet networks.

Actually, the process is a bit more complex. Amazon considers any traffic that crosses a regional boundary to be public Internet traffic, even though both the sending and receiving instances reside within AWS, as shown in Figure 6-3. You can see that traffic between instances that reside within the same AWS region, even if they're in different availability zones (AZs), is low cost, whereas traffic between AWS instances that reside in different regions is considered public Internet traffic and incurs a higher fee.

Internet Network Traffic: Charge

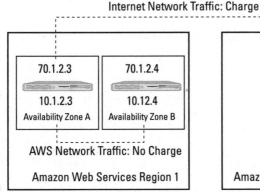
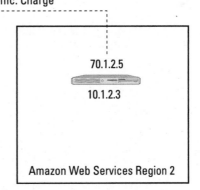

Figure 6-3:
Intraregional and inter-regional AWS traffic.

70.1.2.3	70.1.2.4	70.1.2.5
10.1.2.3	10.12.4	10.1.2.3
Availability Zone A	Availability Zone B	

AWS Network Traffic: No Charge

Amazon Web Services Region 1   Amazon Web Services Region 2

Every instance has a unique public IP address, whereas instances residing in different regions may share private IP addresses. The reason is that private IP addresses cannot be accessed from outside the local environment, and the same address may be safely used in more than one region, because there's no way to access an instance with its private IP address from outside the region. Therefore, instances in both Region 1 and Region 2 have the same private IP address: 10.1.2.3.

And, as though this concept weren't complicated enough, Amazon dropped its charges for inter-AWS regional communication — quite dramatically and literally while I wrote this chapter. For example, the cost of traffic between the US East region and other AWS regions dropped from $.12 per gigabyte to $.02 per gigabyte — an 83-percent reduction.

Users now have three choices for network traffic:

- ✔ **Intraregional:** Traffic between AWS resources within a given region (for example, US East); free for sending and receiving traffic.

- ✔ **Interregional:** Traffic between AWS resources in different regions. For each resource, any traffic it receives is free, but traffic it sends incurs a fee (an admittedly low one).

- ✔ **Extraregional:** Traffic between an AWS resource and a non-AWS resource; traffic to the AWS resource is free, and any traffic sent by the resource incurs a full traffic fee.

Network cost is based on total gigabytes of traffic sent during a month and is based on the price per gigabyte. The first gigabyte of traffic per month is free; traffic ranging from 2 gigabytes to 10 terabytes per month is $.12 per gigabyte. As traffic increases beyond 10 terabytes per month, the cost per gigabyte decreases; at 350 terabytes per month, a gigabyte is only $.05; above that level, you're asked to contact AWS to (presumably) strike a custom-pricing deal.

Instance IP addresses aren't persistent. Every instance that's launched is assigned an address from the general pool of IP addresses — clearly an issue, for two reasons:

- ✔ **People need to be able to find your site if they want to access your application for an extended period.** You want people to access your corporate website (for example, for many years), yet every time you launch an instance that runs your website, it is assigned a new public IP address. In other words, how can you manage the DNS mapping for your website when the IP address associated with your company website (say, www.example.com) changes every time you launch the website's instance? The answer to this question is "Elastic IP addresses — and you can find out all about them in the section titled (curiously enough) "AWS Elastic IP Addresses," later in this chapter.

- ✔ **In a complex application topology, every instance is dynamically assigned a private IP address at launch-time, and it needs to be able to find other instances.** For example, you may have several web servers, a couple application servers, and a couple database servers. If a web server has just been launched and it needs to connect to the two application servers, how can it find their IP addresses so that it can send and receive network traffic to them? The answer to this question is more complex, so you have to see my discussion of techniques for IP address discovery, in the later section "Instance IP address communication."

Reddit OpenClass runs on AWS

Want to know what scaling is? How about 4 billion pages per month? That's what Reddit serves up every single month. The site offers a place for user-created content, along with social sharing and commenting about content.

Reddit runs entirely on AWS. It uses EC2 to host its web servers, EMR for its web traffic analytics, S3 for content hosting, Glacier for content archiving, and CloudSearch to enable users to find content on the sprawling Reddit site.

One of the most popular Reddit features is Ask Me Anything (AMA). AMA sessions feature someone with a particularly interesting background — diplomat, software engineer, hearse driver — you name it — Reddit has hosted an AMA, up to and including President of the United States. That's right: Barack Obama participated in an AMA session, allowing anyone to pose a question.

Among the questions President Obama answered:

✔ What are the job prospects for a recent law school graduate?

✔ What is the recipe for White House beer?

✔ What is the most difficult decision you've been forced to make as President?

✔ And my favorite: Would you rather fight 100 duck-size horses or 1 horse-sized duck?

Reddit is able to leverage the infrastructure that AWS offers to support enormous levels of traffic. AWS handles Reddit's 4 billion page views with no problem. And when a special event, like President Obama's AMA, occurs, Reddit can easily add additional resources to handle user load and network traffic. During the President's AMA session, Reddit spun up an additional 30 EC2 instances in ten minutes to handle the extra user load.

The biggest surprise? Reddit handles all that traffic with a total company staff of 20 persons, or, as Reddit puts it: 200 million page views per employee per month!

AWS IP Address Mapping

In AWS, all S3 addresses take on the public URL format. (Not sure of the finer details of the S3 service? Check out Chapter 5.) However, even though an AWS instance may use the public URL format, AWS cleverly redirects the traffic to the internal AWS network — and imposes no fee for the traffic.

Likewise, if an instance uses the AWS-assigned public DNS name for another instance, it redirects the DNS resolution to the second instance's *internal* IP address rather than to the *public* IP address. This is another example of the clever (and complex) software infrastructure that Amazon uses to run AWS; it intercepts the DNS resolution request with an internal AWS service and returns the internal IP address rather than allow the DNS resolution to occur outside of AWS, where the resolution would return the public IP address of the second instance.

The benefit of this arrangement is that you can, from within AWS, use the public URL of a resource, but, rather than route the traffic outside AWS, over the slower public Internet, and then back to the resource within AWS, AWS maps the public URL to the internal private IP address of the resource and uses it for your communication to the resource. Your interaction with the resource is faster because it stays on the internal AWS network, and you incur no fees for network traffic, for the same reason.

Amazon has rolled out the general DNS service Route 53. I believe that the genesis of this service is its clever IP address mapping, along with Amazon's own internal services, required in order to run its other services (the e-commerce services spread among a number of countries throughout the world, for example). To run this robust and complex DNS capability requires an extremely capable internal DNS service, which Amazon concluded would be useful as a standalone service, launched as Route 53.

Route 53 may seem like an odd name that's perhaps reminiscent of French national highways. The name actually refers to DNS itself — DNS is used to route traffic requests, and DNS traffic communicates on port 53. (Thus the rapier wit of technical types is illustrated!)

AWS Direct Connect

The fact that all network traffic between AWS and non-AWS resources travels over the public Internet poses a significant problem: Even though Internet connectivity is offered by very large service providers that have invested lots of money in their networks, the bandwidth and latency levels available to end users are highly variable and can be unacceptable.

The seeds for these types of problems existed at the birth of the Internet. By its nature, the Internet is a shared network, in which millions of computers' packets are intermingled as they're sent over the network. Your computer's packets jostle with everyone else's. The upside is that a shared network is far cheaper (say Hello to e-mail and Facebook); the downside is that performance and throughput in a shared network are much less predictable.

For you and me, that's not a big deal. If a Netflix video runs a little slowly, it's not an earth-shattering problem, and many of the things we do aren't affected much by network issues. For example, e-mail generally works the same, with network throughput varying by as much as 1,000 percent.

For companies, however, inconsistent network throughput can be a big problem. When you can't watch a video, well, you go about your business and do something else. When an employee can't watch a safety video, however, it may affect her ability to work, and paying someone who can't work is a big problem.

Another problem can occur, from the point of view of many companies: Internet traffic flows over a shared network and can enable inappropriate access to a company's data. For certain companies or certain types of data, sending traffic across a publicly accessible network is a no-no.

Amazon addresses the issue of traffic flowing across the public Internet with *Direct Connect:* It lets a user put a private circuit between his data center and AWS to enable traffic to flow across a dedicated network connection, with no use of the public Internet.

Direct Connect dedicated network connections can be made from AWS to either a company's own data center or to a public carrier, like Equinix. The company requesting the Direct Connect network connection may have its servers located at the public carrier's site or have a second network connection from the public carrier to the company's own data center.

Obviously, a dedicated network connection addresses the issue of packet privacy. A company that uses Direct Connect can be assured that its network traffic is safe from prying eyes. In addition, it can implement a virtual private network (VPN) between its AWS instances and its own data center to further ensure data security. (Describing VPNs and how they work is beyond the scope of this book, but suffice it to say that they use clever software to encrypt data that travels across insecure networks — like the public Internet.)

Amazon offers two levels of Direct Connect bandwidth: 1 Gbps and 10 Gbps. The former should be sufficient for most connectivity needs; the latter is sufficient for all but the most demanding high-performance computing, and it matches the highest throughput level available within AWS itself.

Direct Connect comes with an AWS-like financial arrangement: You use Direct Connect only when you need it, and you pay for it only while you use it.

Direct Connect costs $.30 per hour for the 1 Gbps variant, and $2.25 per hour for the 10 Gbps variant. As you may expect, you don't pay for inbound network traffic, and outbound traffic runs from $.03 to $.11 per gigabyte, depending on region.

Though Direct Connect bandwidth and pricing are extremely attractive, the AWS connection has to be terminated at one of Amazon's Direct Connect partner locations. Your traffic has to reach one of those locations, which you can accomplish by hosting your servers at a partner location or by paying for a dedicated, high-bandwidth circuit from your data center to the partner location. The extra cost you incur shouldn't detract from the value (or cost effectiveness) of the Direct Connect offering itself.

High-Performance AWS Networking

One complaint about AWS networking is related to its performance — in my view, it's the primary challenge of using the entire AWS service. Amazon provides few details of its infrastructure, but I believe that the company has 1 Gbps networking equipment in place in its data centers, which could theoretically provide acceptable throughput for most applications, with higher performance 10 Gbps networking equipment used for more demanding AWS services like the high-throughput instances

However, you must keep in mind that AWS is a shared infrastructure and that many of your fellow AWS customers use the service precisely because they place demands on the infrastructure that are much greater than their own, internal infrastructures can handle. In other words, you're sharing the AWS network with some true bandwidth hogs, and the competition for bandwidth can definitely affect your application's throughput.

Most AWS users generally see around 100 Mbps throughput in inter-instance network traffic during their daily use of AWS. The problem is that, though this average may be perfectly acceptable for many applications, the varying network load can significantly alter that throughput. For some applications, of course, 100 Mbps may be perfectly acceptable; however, even for them, 10 Mbps may be too low. The problem is that you can't reliably predict the network throughput for your application.

Many AWS users have vociferously complained about inconsistent AWS network performance, and many AWS competitors have criticized the company, citing their own network design and capability as superior to AWS's, and therefore providing a reason for users to switch services.

Certainly, Amazon could reconstruct its service to provide higher, more consistent network throughput. A drawback, though, is that it would impose higher costs on all AWS users, including the masses of users who have no concerns about the typical performance of AWS networking.

Consequently, rather than reconstruct the networking service from the ground up, Amazon has created an AWS-like response: an additional set of offerings to address the needs of applications that require high-performance networking. This option leaves the vast majority of AWS users happily using the standard AWS offering while providing another option to the smaller portion of users who need better networking performance.

The key phrase here, *high-performance AWS networking,* is built on three specialized instance types: High I/O, Cluster Compute, and Cluster GPU. (If these terms sound familiar, you've clearly read Chapter 5, where I mention these instance types in my discussion of the Elastic Cloud Compute, or EC2, service.)

These three types are connected to higher-bandwidth networking — 10 Gbps as opposed to the standard 1 Gbps — and experience more consistent throughput. Fewer users contend for a given network segment by sending traffic across it, and Amazon has (I surmise) deployed more network capacity for these types of instances.

As you may expect, using instance types that carry greater network capacity costs a bit more than using other instance types. The least expensive of the instances with high network capacity is the Quadruple Extra Large Cluster Compute type, which costs $1.30 per hour — significantly more expensive than standard instance types. Note that you need to use instances with a lot of horsepower — Amazon makes high-performance networking available only to those who want to apply a lot of computing capacity to their applications.

This arrangement makes a lot of sense — after all, if you need a lot of network capacity, you're probably doing a lot of computing as well. It also makes sense to not impose the higher cost of high-performance networking on users with more modest computing requirements. This approach is consistent with Amazon's: Provide an inexpensive offering for those who don't need more than that, and extend the offering for those who want more and are willing to pay for it. This strategy is in direct contrast with almost all other cloud computing providers, who force all users to pay for expensive equipment, even if a user wants to run only a small or non-mission-critical application.

AWS Elastic IP Addresses

Earlier in this chapter, in the "AWS Network IP Addressing" section, I note a problem with AWS dynamic IP address assignment: If you have a long-lived publicly accessible site (say, your company website), how do you handle the frequent changes in the public IP address as you launch new instances to run your website? In other words, what happens when all the DNS servers out there have your old address and cannot find your site with the new server?

You may be tempted to think that you won't confront this issue and that you'll just leave your AWS instance up and never terminate it. After all, that's what you do with physical servers, right?

Don't think this way. You *will* launch new instances to run your software, and for several reasons, so you're sure to confront the issue of changed IP addresses at some point. First, sometimes instances crash, which is out of your control. Second, you want to update your software. Third, you may need to change the instance type because of the changing load.

How can you solve the problem of changing public IP addresses? I don't bother to cover a few inconvenient techniques here, because AWS itself provides an excellent mechanism to solve this problem: the *Elastic IP address,* which is a public IP address assigned to your account that can be substituted for the temporary public IP address that's assigned to your instance at launch-time. You request an Elastic IP address from AWS, and it's provided to you so that you can assign a permanent IP address to your new instances. You can then create a public DNS entry with your URL (say, `www.example.com`) and the Elastic IP address AWS assigned to your account.

An Elastic IP address works in a straightforward manner:

1. *You request an Elastic IP from AWS.* Within a couple minutes, you receive a new Elastic IP. This address still comes from the general Amazon public IP address range, but it's assigned *for your persistent use.* By default, you're limited to five Elastic IP addresses. You can obtain more from Amazon, but it generally rations Elastic IP addresses because they're part of Amazon's fixed pool of public IP addresses, and it doesn't want to assign them to an account that won't use them.

2. *You assign the Elastic IP address to an instance you run.* You can make the assignment at launch-time or request it after the launch. If it's the former, when the instance is available, it will have the Elastic IP address; if it's the latter, it may take five minutes for the substitution to take place. Note that the formerly assigned general public IP address returns to AWS and is subsequently assigned to a new instance.

3. *You run the instance with the Elastic IP address.* Traffic flows to the address and then to your instance.

That's it! You're running a persistent Elastic IP address. Keep a couple points in mind:

- ✔ If, for some reason, you want to release the Elastic IP address from an instance, AWS assigns a new public IP address to the instance from the overall Amazon address pool. It almost certainly isn't the same public IP address that the instance was initially assigned.

- ✔ If you decide that you no longer want an Elastic IP address, it returns to the unassigned Elastic IP address pool and is subsequently assigned to another account.

Elastic IP address pricing

Amazon prices Elastic IP addresses oddly: It imposes no fee for using Elastic IPs — they're completely free. However, Amazon charges $.005 per hour for *unused* Elastic IP addresses — addresses that aren't actively assigned to running instances. This system motivates users to use the Elastic IP addresses they request, because the addresses are limited commodities. Request only the number of Elastic IP addresses that you need, and release them back to AWS if you find that you don't need them.

Elastic IP addresses and AWS network scope

Essentially, AWS network scope conforms to the regional delimitations of AWS. The public IP addresses assigned to your instance vary by region, but are global in nature — which is to say, like all public IP addresses, they're unique and can be accessed by anyone around the world. For example, if you launch an instance in the AWS US East region, it will have a public IP address from one of the IP address ranges that Amazon maintains in US East. Anyone in the world (including resources within AWS) can access your instance with that public IP address.

Elastic IP addresses are region-scoped as well. You can, by default, have five Elastic IP addresses per region, and the Elastic IP addresses are within the ranges associated with the region in which the addresses are located.

Private IP addresses are also region-scoped. Instances within any availability zone in a given region can communicate with one another using the private IP address associated with the instances, and, of course, they incur no network traffic fees for that traffic.

AWS Instance Metadata

Many circumstances exist in which an instance needs to know the IP address associated with itself. The instance may want to insert its IP address into a database that is used by a content management system to store information about the application it's running or, upon initial launch, the instance may want to publish its IP address to other instances so that they can communicate with it. The first issue is how an instance can find out its own IP address when the address isn't persistent.

Fortunately, AWS offers a convenient mechanism for instance self-discovery of the *instance metadata,* as it's referred to. AWS provides instance metadata at the IP address 169.254.169.254. If you issue an HTTP GET command from within the instance, it will retrieve its own metadata. (HTTP refers to the protocol used by the Web, and GET is a command that can be transmitted across HTTP to instruct a remote resource to execute the GET command against the resource.)

A large amount of instance-specific data is available via the metadata IP address, such as

✔ **The instance's private IP address:** 10.1.2.3, for example.

✔ **The instance's public IP address:** 70.1.2.3, for example.

✔ **The instance's instance ID**

✔ **The instance's security groups:** Used to control network traffic access to instances. (For more on security groups, see Chapter 8.)

✔ **The instance's user data:** Supplied to the instance when it's launched and reflects information that the account owner wants the instance to have during its operation. User data, which is somewhat analogous to command-line parameters, can be used to "pass in" information necessary for the instance to do its work. An example is a URL from which the instance should get data. User data can take the form of text (a string of information, in other words) or a 16 kilobyte or less file from which text can be read.

Instance IP Address Communication

Just as it can be important for an instance to know information about itself, it can be important for other instances to know information about the instance.

The most obvious reason is that one instance may need to send traffic to another; for example, a web server may need to communicate with a database residing on another instance. How can the web server learn the database instance's IP address so that it can make a connection and send traffic? (And, by the way, you would want the database instance's private IP address so that your traffic travels only within AWS.)

Obviously, one method is for the account user to start the database instance via the AWS Management Console, get its IP address, start the web server and log on to it, and manually make the connection to the database instance. Just as obviously, that inconvenient method doesn't align with the whole automated aspect of cloud computing, does it?

Consequently, a number of techniques have been created to handle the dynamic communication of instance information to other instances.

One method, used by some organizations, is the user data option, described in the previous section of this chapter. For example, you may pass a file with the database IP address in it into the web server when it's launched. Of course, the database IP address has to be inserted into the file, which the database server can do by running a text-editing script to insert its own IP address (discovered as metadata) into the file. Alternatively, the file can be manually edited to insert the IP address, but that method only leads to the manual-versus-automated issue again. Put simply, when most organizations begin running fairly complex applications, they discover that manual configuration is insufficient, via the Management Console and user data.

A different but common technique is to move to a configuration management mechanism. One important element of this technique is to enable instances to communicate their IP addresses to one another, but these techniques are also used for other important information that an instance may need, such as the username and password for connecting to a database or which code packages should be loaded onto the instance. Some organizations use this kind of technique to identify a set of scripts that should be loaded onto the instance; these scripts, in turn, download software packages and configure the packages, insert the instance-specific information into the application's configuration management mechanism, and then connect to other resources within the application.

Figure 6-4 illustrates the flow of activities for an instance using this configuration management mechanism:

- ✔ **Launch:** In Step 1, an instance is launched with user data supplied that indicates what kind of role the instance should play in the application (a web server, for example). At this point, it's a bare instance — it has only the bare operating system, but no application software or application configuration information.

- ✔ **Self-discover:** In Step 2, the instance self-discovers its IP address (with the help of the instance metadata IP) as well as any other information it needs to communicate to other instances in the application. At this point, it's a self-aware instance — it has knowledge about its AWS configuration.

- ✔ **Self-configure:** In Step 3, using the role information passed in on the initial launch, the instance connects to the application configuration-management mechanism and downloads software packages, installation scripts, and configuration instructions. It then self-configures to become a *role-ready* instance — in this case, one that's fully configured to be a web server for the application.

- ✔ **Update configuration management:** In Step 4, the instance then communicates information required by other instances in the application to the configuration management mechanism. It would load its own IP address, its role, and possibly other information to the configuration management mechanism. It would then download from the configuration management mechanism information about other instances and resources within the application that it needs to communicate with. It's now an *application-ready* instance.

- ✔ **Connect to other application instances:** In Step 5, the instance then takes the information it retrieved from the configuration management mechanism and sets up connections with other instances and resources that are part of the application. For example, a web server would use the IP address, username, and password information that it retrieved to make a connection to a database instance and set up a connection to the database itself. It may also retrieve information about a load balancer that it needed to register with to begin accepting connections from the Internet and then use that information to register with the load balancer.

At the end of this step, the instance is now an *operational* instance within the application.

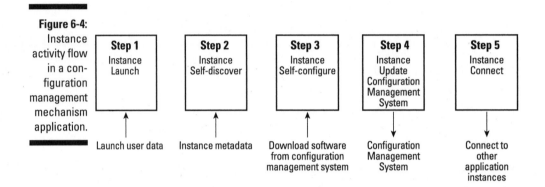

Figure 6-4: Instance activity flow in a con-figuration management mechanism application.

This approach to instance configuration has a lot to recommend it. All application configuration information is stored in one place. Little information is necessary at launch-time to trigger a full instance configuration. The process of full instance configuration ensures that other instances can learn what they need to know about the newly launched instance to communicate with it properly, and the newly launched instance can learn about all the resources it needs to communicate with.

For a technology to support this mode of operation, you have a number of options. Obviously, you can use text documents stored somewhere that's accessible to all instances — S3 comes to mind. The instances can even access storage within your own data center, although that strategy runs the risk, if your data center is inaccessible for some reason, of new instances not being able to join your EC2 applications.

Another common approach to the storage of configuration information is to leverage DynamoDB, AWS's own key-value service. For configuration information, it would be extremely easy to use, and the flexible key-value schema, which allows for flexible records per key, would allow instances to store *instance-specific* information — information required in order to access an external service that supplies data needed by the instance while operating. Though Dynamo hasn't been available for long, I believe that it will be widely used for these purposes. (For more on DynamoDB, see Chapter 4.)

Chapter 7

AWS Security

● ●

● ●

*C*ountless surveys have shown that security is the number-one concern voiced by IT professionals about cloud computing. Deep down, many IT people distrust cloud provider security and believe that *they* are the only ones who can truly implement secure computing environments. And many IT types are most skeptical about the security of AWS. Unspoken by many of them, but part of their visceral reactions to AWS, is, I believe, a kind of disdain for the service, based on a prejudice that a "bookseller" can't possibly offer the same kind of computing security that "real" professionals provide.

Needless to say, I disagree with that point of view. In fact, from my perspective, if you use AWS, you're likely to improve many elements of your computing security. Nevertheless, like almost all other aspects of its approach to computing, the way Amazon implements security is important to understand because it's likely different from yours.

This chapter starts off by covering the concept of the cloud computing trust boundary — the demarcation between the security responsibility of the provider and the security responsibility that lies with you. After I establish those parameters, I describe how AWS implements security. I discuss the AWS Virtual Private Cloud offering, designed to offer greater levels of security than are reflected in the standard AWS service. I also discuss how to determine whether AWS security is sufficient for your requirements. I conclude by discussing six key actions you can take to make your AWS application more secure.

Clouds Can Have Boundaries, Too

The key to understanding the topic of cloud security is the concept of the *trust boundary.* In on-premise computing environments that you may be familiar with, the IT organization takes responsibility for all security throughout the environment, no matter at what level or in which component a particular security requirement resides. By contrast, in a public cloud computing environment, the provider implements, and takes responsibility for, the security of only *a portion* of the overall security situation.

Here's a useful way to frame the discussion: The concept of a *trust boundary* sets a clear dividing line between the service provider's responsibilities and your responsibilities. The provider handles security on one side of the trust boundary, and you're responsible for the corresponding security on your side of the trust boundary.

This concept is by no means unique to AWS. For example, if your company uses Salesforce to manage customer interactions, Salesforce is responsible for a great deal of security for the entire application. In fact, any time you use an external provider's offering, you're handing over some responsibility for security to that provider. In those situations, the obvious concern is how to divide the responsibility with the provider.

The key question then, relating to a cloud computing offering, is where does the trust boundary sit? Intuitively, in a Software as a Service (SaaS) offering like Salesforce, the trust boundary must be located on the spectrum at a spot where more of the security responsibility lies with the provider; after all, Salesforce not only runs the computing environment in which the application runs but also develops, delivers, and takes responsibility for the application itself.

With this logic as a starting point, you'd have to assume that because AWS isn't in the business of running "applications" for clients, the location of the AWS trust boundary is likely a different one than for Salesforce — a place where more of the responsibility lies with the user, to be more specific. So where does the AWS trust boundary reside?

Figure 7-1 (which also appears in Chapter 2) shows the architecture of the AWS computing environment. Given this architecture, you can determine where to place the trust boundary.

For Amazon EC2, the location is simple: The trust boundary is located at the *hypervisor* — the software layer that provides virtualization of AWS instances. Security below the hypervisor is Amazon's responsibility; everything above the hypervisor is your responsibility.

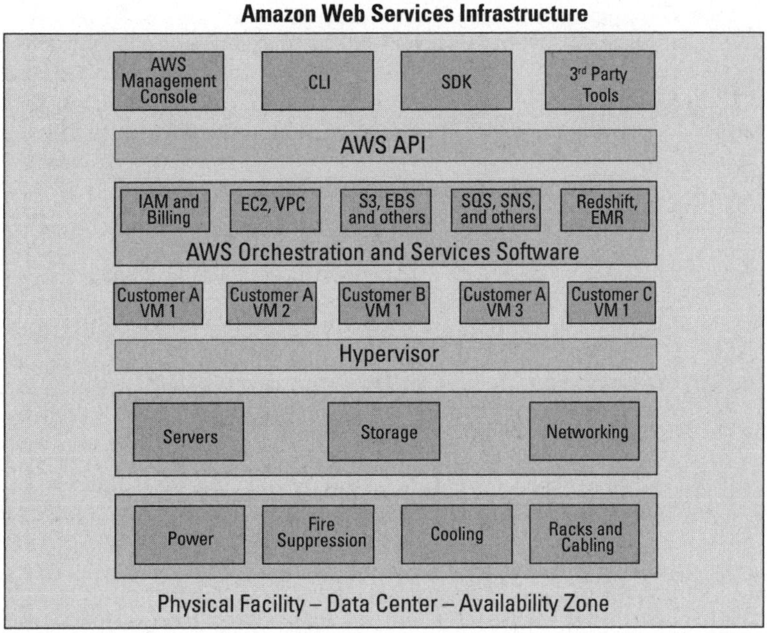

Amazon Web Services Infrastructure

Figure 7-1:
The AWS
computing
environment
architecture.

To my mind, that's generally true, but a bit glib. It does, however, accurately make obvious a truth of cloud computing: Security is a shared responsibility, and each party must do its job properly for an application running in a cloud computing environment to be secure.

A more accurate description is that Amazon takes responsibility for the AWS instance and everything that surrounds it, whereas you must take responsibility for the security of all software and configuration that resides inside the instance. You must also take responsibility for network traffic that moves in and out of the instance. (I tell you more about this topic in the "AWS Security Groups" section, later in this chapter.)

The placement of the trust boundary at the instance means that Amazon takes responsibility for the security of these parts of the computing environment:

✔ **The physical facility:** The data center; its access controls for people; and all power, cooling, and Internet connectivity and networking from the building's perimeter to the rack containing computing equipment

✔ **The computing hardware:** All servers, storage, and networking devices

✔ **The hypervisor:** The instance manager and the virtual machines within which instances run

✔ **The surrounding software infrastructure:** The software that manages all AWS services and provides the automation that allows you to operate your application without ever needing to interact with another human

✔ **The Application Programming Interface (API):** The true AWS interface, where all outside interaction with AWS is controlled

If you think about it, this concept is fantastic: Amazon takes on a huge amount of the security load that you're ordinarily responsible for, which reduces the amount of work you have to do — and the investment you need to make.

Of course, as noted, security is a shared responsibility, and some security elements remain with you. Here's a brief list:

✔ **Your application's software packages:** They contain all the software that makes up your application, including any software components you write.

✔ **Your application's configuration:** To maintain an application's protection, it's often critical to configure software packages correctly in order to ensure that no malevolent actor can access them and cause havoc.

✔ **Your application's operating system (possibly):** This one is a bit tricky — and it relates directly to my earlier characterization of your security responsibility as "starting with the hypervisor" as being "a bit glib." It all depends on who is responsible for the image you use. If you use an image created by someone else (either Amazon or a third party), the security for the operating system and operating system packages resides with the image provider, including not only the general operating system (Windows 2008, for example, or Ubuntu Linux) but also all patches to the operating system, system software (the identity management system, for example), and, possibly, middleware (say, the Tomcat Java application server).

An Amazon Machine Image (AMI), or image for short, is the template from which a running instance (also known as the virtual machine) is launched. The image contains all of the information necessary for AWS to construct a running instance: the operating system, any software components that are contained within the image, and all configuration settings for the operating system and software components that were set at the time of image creation.

The Deperimeterization of Security

When calculating your various security responsibilities, you may have to consider the effects of a concept known as the *deperimeterization* of security. (Of course, you may have to ask yourself how you're supposed to consider a concept that you can't even pronounce?)

Let me give you a little background: The concept of deperimeterization grows out of work done by the industry research group Jericho Forum, which is part of The Open Group. The core conviction of its founders is that traditional computing security measures, which are focused on stopping threats at the perimeter of the data center, are insufficient in today's computing environments.

With the rise of repeated attacks by criminal and state actors, the covert installation and ongoing monitoring by advanced persistent threats (APT), and the constantly evolving viruses and malware that present *zero-day* dangers (dangers that require immediate responses instead of letting you wait for updates to virus scan databases or malware detection services), you can no longer assume that security measures on the outside of your computing resources are sufficient.

The Jericho Forum recommends that everyone recognize the successful deperimeterization of security and acknowledge that, consequently:

- ✔ Security measures must be present on every computing resource.

- ✔ These measures must be capable of protecting the resource without depending on external, perimeter-based security services.

If you're acquainted with the Old Testament, you may catch the reference in the Jericho Forum's name to the famous walls of Jericho that "came tumbling down." The walls were inadequate to protect the city; likewise, the usual protective security measures at the perimeter of a data center are inadequate to protect the resources inside it. (It's more evidence of technically minded humor.)

I think it's fair to say that conformance with the Jericho Forum's recommendations is "more honored in the breach than the observance." Many organizations continue to rely on security measures "on the perimeter" (outside their own computing resources) for reasons ranging from concern about resource performance to general apathy.

Why is this topic relevant to AWS? Simply because, unlike many computing environments where it's possible to place security systems (commonly, hardware appliances) within the data center's network, in AWS it's impossible for a user to place specialized devices (or, indeed, any hardware) within the AWS data centers. By default, any security measures you want to take have to be located within your application and computing resources.

The prototypical example of the kinds of protection you can locate within your application and computing resources is IDS/IPS (Intrusion Detection Software/Intrusion Protection Software). Many organizations install IDS/IPS hardware appliances as gatekeepers through which all outside network traffic must pass before being sent on to specific servers or virtual machines.

The IDS/IPS security products scan the packets to see whether they appear malevolent. If the packets don't appear malevolent, they're forwarded to their destination; if they do, a variety of measures are taken, ranging from logging the activity to blocking the packet and raising an alarm to alert operations personnel.

Amazon doesn't let you install an IDS/IPS device in its network, because

- ✔ It would view that action as inappropriate for its service and for the control it requires in order to operate AWS properly.

- ✔ Even more important, other AWS customers would regard your security device as a security threat to *their* applications. Any security appliance that monitors traffic would be seen by other users as an intrusive device that is attempting to examine *their* traffic, which they would find unacceptable.

The way to address this problem is to install *host*-based *intrusion detection software*, or HIDS, on your AWS instances. (The letters *IDS* also incorporate IPS — even techie types couldn't stomach a HIDS/HIPS acronym.) HIDS performs exactly the same function as an IDS/IPS appliance, but doesn't require installing any hardware within the network.

How does deperimeterization affect that crucial trust boundary between your zone of responsibility and Amazon's zone? It doesn't, to be honest. The concept of deperimeterization provides the context for what's going on, but doesn't truly change the fundamental nature of your partnership with Amazon, because

- ✔ **Amazon is still responsible for all security of the computing environment, up to and including the hypervisor.** Actually, as I point out earlier, that's not entirely accurate because Amazon is responsible for creating and operating the virtual machine. Also, if you're using an AWS-supplied image, Amazon is also responsible for the security of the image. It must ensure that it incorporates the correct version of the operating system, all necessary patches, and appropriate configurations. Amazon manages and configures all hardware and software, and you have to do nothing (and, indeed, *can* do nothing) about AWS security.

- ✔ **You're still responsible for the security of the running instance and the overall application.** This includes all software running in the instance, whether you (or your organization) developed it or it's sourced from a third-party supplier (commercial or open source community). You manage and configure all your software, and Amazon has to do nothing. (Indeed, it *should* do nothing, because accessing your resources would be a significant betrayal of trust and a valid reason for customers to abandon the service.)

However, in one place, you and Amazon share some responsibility for security: at the interface between Amazon's area of responsibility and yours. That interface is, logically enough, the *network interface* — where network traffic leaves Amazon's environment and enters your instance.

AWS Security Groups

An AWS virtual network interface is located within each instance, and Amazon installs a software firewall on every instance. The firewall is there to manage traffic to and from the instance.

Every instance launches by default with a firewall that's clamped shut — no traffic can enter the instance. As you might imagine, that often makes it useless, unless it's doing self-contained computing activities.

Consequently, you must deliberately enable network access to your instance. (If you've ever had the misfortune of administering a software firewall on a Linux machine, take heart: Amazon makes this task much easier by using security groups.)

Actually, you may have done enough work with Linux firewalls to believe that managing a firewall isn't a big deal; after all, after you know what you're doing, Linux firewalls can be managed logically and handily (via a set of rules known as iptables). Of course, the same statement can be made about calculus: After you understand it, it's logical and useful. The challenge lies in reaching the point of understanding. Fortunately, Amazon has recognized that expecting users to build an understanding of Linux firewalls sufficient to be able to use AWS would be, as they say, "non-revenue-enhancing," so it developed security groups, which are *much* easier to use — and they get the job done.

Security groups control network traffic associated with every instance, and you must understand that only traffic associated with a specific instance is directed to that instance. The mechanisms you use to define the security rules that control this traffic involves security groups.

Security groups are asymmetric, in that they apply to *inbound* traffic (traffic being sent to the instance). At this time, no controls are placed on traffic sent from the instance. (Note that this is not true with VPC; please see the VPC section below to understand how it handles outbound network traffic.)

Security group rules control the following elements of network traffic access:

- ✔ **Traffic protocol:** Security groups support and apply to three types of network traffic:
  - *Transmission Control Protocol (TCP):* I discuss it in Chapter 6.
  - *User Datagram Program (UDP):* This network protocol, less sophisticated than TCP, is hardly used, so you can safely ignore it.

- *Internet Control Message Protocol (ICMP):* This protocol is used to support certain diagnostic network commands and for applications to send error messages. (My guess is that you probably won't use this protocol much, either.)

✔ **Traffic source:** The idea is to control those sources from which a security group accepts traffic. The security group can be set to allow traffic from everyone, from only a specific IP address, from a range of IP addresses, or from other members of the security group. (I tell you more about traffic sources in the next section of the chapter.)

✔ **Traffic port:** TCP traffic moves between *ports,* which can be thought of as individual network connections within overall network connectivity. Ports are typically associated with specific applications, and all traffic to a specific port is directed toward that application. For example, Port 80 is used to support web traffic (or, more precisely, HTTP traffic). Everyone tries to confine a port's traffic to a single application; otherwise, you run into problems when two applications try to read network traffic on a single port — where should the packet be sent?

Security group traffic sources are extremely important and are certain to occupy your attention when you design an application. When you understand how traffic sources and security groups work, you can make your application much more secure.

The traffic protocol limitations discussed here apply to EC2 security groups. In AWS's Virtual Private Cloud (VPC), any protocol can be used. (VPC is discussed later in this chapter.)

Security groups

Every account has one predefined security group: default. Default starts out with no traffic being allowed to access the instance, so whenever you launch an instance with the initial default security group controlling what network traffic is accepted, no traffic can reach the instance.

You can also create additional security groups and place rules within the new security groups. An AWS account can have up to 500 security groups and 100 rules per security group.

Security group rules

To allow traffic into an instance, open one or more ports by creating a security group rule for the default security group. For example, you can create a rule to allow HTTP traffic to enter the instance.

Obviously, you can use the AWS API to implement this rule. However, most people use the AWS Management Console to define rules. Figure 7-2 shows you how rules are set. (For more on the basic operation of the AWS Management Console, including how to access it and navigate its various features, check out Chapter 3.)

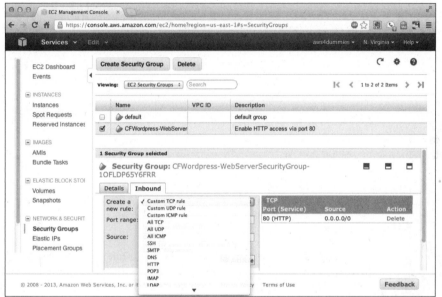

Figure 7-2: Setting security group rules.

The figure shows that I've selected the CFWordpress-WebServer security group and clicked the Inbound tab, which brings up a dialog box listing a number of common TCP protocols (including DNS, HTTP, and POP3, a popular e-mail protocol) that allow me to make rules for data access. You can select a predefined protocol or create a custom rule based on either TCP, UDP, or ICMP.

If you create a rule for a predefined TCP protocols, the Port Range field is filled in with the port associated with that protocol. (Figure 7-3 gives you a better view of the Port Range field.)

In the Source field, you can define the IP address or addresses from which to accept traffic. (The next section discusses security group traffic sources.)

After you're satisfied with the rule, click the Add Rule button to add the new rule to whichever security group you're targeting. You can then use this security group as part of an instance launch definition, and traffic that fits with this rule is accepted into the instance.

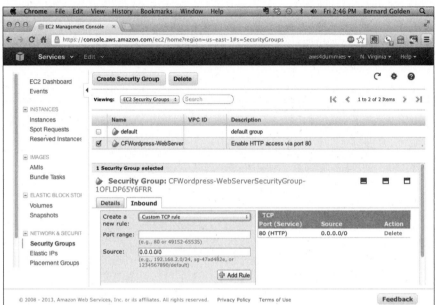

Figure 7-3:
The port
range field.

You can add or remove rules from a security group at any time, and any instances running with the security group will have the rule changed almost immediately. You can then add a new rule, and the instance can accept new traffic quickly. You cannot, however, add an entire security group to, or remove it from, a running instance.

Security group traffic sources

The AWS Management Console lets you control where the instance accepts traffic, which makes a lot of sense. For example, you may accept traffic from anyone who visits your corporate website; as for administrative access to the instance on which your corporate website runs, you may restrict such traffic to your company's own IP address.

Fortunately, AWS provides a lot of flexibility regarding traffic sources for security group rules.

The most obvious source of traffic is from other instances in your application or account. For two instances to communicate within AWS, they must either belong to the same security group or you have to configure an instance's security group to receive traffic from another security group owned by the same account. (The latter option allows you to set an instance's security group so that it can receive traffic from every instance that has the source security group attached to it; if they do, they can automatically send and receive traffic to and from each other.) But what if the source of the traffic isn't another AWS instance? Then another set of rules comes into play — one that uses IP addresses rather than security groups to identify the source of acceptable network traffic.

If you want to accept network traffic from anywhere, simply enter 0.0.0.0/0 as the traffic source. If you want to accept traffic from a single address — say, 123.45.67.89 — enter 123.45.67.89/32. Wait — why does one end in /0 and one end in /32? The numbers following the slash (/) refer to CIDR (Classless Inter-domain Routing, if you're curious). IP addresses always consist of 32 bits and are commonly segregated into four 32-bit segments. CIDR treats the 32 bits differently, using a mask placed on the 32 bits to identify a range of addresses without needing to specify each address. The mask, which is placed from the leftmost bit in the address, identifies how many of the left-hand bits should be considered part of a general pool of addresses; conversely, the remaining bits can be used to identify specific IP addresses within that pool. CIDR notation is used to identify the size of the common pool.

Clear as mud, right? An example will help.

Again, placing a mask on a range of the 32 bits affects the size of the pool — the length of the mask reflects how many bits can be used to identify individual IP addresses. If you place a mask consisting of the full 32 bits on the IP address 123.45.67.89, it occupies the entire address; 32 bits covers the entire IP address. Only the single IP address, therefore, can be defined by a CIDR notation of 123.45.67.89. For AWS purposes, only traffic from that single address is accepted by that group.

Conversely, in a CIDR mask of 0, all bits are accepted to comprise an IP address from which traffic is accepted; combined with the 0.0.0.0 as the address portion of the CIDR notation, traffic is accepted from any IP address.

When a CIDR mask of 24 bits is used, 8 bits remain for IP addresses to fall within that CIDR group — a total of 256 IP separate addresses.

From the perspective of AWS security groups, if your company's IP address is 123.45.67.89 and you set a security group traffic source of 123.45.67.89/24, you allow 256 computers within your company's IP address range of 123.45.67.X (where X is the specific IP address) to access your instance. Depending on how fine-grained the level at which you want to control access, you can use more or fewer bits in the CIDR mask. And there's no requirement that the IP address be your company's — you can set the IP address as a partner's, and then traffic from that address follows the CIDR mask rule you define.

Using Security Groups to Partition Applications

Security groups are used to control access to EC2 instances. Because AWS uses flat Layer 3 networking, any instance within a user account can communicate with any other instance — unlike many corporate IT networks, which are partitioned via VLANs so that many virtual machines can communicate only with other virtual machines residing on their VLAN. In that particular corporate world, communication with other virtual machines must pass through a router or a gateway server that has two network interfaces and can pass traffic back and forth.

The reason many organizations choose to implement this type of arrangement is to prevent inappropriate access to computing resources. In particular, most organizations consider it important to prevent outside access to servers providing data access, so they allow public network traffic to application web servers but prevent public network traffic to database servers. The web servers and database servers reside on different virtual local-area networks (VLANs), and traffic between them must flow over a router or a gateway server.

For a host of reasons, AWS doesn't provide this kind of VLAN capability — check out Chapter 6 for the specifics. For now, though, the challenge is what you can do to improve network traffic security.

A common technique is to use multiple security groups to partition traffic. Suppose that you have a three-tier application, along the lines of the one shown in Figure 7-4: The Web tier offers web access to the web servers, the Business Logic tier runs a Java application, and the Data tier manages data in a MySQL database. Your goal is to prevent public access to the Business Logic tier and the Database tier, and to ensure that the only way outside traffic can interact with those two tiers is via the established routes of the application itself. How would you accomplish that task?

HTTP traffic operates on Port 80. In this example, assume that the Java application accepts traffic on Port 4555 and that MySQL accepts traffic on Port 3306.

Look at the steps you'd use to define how security groups can implement application partitioning:

1. Define a security group that's open to TCP traffic on Port 80.

   Name it **WebTierSecurityGroup**.

2. Define a security group that's open to traffic on Port 4555.

   Name it **BusinessLogicSecurityGroup**. Configure this security group to receive traffic from any instance that is a member of the WebTierSecurityGroup.

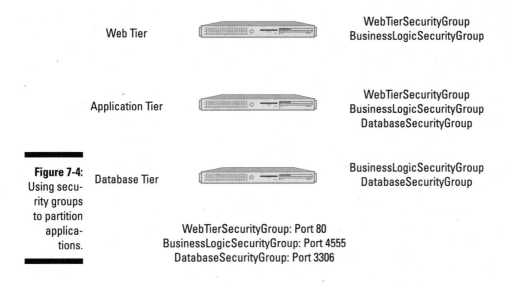

Web Tier — WebTierSecurityGroup
BusinessLogicSecurityGroup

Application Tier — WebTierSecurityGroup
BusinessLogicSecurityGroup
DatabaseSecurityGroup

Figure 7-4:
Using secu-
rity groups
to partition
applica-
tions.

Database Tier — BusinessLogicSecurityGroup
DatabaseSecurityGroup

WebTierSecurityGroup: Port 80
BusinessLogicSecurityGroup: Port 4555
DatabaseSecurityGroup: Port 3306

3. Define a security group that's open to traffic on Port 3306.

   Name it **DatabaseSecurityGroup**. Configure this security group
   to receive traffic from any instance that is a member of the
   BusinessLogicSecurityGroup.

4. When launching a server in the Web tier, attach WebTierSecurityGroup
   to it.

   This step ensures that the server can accept public HTTP traffic from
   the Internet.

5. When launching a server in the Business Logic tier, attach the
   BusinessLogicSecurityGroup. Because this security group has been configured to accept traffic from instances in the WebTierSecurityGroup, it
   can send and receive traffic from the web instances in the application
   without being exposed to port 80 traffic.

6. When you launch a server in the Data tier, attach
   DatabaseSecurityGroup to it.

   Because the DatabaseSecurityGroup was configured to accept traffic
   from any instance that is a member of the BusinessLogicSecurityGroup,
   any Data tier instance will be able to communicate with instances
   in the Business Logic tier. Note that by not having made the
   DatabaseSecurityGroup accept traffic from the WebTierSecurityGroup,
   these instances aren't accessible from the public Internet, even though
   they have a public IP address; any attempt to send HTTP traffic to one of
   these instances is rejected because it doesn't have that port open.

As you can see from this arrangement, no web traffic from outside AWS can
access the database server without going through the Web and Business

Logic tiers. Often referred to as *defense in depth,* in this type of partitioning, a security attack has to successfully penetrate several layers to obtain access to critical resources.

I've simplified this example to illustrate the concept of using security groups to partition applications. For actual production use, you'd probably have many more security groups (or more rules in the existing groups) for your application. For example, you'd almost certainly have a dedicated security group for Port 22 (SSH) access that would be IP-traffic delimited to allow Port 22 traffic only from your corporate offices; this strategy would prevent malicious attacks from other traffic sources.

Another activity that would be more complex in real life is running several versions of an application: a development version where new code is being worked on, a testing version for quality assurance, and a production version for customers to interact with. You then subdivide the security groups and have Development, Test, and Production versions for each tier and attach the appropriate security group to the version you're running. For example, you'd use DevWebTierSecurityGroup, BusinessLogicSecurityGroup, and DevDatabaseSecurityGroup so that only development traffic would access these instances and, in particular, no development traffic can access production instances.

Using security groups to partition applications is an excellent approach to increasing application security, and I highly recommend it. It can significantly increase the security of your applications. It's not perfect, however.

You may have noticed one vulnerability that cannot be addressed by security group partitioning. Each instance still retains a public IP address, making it — at least theoretically — vulnerable to direct attack and penetration. For all the cleverness of shielding the Data tier by ensuring that application traffic has to flow through two other instances before accessing precious data resources, a drawback is that another, much more direct method of attacking instances in the Data tier exists: a direct attack against the public IP address that every instance in AWS carries. That's quite a shortcoming, isn't it?

Fortunately, you can address this vulnerability, by using the AWS service Virtual Private Cloud (VPC), which I discuss later in this chapter. For now, be aware that security group partitioning, though important, doesn't offer perfect protection of your applications.

Security group scope

Security groups are scoped regionally, so you need appropriate security groups in every region in which you plan to operate applications.

Security group cost

Hey, security groups are a bargain — they're free! Go ahead — use as many as you like.

Security Group Best Practices

The security group is a critical feature because it performs a vital function: It controls traffic into your instances. Understanding and applying security groups is important to ensure that your applications operate properly and safely. Follow this set of best practices regarding security groups:

- **Avoid using the Default security group.** Though you can open ports on the Default security group, avoid doing so — create separate security groups instead for all network traffic rules. Using default configurations is a sloppy technique and leads to poorly-thought-out design and practices.

- **Use meaningful names.** It's much easier to decide which security group needs to be applied to which instance when you use names that provide helpful information. This may not seem difficult, but, believe me — when you start managing upward of 100 different security groups, you'll appreciate any help you can get.

- **Open only the ports you need to open.** This time-honored recommendation has nothing to do with cloud computing. Reducing the number of open ports reduces the attack opportunities for malevolent actors, so open ports only for the services or applications you need.

- **Partition applications.** Using security groups to partition applications is a good practice to implement defense in depth and reduce the possibility of malevolent actors being able to access important application resources. Be sure to create versions of security groups to support the different application versions that you'll end up running. (For more on defense in depth, check out the "Using Security Groups to Partition Applications" section, earlier in this chapter.)

- **Restrict system administrator access.** By using CIDR masks, you can restrict system administrator access to your instances to computers that are located in places you trust, like your corporate offices. If employees are working from home or on the road, you can set up a virtual private network (VPN) from their computers to the corporate network and then forward AWS system administrator traffic via the corporate network, where it conforms to the CIDR masking you've implemented.

NASDAQ runs on AWS

You often hear it said about AWS that financial services companies are reluctant to use it because of security concerns and considerations. The theory is that financial data is so important that a financial firm can't rely on AWS to treat it with appropriate controls and processes.

The only thing wrong with this theory is that it's inaccurate. NASDAQ, one of the largest financial exchanges in the world, runs the FINQLOUD application on AWS; it's a site for NASDAQ customers to perform custom analytics on NASDAQ financial data.

It's difficult to comprehend the scale of NASDAQ: As the largest exchange company in the world, it owns and operates 24 markets, three clearing houses, and five central securities depositories spanning six continents. It carries data for much of the world's financial transactions and clearly understands the compliance and regulation requirements associated with providing financial services. However, even a gigantic institution like NASDAQ faces the same challenges as many smaller companies: the lack of computing capacity, long provisioning timelines, and high costs. For these reasons, it turned to AWS when it moved forward with FINQCLOUD.

But wait — what about the putative security issues associated with cloud computing? NASDAQ addresses them by encrypting data to be stored in S3 at the company location; only the encrypted version is stored in S3. And NASDAQ ensures the security of the data during transmission by using secure connections to AWS so that no possible intruder can access NASDAQ data on its way to or from AWS.

NASDAQ characterizes AWS as super-secure, easily meeting the best that NASDAQ could implement on its own. And in addition to the level of security that NASDAQ achieves with AWS, the firm estimates that it saves 80 percent compared to the costs of implementing a system on its own.

AWS Virtual Private Cloud (VPC)

As useful as EC2 undoubtedly is, many customers prefer a more secure offering. As I noted in the earlier section "Security Group Best Practices," even with the best security practices regarding security groups, a potential vulnerability in applications is present when each EC2 instance has a public IP address.

Fortunately, AWS addresses this problem with its Virtual Private Cloud (VPC) offering. In broad terms, VPC lets users segregate their instances and shield them from direct Internet access. VPC makes it possible to implement AWS applications that are more secure.

Educate yourself about VPC. Amazon announced this change in early 2013: From now on, new accounts don't use "traditional" EC2, but instead are assigned to use VPC. Existing accounts can continue to use EC2 within regions they have already used, but when existing accounts access new regions, they need to use VPC as well. Amazon's long-term AWS direction is to make VPC the foundation of its service, so it's vital that you become familiar with it and become comfortable with its characteristics.

VPC overview

VPC operates by providing you with a virtual network topology that's separate from the general AWS environment. Another way to say this is that via the use of clever software, AWS provides you with a segregated computing environment. Instances are located within your own, private VPC, with no access to them other than via the VPC environment. In a certain sense, what you end up with isn't dissimilar from a VLAN environment.

Using a VPC, you can create a separate set of resources that carry private IP addresses within a range you select. You set rules for how traffic enters and leaves instances within the VPC. You can choose to make instances accessible to the public Internet via Elastic IP addresses. Moreover, you can create subnets (in effect, subdivisions of the overall VPC) and control access to and from the subnets and between subnets. (Curious about Elastic IP addresses? Check out Chapter 5.)

You can also make a VPN connection between your own data center and your VPC running over a private circuit. You can use this capability to ensure that no traffic between the two sites is exposed to public access, and you can use your ability to select the private IP address range to align your VPC addresses with your internal company address scheme. The VPC can then act, in effect, as an extension of your corporate computing environment.

There's no question that VPC is an innovative offering and one that addresses many of the concerns that people raise regarding AWS. To be clear, however, your VPC still runs within AWS and is implemented via network partitioning and packet routing — in other words, the security is based on clever software, not on a physically separate environment. Some people undoubtedly find VPC (attractive as it may be) insufficient for their security concerns. On the other hand, VPC is based on techniques that aren't enormously different from those used by hosting companies and other cloud providers, so a refusal to find VPC sufficiently secure consigns users to their own on-premises data centers.

How VPC works

VPC is straightforward conceptually, though a number of details make it more challenging than "vanilla" EC2. As you make your way through my explanation, keep Figure 7-5 in mind, which should make it easier for you to follow along. (Note that Amazon goes out of its way to make managing VPCs easier by including VPC administrative capabilities within the AWS Management Console.)

You start by declaring a VPC within your account. You identify the address you want to use and a CIDR mask to define how many IP addresses you want within your VPC. (See the little cloud within the larger cloud in Figure 7-5? That's your VPC.) Traffic to and from your VPC is sent via a "virtual router" (Amazon's term), although a better way to describe it is as a set of rules used to control traffic for your VPC.

Every VPC can have one or more subnets, which can then be used in these four VPC scenarios, based on the types of subnets the VPC contains:

- ✔ **VPC with public subnet:** A public subnet is accessible to the public Internet, and instances within a public subnet can directly access the Internet with inbound or outbound traffic. By default, every VPC is created with a public subnet.

- ✔ **VPC with public and private subnet:** A private subnet is located within a VPC and cannot access the Internet. Instances within the subnet are limited to sending traffic among themselves, unless an instance offering NAT support is available in a public subnet within the VPC.

  NAT, which stands for *n*etwork *a*ddress *t*ranslation, is a service commonly used to send and receive traffic from servers or virtual machines (or, indeed, AWS instances, in this case). If an instance supporting NAT is in the associated public subnet, instances within the private subnet can route external traffic through it.

- ✔ **VPC with public and private subnet and hardware VPN access:** It's similar to the scenario in the preceding bullet, but a direct connect also exists between the VPC and an external location (your corporate data center, for example).

- ✔ **VPC with only private subnet and hardware VPN access:** This scenario allows AWS resources to be completely isolated from public Internet access but to be accessible from an external location, such as your corporate data center.

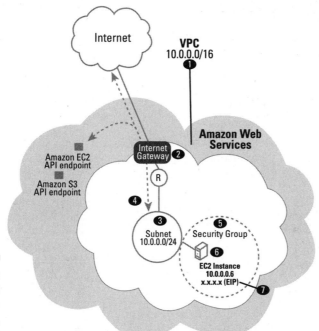

Figure 7-5:
The AWS
virtual pri-
vate cloud.

As with standard "vanilla" EC2, you must declare security groups to control traffic for your instances. There's a major difference between EC2 security groups and VPC security groups, though: Whereas EC2 security groups control traffic into instances but allow all traffic from instances, VPC security groups control traffic to *and* from instances. If you want your instance to be able to download software updates from a particular site, you must put the site's IP address into a security group that's attached to the instance. That is for direct outbound traffic; for traffic that carries responses to inbound traffic (traffic responding to an HTPP request on Port 80, for example), VPC automatically allows traffic from a VPC instance to return traffic to the IP address from which the request originated.

VPC security groups are completely different from EC2 security groups, and one type cannot be used with the other type of AWS computing environment.

Each VPC instance is assigned an IP address within the range you defined when you created your VPC. AWS provides a DHCP service that provides the specific private address for your instance from the range you defined when you created the VPC. (DHCP, which stands for Dynamic Host Configuration Protocol, is a service that assigns IP addresses on the fly.) In Figure 7-5, you can see that the entire VPC has been assigned an address beginning with

`10.0.0.0`, with a CIDR mask of 16 bits, allowing 65,534 addresses within the VPC. One subnet has been created, with the same beginning address and a mask of 24 bits, allowing 255 addresses to reside within the subnet. One instance has been created within the subnet, with an IP address of `10.0.0.6`.

This particular instance has the given private IP address and no public IP address. To make this instance accessible from the public Internet (and reside within a public subnet), you can attach an Elastic IP address to it. Elastic IP addresses are similar to security groups, in that VPC and EC2 Elastic IP addresses are different and cannot be applied to the other AWS computing environment.

Because VPC instances can have more than one Elastic IP, you can load multiple applications on a single server and have each application associated with a given Elastic IP; then you can perform more useful work on a single instance.

VPC subnets

Even though VPC offers a virtual private cloud, all VPC computing is done within a subnet of a VPC. In other words, your instances all reside within a subnet of the VPC and interact with one another and to the Internet via the subnet. (Your overall set of IP addresses must be partitioned into one or more subnets; every instance in a VPC must reside within a subnet.)

AWS makes it easy to create subnets, in that the VPC wizard in the Management Console provides a dialog box with choices that reflect the subnet types I just discussed. However, your choices aren't limited to the default topologies listed in the dialog box, because you can add or delete subnets on the subnet page associated with each VPC in your account.

Communication from instances within subnets

Although you can associate an Elastic IP address with an instance within a public subnet, packets from the instance don't move directly to the Internet. They travel through an Internet gateway associated with the VPC. The Internet gateway *isn't* part of any subnet, but resides within the VPC, and all subnet instances that want to send traffic to the Internet have to send it through the Internet gateway. (Refer to the Internet gateway shown at the top of Figure 7-5.)

The concept of communicating to the Internet from an instance in a public subnet is simple: Because the instance has an Elastic IP, it can send and receive traffic from the Internet. Note that an Elastic IP is required even if you want to send traffic to the Internet only from a public subnet.

But what happens if you have a private subnet? Private subnets are shielded from the Internet, and it's impossible to attach an Elastic IP address to an instance within a private subnet. It probably isn't a problem if the instance can't receive Internet traffic; if you wanted it to do so, you could have put it in a public subnet. But what if you want it to be able to *send* traffic to the Internet (to download software updates and patches, for example)? Is this not possible if the instance resides in a private subnet?

The answer is that the instance can't contact the Internet, though it can talk to a NAT server that can, in turn, forward traffic to the Internet gateway, which makes it possible for the instance to communicate with the Internet. (A NAT server, by the way, is an instance that performs NAT — *n*etwork *a*ddress *t*ranslation; NAT is discussed near the beginning of this section of the chapter.)

How do you configure the subnets to communicate with other instances and the Internet? You do it with the help of an item called a routing table.

VPC routing tables

Each VPC comes with a *virtual router* — a (virtual) device that controls all traffic to and from instances. Each subnet must have a specific routing table associated with it to configure how instances within the subnet communicate over the network. The ability to assign a specific routing table to each subnet makes it easy for you to tailor your VPC operation to the needs of your applications. (In Figure 7-5, the routing table is depicted as a circle containing a capital letter *R.*)

Naturally, each VPC comes with a default routing table; if you don't explicitly assign a routing table to a subnet, the default routing table is assigned to it. Upon creation, the default routing table has a single rule; this rule enables communication between instances within the subnet.

Just as I recommend that you avoid using the default security group for your security group rules, I also recommend that you avoid using the default routing table for your VPC subnets. You're always better off creating your own resources with respect to security, because it forces you to think things through more thoroughly and enables better security partitioning.

If, after you've created your own routing table, you can — if your subnet is a public subnet — include a rule to allow the subnet instances to communicate with the Internet gateway and thereby communicate with the Internet.

Internet gateway

The *Internet gateway* is a resource that can be attached to a VPC to enable all subnets to communicate with the Internet. If you use the Management Console to create your VPC, an Internet gateway is automatically created and associated with your VPC.

For any subnets that you want to communicate with the Internet, you must add the Internet gateway to the subnet's routing table. (Remember that you must also attach an Elastic IP to every instance that you want to communicate with the Internet; an instance with an Elastic IP attached to it can then communicate with the Internet gateway, which in turn forwards traffic to the general Internet.) Any time your instance makes a call to an address outside the bounds of the subnet containing it, the traffic travels through the Internet gateway and then on to the Internet. Likewise, any traffic directed toward your Elastic IP must transit through the Internet gateway.

NAT servers

What if you've created a private subnet and want it to communicate with another subnet or the Internet? Are you prevented from doing so because you have a private subnet? Not at all, but you do have to use a special instance that sends traffic back and forth between the two subnets — a NAT instance. Figure 7-6 shows a more complex VPC configuration than the one depicted earlier, in Figure 7-5. In Figure 7-6, you can see that a NAT instance has been included in the public subnet `10.0.0.0`, allowing for traffic from the `10.0.1.0` subnet to transit to the Internet via the Internet gateway.

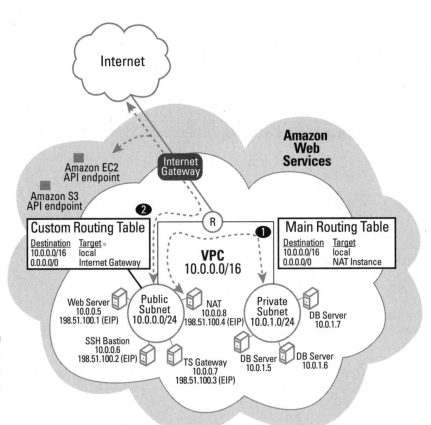

Figure 7-6:
A more complex VPC configuration.

A NAT instance is, in effect, a traffic cop that resides within a public subnet and accepts traffic from instances on private subnets. As you may already have guessed, for the NAT instance to do its job, you need to create a security group for it. The security group includes which ports the NAT accepts traffic on, but also the source — the private subnet address used to forward traffic to the NAT instance. You need to add multiple rules for, say, Port 80 (web traffic) — one for each private subnet that the NAT instance will accept traffic from.

NAT instances also require a bit of tweaking in that regular EC2 instances are set up for source/destination checking. As Amazon states in its VPC documentation about source/destination checking: "This means the instance must be the source or destination of any traffic it sends or receives. However, the NAT instance needs to be able to send and receive traffic where the eventual source or destination is not the NAT instance itself. To enable that behavior, you must disable source/destination checking on the NAT instance." Essentially, EC2 instances always expect to generate or respond to traffic, but never to act as a gateway that passes traffic along. They are configured to accept only traffic that the instance sends or receives and respond to the sending address directly. A NAT instance acts as a gateway and receives traffic from an instance and sends it along to a server on the Internet, so it "breaks" the source/destination checking. For that reason, after you launch the NAT instance, you have to disable this checking: Select the instance within the AWS Management Console, right-click, and then click the Change Source/Destination Check option in dialog box.

The VPC configuration shown in Figure 7-6 illustrates the power of VPC. You can see that the VPC contains two subnets: one public and one private. The public subnet contains a number of instances, all of which are exposed to the Internet. The application's database servers, however, are segregated into a private subnet, and none of them carries public IP addresses. No traffic from the Internet, therefore, can directly access the database servers, thereby increasing their security. This approach is an improvement over the security-group-based tiering (which I outline earlier in this chapter) because with no public IP address exposure, malicious traffic faces much more difficulty in accessing a VPC private subnet instance. Note that in Figure 7-6, the public subnet has a custom routing table that provides traffic routing rules for the instances as well as the Internet Gateway, whereas the main routing table is attached to the private subnet and includes the NAT instance information to enable access to the public subnet and subsequently to the Internet itself.

VPC Network Access Control Lists (ACLs)

VPC offers another traffic controlling mechanism beyond security groups. You can create a Network Access Control List (network ACL) to control traffic flow for an entire subnet. You may use a network ACL to impose a strict security regimen at the subnet level to ensure that, even if someone becomes sloppy with instance-level security groups (say, by opening a wide range of ports for public access from the Internet), you would ensure that no inappropriate traffic can access subnet instances, because the ACL prevents it from even entering the subnet.

To manage an ACL, you create a set of rules that are evaluated in order according to rules numbers you assign to each rule. An ACL essentially offers a Linux-like firewall, with all the fun of managing rules, ensuring that they're applied in the correct order, and that a later rule doesn't undo the work of an earlier rule. Good times.

Elastic Network Interfaces

Unlike EC2, which restricts instances to a single virtual network interface card (NIC), a single private IP address, and a single public IP address, VPC allows multiple virtual NICs and multiple IP addresses. Each of these virtual NICs (referred to as elastic network interfaces) can have its own security groups, which enables you to allow public Internet access on one elastic network interface, open on Port 80 to the world, with another elastic network interface with a different security group that has Port 22 (ssh) open only to your corporate network.

Another scenario is that you can have an instance that acts as a gateway between two subnets and passes traffic back and forth. Though this may seem like a NAT instance, a gateway instance with two Elastic Network Interfaces may be used for an all-private subnet scenario in which instances in one subnet (say, a sales group) sends data requests to a database server in the other subnet, which belongs to the finance department. The finance department doesn't want to allow general access to servers from the sales department, so it sets up a gateway server that shields the database server from direct access.

Elastic network interfaces can be used to partition subnets, and then should be used in environments where the separation of computing resources is important for security or compliance reasons.

VPC access to other AWS services

A theme of this book is that one of the great benefits of AWS is the range of services it provides. Chapters 8 and 9 cover these services in greater detail, but trust me for now: There are a lot of great AWS services. How can a VPC instance access an AWS service such as Simple Queue Service (SQS)?

The answer is that access to other AWS services is routed through the Internet gateway. However, your request to AWS services doesn't go all the way out to the Internet and back into AWS (which would incur network traffic charges on traffic); instead, the Internet gateway recognizes that the traffic destination is within AWS and takes a shortcut to the AWS service without sending traffic outside of AWS. Cool, right?

VPC scope

VPC is, like most other AWS services, region-scoped. You can have a VPC in US East and a separate VPC in US West-Oregon. Traffic between them travels over the public Internet and incurs a network charge (although it's a much lower charge than if the traffic were going to a non-AWS location).

VPC cost

The best thing about VPC is its cost: nothing. Amazon provides a way for you to improve your AWS security and doesn't charge you a cent for it. You pay a fee for any unused VPC Elastic IPs, just as you do for EC2 Elastic IPs, but this fee is nominal. And, of course, you pay normal fees for all AWS resources — an instance running in VPC racks up instance charges. But for VPC itself? Nothing.

Using VPC

VPC is an excellent solution to an issue highlighted earlier in this chapter: How to avoid exposing instances and data that you prefer to shield from outside Internet access when every EC2 instance has a public IP address.

Using VPC, you can implement a dual-subnet application topology, in which the appropriate Internet-facing instances — the web servers — are placed in a public subnet, whereas instances that you'd prefer to not be accessible to the Internet — database servers, of course, but potentially other types of instances as well, such as cache servers and the like — are placed in a private subnet. A viable deployment strategy that you can pursue is to leverage VPC heavily and use a private, subnet-focused application design, where you place in a public subnet only those instances that need to be accessible to outside traffic and you place all other application instances within a private subnet, where they're shielded from all outside traffic. Any Internet access necessary for private subnet-based instances (to download software updates and patches, for example) can take place via a NAT instance.

I believe that VPC use will increase significantly when people understand it better. It's more complex than vanilla EC2, but offers greater security.

AWS Application Security

AWS requires a shared security responsibility, with Amazon taking responsibility below the trust boundary and users taking responsibility above the trust boundary. In this chapter, I describe Amazon's security offerings that address *its* area of responsibility. But how about *yours?*

Many people are unsure what steps to take to improve security for their applications. This uncertainty is troubling because Amazon (and every other cloud provider in the world) rightly refuses to take on user security responsibility. The company cannot possibly know what users do inside their applications, of course, so Amazon and other cloud providers leave application security to the user.

Given this situation, follow my recommendations to increase your AWS application security:

✔ **Use security groups appropriately.** Obviously, you should avoid using the Default security group for applications. Every security group should be identified explicitly with a name that indicates its purpose. This strategy makes it easier to audit the security groups to ensure that they're appropriately configured. If you see a security group for web servers and it has Port 21 (FTP service) listed in addition to Port 80 (HTTP service) and 443 (HTTPS service), it's probably incorrect. Earlier in this chapter, I discuss the use of security groups to partition your application to implement defense in depth, and I strongly urge you to follow that strategy. Limiting traffic to appropriate IP address ranges is a good practice to follow as well.

✔ **Implement data encryption in transit.** If you encrypt your network traffic, both external to AWS and within AWS, you prevent anyone from reading your packets. Though AWS's record in maintaining packet security is exemplary, you still may implement encryption — just to be certain. Trust but verify.

✔ **Implement data encryption at rest.** If you encrypt data that's stored within AWS, you protect it from being examined by other AWS users as well as by AWS personnel. One of the strongest arguments against encryption is the performance penalty it imposes, so evaluate your data to see whether it has particularly sensitive portions for which a performance hit would be acceptable.

✔ **Manage security keys carefully.** Administrative access to AWS Linux instances is typically via shared key SSH. Stories abound about organizations in which keys are widely shared by many administrators, placed on individual user's drives, and never rotated. Even worse, many organizations fail to change the keys they're using when an employee quits (or, even worse, is fired for a serious reason) and the former employee still has a copy of the key used to administer AWS instances. This neglect constitutes playing with fire, and any organization that fails to manage its keys carefully deserves to have its fingers burned. Many key management solutions exist in the marketplace — and several open source options — so implement a solution to manage your keys.

✔ **Install and configure your software packages correctly.** It's a cliché that many IT organizations install software and leave default passwords in place, leave unnecessary ports open, and fail to configure the software packages to properly protect them against attack. Don't make that mistake. Evaluate every component of your application (including the operating system in the image) and ensure that you've installed and configured them correctly and securely.

✔ **Implement on-instance security.** The move to deperimeterized security emphasizes the need for every resource to be appropriately protected against security issues. It's critical that you put Host-based Intrusion Detection/Prevention Software (HIDS) in place to track and respond to attacks. If you're running Windows-based instances, you should also ensure that you have antivirus and antimalware software operating as well. Frankly, this area is the one where most organizations commonly fail, and it often reflects the unwarranted assumption that AWS is responsible for security. For its portion of the environment, it is responsible. For your stuff, it isn't. Be sure to have on-instance security in place.

✔ **Manage your instance code properly.** Too many organizations create an image and then use it, untouched and unchanged, for months (or years!) on end. That's a huge problem. First, this level of carelessness neglects the installation of important security patches and can leave your application exposed to security holes. Second, if you don't manage your application code correctly, you can't be sure what version of your application is running, and that's a big problem. Many organizations address it by creating new images, but that strategy poses a different problem: image sprawl. A better approach is to implement the techniques described in Chapter 6 for managing instance code, to ensure that you have better security in place and always know what you're running.

Chapter 8

Additional Core AWS Services

• •

In This Chapter

▶ Introducing other AWS services

▶ Integrating additional core services into your application

▶ Dealing with AWS lock-in

• •

AWS has its core services — S3, EC2, Amazon Glacier, and Amazon EBS, for example — but that's not the end of the story. Amazon operates according to the principle "Variety is the spice of life," so it offers quite a range of services in addition to the big players. This chapter takes you on a mini-tour of the rest of the AWS services. The idea is to help you understand the breadth of products that Amazon provides and give you the confidence of at least being acquainted with every product in the most comprehensive cloud service offering in the industry.

As part of this tour, I address one key concern about AWS that many people have: *lock-in,* or the extent to which your use of various AWS services can prevent you from choosing to place your AWS applications in another cloud environment. I evaluate how serious the issue is and then offer strategies for dealing with any potential issues that may arise.

Finally, I pull back to offer some Big Picture advice about which AWS services you should use as part of your application. I show you how to assess the value you obtain from a given AWS service, how to measure your concern about lock-in, and how potential plans for changing the location of your application deployment should affect your AWS strategy.

Understanding the Other AWS Services

My take on AWS is that certain foundational services — EC2, S3, Amazon EBS, and Amazon Glacier — are at the center of the AWS universe. I refer to them as *foundational* for two reasons:

✔ **They include the first AWS services introduced to the marketplace.**
AWS launched with S3 and followed within the year with EC2. AWS networking and security were critical components of how the entire AWS
environment operates and were components of S3 and EC2. Several
storage options I cover weren't part of the early AWS services, but were
included with S3 for the sake of consistency.

✔ **These services represent the foundation of how you use AWS. Though
it's certainly possible to leverage other AWS services without using
storage and computing, the vast majority of people use those services
in conjunction with storage and computing.**

Because I'm talking about other AWS services, this spot is as good as any to
tell you about www.bernardgolden.com. As you may expect from the name,
this is my website. It offers a section covering any new AWS services that may
be released after this book is published. Look at my site to find out about new
AWS services and how to apply them to build even better AWS applications.

The "additional" services — the focus of this chapter — integrate and make
the foundational services more useful. They help you build better applications by using the foundational storage and computing services offered by
AWS. For example, Elastic Load Balancer (ELB) is an additional service that
Amazon offers in order to distribute traffic to multiple web servers, enabling
your application to support more traffic than can be handled by a single web
server. You don't *need* an ELB to deploy a basic AWS application, but the service makes it much easier to run a high-traffic, AWS-based web application.

If you were to use a "traditional" PaaS solution, it would provide load balancing automatically — you probably wouldn't even be aware of it being in place,
but the service would arrange for enough web server resources to support
your application's traffic, and it would put in place a load-balancing mechanism to distribute the traffic among those web servers. That's all fine and
dandy, except that there are many choices for traffic distribution. Sometimes
it's round-robin (each server receives traffic in turn), sometimes it's based
on the processor load of the servers (lightly loaded servers receive more
traffic), and sometimes it's based on which server has the least number of
active connections. In a traditional PaaS system, you're stuck with whatever
distribution method the service offers, and if it doesn't suit your application's
needs, you're out of luck.

So Amazon, in its desire to provide more services to its customers, offers
ELB, which provides a lot of functionality, is easy to use, and is cheap.
However, if it doesn't suit your application's requirements, that's no problem — you're free to implement your own solution (or to leverage one of the
many open source or commercial offerings that other organizations make
available within AWS). The key difference between Amazon's platform

offerings and what you may expect from the traditional Platform as a Service (Paas) offerings is that Amazon provides a service designed to help you develop and operate your application, but doesn't force you to use it. You're free to address your application's load-balancing needs in another way, if you want. And this is true of all AWS services — they provide commonly needed services, but you're the in the driver's seat. Feel free to use them or not.

This approach appears to be the right one for these kind of services — rather than offer a set of handcuffs that constrain how you achieve your requirements, AWS offers a stepladder to make it easier for you to reach your objectives. Hokey images aside, the bottom line is this: AWS has a number of services that you can leverage to assist in building your application, but you have complete control and choice regarding them — if they're helpful, that's great, but if you want to do something else, that's fine, too. Amazon doesn't dictate how you must achieve your goals.

Deciding whether it makes sense to use other AWS services

It's time for brass tacks: What are the advantages you can realize by using what Amazon offers instead of implementing your own application functionality? Alternatively, what are that reasons that you wouldn't use these services? Listing all the pros and cons may help. First, here are some important reasons that you'd use AWS core and extended services — because they can

- ✔ **Offer needed functionality outside your area of expertise:** The extended services provide something you need for your application in an area that you don't know much about — and don't have time to learn. For example, you may need load balancing but have never implemented it. (And believe me, operating load balancing properly is an arcane art; one application performance expert told me that the number-one performance bottleneck he sees is misconfigured load balancers.) Rather than devote time to learning about load balancing, use Amazon's service — you *know* that it has world-class experts working on its Elastic Load Balancer.

- ✔ **Simplify application development:** Using Amazon's service makes it easier to create your application. Leveraging AWS core and extended services makes it easier to develop the whole application.

- ✔ **Speed the time to market:** Using AWS services means less work for you, which enables you to deliver your application more quickly. There's *always* time pressure on application delivery, and using AWS services makes it possible to deliver your applications sooner. In a sense, it's an extension of the general argument for using AWS — just as the AWS foundation services speed the provisioning of fundamental computing capability, the additional core and extended services speed the creation of application capability.

✔ **Achieve scalability:** Managing scalability is difficult, and it can be even more difficult to manage high load variability, which requires the constant growing and shrinking of capacity. Amazon not only makes it easy to consume just as much of a service as you need but also handles all the plumbing details for you.

✔ **Integrates with other AWS services you're using:** If you're writing an application in AWS, you can be sure that both core and extended AWS services work well with not only AWS storage and EC2 compute but also with one another. Not having to jury-rig different applications to get them to work with one another is a definite benefit of using AWS services.

✔ **Save you money:** AWS provides only the services it can deliver via automation, so no (expensive) manual interaction is required on the part of Amazon personnel. The company is relentlessly focused on cost reduction. Consequently, the AWS service is likely to be less expensive than if you were to implement it yourself.

✔ **Allow you to focus on differentiated application functionality:** Most of the additional AWS services fall into the category of necessary-but-unexciting-functionality. Put another way, AWS services comprise the plumbing of your application — it's critical but nothing that your application users would ever view as something special associated with your application. In Silicon Valley-speak, these services are *undifferentiating* — they do nothing to make your application stand apart from any other application. To extend this example, no application user has ever said, "Boy, the reason I like this application is that it does an awesome job of load balancing!" If you use AWS services to provide undifferentiating functionality, it gives you more time to focus on functionality that differentiates your application from others. This benefit is perhaps the most important one of the additional AWS services — they free you up to focus on the most important aspects of your application.

Of course, you may not choose to use AWS services, so it's only fair to examine your reasons. You may choose not to use the core and extended AWS services because they

✔ **Lock you in to AWS:** The topic of lock-in is significant enough that I deal with it at the end of this chapter, but take the following as the thumbnail version of the argument: Every additional AWS service you use makes it that much more difficult to move your application to another cloud provider. In part, the reason is that every cloud provider does everything somewhat differently, so using Amazon's version of a service makes you have to adjust your application if you move it elsewhere. The greater issue is that most other cloud providers offer far fewer services than Amazon, so if you take advantage of an AWS service and subsequently decide to move to another environment, you have to figure out how to implement the functionality yourself. It's a concern, no doubt, but it's more of an indictment of the inadequacy of other cloud provider offerings than a problem with AWS proper.

✔ **Provide inadequate functionality:** Amazon's AWS technical strategy is to offer basic functionality that satisfies the needs of the largest, least-demanding part of the market. It may well be the case that you need functionality that the AWS offering cannot provide, which precludes you from using the service. Nothing in AWS forces you to use an AWS service offering, so inadequate functionality means only that you have to implement the service yourself (or use another vendor offering that's available in AWS).

✔ **Cost too much:** Sometimes people feel that a particular AWS offering is too expensive. And it's true that using multiple AWS services can drive up your overall AWS cost. This concern is certainly valid, and you should be aware of what a service costs you; on the other hand, you should also evaluate what it would truly cost you to implement the service yourself. People notoriously underestimate the time and expense of implementing technical functionality themselves, and it's easy to say, for example, "Running a load balancer isn't difficult — I run HAProxy, an open source load balancer, and it's free," completely missing the value of the investment of time required to install and configure a solution, operate it in production, and ensure that it's scaling as necessary. Simply put, while a cost comparison is appropriate, it's important to make sure you account for all of the components in your cost when you compare it to AWS.

With all the pros and cons out of the way, it's time to move on to an examination of all those "other" AWS products. I apologize in advance for the brevity of the discussion for each of the following services, but in my defense, addressing each of the AWS services in the depth it deserves in this book would make *War and Peace* look like a pamphlet! The strategy I have followed is to first describe the service in enough detail that you can understand its high-level functionality and benefit, and then provide recommendations regarding how you can apply it usefully.

If you need more detail on a particular offering, Amazon provides comprehensive — at times, *overly* comprehensive — documentation on all its services. The primary criticism of Amazon documentation is that although it provides in-depth information, the descriptions of its services aren't necessarily easy to comprehend. My goal in this chapter is to make the incomprehensible comprehensible — and to give you the context necessary to make sense of the pages and pages (and pages) of information that Amazon provides for specific services.

Working with Identity and Access Management (IAM)

I've long argued that the genius of AWS is that it makes it simple to obtain the resources to create and launch applications. Sometimes, however, the blessing of simplicity brings with it a bit of curse — potentially, at least. It turns out that when AWS was first launched, one way that AWS made its use "simple" was in handling account and user management: For every account, there was to be one (and only one) user, and that individual was assumed to "own" the account and all resources associated with the account. Though this setup seems logical, it presents a significant shortcoming to many companies using AWS, particularly those referred to in the technology industry as *enterprise*.

Enterprises typically have *multiple* organizations involved in the lifecycle of applications — development, for one; operations, quality assurance, and testing, for others. Within each of these organizations, multiple individuals may perform administrative functions on the application. When AWS was originally launched, it meant that between 10 and 40 individuals may administer the application and the AWS resources it ran in, but everyone had to share a single identity.

Moreover, most organizations would use a single private key to control administrative access to AWS instances and the software components incorporated in the instances. This single, private key would then have to be shared among all users.

Are you beginning to see the problem? You have a situation where perhaps 40 people share a single user identity and that identity just happens to allow the user full control over all AWS resources. There's no way, in other words, for you to restrict a specific user's access to only certain resources. Alarm bells may ring in many IT organizations because they may be perfectly willing to provide developers with full administrative access to development instances, but will want to forbid developers administrative access to instances that are parts of a production deployment.

An even bigger problem for organizations is what to do when someone leaves the organization. Clearly, a former employee shouldn't be able to access resources, yet denying access to him would require reissuing new credentials and keys to all remaining employees. In an IT organization of dozens or hundreds (or thousands!) of employees, having to reissue credentials every time an individual leaves would be a nightmare.

Even worse is that all existing resources (running instances, for example) would need to be terminated and relaunched with new credentials, which would affect application uptime.

As you can see, the "simple' way of doing things — going with a single user identity and credential environment — brought with it a boatload of complications. Luckily for us, to deal with these complexities, Amazon created its Identity and Access Management (IAM) service, a way of tweaking access control and the AWS credential environment in ways that made the system more hospitable to enterprise users. IAM is automatically included with every AWS account, and you don't need to do anything to activate it.

IAM functionality

IAM offers these excellent features:

- **User management:** You can create multiple users within a single account and provide them with different account resource access controls. Users can also be assigned to groups, and access controls can be assigned at the group level, which then implements those controls for each person within the group.

- **Centralized control of user identities and access credentials:** IAM is used to manage all user identities and access credentials, thereby centralizing and simplifying a complex and important control mechanism.

- **AWS resource controls:** You can control what users can access given AWS resources by placing controls on specific AWS resources. You may, for example, allow certain users within your organization to access company data stored in S3, while preventing other users who have no need to access the data from being able to interact with the S3 object.

- **AWS resource creation controls:** You can restrict where users can create AWS resources. If you want to ensure that only users in the US West region launch new instances, for example, IAM can be used to enforce that rule.

- **AWS resource sharing across accounts:** You can provide access to AWS resources within your account to people in other accounts. This may be useful if you want your organization to collaborate with a partner company or if your company uses different accounts for different departments.

- **Consolidated billing:** You can receive a single bill for all user activity within AWS, rather than an individual bill for each user. Consolidating billing simplifies your cost management because it allows easy examination of all AWS costs in a single billing statement. It also reduces your overall AWS cost because you can take advantage of reduced pricing associated with higher levels of AWS resource use and allows you to take better advantage of reservation pricing.

When you implement IAM, each user gets a unique identity and password, and a user-specific set of security credentials. You create IAM policies that are applied as users attempt to access AWS resources. The policies define access controls and can be written to apply to specific users or to groups of users.

Using IAM

IAM is a service that you may not see a need for until, all of a sudden, you realize that you needed it *yesterday,* as your AWS use spirals out of control and you don't know who is doing what. Don't implement IAM as you first begin experimenting with AWS, however, but do closely track how your organization continues to use AWS. When you begin to have multiple groups involved with AWS, when you're running multiple applications in AWS, or you're deploying production applications within AWS, you should strongly consider moving to IAM. It's definitely somewhat more complex than vanilla AWS identity management, but it offers real enterprise functionality as your AWS use scales both in volume and in numbers of users interacting with AWS.

IAM cost

IAM is free to users.

Elastic Load Balancer (ELB)

One useful benefit of cloud computing is that it supports *scalability* (the ability to provision large amounts of computing capacity) and *elasticity* (the ability to easily and rapidly grow and shrink the computing capacity assigned to your application). And one benefit of AWS is that it supports these aforementioned benefits more than any other cloud provider in the market. You can easily start and stop instances and add them to, or remove them from, your application, paying only for the computing capacity you consume.

One key requirement for taking advantage of these benefits is the ability to direct network traffic to these instances, and a load balancer is the solution to this requirement. A *load balancer* spreads load across multiple computing resources that offer the same functionality, improving the overall application performance. If you have four instances that operate as web servers, for example, a load balancer directs traffic to each of the four so that no web server is overloaded and all users experience better performance.

One challenge of using AWS is that, because of its elasticity support, instances may frequently join or leave a resource pool, so a load balancer needs to easily allow both registration and deregistration. *Registration* refers to the process of a computing resource (in this case, an AWS instance) making the load balancer aware of the instance's availability and setting up the network connection between the load balancer and the instance so that traffic can flow between them. *Deregistration* performs the process in reverse — it removes the instance from the load balancer's connection list, which causes the load balancer to stop sending traffic to the instance.

Load balancing is a long-established technology, and many products, both commercial and open source, are available on the market. However, using these products requires user administration and may impose inconvenient billing arrangements — separate billing distinct from AWS, in other words, which can make it difficult to accurately track costs.

A larger problem is that load balancing itself can suffer from the same kinds of scalability and elasticity constraints that load balancing is designed to solve. As your application's traffic grows and shrinks, you'll need more or less load-balancing capacity. So the problem becomes one of managing your load-balancing capacity, and you're back to the same issue — the same hassles — that drove you toward load balancing in the first place. In the name of eliminating these hassles once and for all, AWS launched its own load balancing service, called Elastic Load Balancing (ELB), designed to offer these benefits:

✔ **Load balancing as a service:** ELB is designed to make it easy to support load balancing without requiring AWS users to manage load balancer resource pools. As is typical of Amazon, it designed a service to simplify important application functionality, thereby giving users an easier way to use AWS.

✔ **Automated load balancing scalability and elasticity:** Instead of users having to manage load balancer pools, requiring constant monitoring and administration, Amazon designed its load balancing service to automatically support more (or less) traffic with no user interaction required.

✔ **Easy registration and deregistration:** ELB reduces the overhead of getting an instance known to a load balancer so it can register and deregister the instance. ELB automates that process, making setup and teardown much faster and less error-prone.

✔ **Low cost:** Consistent with Amazon's overall AWS philosophy, ELB isn't only inexpensive, but you also pay for only the ELB capacity you use. For more details on ELB cost, see the later section about ELB costs.

Amazon supports ELB via the AWS API and Management Console.

ELB functionality

ELB provides these features:

✔ **Easy creation of ELBs:** A simple API call or use of the AWS Management Console allows users to automatically create an ELB. Upon creation, the ELB is assigned a DNS identifier, such as `LB1-26746260.us-east-1.elb.amazonaws.com`. Traffic sent to this DNS domain is automatically spread among all instances registered to the ELB.

✔ **Easy registration and deregistration of instances:** AWS makes it easy to connect an instance with an ELB or to remove the connection. This makes leveraging AWS's scalability and elasticity easier for users, which is good for everyone.

✔ **Support of multiple availability zones (AZs):** The instances registered with an ELB can be placed in multiple AZs, providing better application robustness and protection against downtime in the event of an entire AZ going offline.

ELB distributes traffic evenly between AZs. If you decide to use the ELB multi-AZ support, you should understand that each AZ will receive roughly the same amount of traffic; therefore, you should plan to have roughly equal numbers of instances running in each AZ to avoid one AZ's instances from being overwhelmed with traffic.

✔ **Support of encryption via Secure Socket Layer (SSL) technology:** ELBs offer automated support of Secure Socket Layer (SSL) encryption, which, if you've ever had to manage SSL certificates, you'll know isn't trivial. If you have ELB encryption support, you can make your applications more secure while still achieving high scalability and elasticity.

✔ **Support for session affinity:** Session affinity (also known as *sticky sessions*) refers to the ability to associate a user's connection to a particular instance, directing all subsequent user traffic back to the same instance that the first connection from the user was sent to. Applications can then store session state information (username and ID, for example) in the instance, allowing easier application design and better performance.

✔ **Domain name assignment:** Even though ELB assigns a DNS name to your ELB, you wouldn't want all of your customers who want to contact your corporate website to have to enter `LB1-26746260.us-east-1.elb.amazonaws.com` in their browsers. ELB makes it easy for you to associate a more user-friendly domain name (`www.yourcompanyname.com`) to the ELB DNS name, allowing user traffic automatically to be redirected from your domain name to the highly scalable ELB.

✔ **Instance health monitoring:** AWS monitors instances registered with an ELB; if an instance stops performing, the ELB automatically stops sending traffic to it. This prevents traffic from being directed to an instance that won't respond and reduces the likelihood of having dissatisfied application users.

✔ **Support of autoscaling:** AWS offers *autoscaling,* which uses application load to automatically trigger additional instance launches to support application traffic. If you configure your application to use autoscaling, AWS automatically adds (or subtracts) instances as necessary.

Instance IP addresses are *ephemeral:* AWS assigns each new instance an IP address at random. If you stop and restart an instance that's registered with the ELB, therefore, the ELB is unaware of the new instance and, consequently, doesn't send traffic to it. The right way to handle this situation is to deregister instances upon shutdown and to be sure to register new instances on start-up. (The AWS Auto Scaling service also alleviates this issue; Auto Scaling is covered in Chapter 10.)

ELB scope

ELBs are regional in scope. This concept is quite important to understand in that an ELB cannot distribute an application's traffic across multiple regions. To distribute traffic across multiple regions, you should look at other solutions, including the use of one of the load balancer products available as images within AWS.

ELB cost

ELB cost varies by region, but, overall, the cost of ELB is quite reasonable. An ELB costs, per hour (depending on region), between $.028 and $.034. There's also a traffic charge for ELBs, which runs between $.008 and $.011 per gigabyte.

Route 53

Route 53 is Amazon's own Domain Name Service (DNS). A DNS provides a straightforward, yet crucial service by translating domain names (`www.example.com`) to IP addresses of specific computing resources (`71.57.3.17`). Computing resources communicate by sending packets to specific IP addresses, so knowing the right IP address for a given computing resource is critical. On the other hand, humans have difficulty remembering — or even typing! — complicated sets of numbers, which makes an IP address a poor choice for identifying computing resources. Humans easily remember names, though, so DNS allows easily remembered names to be mapped to difficult-to-remember IP addresses.

A domain name must be registered before you can use it, which makes sense. It turns out that there are any number of DNS register services in the world; you can go to any of them to register a specific domain name. Before you can use a domain name you have registered, though, you must list it with a DNS service that responds with an IP address whenever someone requests a translation of the domain name.

DNS offers a *hosted zone,* which refers to the collection of definitions associated with a given domain name. For example, for the domain example.com, `www.example.com` is a fully qualified domain name, or FQDN — it has a full listing of the resource requested.

The hosted zone may have just the www record associated with the domain name, but it's more likely to have additional services as well. E-mail is a common service and gets a `mail.example.com` FQDN record. Likewise, additional services associated with the domain name would get additional records as well. You can create a FQDN for your company documents called `documents.yourcompany.com`, identify an IP address for that subdomain, and place all your documents on a server at that address. Anyone who entered `documents.yourcompany.com` in a browser would be directed to that server to obtain any of your company's documents.

As you may expect, a domain record can direct to a load balancer IP address, which then distributes traffic meant for that subdomain to any number of servers attached to the load balancer.

Every domain must have DNS name servers associated with it that serve as the authoritative place to request the *DNS lookup* for a particular domain — the process whereby a domain name gets translated to an IP address. Route 53 provides four DNS name servers that need to be identified to the domain name register, so that requests for DNS lookup are sent to an appropriate server to retrieve the right IP address.

So far, so good. As you can see, DNS is an incredibly useful service. If it didn't exist, the Internet as we know may not exist. But why does Amazon offer a DNS product? After all, DNS existed before AWS, and it will certainly exist long after AWS.

The answer is that, like so many other AWS products, Amazon wants to make using DNS easier, and, by extension, make using AWS easier. Before Route 53, inexpensive (or even free) DNS products didn't scale well, and scalable DNS products cost a ton of money. With the rise of AWS and a whole new set of webscale companies that have huge amounts of traffic but not that much revenue (Pinterest, for example), there was a need for a highly scalable yet inexpensive DNS product, especially because many of these webscale companies are hosted in AWS. After examining its global footprint of AWS regions, Amazon recognized that it could step in and create a DNS offering to better address these needs.

The critical aspect of Route 53 isn't that it's an innovative service — other AWS offerings are far more clever, to be honest. Route 53's selling point is that it commoditizes an important building block of the Internet and makes highly scalable DNS products available at a cost-effective price. DNS is the type of service that typically is set up early in a company's life or application's life and isn't touched for months or years; it usually lurks in the background, quietly operating and resolving DNS requests with no problem. That is, until a problem occurs, usually associated with insufficient scalability or failed infrastructure (the name servers associated with a domain name crash, for example), and then *big-time* problems pop up. Route 53 leverages Amazon's enormous infrastructure and resiliency to keep DNS humming along.

Saying Route 53 isn't that innovative isn't exactly right; by running its own DNS service, Amazon is able to tune it to work better with the rest of its services. For example, it can allow you to specify a load balancer for your FQDN directly, rather than having to use a CNAME mapping; and, of course, that load balancer can, yes, be an AWS Elastic Load Balancer.

Using Route 53

For the most part, using Route 53 is dead-simple. You register your domain name with a domain registrar, list the name servers that your domain name will use for address mapping, and then create subdomains and create zone records that list your subdomains and the IP addresses you want serving the subdomain service. Typically, this set-and-forget effort is completed early in a company's or application's life and is rarely touched thereafter. You'll most likely use the AWS Management Console for this particular task.

Amazon limits calls to the Route 53 API to five per second per account, so if you have an application with many instances within it, you should have the instances configured so that they retry their DNS calls in case of a failed response due to such API limitations. (The technical term for these limitations is *API throttling*.)

Route 53 scope

Router 53 is a global service. Amazon uses its data centers spread throughout the world to execute Route 53 calls so that when you perform a Route 53 action, it executes it so that the information is available throughout all locations in which it hosts Route 53. One clever aspect of Route 53 is that it tracks the location of requests to the Route 53 service and serves up the response from the AWS data center that's closest to the requestor. In this way, Route 53 reduces to a minimum the network latency for DNS lookups. You don't have to do anything to leverage this geographic distribution; AWS takes care of it for you.

AWS offers a cool feature that extends its geographic distribution. You can host your application in several regions, and DNS lookups for your application automatically return an IP address associated with the region nearest to the user. Amazon refers to this as *latency-based routing,* and it's designed to minimize network latency for your application's users.

Route 53 cost

Route 53 is quite cost-effective:

- ✔ $.50 per hosted zone for the first 25 zones and $.10 per hosted zone above 25 zones

- ✔ $.50 per million DNS queries for the first billion queries per month and $.25 per million DNS queries above a billion

- ✔ $.75 per million latency-based queries for the first billion queries per month and $.375 per million queries above that amount

CloudFront

The issue of *latency* — the length of time a network request takes to complete its roundtrip — is always a big deal as it relates to network traffic. If it affects minor elements, such as DNS queries, which are quite small and don't even require a great deal of bandwidth, you can imagine how much it affects actual content — factors such as documents, images, and (heaven forbid) videos. When the Internet first became popular, all content was served up from the central web server; user requests were often served from locations halfway around the world. The impact on latency by sending packets a long distance — and via so many different routers — created a lag in user performance. It wasn't long before latency became a major issue because large websites that used traffic to sell ads or perform e-commerce transactions found that people became frustrated by slow websites and simply abandoned them.

The solution to this problem occurred with the creation of the *content delivery network (CDN)*, which places servers around the world and allows companies to locate their data on the servers. For example, a company located in the United States could use a CDN to place images in Australia; when an Australia-based user accessed the U.S.-based website, the pages were sent (provisionally) without images, and the images were then placed into the pages on their arrival in Australia. This approach allows important or changeable data to reside in the central location and allows static or infrequently changed large content files to be located near the user.

Overall, the use of CDNs can reduce network latency enormously. As you may expect, their use has grown significantly over time. A number of large CDN providers now provide thousands of endpoint locations around the world. These highly sophisticated solutions can be used to reduce latency for web applications, with users able to specify exactly which geographic locations should be the final destinations for distributed content. On the other hand, one common challenge regarding CDNs is their complexity, which brings these issues to the fore:

- **CDNs require sophisticated configuration and tuning.** These "high-maintenance" needs tend to limit the use of CDNs to larger, more technically capable IT organizations that can devote a resource to learning the ins and outs of the product.

- **CDNs can be expensive to use.** Sticker shock makes them difficult to afford for small companies and even small groups or projects within larger organizations.

- **CDNs are typically sold in an enterprise fashion.** By *enterprise,* I mean that customers have to make a lengthy commitment to the service, estimate total usage over the length of the contract, and interact over an extended period before starting to use the service.

✔ **CDNs can be overkill.** If your organization wants improvement in latency but isn't looking to implement a highly sophisticated solution, a CDN isn't the best option.

In sum, CDNs are incredibly important and useful, but many who could potentially benefit from the technology are prevented from leveraging them because of cost and complexity issues.

Two years ago, Amazon launched its attempt to address this dispiriting state of affairs: CloudFront. CloudFront is easy to use and inexpensive, and it makes CDN technology available to entire new user bases that were previously unable to use existing CDN solutions.

CloudFront features these capabilities:

✔ **It serves both static and dynamic content from CloudFront.** Static content is served by S3, whereas dynamic content is served from EC2 instances. Static content can be downloaded or streamed to the content user.

✔ **It supports three content protocols — HTTP, HTTPS, and RTMP.** You'd expect HTTP and HTTPS, but RTMP — the protocol used to stream Adobe Flash–based videos — is a nice addition.

✔ **Content can be made publicly available or restricted to certain users.** Content control is helpful in situations where you want to make content available only to employees or company partners.

In a further extension of this content-control feature, you can create an Origin Access Identity (OAI) to restrict access to your CloudFront objects so that only someone getting a special URL can access the object. The access can be further restricted to only being available to access from specific IP addresses and for a limited time to the special URL. This controlled access is typically used by organizations for commercial reasons to ensure that content access is restricted to subscribers or made available for a limited time.

✔ **Content can be set with an expiration date.** It's an easy way to set things up so that, after a certain date, the content is no longer available. For short-lived content, such as certain kinds of marketing campaigns, this enables control of how long the content is available or ensures that content that is served up by CloudFront is the most recent version (or "freshest," in CDN-speak).

✔ **Content access can be logged.** The ability to log content access means that the content owner can easily track how CloudFront data is being used.

Using CloudFront

In contrast to the more established commercial CDN alternatives, using CloudFront is straightforward. You merely use the AWS Management Console or API to define a distribution. You then associate the distribution with the origin of the content. The origin can be either S3 or EC2; I focus on S3 here. If you want, you can set additional restrictions as discussed earlier, along with an expiration period, which is 24 hours by default. You set permissions on the origin to allow public access (unless you want to restrict permissions so that only certain people can access the content). That's it.

CloudFront returns an identifier URL for you to use to enable access to your content. The identifier takes a form similar to this:

```
d111111abcdef8.cloudfront.net
```

You use this identifier along with the name of the specific object you want served up to deliver it from CloudFront. So you may identify a JPEG image of a cat on your website as d111111abcdef8.cloudfront.net/catimage.jpg. When someone accesses your website and wants to see a picture of the kitty, the call to that URL would return the image from the nearest location to the requestor.

You can create a CNAME alias to make the CloudFront identifier appear as though it's part of another URL. You can then map the CloudFront identifier I just mentioned to mask your use of CloudFront:

```
www.yourcompanydomain.com/images
```

For more information on CNAME DNS records, check out Chapter 7.

That's all that's required to set up a CloudFront distribution. When someone accesses an object that's part of a CloudFront distribution, CloudFront checks to see whether the object is located in a CloudFront cache near the requestor. If the object is in the cache, CloudFront serves it up from there. If it isn't in the local cache, CloudFront fetches it from the Origin S3 bucket and brings it into the local cache and then serves it up to the requestor. Thereafter, CloudFront returns the object from the local cache for requests that are geographically nearby. If the expiration time on the object copy in the local cache has passed, CloudFront checks to see whether the Origin object has changed. If it has, it fetches the object into the local cache; if not, it returns the object copy that's in the local cache.

Amazon offers CloudFront from around 40 places *(edge locations)* around the world, including North America, South America, Europe, and Asia. The number of locations is fewer than some of the big-name competition, but CloudFront performance appears to be satisfactory for most end users.

CloudFront scope

CloudFront itself is a global service — using it automatically places content around the world (excepting any edge locations that you identify as wishing to not have your data placed in). The source of the CloudFront data is regionally scoped; so, for example, you may use CloudFront to distribute your video content throughout the world, so it would be globally available; however, the bucket that contains your video is located in a particular region.

CloudFront cost

The cost of network traffic from CloudFront is only slightly higher than the cost to stream the same traffic directly from S3. For the first 10 terabytes (TB) of network traffic per month, the cost ranges from $.12 (North America) to $.25 (South America). This fee drops to as low as $.02 at volumes above 5 petabytes (PB).

In addition to network traffic, Amazon charges for access requests, on a per-10,000 access request basis, ranging from $.0075 (North America) to $.016 (South America). Access requests are pretty much what they sound like — requests to retrieve data managed by CloudFront.

You can reduce your network traffic costs if you restrict the number of edge locations that your content is cached in, and you can save money by committing to a certain volume of traffic each month.

Though CloudFront pricing is certainly attractive, Cloudfront's true selling point is its reputation for flexibility and ease of use when compared to the established CDN providers.

Hudl runs on AWS

One of the most interesting aspects of AWS is how it enables innovation and the development of companies that leverage AWS to create new businesses — and the new businesses often take advantage of different services as their basis.

The growth of inexpensive bandwidth and storage has jump-started online video — as anyone who has watched YouTube can testify. Though YouTube mostly represents the world's collection of consumer videos (all the cat videos you could ever possibly want to watch, for example),

other companies use these factors as the basis for commercial offerings, and many of them use AWS extensively for their infrastructures.

One example of this kind of innovative start-up is Hudl. You may not have heard of Hudl, but in the world of high school football, it is a powerhouse. Football uses video extensively, even in high school, for player analysis, play review, and opponent research. Traditionally, managing video at high schools is a pain — it's expensive, uncoordinated, and hard to access. Hudl came along and changed all that.

(continued)

(continued)

High school practices and games are now recorded by local high school representatives, who then upload their videos to Hudl. Hudl stores all the video, tags it with player identification, and creates a database listing every player with all his videos. Someone who wants to scout a player or an upcoming opponent can go to Hudl and easily access the appropriate video from a centralized location rather than root around in a dozen different sites.

Behind the scenes, Hudl is a completely AWS-based application. It not only uses EC2 and S3 for compute and storage but also bases its entire video streaming distribution on CloudFront — every video is stored in a CloudFront-enabled S3 bucket. When someone accesses a specific video, AWS identifies the nearest Amazon edge location to the video requestor and streams the video from that location. In this way, Hudl achieves the best possible streaming performance.

The striking aspect of Hudl is how big it is. As I said, you may not be familiar with the company, but it's a big deal in its domain. Every month, Hudl serves up 600 million videos to its users from its 500 terabytes of video, which totals 1. 8 petabytes of network traffic. To me, this scale of operation is mind-boggling; perhaps most striking is that, despite Hudl's scale, it isn't even a large AWS customer.

The easy access and low cost of AWS enables thousands of innovative start-ups to get a foot in the door. Though IT resources once represented a barrier to entrepreneurship, that barrier has fallen, thanks to Amazon.

Relational Database Service (RDS)

The AWS relational database service (RDS) is set up for a single purpose: to make it easier to run relational databases in AWS. Though that purpose seems obvious, it's important to understand Amazon's motivation for creating the service.

Though the use of nonrelational databases (also known as NoSQL databases, as witnessed by Amazon's own DynamoDB service) is growing, an enormous percentage of applications throughout the world rely on relational databases.

Traditionally, companies employed database administrators to handle the administrative tasks associated with running a relational database: configuring them, backing them up, and monitoring resource consumption and performance, for example. This approach has only two problems: It's expensive and it's error-prone. Nevertheless, companies continue using this approach because, well, because that's the way it's always been done — and even though the typical tasks of a typical database administrator are the same, day in and day out.

It's exactly the kind of opportunity that Amazon looks to address, so it created RDS to help companies take advantage of a less-expensive way to manage their database needs. Left unstated are two other reasons Amazon may offer RDS: Using automation to avoid errors stops people from making mistakes and blaming Amazon for security problems with their poorly administered databases, and it helps AWS users consume more AWS — and makes Amazon more money.

RDS is breathtaking in its simplicity, as this list of features points out:

- ✔ **It supports MySQL, SQL Server, and Oracle.** I'm talking about three popular relational databases here.

- ✔ **Any required patches and updates to the database software are made by RDS.**

- ✔ **RDS makes backups of the database according to a schedule you set.** All backups are stored in S3, where they can be retrieved at any time. (Amazon also performs EBS snapshots to enable database transference, if you want.)

- ✔ **RDS can be run on different instance types.** This flexibility ensures that you have sufficient processing power to support the database performance that your application requires, and that you can scale up or scale down as your needs change.

- ✔ **RDS storage can be standard or Provisioned IOPS.** You can choose the latter storage type if low latency is a critical requirement for your application.

- ✔ **In the case of MySQL and Oracle, RDS lets you seamlessly increase the amount of storage associated with your RDS service.** Unlike traditional database administration, where deploying additional storage to a database is an extended, complex operation fraught with anxiety, RDS makes the process pain-free.

- ✔ **RDS supports multi-instance deployments with a master/slave arrangement, increasing performance and system resiliency.** The master and slave can be placed in separate AZs to further increase resilience. If a database instance crashes, Amazon automatically restarts a new RDS instance and any associated read replicas configured for the RDS instance.

Using RDS

Using RDS is quite straightforward. You can use the AWS Management Console or API to create a database security group, which identifies which IP address (or addresses, which can be defined using a CIDR group) can access the RDS database instance.

After configuring the instance by defining which kind of database you want RDS to manage — along with instance size, licensing conditions, and backup frequency, for example — you launch the database instance. Upon successful launch, AWS provides a unique URL for your database instance that's used to communicate with it. From that point on, you use your RDS database instance as you would a typical database.

RDS scope

Because RDS is a regionally scoped service, RDS databases run inside a given region. Unless the multi-AZ option is selected, the database instance runs inside a single AZ, which you can choose. Use of the database instance URL within the region (from EC2 instances within the region, for example) keeps network traffic within AWS, and you incur no traffic charges. Access from outside the region incurs outbound traffic charges.

RDS cost

RDS imposes a few types of charges:

- ✔ **Instance charges:** You pay a charge for every RDS instance, just as you pay for standard EC2 instances. AWS charges more for RDS instances than the comparable EC2 instance; you can think of the difference in cost as a surcharge for the convenience of RDS. A small, standard MySQL instance costs $.09 per hour, whereas the comparable EC2 instance is $.065 per hour, indicating a $.025 "uplift" for the RDS service itself. The uplift is higher for larger instances, as you may expect.

  You can reduce the overall cost of your RDS database instances by using *reserved* database instances, which operate similarly to EC2 reserved instances.

  Multi-availability zone deployments incur a larger charge, which makes sense, given that you're running multiple instances. If you use RDS with a commercial database support option, there's a further additional charge to cover the database's licensing fees.

- ✔ **Storage:** You pay for standard or Provisioned IOPS storage at normal rates; normal storage is $.10 per gigabyte per month, whereas Provisioned IOPS is $.125.

- ✔ **Network traffic:** You pay standard network traffic rates for data flowing from the database instance. Inbound traffic incurs no charge, whereas outbound traffic starts at $.12 per Gigabyte and declines with volume.

That's it. Really, RDS is so simple and imposes so little extra expense that it doesn't seem worth it to manage your own database setup. RDS adoption is skyrocketing as more and more companies gauge the value that RDS offers versus the minimal incremental cost.

ElastiCache

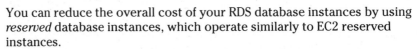

The most common performance bottleneck for webscale applications is the database. It's really a reflection of the laws of physics — queries against databases end up reading data from a spinning disk, which imposes delays because of disk rotation speeds and data transfer speeds, not to mention the overhead of relational database queries. Some tricks can be applied to address this issue; for example, you can set up a master/slave database configuration or set up more slave database servers. At a certain point, however, the overhead of updating all those slave database servers outweighs the performance gains they provide.

Amazon offers some solutions that can be used to mitigate database performance issues. You can use the *high-performance* instances — the ones that have solid-state storage rather than disks. You can also switch to using the DynamoDB service, which offers a high-performance, key-value database that runs on solid-state storage instances. But what if you want to stick with the relational database model but need better performance than you can get with master/slave-based systems?

The answer is *caching* — placing data in high-performance memory so that frequent queries are served without having to go out to a spinning disk to be retrieved. You may have seen the use of caching earlier in this chapter, in my discussion of CloudFront. Database caching uses the same technique to solve a different problem; whereas CDNs are designed to address the issue of accessing data in widely dispersed locations, database caching is used to address the issue of accessing data in centralized locations that require a solution beyond hard drives.

A decade ago, an engineer working on an early webscale application recognized the potential for caching to address his database performance issue; his solution is called *memcached.*

What's the secret to memcached? Essentially, rather than repeatedly query a database to provide the same information to a specific user or to multiple users who want the same data (a list of today's blog entries on an industry news site, for example), you use memcached to store data that's repeatedly accessed in a set of servers that are configured to store the data *in memory.* (That's the *mem* part of memcached.) After the initial retrieval of the data from the database, subsequent queries go to memcached to retrieve the data, thereby achieving much higher levels of performance.

The genius of memcached is that it can be used to accelerate application performance dramatically but doesn't require significant application changes to be implemented — in other words, little application pain, much application gain. The primary change is that database queries add a step before the database query to see whether the necessary data is in memcached; if it is, it's retrieved from memcached; if not, it's retrieved from the database and, before being returned to the requesting application, is placed in memcached. This enables subsequent queries to find the data in memcached and avoid accessing the database.

Memcached is widely used in many applications to improve performance — Wikipedia, Twitter, Flickr, and Craigslist all incorporate memcached in their application architecture. For many of the webscale applications that run on AWS, memcached would be an excellent performance tool.

As with so many other useful technologies that I discuss, even though it's extremely valuable, memcached can be a burden to install, configure, and manage. Therefore, you shouldn't be surprised that Amazon rolled out a service it calls ElastiCache, designed to make using memcached easier.

ElastiCache is *protocol-compliant* with memcached — it supports the same commands as memcached, and existing language libraries that work with memcached also work with ElastiCache. This benefit is important because it means an application can be migrated to ElastiCache without modification.

Perhaps a good way to think about ElastiCache is that it's similar to RDS: an Amazon-managed, operations-simplified service to make services commonly required by many applications both easy and inexpensive to use.

ElastiCache offloads the administrative overhead of running a caching service by

✔ **Creating the server pool based on commands issued via the AWS Management Console or API:** The server pool can be arbitrarily large, composed of servers ranging from micro-instances (213MB of memory per node) to High-Memory Quadruple Extra Large instances (68GB of memory per node). The number of nodes is limited to 20 per AWS account, but more can be requested if needed.

✔ **Managing the pool to ensure caching server availability:** If a server crashes or becomes unavailable, it automatically starts another to replace the failed server. . (Note that this service is available only with caches contained in a single AZ; spreading a cache geographically is not supported).

✔ **Automatically patching servers with necessary software changes and migrating your data from an unpatched version to a new, patched version:** This occurs at infrequent intervals, although at a time and weekday you define, which should be during a low-load period. During this maintenance window downtime, your application retrieves all data directly from the database instead of from ElastiCache.

✔ **Allowing you to grow or shrink the pool with a simple command:** It rebalances your data across the larger or smaller number of servers, all without interrupting service.

Using ElastiCache

ElastiCache is straightforward to use. Using either the AWS Management Console or API, you define the initial ElastiCache configuration, choosing the type of servers you want (in terms of memory capacity) and the number of servers you want in the ElastiCache pool. You then have to associate an ElastiCache security group with one that's associated with your account. After you finish this configuration work, Amazon returns an *endpoint identifier* — a resource name that your applications use to interact with your ElastiCache pool. Using this endpoint identifier, you can then create and retrieve ElastiCache records using key-value techniques.

Why do you have to create an ElastiCache security group and associate it with an account security group? ElastiCache is a service that's separate and distinct from the account used by your applications. It has to be configured to accept traffic from your account, which is why it has its own security group that must be associated with a security group from your account — and preventing your ElastiCache pool from being accessed by anyone else.

ElastiCache scope

ElastiCache is available in all AWS regions.

ElastiCache cost

ElastiCache imposes a cost per server for each server within an ElastiCache pool, ranging from $.022 per hour (micro-instance type) to $2.02 per hour (Quadruple Extra Large type — 64GB memory). Prices vary somewhat by region.

In addition to the server charges, you face network traffic charges for traffic between an EC2 instance in one AZ and an ElastiCache pool in another AZ. The charge is $.01 per gigabyte of data transferred. Each account can transfer 15GB of traffic per month at no charge.

Integrating Additional AWS Services into Your Application

One major benefit of Amazon's approach to application services is that it provides them on a use-if-you-choose basis. Nothing prevents you from using another product or service to implement identical functionality to that offered by one of Amazon's services — even if you decide to run that product or service in AWS.

Two tasks are present in using an AWS core services in your application:

- ✔ Create and configure the service itself.
- ✔ Use the service from within your application.

With respect to the first task, it's typically much easier to use the Amazon alternative for a given service compared to setting up your own. For example, filling out a brief wizard to create, say, a large memcached pool and letting Amazon take care of creating the instances, installing the memcached software, configuring them to talk to one another, and managing their uptime, for example, is far easier than performing all those tasks yourself.

I'm not even mentioning the fact (okay, I am) that your interest is in the functionality of the service, not in managing the service per se. In other words, if you do it yourself, to gain the benefits of the core service, you have to do all the work yourself. By contrast, using the Amazon variant, you gain the benefits of the service without needing to invest any of your precious time administering it.

Depending on your valuation of your time, you can make an evaluation of the financial benefits of allowing Amazon to take on responsibility compared to the cost of the Amazon service. I believe that in most cases you'd be better off using the Amazon service, financially speaking.

With regard to the second task — using the service from within your application — Amazon's approach to offering these services shows its intelligence. Rather than create a different or comprehensive solution that requires you to learn an offering-specific use model, Amazon has typically left the use model undisturbed, or similar to the model used by the alternatives you would use if you decided to implement the functionality yourself. For example, though Amazon's RDS service offers real benefits in terms of database administration tasks, it imposes no change on you for interacting with the databases that are managed by RDS.

It's fair to say that the differences between the established products that Amazon mirrors to create its core services and the Amazon variant is small enough that using the core service isn't especially difficult and doesn't impose a difficult learning curve.

This approach is quite different from the other one to these services, which fall under the Platform-as-a-Service (PaaS) umbrella. In those offerings, similar functionality is offered, but it's so tightly coupled to the PaaS offering that using it requires learning a new approach and sometimes a completely different method for achieving the same result as with established products. As you can probably tell, I'm a strong proponent of the Amazon approach because I feel that it offers the greatest productivity and financial benefits while imposing the smallest disruption in application design and implementation or skill building.

Choosing the Right Additional AWS Service Integration Approach

Taking the right approach to choosing AWS core services to leverage is important. These services are enormous boosts to productivity, but integrating them into your application needlessly doesn't make sense. Here are the guidelines I recommend:

✔ **If this service area is one in which you have no expertise, rely on the AWS experts to run it.** We all are pressed for time, and learning a new skill while under the gun is inefficient and pointless. You're unlikely to be better at it than Amazon is, and you can invest your time more productively in areas where you have the expertise.

✔ **If this service area doesn't provide unique functionality or differentiate your application, rely on the AWS service.** Though your application may be much more satisfying to your users if you have its content locally cached, nobody will buy your service because you personally implemented a set of geographically distributed servers to support low-latency access. You'll be better served by focusing on what's in the content, not on how the content is delivered. Rely on CloudFront for what it's good at, and direct your energies toward something that provides user value.

✔ **If this service is one that you aren't certain you can provide significantly less expensively than Amazon can, rely on Amazon to implement it.** Most IT organizations are terrible at estimating their true costs to deliver a service, and if there's even a chance that Amazon may be more cost-effective, you're better served by leveraging AWS, because Amazon likely runs it far less expensively than you can.

Dealing with AWS Lock-in

Some people are concerned that, by using some of the AWS core (or for that matter, extended) services, they're locked in to AWS for all eternity. That is to say, it will be difficult to shift an application from AWS if they use other AWS services.

Though lock-in is a fair concern — and one that's a perennial worry for IT organizations — I believe that, for most people, the benefits of using AWS far outweigh the issues presented by the potential for lock-in. This statement is true for these reasons:

✔ **Acknowledge your concerns.** When people use the term *lock-in,* most are concerned that if they want to migrate their applications to another location, they'll be unable to do so. My first recommendation is to accurately assess the extent to which your application is locked in — that is, how much your use of AWS services forces your application to run only in AWS. Several AWS services are useful no matter where your application runs. For example, Route 53, the DNS service, can be useful no matter where your application runs. Likewise, CloudFront, the AWS CDN service, can be used even if your application runs elsewhere. In fact, many applications that run in other cloud environments or within on-premises data centers use CloudFront. Consequently, it's important to understand what and how much you're truly locked in by your use of specific AWS services.

✔ **Design for portability.** Make it easy to migrate your application. One time-honored strategy for avoiding lock-in is to create and use an encapsulation layer rather than write directly to a provider API. That way, you can place another set of API calls within the encapsulation layer without disturbing the mainline code within your application. Given the fact that Amazon's services tend to mimic other functionality that you can obtain by implementing software yourself (ElastiCache, for example), this strategy is fairly easy to pursue within your application, and it's certainly far easier with AWS than with alternative PaaS offerings.

✔ **Always understand both sides of the cost-benefit equation.** People put up with lock-in because of the benefits an offering provides compared to the downside of a long-term commitment to the offering. Amazon offers tremendous ease of use and cost effectiveness, so perhaps incurring some lock-in is a trade-off that you're willing to accept.

✔ **Recognize the fear of financial gouging.** The primary reason that people avoid lock-in is a well-founded fear of being taken advantage of, financially speaking. Traditionally, vendors, after achieving lock-in on the part of their customers, inevitably and rather ruthlessly exploited that commitment to increase their financial performance. Fees for forced upgrades, application modules that the customers had no desire for but were forced to pay for as part of a version upgrade, or arbitrarily increased maintenance fees are part of the litany of customer complaints about lock-in. Though there's no way to predict what Amazon may do, to this point its prices have always headed downward — people now pay roughly one-half to two-thirds for an EC2 instance than they did three years ago. Certainly, it's always wise to be concerned about potential financial gouging, though it hasn't been an issue with AWS.

Part III
Using AWS

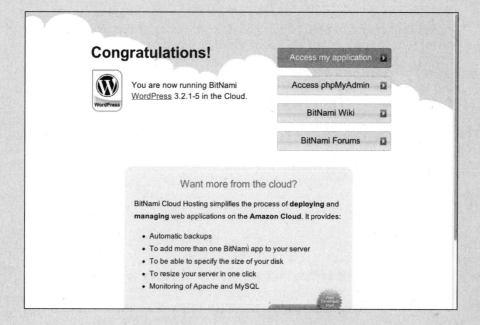

In this part . . .

You have an opportunity to explore AWS in a hands-on manner. You'll start with the basics — locating an AWS application that you will use as the basis for your exploration. But you'll move far beyond that. You'll learn about setting security, connecting to your running application, and even how to easily modify it with additional AWS services to improve its robustness and performance.

✔ Take advantage of opportunities to explore AWS in a hands-on manner.

✔ Learn about setting security for your running application.

✔ See what's what with AWS networking.

✔ Find out how easy it is to modify your application with additional AWS services to improve its robustness and performance.

✔ Check out the article "Pearson OpenClass Runs on AWS" (and more) online at www.dummies.com/extras/amazon webservices.

Chapter 9

AWS Platform Services

● ●

In This Chapter

▶ Sorting out the AWS platform services

▶ Seeing what CloudSearch can offer

▶ Managing video formats with Elastic Transcoder

▶ Making your way through the Simple services

▶ Managing big data with Elastic MapReduce

▶ Data warehousing with Redshift

● ●

A mazon Web Services (AWS) gives you the core services S3, EC2, and Amazon EBS and then all the additional services I cover in Chapter 8, such as IAM, ELB, and Route 53. The AWS *platform* services, however, are the focus of this chapter — they dial up the level of sophistication, by concentrating on these three areas of functionality:

✔ **Services that provide additional application functionality:** For example, Amazon's Simple Queue Service (SQS) provides functionality to enable asynchronous communication between your application and its users or perhaps another application. I call them *extended* services.

✔ **Additional applications that commoditize traditional software offerings that are important but have typically been expensive and complex:** An example is the recently launched Redshift business intelligence application. Many established vendors occupy this space, and their applications have two characteristics in common: They cost a lot, and they're difficult to use. Redshift aims to simplify the building and running of a business intelligence application and to make it much less expensive to operate.

✔ **AWS management tools:** The AWS API and Management Console are useful for managing specific AWS services (individual EC2 instances, for example), but they don't provide much help in managing an aggregation of AWS resources that make up an application. How can you define and manage the collection of resources that comprise your application? Amazon offers three separate tools: Elastic Beanstalk, CloudFormation, and OpsWorks. You should understand the differences between them so that you can select the right one.

AWS platform services offer the same benefits (and generate the same problems) as the core services. Though they provide useful, easy-to-use functionality at a reasonable price, they present the potential for *lock-in* — the investment of so many resources in a solution that changing course is almost impossible. In fact, the lock-in potential is probably greater for platform services because they're more closely tied to the AWS environment than many of the additional AWS services discussed in Chapter 8. Therefore, you must carefully evaluate whether the benefit you receive by embracing these services outweighs any concerns you may have regarding AWS lock-in.

Searching with CloudSearch

Search is one of the most useful capabilities on the web, and huge businesses have been built on search. (Ever hear of Google?) However, not all searches need to cover the entire Internet, and some searches shouldn't be public. For example, you may want to make content on your company's website searchable — or limit who can see the results of a search.

The challenge for many companies that want to enable search on their websites or other content repositories is that the quality of the typical search tools associated with content management systems is, to put it bluntly, awful. The situation is worse for companies that want to make a *content repository* — a big collection of documents dropped down into a file system, rather than an actual content management system — searchable. These environments have no search mechanism (no matter how flawed) available.

Traditionally, if you wanted to make a sophisticated search capability available for your content, whether contained in a content management system or plopped down in a disorganized content repository, your options were unappealing:

✔ **Buy expensive proprietary search software and use it to organize search capabilities for your content.** This option requires a large financial outlay and makes sense only for high-value content.

✔ **Download and use open source search software, which is both capable and inexpensive.** This option makes search financially viable for content that isn't necessarily high-value but can be made more useful with search capabilities.

The downside is that you still have to

✔ **Locate hardware on which to install the search software.** You may have to purchase equipment to support your search software.

✔ **Install and configure the search software on the hardware you obtain.**
You need to have detailed knowledge of the search software. Most
people have little expertise in this arcane area, but it can't be avoided if
you want to enable search on your content.

✔ **Manage the hardware and software to ensure that your search software remains up and running.** If your content repository grows to the
point that the indexes associated with it outgrow the hardware you
obtained originally, you're back to the same (unappetizing!) buy-hardware-and-configure-the-software routine you started with.

Obviously, this situation is unsatisfactory — and ripe for disruption. Amazon,
sensing an opportunity, launched CloudSearch early in 2012. CloudSearch
is based on technology that Amazon uses on its own website, which should
indicate its capability as well as its scalability.

CloudSearch is based on *A9,* a search company that Amazon incubated a
number of years ago, when it realized that the ability to search — and search
accurately — would be important to its business. A9 is used for searching on
Amazon and its subsidiaries. Though the original A9 focused on text search
and relevant results, the A9 technology team has branched out to image
search and social search, a category that relies on user interaction to add context to regular text search.

CloudSearch is capable of searching structured content, such as word processing files, and unstructured content — commonly referred to as *free text,*
or unstructured collections of text-like web pages or forum posts.

Using CloudSearch is relatively straightforward, though a bit tricky to understand. The content you want to search has to be indexed (the data within the
content is evaluated so that individual words can be located) so that indexes
about the word (as well as the documents associated with the word) can be
built. For example, if you want to be able to search a large number of documents about zoos, you need to build an index so that in a search for the word
elephant, the search software can return every document containing the
word *elephant.*

You upload the data you want to search into a CloudSearch domain, where
the given domain name is the name of a searchable documents database. For
data uploads, CloudSearch uses SDF (short for Search Data Format). Though
CloudSeach can create SDF on the fly for certain types of data, such as PDF
and Word files, for others you have to create the SDF documents yourself in
order to upload your data. SDF documents can be formatted in either XML
or JSON — two common standards for describing data collections. An SDF
record is nothing more than a formatted set of key-value items describing the
data you want to be able to search on.

After you upload the SDF documents, CloudSearch analyzes them and creates indexes of all the items you've indicated you want to be able to search on. For example, if you create a set of SDF documents outlining all players in a sport for a given year, you may search on the position played or the number of games played in the year. CloudSearch creates indexes on all fields you identify as searchable. Then you can execute searches against your domain on the fields you've identified as searchable.

You must also create *access policies,* which are analogous to EC2 security groups. You define the IP addresses that you want to allow access to CloudSearch, for both search access and domain administrative access. (Typically, you'd allow *all* IP addresses to search via CloudSearch because the most common use case is allowing visitors to a website to search information on the website, but you may restrict search access to employees of your company or a small number of partners.)

Though you can execute searches from the AWS management console, the most common search is conducted via the CloudSearch API or the CloudSearch CLI (command-line interface). If you're adding search capabilities to a website, you use the API method to perform searches on your CloudSearch domain.

CloudSearch resources

CloudSearch maintains a high performance level by keeping all indexes you've created within the memory of EC2 instances. Now, the obvious question is exactly how many EC2 instances will the CloudSearch domain require? This number, however, isn't one that you control; AWS automatically calculates how many instances your search domain requires and their size. CloudSearch supports three instances sizes: Small, Large, and Extra Large. If required, CloudSearch splits your domain indexes across multiple instances in order to retain them in memory and support fast search performance.

CloudSearch scope

CloudSearch is regionally scoped, which affects where you deploy your CloudSearch domain. If the website you're enabling with CloudSearch is in a particular region, there's no fee for network traffic if your CloudSearch domain resides in the same region. Of course, given that CloudSearch is accessible via an AWS API, searches can be executed from anywhere on the Internet, as well as within other AWS regions.

CloudSearch cost

Here are the hourly instance prices:

- **Small search:** $.10 per hour
- **Large search:** $.39 per hour
- **Extra Large search:** $.55 per hour

PBS runs on AWS (CloudSearch)

If you've joined the *Downton Abbey* craze on public television, you know how popular PBS is. PBS presents quality programming on public television stations throughout the United States, and it's renowned as the home of many highbrow British dramatic series. Part of the PBS strategy is to complement successful series with additional material and video content so that it can build more loyal audiences and increase viewership.

PBS offers streaming video on the web; in addition, over the past few years it has begun to offer streaming video to portable devices like mobile phones and tablets. For all the video PBS serves up, it uses AWS. PBS not only uses EC2 and S3 for processing and hosting videos but also leverages CloudFront to distribute video content — up to a petabyte of content every month.

More recently, as part of an initiative to more deeply support mobile devices, PBS has placed additional emphasis on creating mobile applications. Part of this mobile initiative requires better-quality searching to enable users on limited form factors to still be able to find and enjoy targeted video content. As part of this mobile initiative, PBS uses ElasticSearch to enable search. ElasticSearch offers greater scalability and better performance, and it frees PBS personnel from having to manage search software and infrastructure.

And here are the data transfer prices per month:

- ✔ **First 10TB:** $.12 per gigabyte
- ✔ **Next 40TB:** $.09 per gigabyte
- ✔ **Next 100TB:** $.07 per gigabyte

The issue of traffic prices may not be significant, because search results return text documents (both XML and JSON are text-based), which do not require much network traffic to send, so your traffic charges will probably not be that high.

You face incidental charges for batch uploads and re-indexing, which shouldn't add significantly to your overall CloudSearch bill.

Managing Video Conversions with Elastic Transcoder

Elastic Transcoder, a relatively new service (started in 2013), is conceptually quite simple: It converts video files from one format to another.

Video transcoding is a widely applied computing task. You'd have to have been living under a rock not to have observed that video is everywhere. Though people have used dedicated video-recording devices for more than 40 years, the rise of smartphones (initiated by the launch of the iPhone in 2007) has supercharged the video trend. Spurred on by the iPhone and, more recently, the iPad, video-enabled smartphones and tablets have flooded the market. Amazon even provides a family of tablets branded Kindle Fire. Every one of them is now a video recording device.

The ease of sharing video via video-hosting services has skyrocketed as well; at the time this book was written, 72 hours of video were uploaded to YouTube every minute of the day. Though it may seem now and then that all 72 of those hours feature cats in funny or heartwarming videos, the truth is that video is now a communication medium used by all types of organizations for all kinds of purposes — entertainment, education, documentation, evidence, and a thousand others.

For many video creators, this explosion of video presents an embarrassment of riches — so many output devices are available, each of which has its own preferred format, that making all the required versions of video to support customer preferences is challenging. Thus, *transcoding* — the conversion of one video format to another — is now a critical capability for video-producing entities. Being able to take a source video and prepare all the versions required for widely used display devices is now critical for organizations that want to leverage the power of visual communication.

AWS has been part of the transcoding mix for a long time. In fact, when Netflix first started its video-streaming service, AWS was there as part of its video-transcoding strategy. AWS combined with video transcoding is a natural fit: S3 is a great choice to store the original and transcoded versions of a video, and EC2 can naturally host the compute-intensive transformation process. No statistics are available to indicate what percentage of total AWS workload is represented by video transcoding, but it's probably a significant portion.

The workload associated with transcoding can be erratic — in fact, depending on the organization and the type of videos it creates, transcoding workloads may vary by as much as 1,000 percent over a given timeframe. If your organization is using AWS for transcoding purposes, the service may be perfect from an ease-of-access point of view, but such highly variable workloads impose significant management challenges. Translation? You'll likely need to grow and shrink your EC2 processing pool quite a bit to meet transcoding requirements.

Given these facts, the launch of Elastic Transcoder was a foregone conclusion: It helps organizations perform useful video transcoding in AWS but removes the management overhead.

Elastic Transcoder, which is designed to simplify common transcoding tasks, lets you designate videos that need to be transcoded and automatically pulls individual videos from S3 storage, performs the transcoding operation, and then places the transcoded versions into S3 storage.

Using Elastic Transcoder, you specify the characteristics of the output format you want for your videos, though it also provides a number of preconfigured popular output formats for iPhone, iPad, and, of course, Kindle Fire.

You can operate Elastic Transcoder from the AWS Management Console, but it also offers a RESTful interface so that applications can call the service on their own. The RESTful interface is likely to represent the majority of the service's use because many online video applications will transition to Elastic Transcoder, given its ease of use. Amazon provides language SDKs (software development kits) in a number of languages such as Python and PHP to reduce the burden on developers; instead of having to call the RESTful service directly.

Every transcoding job submitted to Elastic Transcoder is represented as a JSON object, containing the name of the bucket that holds the file to be transcoded, a set of configurations that you want applied to the file (the output formats you want, for example), and a location in which to place the transcoded video.

Elastic Transcoder operates quite simply:

1. Identify the video(s) you want to convert.

2. Create an Elastic Transcoder pipeline or use an existing pipeline.

   A *pipeline* in this context is simply a service endpoint to which jobs are submitted. An AWS account can have several different pipelines, which allows you to separate and prioritize transcoding tasks, if you want. You can, however, have only one pipeline.

3. Use AWS Identity and Access Management (IAM) to create a role for Elastic Transcoder. (For more on IAM, check out Chapter 8.)

   This step enables Elastic Transcoder to access your resources (say, video files in S3 buckets) to perform transcoding services. If Elastic Transcoder isn't given appropriate access rights, it cannot access your resources and perform transcoding.

4. (Optional) Create a preset containing the settings that you want Elastic Transcoder to apply during the transcoding process. If you are using an existing pipeline, you can use an existing preset or create a new preset.

   Amazon provides presets to support popular transcoding operations such as formatting for the iPhone, which can be used instead of creating your own preset.

5. Create a job, which represents the transcoding operation for a specific video.

   The job is submitted in JSON notation. When the service was originally launched, each output format required a different job; today, you can request multiple outputs in a single job, which reduces your network transfer costs a bit.

6. (Optional) Configure Elastic Transcoder to use AWS's Simple Notification Service (SNS) to provide you with status updates as the job is executed.

7. After the transcoding job is complete, do something with the output videos stored in S3.

   You can retrieve the video objects from the S3 buckets in which they've been placed, or you can allow access to them from the bucket (with appropriate Access Control List [ACL] settings to allow access, of course). You can even configure the S3 bucket to serve as a CloudFront origin bucket, which then caches the video at the AWS CloudFront end-points. (For more on CloudFront, see Chapter 8.)

That's all there is to using Elastic Transcoder. Amazon takes care of managing the service, the instances on which the service runs, and the queues (pipelines) associated with submitting jobs to the service. You're only responsible for managing the original video file, interacting with Elastic Transcoder, and doing something with the output video files. In other words, Elastic Transcoder enables you to benefit from the process of transcoding videos without suffering the headache of having to manage its details.

Elastic Transcoder scope

Elastic Transcoder is *regionally scoped:* An individual pipeline resides in a single region, although the service, because it has a RESTful interface, can use S3 buckets associated with your account in other regions.

At the time this book was written, Elastic Transcoder wasn't available in all AWS regions, though you can expect that Amazon will soon make Elastic Transcoder available throughout all AWS regions.

Elastic Transcoder cost

Elastic Transcoder offers quite a simple cost model: AWS charges a fixed price per minute of transcoded video. For standard-definition (SD) video, the cost is around $.015 per minute; for high-definition (HD) video, the cost is around $.030 per minute. The cost is slightly higher in certain regions, but no SD transcoding (as of this writing) costs more than $.018 per minute, nor does HD transcoding cost more than $.036 per minute.

Amazon offers a free tier of Elastic Transcoder use. Every month, the first 20 minutes of SD transcoding, or the first 10 minutes of HD transcoding, is provided for free.

Simple Queue Service

It's time now for my favorite AWS service: Simple Queue Service. (It's a geeky choice, I know — but what can I say?) The queue is an awesome system capability, vastly underused by most application designers — which is unfortunate because you end up with complicated, fragile applications that could be improved if they were integrated with queue services.

Now that you're undoubtedly excited about the queue, what exactly is it? The *queue* concept is dead-easy to understand: It's a communication mechanism between two processing resources that allows them to collaborate on work without needing to operate in a synchronous manner. This description may seem complicated, but the fact is that you use queues in real-life all the time.

Say you need your shirts laundered. You can go to the laundry service, hand over your shirts, wait around for the service to finish washing and pressing them, and then take them home. That's one way to do it, but I think you'll agree that it wastes a tremendous amount of your time. You can refer to this mode of operation as *synchronous:* You call on the laundry service and then wait for it to be complete.

A different way to get your shirts laundered — and the way this service gets done universally throughout the world — is that you take your shirts to the laundry, drop them off, get a claim ticket along with an estimate of when to return to pick them up, go do other errands (which may include dropping off your shoes at a shoe repair place to get new heels installed), and then return on the estimated readiness date to pick up your nice, fresh, clean shirts.

This second mode is *asynchronous.* You aren't forced to wait for your shirts to be finished — you just put them into the laundry service's work queue and you get a ticket that is then used to track the job. You return at the given time, having allowed the laundry to do its work while letting you go off and do other (hopefully) productive work.

The queue is the ideal tool for a job that's performed by one service and doesn't require the calling service to wait for the results. Elastic Transcoder, the AWS service I discuss in the earlier section "Managing Video Conversions with Elastic Transcoder," is a good example. Many applications that can use video transcoding don't wait for the transcoding process to complete. Imagine a community website that allows you to upload a video and then makes it available to visitors in formats that are convenient to them, such as iPhone, iPad, Kindle Fire, or a webpage. If you're running the website, you don't want to force users to wait around while videos are transcoded, do you? Especially because the videos being submitted for other people to view, there's no point in making people wait for the transcoding process to complete. The video can be submitted and placed on the queue to be transcoded, leaving the submitter free to do something else (such as explore the rest of your website).

Many, many processing tasks conform to the asynchronous use pattern; as I hint in my Queue Love confession, there are undoubtedly more potential queue use cases than aren't taken advantage of by application designers, which is too bad.

Simple Queue Service overview

SQS lets you create a queue in AWS and then place and retrieve messages from that queue. However, you can also set permissions on a queue to allow access to it that's broader than your account. Being able to enable a broader population to use your queue is useful when you want to allow outside entities, whether a restricted group (say, partners of your company) or the general public, to access it — particularly, being able to submit tasks to your application while not requiring the submitter to wait until the job is complete.

Naturally enough, Amazon has designed SQS to be extremely robust with very high uptime, which imposes some design constraints that, in turn, affect the way SQS operates. You should understand the operation of SQS to ensure that you aren't taken by surprise by the service's behavior.

SQS allows multiple message submitters and retrievers to share a queue, which is a fancy way to say that you can allow your queue to have multiple processes placing messages on the queue and removing them. You can, for example, operate a number of AWS instances designed to retrieve uploads of videos for Elastic Transcoder, ensuring that no transcoding request is delayed by a large job ahead of it in the queue.

One way that Amazon makes SQS robust is that it implements redundant queues behind the scenes; if one queue fails, another, mirror queue can continue operating until the failed queue is restarted. This strategy ensures that no resource failure can ever make SQS unavailable.

However, because messages may be spread across the redundant resources, they may not be delivered in the order they were placed on the queue. Unlike some other queue products, SQS doesn't guarantee first-in, first-out (FIFO) delivery. If a submitter splits a job into several messages, the receiver cannot be sure that they will be retrieved in the proper order.

Though nonguaranteed delivery order isn't a problem for many queue-based applications, those that require an ordered sequence of messages need to create a *supra-queue* coordination mechanism; a sequence order number that's part of the queue message would be appropriate. A message submitter who places multiple messages that are part of a single overall job may place a sequence order number of *one* in the first message and a total message number of *three* in that message, indicating to the reader that it needs to receive three messages to make up the entire submission. The receiving application would read the total message number in the first message, recognize that it needs three messages to receive the complete submission, and continue reading until it had retrieved messages two and three.

Despite the lack of a FIFO mechanism. Amazon guarantees that each message is delivered at least once. Until the message is retrieved, it's retained in the queue, waiting to be read.

The potential for messages to be retained until they're read can cause a problem if no reader ever requests a message. If this situation occurs often enough, the queue can become backed up with unread messages — and with enough unread messages, even AWS can get overloaded. Therefore, SQS has a message time-out period that defines how long a message is retained in the queue. The default retention period, set at four days, can be adjusted to meet the requirements of the application.

Another SQS characteristic to be aware of is that queue messages remain in the queue until they're deleted — even when they've been read. AWS does this because, even if a message is read, it may not be fully acted on — the reading application may crash or otherwise fail to complete the task associated with the message. To avoid situations in which the queue message is read but not fully acted upon due to resource failure, AWS implements a *visibility time-out:* While a message is being read, it's locked for a period to ensure that no other reader can access it. However, one key task for a reader is to delete the message when the task associated with the message is complete; if the reader fails to delete the message, another process can — when the visibility time-out expires — read the message again and perform the task associated with the message.

Obviously, redundantly performing work isn't a good idea (generally speaking) and, depending on the application, may even cause problems. Therefore, your reading applications *must* delete SQS messages after they have completed their tasks. The message size in SQS is restricted to 64KB — for many applications, perhaps not a significant restriction; if the complete task is to place someone's name in a database, 256KB is probably more than ample. On the other hand, you can easily envision queue-based tasks that can be far larger. In the video transcoding example from earlier in this chapter, almost every video submitted would be far larger than 64KB. The reason for this size restriction is, again, to prevent SQS from being overloaded with requests — too many overlarge messages can cause SQS to choke.

So what can you do to overcome this size restriction? It's straightforward: Rather than place the large data payload (in the example, the large video file) in the message, you can, for example, put it in an S3 bucket. You then place the S3 bucket name in the message and place the message in the queue. The queue reader reads the message and retrieves the video from the S3 bucket based on the information contained in the message. This indirect pointer technique is well-established and commonly used with SQS.

SQS scope

SQS is regionally scoped. Each queue is associated with a particular region; when you create an SQS queue, you define which AWS region will serve as your queue's home. However, because SQS is an AWS-provided service, you don't have to place it in a particular availability zone. In fact, Amazon undoubtedly runs each SQS queue in multiple availability zones to ensure robustness and to prevent failure in the unlikely event of an entire availability zone going offline.

The restriction of an SQS queue to a particular region shouldn't be viewed as a problem; each queue comes with a URL to which users can submit jobs from anywhere. Given that AWS doesn't charge for inbound traffic — and therefore no traffic charge is associated with submitting jobs to an SQS queue — the region restriction of SQS has no significant repercussions.

On the other hand, if you're planning to have an EC2 instance within your own account submit messages to the SQS queue, you want the instances and the queue to reside in the same region. Otherwise, the EC2 instances incur charges for traffic sent interregionally — even if they're at the smaller inter-regional cost.

SQS cost

SQS costs $.50 per million SQS requests, where a *request* is any kind of SQS API call. That means both message submission and retrieval, as well as set-ting a queue attribute and the like would incur a charge. Naturally, message submission and retrieval represent the vast preponderance of SQS API calls, so those are the sources of most SQS costs. Up to ten messages (if they're less than the 64KB message limit) can be batched together to count as only one submission.

SQS also offers a free-use tier; you receive up to 1 million SQS requests per month for free.

Don't forget that you also pay for traffic sent out of AWS, starting at $.12 per gigabyte and descending as more traffic is sent. The first gigabyte of out-bound traffic is free each month.

SQS use

I hope that my introduction to SQS and my overview of the service piques your interest in using it. Queues are extremely useful, and SQS is useful, robust, and extremely cost-effective.

The most daunting challenge for most people in using queues is to think about application design differently. Rather than picture a serial progression of tasks within an application, with each task waiting on a previous task to be completed, you have to consider how to disconnect two tasks, make it possible for them to communicate, and notify one another when work is to be done.

Using a queue allows an application to avoid all this waiting around and offer a better user experience — which is important. I encourage you to experiment with SQS to see how you can partition your applications into independent entities that use queues to submit tasks to, and retrieve tasks from, one another. After you get the hang of using queues, you'll start to see lots of opportunities to use them, and you'll likely rethink many of your application design decisions.

Simple Notification Service

As the saying goes, Simple Notification Service (SNS) does what it says on the can: It sends notifications about an event via a convenient mechanism as a way of alerting a person or a computer program that something interesting just happened.

The simplicity of this description belies the power of notifications, however. Consider the case of a system administrator who's responsible for the proper operation of an application within AWS. Clearly, if something stops working properly, she needs to know immediately.

One way to make the administrator aware of application problems is to have her be logged on to AWS at all times, to obsessively check the state of the application every second (which is neither efficient nor fun).

Another way is to use a notification: After defining at least one condition that the administrator needs to know about (and, presumably, respond to), you create a mechanism to respond to the condition(s). When the mechanism identifies one of these conditions — errors show up on database reads, for example — it sends a notification to one or more people to evaluate the issue and decide whether to take action.

Notifications can be sent in a variety of ways — via e-mail or SMS messages, for example. Moreover, notifications don't even have to be sent to humans; they can be sent (via e-mail) to a program that takes action whenever it receives a message with a given subject.

The notification is a simple concept but extremely powerful in use. System administrators swear by them (and, occasionally, *at them,* such as when they receive them at 3 in the morning or while on holiday).

You may notice a similarity between SNS and SQS — don't both involve an entity submitting a message to a service that then delivers it? Yes, but with SQS, the entity receiving the message has to take action in order to receive it; with SNS, the service sends the message to the receiving entity automatically, with no action required on the part of the receiving entity. This concept is referred to as *pull* versus *push*: With SQS, the receiving entity has to pull the information; whereas with SNS, the information is pushed to the receiving entity.

The distinction between pull and push is useful in situations where the event that the receiving entity is on the lookout for is infrequent but extremely important. You wouldn't want a receiving entity polling a message queue every second for an event that occurs once a month; it would be extremely expensive in terms of processing to pay for constant polling on the off chance that this month's event will happen in the next second. With a notification service, receiving entities (which, again, can be either humans or computer programs) can perform their other work, secure in the knowledge that they'll know almost immediately when the occasional event occurs.

SNS overview

I hope that the foregoing makes clear that notifications are extremely useful. On the other hand, they're a fair amount of work to set up and, if a large volume of notifications are being sent, they can be a lot of work to manage. Sounds like a perfect opportunity for AWS, right? You are correct.

SNS operates as an AWS service that you create within your account. After you create the service, you're ready to begin distributing notifications.

You can — and probably will — have multiple notification streams within your notification service. You may have one stream for events and messages from your application to system administrators to alert them to possible problems with your application. You may have another notification stream for your application to send messages to users of your application. You almost certainly wouldn't want to mingle messages for those two very different audiences such that one could read notification messages intended for the other.

SNS allows you to send messages to different audiences (or, indeed, to different individuals within the same audience) by setting up separate topics. A *topic,* in this context, is a specified stream of notifications that one or more entities can publish. I use the term *entities* because the topic publisher can be a software component (say, a database that sends notifications whenever certain conditions occur) or a person (someone who logs on to the AWS Management Console and uses it to send a message, for example). Likewise, the notification recipient can be either a human or a software component.

Queue messages — like the messages in Amazon's SQS service — can be retrieved by only one entity; by contrast, notifications such as the ones sent by SNS are sent to any entity that is signed up to receive notifications about a particular topic.

Obviously, one key requirement for (successful) notifications is the ability to control who can send or receive notifications — and just because someone wants to receive notifications doesn't mean he should.

The method that SNS uses to control who (or what) can send or receive notifications on a given topic is the *topic policy.* As the owner of the topic, you can create policies to control who can sign up to send or receive a topic's notifications. (The entities that do the sending or receiving are known within SNS as principals.)

This list describes your choices for who receives topic notifications:

- ✔ **Individual:** You can identify by policy specific individuals within your account who are permitted to send or receive notifications. SNS is integrated with AWS Identity and Access Management (IAM) to manage the individual identities that are SNS principals.

- ✔ **Accounts:** You can identify AWS accounts that can act as principals with respect to a particular topic. The AWS account identifier is used to denote an account that can act as a principal for the SNS topic.

- ✔ **Public:** You can allow anyone to act as a principal for your SNS topic. It's probably a bad idea for the public to be able to *send* notifications, but it could very well make sense to allow anyone who is interested in a given topic to receive notifications. Though my SNS examples thus far focus on technical personnel who may need to receive notifications (such as system administrators), you may like a large audience of individuals who aren't part of your account to be notified of an event. An obvious example is to send an e-mail to all subscribers notifying them of a special offer your company is making available — you would simply publish the notification once, and then every person subscribed would receive a notification.

Speaking of everyone getting a notification, you may ask exactly how notifications can be received. SNS is rich in notification protocol options:

- **SMS messages sent to a phone number:** The phone number has to be registered with SNS, naturally enough, but SNS can send topic notifications via SMS. (Charges for receiving the SMS message apply, of course.)

- **E-mail sent to an e-mail address:** This is a common and popular method of sending notifications. The person who registers to receive the notification receives them via whatever e-mail application she uses.

- **HTTP/HTTPS:** A web application can receive notifications over the general public Internet or via secure HTTP. The assumption is that you have a web-based application receiving traffic directed to a URL that's listening on the appropriate port; when a notification is received, the web application displays the message on a web page. Of course, the web-based application doesn't have to display it; it can do any number of other things with the notification, including forwarding it via another protocol or storing it in a database. A good use case for this notification protocol is system administrators who want an ongoing and constantly updated display of application and system events.

- **Simple Queue Service (SQS):** This hero of the previous section can also be a notification recipient. You may wonder why you would want to use SQS as an SNS recipient. It makes sense if you consider this scenario: You need to be sure that you receive and act on important notifications. If you have an application that *must* be sure that recipients receive notification of events, how can you be sure that the notifications will occur? After all, e-mail may not reach its destination; SMS (at least in my experience) often seems flaky, and it's not easy to be sure that a web application is running at the right time to receive a notification. Using SQS ensures that a notification is available and can be acted on no matter what; the queue message remains in the queue (up to the message discard time) for as long as it takes for a second entity to retrieve the message. The use of SQS as the SNS delivery protocol increases SNS robustness.

One important requirement to keep in mind with regard to SNS is that any initial recipient sign-ups have to be confirmed, to prevent malicious SNS sign-ups that can flood the recipient with unwanted notifications or, worse, impose significant costs (such as SMS fees). Each notification protocol requires confirmation from the recipient that they (or it) want to receive notifications on the topic. This strategy can be a bit challenging for nonhuman recipients. For example, a web application still receives an initial confirmation message from SNS and must be able to receive, decipher, and respond to the message before beginning to receive notifications. The application's code first must be able to differentiate between the initial invitation and subsequent notifications and then respond correctly to the invitation. Otherwise, SNS decides that the topic subscription was a mistake and refuses to forward notifications to the application.

SNS scope

SNS is a regionally scoped service. However, SNS operates as an AWS service and is accessible from outside the region; therefore, external programs can use SNS. Each topic, upon creation, is assigned an Amazon Resource Name, or ARN. An entity, either human or application, that wants to publish a notification calls the SNS service with the topic's ARN as one of the arguments. Likewise, notifications can be received outside of AWS; SNS forwards them via the selected protocol to wherever the notification recipient is located.

SNS cost

SNS has probably the most unusual pricing of any AWS service because of the various protocols it supports for notification delivery.

The basic service is cost-effective: $.50 per million SNS API requests and you don't pay for the first million SNS API requests per month. However, the cost of the notifications themselves varies, depending on the protocol:

- ✔ **HTTP/HTTPS ($.06 per 100,000 notifications):** The first 100,000 notifications per month are free.

- ✔ **E-mail/e-mail-JSON ($2.00 per 100,000 e-mail/e-mail-JSON requests):** The first 1,000 requests per month are free. You would use an e-mail-JSON request to send an e-mail notification to an application rather than to a person; the application parses the JSON text to evaluate the notification and then takes an action in response.

- ✔ **SMS ($.75 per 100 notifications):** The first 100 notifications per month are free.

- ✔ **SQS:** No charge.

Protocol	*Cost*	*Note*
HTTP/HTTPS	$.06 per 100,000 notifications	The first 100,000 notifications per month are free.
E-mail/E-mail-JSON	$2.00 per 100,000 E-mail/E-mail-JSON requests	The first 1,000 requests are free each month. You would use an E-mail-JSON request if you were sending an e-mail notification to an application rather than a person; the application parses the JSON to evaluate the notification and then takes some action in response.
SMS	$.75 per 100 notifications	The first 100 notifications per month are free.
SQS	None	

For notifications sent outside AWS, a typical outbound traffic charge applies.

Simple E-Mail Service

Let's face it: E-mail is the hardest-working service on the Internet. Though people complain endlessly about it and continually talk about the up-and-comers that will make e-mail obsolete (Facebook, anyone?), e-mail continues to flood the Internet — and it's growing all the time.

E-mail is an extremely effective way to communicate. It excels at transmitting large amounts of data (large as compared to Twitter, for example), and it has the virtue of providing a long-lasting record of communication, making it easy to refer to a communication from the past or to reinitiate a discussion by forwarding a previous e-mail.

Beyond its virtues as a personal communication tool, e-mail is an excellent vehicle for business communication. Many businesses use e-mail to send information to their customers for many purposes — to acknowledge an order, track a package, respond to a question, and so on.

When tied to recipient demographics, e-mail can be a powerful marketing tool. You can carry out tightly targeted communication at a fraction of the cost of traditional direct marketing mechanisms, with e-mail delivery almost instantaneous compared to "snail mail" timeframes.

One fly remains in the e-mail ointment, though: managing the e-mail server software. It's finicky, it requires constant configuration and tinkering, and it's difficult to manage when e-mail traffic can fluctuate wildly. Companies can use e-mail services, thereby avoiding the management headache, but the high cost of such services can create other headaches.

So there you have it — a core service, one with high and highly variable loads and one that is difficult to manage and costly to boot. It sounds like a job for AWS. And Amazon has stepped up to tackle the job, providing an AWS-based service that provides enormous scalability at a reasonable price: Simple Email Service (SES).

SES provides an easy-to-use e-mail service that can support a high volume of e-mail. It probably wouldn't surprise you to learn that SES is based on Amazon's own internally developed e-mail application, because Amazon sends out a ton of e-mail every day. Amazon merely polished up its existing service so that it could be used as part of AWS.

SES overview

SES is straightforward, conceptually. E-mail is a well-established set of standards and protocols, so SES implements and supports established e-mail practices. SES supports the Simple Mail Transfer Protocol (SMTP), a venerable protocol for sending e-mail. You submit your e-mail to SES, using one of the supported integration mechanisms, and it sends the e-mail to the recipient — easy as pie.

Of course, this simple story has a few complications, all related to the seductive usefulness of e-mail. Just as companies have found e-mail to be an incredibly easy way to engage with customers and prospects, so too have malefactors who send endless amounts of spam. The potential for SES to be used to distribute spam is quite high, with these potentially terrible consequences for Amazon:

✔ SES can be perceived as a haven for spam, which can lead to customers not wanting to use SES, or perhaps AWS itself.

✔ In an attempt to limit spam, outside parties, such as ISPs, may refuse to accept e-mail from AWS on behalf of their customers.

✔ If an ISP's refusal to accept e-mail makes SES unusable, honest users of SES would be unfairly penalized for using the same AWS service as spammers.

Obviously, none of these outcomes is acceptable to Amazon, so it has implemented a number of SES requirements to avoid problems. Because of these requirements, getting started and then using SES requires you to deal with these constraints that are important to understand as you prepare to use SES:

1. When you sign up to use SES, you must register the domain from which you will send e-mail (say, `example.com`). Amazon approves your domain registration in a day or two, so be prepared to work on something else while you're waiting. Amazon refers to this process as *verifying your domain.*

2. After your domain is verified, the individual e-mail addresses from which you'll send e-mail must be verified as well. SES sets a limit of 1,000 verified addresses, so the service is more appropriate for marketing campaigns and application output than for general corporate e-mail support.

3. When you get started, Amazon places you in an SES *sandbox,* in which you're limited in what addresses you can send e-mail to — these addresses need to be from within your own domain, which prevents you from immediately spamming someone. During the sandbox period, you're limited to 200 e-mails per day, all of which have to be sent to e-mail addresses that are verified by Amazon.

4. When you have established your trustworthiness, Amazon will move you to the Big Leagues: production SES.

Even though you're no longer rationed to the sandbox limits, you're not permitted full, unfettered SES use. As you begin, you're limited in the number of e-mails you can send in any single day, and you're limited in how many you can send in any single second. As Amazon gains more confidence in your use of SES, it raises these limits.

AWS offers four ways to interact with SES and send e-mails:

- ✓ **The AWS Management Console:** The console allows you to create and send e-mails. This method, which isn't very efficient, is offered primarily to let you test your SES setup and service.

- ✓ **The SES API:** You can write directly to the SES API in order to make web service calls and interact with the SES API interface.

- ✓ **Programming language SMTP modules:** SMTP is a venerable protocol — most programming languages have modules or libraries that enable the sending of e-mail via SMTP. Note that the use of a programming language SMTP module requires a special SES username and password (different from the account username and password), which must be requested via the AWS Management Console.

- ✓ **AWS programming language SDKs:** Amazon itself offers SDK libraries encapsulating the SES API, which can be used in writing programs to interact with SES.

No matter which interaction method you use, SES dutifully sends off however many e-mails you tell it to. In addition to faithfully sending e-mail, SES collects a number of statistics for you — the number of messages that were delivered, bounced (both temporarily and permanently), or rejected and the number of *complaints* (e-mail refused by a receiving ISP based on its perception of your e-mail as spam). As for rejected e-mails, before sending your e-mail, SES passes it through content filters designed to weed out spam and content that may be perceived as spam; SES lets you know if any sent message is rejected.

Sending e-mails via a programming module or an AWS SDK is relatively easy. It usually calls for setting some variables (the send-to e-mail address, sent-from e-mail address, e-mail body content, and the like), and a call to "send" the e-mail to the SMTP service.

Usually, the most difficult part of sending an e-mail is composing the message body — deciding whether it should be plain text or HTML, or both, and how to format the body so that the recipient finds it interesting enough to open. SES doesn't help you with that decision, although it supports both HTML and plain text e-mail. On the other hand, people tend to futz around with e-mail a lot, to get the formatting correct, and then don't touch the formatting settings for months (or years). This task is where the sandbox comes in handy — it's a place to experiment, to be sure that you nail the appropriate e-mail design.

SES scope

SES is regionally scoped and, like all platform services, is accessible from anywhere on the Internet, so it's quite conceivable to use SES as a stand-alone service, with e-mails sent from an application residing in your own data center.

SES cost

SES costs $.10 per 1,000 e-mails. If you use EC2 or Elastic Beanstalk, you can send 2,000 e-mails free per day.

Standard outbound network traffic charges apply to SES messages, which are based on total traffic size. If you send humongous e-mails, you'll rack up more of a charge than if you send tiny, one-line e-mails.

You're also charged for sending e-mail attachments, at the rate of $.12 per gigabyte.

SES considers an e-mail message to be one message sent to one e-mail address. So if you send one e-mail to 100 different recipients, it counts as 100 e-mail messages.

Simple Workflow Service

Simple Workflow Service (SWF) addresses a common challenge in large, distributed applications: how to coordinate all the work between the components of the application, especially when some of the work carried out by a component may depend on the successful completion of work by another component. SWF is the commercial offering of a service that Amazon implemented for its own, internal operations. SWF is a powerful service, but I would say that the initial letter in the acronym (S for Simple) isn't accurate. Unlike most AWS services, SWF isn't simple to understand or use. On the other hand, the problems that SWF was designed to address are fiendishly complex and undoubtedly require a complex tool to master them.

One traditional way to manage complex workflows is to have a human do it. A person kicks off one task, waits for it to complete, starts a second task, waits for it to be done, and so on. This process has a couple very basic problems: It's slow, and it's boring. It also doesn't scale well.

Another method, used in the past, is to write a custom workflow via scripting or code. That approach definitely addresses the challenges of the previous method, but has its own set of challenges. It supports the workflow it's designed for, but as soon as you want another type of workflow, well, you're out of luck. Or you end up trying to generalize your custom workflow and pretty soon you're working full-time on trying to maintain your simple workflow product rather than on doing any . . . you know, work.

Of course, many commercial workflow engines are available to solve these two problems. Though these engines are quite capable, they commonly carry hefty price tags and, given their esoteric nature, aren't easy to get funded.

SWF addresses this problem with a general workflow functionality that's offered and priced like all other AWS services: Use it when you want, and pay for only what you use. If you have a complex workflow that you need to execute, SWF can be a big help.

SWF overview

SWF is a generalizable workflow coordinator, commonly called a *workflow engine*. To use it, you create these two elements:

 ✔ **Decider:** Defines the tasks that your workflow needs to coordinate

 ✔ **Tasks:** Do the work that the decider coordinates

Though SWF needs to run in AWS (after all, it's an AWS service, right?), the tasks aren't limited to running within EC2. They can run anywhere. In fact, they don't even have to run — a task can be a human-powered thing. For example, if you implement a printing workflow, one task can be Review Proof with Client, which is a face-to-face task. After receiving positive feedback from the client, the printer's employee can open a web page and click the Approved button for the Review Proof task, and the remainder of the workflow can proceed in an automated fashion. The workflow need not be a sequential series of tasks, either; it can handle concurrent tasks that are run in parallel. A workflow can also include task dependencies, in which a given task cannot start until one or more previous tasks successfully complete.

An SWF decider can include logic to handle task errors and time-outs, for example, enabling it to handle problems that occur within individual tasks. Naturally, you can write workflows to accept input parameters that control how the workflow executes. You can also incorporate timers, signals, and markers in your workflow to help coordinate tasks.

Though SWF provides an API to interact with the service, Amazon has built a fairly full-featured management capability into the AWS Management Console. I think it's fair to say that it expects most SWF users to manage their workflows via the Management Console. SWF can manage workflows that are arbitrarily complex and that may be quite long-running; therefore, it stores the state of the workflow, which can be accessed from the AWS Management Console or via the API so that you can determine where things stand with a given workflow execution. Completed workflow information is also retained and is available for inspection, although you may prefer to delete retained information because AWS imposes a small charge for retaining completed workflow information.

Workflows can be defined in programming languages or CloudFormation (an AWS management tool discussed in Chapter 10).

I must warn you: SWF isn't for the faint of heart. However, the SWF section of the AWS Management Console *does* have a simple application example that demonstrates the power of SWF. This image processing application accepts an input image and converts it to sepia or gray-tone, depending on input it receives via a dialog box. To see SWF in action, check out the example.

SWF scope

SWF is regionally scoped, although it can access AWS resources in other regions as well as non-AWS resources.

SWF cost

AWS imposes several types of charges for SWF, although the aggregate cost is extremely low, unless you execute vast numbers of workflows.

For every executed workflow, AWS charges $0.0001. However, you receive 1,000 free workflows per month. If a workflow remains open beyond 24 hours, AWS imposes a $0.000005 fee per day. If a workflow is retained beyond completion, AWS charges the same $0.000005 per day. AWS provides 30,000 open or retained workdays for free.

AWS also imposes a fee for individual tasks, markers, timers, and signals — $0.000025 per task, signal, timer, or marker. AWS provides 10,000 of these items for free per month.

These costs vary slightly by region, but not significantly.

Dealing with Big Data with the Help of Elastic MapReduce

You have to have been living under a rock not to have heard of the term *big data*. It's a deceptively simple term for an unnervingly difficult problem: how to make sense of the torrents of data flooding into today's applications.

Let me quote a couple factoids to outline the dimension of the big-data challenge. In 2010, Google's chairman, Eric Schmidt, noted that humans now create as much information in two days as all of humanity had created up to the year 2003. Moreover, the research firm IDC projects that the digital universe will reach 40 zettabytes (ZB) by 2020, resulting in a 50-fold growth from the beginning of 2010. In other words, there's lots and lots of data, and its growth is accelerating.

The challenge that big data presents is that most of the established data analytics tools can't scale to manage datasets of the size that many companies want to analyze. For one, traditional business intelligence or data warehousing tools (the terms are used so interchangeably that they're often referred to as *BI/DW)* are extremely expensive; when applied to very large datasets, you soon face national-debt-type numbers.

Humor aside, the established BI/DW tools have a more serious scalability shortcoming: They're architected with a central analytics engine that reads data from disks, performs analysis, and spits out results. Today, data sizes are so huge that simply sending the data to be analyzed across the network takes too long to perform any useful work. By the time the data is transferred, the insights that can be gleaned from it are obsolete.

Clearly, a new BI/DW analytics architecture and problem approach was called for, and for inspiration the industry reached out to Google. Google has implemented a different approach to gathering data. Its architecture, *MapReduce,* is based on this simple insight: With so much data, it makes sense to move the processing to the data rather than attempt to move the data to the processing. MapReduce takes a very large datastore that may be spread across hundreds or thousands of machines and formats the data to structure it for the type of analysis you want to perform (that is, it maps the data into an analyzable format), and then you *filter* the data (reduce the mapped data, in other words) to isolate the information you want to examine.

Google treats its MapReduce implementation as proprietary, but, based on a paper it published, one person implemented an open source version of MapReduce called Hadoop. It's no exaggeration to say that Hadoop has revolutionized the BI/DW industry. In fact, an entire ecosystem of complementary products exists to make Hadoop even more useful.

You've probably already cut to the chase and recognized a familiar refrain: Hadoop is useful, but complex to install, configure, and manage. Gee, wouldn't it be useful if someone created an easy-to-use, cost-effective Hadoop solution that integrates with the existing ecosystem, allowing established tools that complement Hadoop to be used with this service?

Yes, it would, and Amazon calls its Hadoop solution Elastic MapReduce (EMR). The concept is straightforward:

1. Identify the data source you want to analyze.

   This is data located in S3. EMR can handle petabytes (a petabyte is 1,000 terabytes) of data with no problem.

2. Tell EMR how many instances (and of what type) you want the EMR pool to contain.

   EMR can use EC2 standard instances or one of the more exotic types, such as High-IO or High-CPU. Each instance offers a certain amount of disk storage for running the Hadoop Distributed File System (HDFS). The total amount of data you want to analyze dictates the number of instances you require.

3. Set up an EMR job flow.

   A job flow can be either of two types:

   - *Streaming:* Programming language mappers and reducers are introduced into EMR and processed across EC2 instances and the data they include.

   - *Query-oriented:* A higher-level data warehouse tool, such as Hive (which provides a Structured Query Language-like interface) can be used to run interactive queries against the data. The output of either type can be stored in S3 and then used for further analysis without requiring an active job flow.

4. Continue running the job flow, running MapReduce programs or higher-level query languages against the data, until you're finished using the job flow.

   A job flow can be terminated, which terminates all instances that make up the EMR pool.

Amazon manages the instances within the EMR pool. If an instance terminates unexpectedly, Amazon starts a new instance and ensures that it has the correct data on it to replace the terminated instance. And, of course, Amazon takes care of starting the EMR pool, connecting the instances to one another, and running MapReduce programs or providing higher-level tools for you to use for analysis.

EMR supports these programming languages: Java, Ruby, Perl, Python, PHP, R, Bash, and C++. With respect to these higher-level tools, Amazon provides a wide variety. In addition to Hive (as just mentioned), Amazon also offers Pig (a specialized Hadoop language). Finally, if you want, you can use EMR to output data that can then be imported into a specialized analytics tool like (the curiously named) R.

EMR is one service in which Amazon's pay-only-for-what-you-use philosophy may not be optimal, because transferring and formatting very large datasets to the EMR EC2 instances may take a long time. When you end a job flow, the instances on which the EMR pool is running are terminated and the data discarded. The next time you want to run an analysis, you have to rebuild the EMR pool. So you need to establish a trade-off, to balance the cost of keeping your EMR pool up and running versus the cost of rebuilding it. Clearly, if you plan to run multiple analyses over time against a data pool, it probably makes sense to keep your job flow active.

One interesting characteristic of EMR is that it differs from the other platform services I've already described. The others are "helper" services — useful services that help you build better applications more quickly. By contrast, EMR represents a stand-alone application that's not intended to support an application that the user is writing. Another example of this type of "non-helper" stand-alone application is Redshift, covered next. I expect that you'll see more of these stand-alone applications, for these reasons:

- ✔ **Its serious reputation:** Amazon feels that AWS is now accepted as a serious IT player, and IT is willing to trust it with important use cases. The company is now ready to branch out into areas that provide more direct user benefit in addition to its established infrastructure components that enable users to build their own applications.

- ✔ **The opportunity to expand:** Amazon perceives many application domains as ripe for automation and commoditization. As it provides offerings in these domains, its users increasingly benefit, and AWS can become more useful to them, thereby cementing its place as a critical part of their IT environments.

- ✔ **Strategic pricing strategies:** AWS recognizes that the high price of current offerings in these application domains prevents many potential users from taking advantage of them; its offerings democratize access to these domains. I'll let you decide whether Amazon is acting purely altruistically in this regard, or perhaps with an element of self-interest.

EMR scoping

EMR is regionally scoped. You should locate your EMR use in the same region where your data resides, if you want to avoid data transfer fees. (Given the kind of data volumes that EMR supports, avoiding these fees can be a big deal.)

EMR cost

The primary cost of EMR is the cost of the EC2 instances on which your EMR pool runs, as well as the S3 storage for your input data and results (assuming, reasonably, that you output results to S3).

In addition, you pay an additional EMR fee per instance. Think of it as an instance surcharge that Amazon imposes to manage the EMR service, install and configure the EMR software on the instances within your EMR pool, and transfer data between all the instances and S3. The EMR surcharge is approximately 25 percent of the instance cost, making it (in my opinion, at least) a modest cost for such a powerful application, compared to the cost of managing Hadoop on your own.

Redshift

Elastic MapReduce (EMR) is a useful analytics tool; however, SQL remains the lingua franca of the IT world. EMR's architecture requires writing filters in a programming language, along with following the MapReduce approach to data analysis. Though many engineers are comfortable moving from SQL to the EMR approach, many others are less so. Less technical personnel such as data analysts may not have the skills to take on the more technical requirements of creating EMR analyses. Moreover, many popular analytic tools are designed to work with SQL databases and are unavailable for EMR. For all these reasons, it makes sense that SQL-based data warehouse (DW) environments continue to be popular.

This isn't to say that today's SQL-based DW products don't suffer from the same problems accompanying the rise of big data (outlined earlier in this chapter, in the section "Dealing with Big Data with the Help of Elastic MapReduce"). In response to this cascade of data, SQL DWs have changed significantly over the past decade. Rather than have data attached to a single server and analyzed by a single DW software instance, new products where analytics are performed on multiple data sources in parallel are now used. Improved performance, via innovations such as bit-mapped columnar databases, supports the much larger data pools that are managed by SQL DWs.

 A *bit-mapped* database groups a large number of entries into a small entry in a column by using the individual bits of the storage for that entry to track and point to data. The use of bits allows the "compression" of data and enables far higher performance because the DW engine can analyze much smaller amounts of data to identify rows that meet particular selection criteria. In addition, the filtering can be achieved by simply looking at the compressed bitmap rather than reading in each row that meets the filter criteria. Instead, only the bitmap needs to be examined, and full rows read in only for those values that fit the filter criteria.

The big-data explosion in SQL DW carries associated complexities, which cause significant challenges for users:

- ✔ **Data volume:** The sheer volume of data mandates large amounts of equipment for processing. In many companies, DW activities aren't high priorities, so obtaining sufficient resources is difficult.

- ✔ **Resource management:** Beyond obtaining resources, managing them is difficult, too. Trying to administer a pool of dozens or hundreds of machines can be more than a full-time job — one that, by the way, supports DW but doesn't directly perform analytics work.

✔ **Planning difficulties:** It's hard to predict how much data is likely to reside in the DW, which causes problems in changing your DW environment down the road. And unloading and rebalancing parallel databases is typically time- and labor-consuming (and you need to take the DW offline while changes are made).

✔ **Relatively high prices:** Did I mention how much SQL DW software costs? Well, let's just say it's not cheap — not by a long shot.

Any time an important IT use demonstrates these kinds of challenges, you can expect Amazon to step forward with a service — and it has. Redshift is the new service from AWS that addresses the SQL data warehouse market. Though Redshift is a relatively new service, it's attracting a lot of attention.

Redshift overview

Redshift, a columnar SQL DW service, can operate on DWs as small as a single terabyte and can scale up to multipetabyte size. Standard SQL is used to query Redshift, which makes its potential user base larger than what you'd see for EMR.

You may ask, if Redshift is SQL-based, why you have to use a special service for analysis. Why can't you use a regular SQL database, like MySQL or Oracle?

The reason to opt for a specialized DW database is that it's biased to support DW use cases. I've already mentioned the bitmapping columnar feature, which reduces the amount of data that needs to be read to perform a filtering operation. Another difference between DW and standard databases is that DW workloads have a higher proportion of queries versus updates or deletes, and the queries are often more complex. Consequently, the SQL parser in these products is focused on query optimization to accelerate data reads. Though it's not impossible to use a standard SQL database for this use case, it's not nearly as efficient as using an SQL DW database.

As described in the following list, Redshift is designed to address the SQL DW challenges outlined earlier:

✔ **It operates in Amazon's virtually limitless infrastructure.** Unlike on-premise environments, there's never a problem with obtaining sufficient resources to support your DW. Redshift data is loaded from S3, which can certainly scale to support any imaginable DW size.

✔ **It's robust, with each individual node in the Redshift cluster supported by EC2 instance redundancy.** Even if an individual instance within the collection of servers used to support your Redshift environment goes down, your DW continues operating.

✔ **Its cluster can be resized at any time.** If you decide to increase (or decrease) the size of your Redshift cluster, you simply execute a resizing command and Redshift takes care of it. It puts your DW into read-only mode so that no changes are made to the data during the conversion process. It then starts up a new cluster with the requested number of nodes. When those nodes are operating, Redshift copies your data into the new cluster and makes it available. After the new cluster is available, Redshift shuts down the old cluster and releases its resources back into the general EC2 resource pool.

✔ **It automatically "snapshots" (makes a direct copy of) your DR into S3 to ensure that Redshift can recover from any unanticipated situation.** These snapshots aren't available to users and cannot be used by them. A user can also initiate a snapshot to create their own copy of the Redshift data, and the snapshot can be used as the basis of a fresh Redshift instantiation.

✔ **You pay only for the resources you use.** If you shut down your Redshift cluster, you incur no further fees.

✔ **Redshift is supported by a large ecosystem of DW tools that make performing analytics easy.** If you want to query your Redshift cluster directly, you can execute SQL against it via ODBC or JDBC.

Here's one potential drawback you may have thought about: If you create this very large Redshift DW cluster, are you stuck running it all the time because you'll lose data if you shut it down? Doesn't the overhead of loading all the data prevent you from benefitting from the pay-for-only-what-you-use feature in Redshift?

Yes and no. Just before terminating your Redshift cluster, you can execute a snapshot. When you're ready to run further analysis on your DW data, you can create a new Redshift cluster from your snapshot. As soon as you launch the new cluster, Redshift makes it possible to run queries. On the other hand, the query performance will likely be quite low until the data is fully loaded into the Redshift cluster. If you plan to use your cluster on an ongoing basis, work out a plan to keep it up and running. In the later section "Redshift cost," I discuss the use of Redshift reserved instances to reduce the overall operating cost of the service.

The DW market has been ripe for disruption for a long time. Analytics are hugely valuable, and most companies can usefully apply analytics much more broadly than they do. Unfortunately, because the cost of current solutions makes it difficult to justify using such products, analytics are typically applied to only the highest-value domains.

The advent of Redshift reduces the cost of DW significantly, and makes the power of analytics much more widely available, with the enormous potential for organizations for which analytics was previously unaffordable. It's too early to see the impact of Redshift, but I predict that it will be a gigantic success.

Redshift scope

Redshift is regionally scoped. Though it isn't yet available in all regions, it's being rolled out rapidly Because Redshift data comes from S3; you should attempt to locate Redshift in the same region as your data. However, many users are likely to upload data from off-premises into S3; in those cases, they should choose a region that's convenient for their use.

Redshift cost

The price of Redshift is set by the cost of the node that's used for the Redshift cluster. Redshift supports two node types: XL (2TB of storage) and 8XL (16TB of storage). With on-demand pricing, the former costs $.85 per hour; the latter, $6.80 per hour. You can also purchase reserved node pricing by making an upfront payment, which creates a lower per-hour cost. Redshift reserved nodes are available in one- and three-year commitment lengths.

The typical method of evaluating costs in the data warehouse industry is the price per terabyte per year. By this measure, Redshift on-demand results in a $3,621 cost per terabyte per year. With the use of three-year, reserved node pricing, the cost per terabyte can be reduced to just under $1,000.

That price may seem to be significant. However, it's important to evaluate the price of Redshift in terms of the current vendors in the market. I have seen DW pricing typically range *between $12,000 and $57,000* per terabyte per year. One vendor recently trumpeted a reduction of its annual cost to less than the magic $10,000 price point. Shown in that light, Redshift obviously represents an enormous cost advantage versus the incumbents.

Of course, the established vendors will raise the usual FUD (*f*ear, *u*ncertainty, and *d*oubt): "Can you trust Amazon? We have a long history in this market, and Amazon is still wet behind the ears. We are a known brand and so on and so forth."

Notwithstanding this bluster, I predict that Redshift will disrupt this market significantly and will divert significant market share from the established players. More important, its much lower pricing will enable organizations that previously were unable to afford analytics to take advantage of data warehousing for the first time. I believe that the bigger impact of Redshift will be to grow the DW market by a factor of 10, or even 100, as it democratizes what has been a pricey, even clubby, vendor community.

Chapter 10

AWS Management Services

*T*he chapter title I've chosen should provoke an obvious question: Given the richness of the AWS resources now available (a richness spelled out in detail in the opening chapters of this book) and the AWS Management Console (which I cover quite thoroughly in Chapter 3), why would you need any additional management services?

That's kind of a trick question, in that the answer lies in the question itself — it's because of the richness of the collection of the AWS offerings that more capable management services are themselves necessary.

In the past, in order to create or run an application, you had to do a ton of work, none of which was directly tied to application functionality: Install software components, configure them, and then connect them to other software components. After the application was up and running, you then had to manage its components, keep them running, respond in the event of a resource failure, back them up, and so on. It was as if every time you wanted to drive to the grocery store, you had to build a new car and sweep the road — just to get a quart of milk!

The revolutionary aspect of AWS is that it decouples the installation and management of application components from the act of *using* those components. Amazon's bright idea was to automate the infrastructure administrative overhead and free you to focus on functionality.

Why then do you need sophisticated AWS management services? Well, because the administrative effort has now shifted up one level, that's why. Rather than manage software components and make sure that they play well together, now you have to manage your AWS products and make sure that *they* play well together. The rest of this chapter offers a few strategies for accomplishing just that.

Managing Your AWS Applications

Just suppose you've written an application and now you want EC2 instances to talk to an SQS queue and insert and retrieve S3 objects. Well, Amazon makes it easy to create those resources, and it's relatively straightforward to connect an EC2 instance to the queue and to the S3 bucket it will use. But (and it's a big *but)* that's for only the lone instance. What if you terminate and restart the instance? Well, it needs to be connected to the queue and S3 bucket once more. And what if your application is hugely successful? Then you've got to connect a bunch more instances, and as those instances terminate and restart . . . well, you get the picture. It's a lot like Mickey Mouse as the Sorcerer's Apprentice in the Disney movie *Fantasia.* Or, to use a more classical allusion, it's like Sisyphus endlessly rolling his rock to the top of the hill and watching it tumble to the plain below. In other words, it's a ton of repetitious work. Humans don't excel at performing repetitive manual work. They make mistakes, which means that you're likely to break your own application as you try to keep up with what needs to be done.

So you have endless work, and in doing this work, you're likely to cause new problems. Wouldn't it be great if you could find something to manage the AWS side of it for you, making it easy to ensure that the applications have the right code components, that the different services are automatically connected to talk to one another, and that they were all scaled as necessary to meet varying application load?

The good news is that this something exists — in fact, Amazon provides three AWS management services, each designed to address a particular user segment and to help it more effectively manage AWS applications.

In this section, I address all three of these services to help you understand their characteristics and know when to use them. Before diving in to the individual services, though, I want to introduce two AWS services that underpin the others: CloudWatch and Auto Scaling.

Watching the cloud with AWS CloudWatch

CloudWatch is an AWS component that monitors your AWS resources. (Hot tip: It can also be used to monitor AWS applications.) It watches — get the allusion? — over AWS resources and provides information to users in the form of data and alerts. The data can be accessed directly, as text and numerical output that can then be analyzed or manipulated, or viewed in more mediated formats, such as graphs.

What kinds of monitoring am I talking about? A good example is the EC2 instance load. You can have CloudWatch keep an eye on the processor load of an EC2 instance. The metric can be configured to generate an e-mail alert if the processor load percentage rises above a certain level or even trigger a programmatic action such as an Auto Scaling event. (Auto Scaling is discussed in the next section of this chapter.) Nice, right?

Need more metrics examples? Here's a list of some other AWS characteristics that CloudWatch can monitor. CloudWatch can track metrics across time — notice that many of the preset metrics capture data at 5-minute intervals, though you can choose another interval, if you like. All these metrics are free, except for the first one; I discuss the whole CloudWatch pricing issue later in the chapter. Anyway, here's the list:

- ✔ **EC2 instances:** Ten preselected metrics at 5-minute intervals

- ✔ **Amazon EBS volumes:** Eight preselected metrics at 5-minute intervals

- ✔ **Elastic Load Balancers:** Ten preselected metrics at 1-minute intervals

- ✔ **Amazon RDS DB instances:** Thirteen preselected metrics at 1-minute intervals

- ✔ **Amazon SQS queues:** Eight preselected metrics at 5-minute intervals

- ✔ **Amazon SNS topics:** Four preselected metrics at 5-minute intervals

- ✔ **Amazon ElastiCache nodes:** Twenty-nine preselected metrics at 1-minute intervals

- ✔ **Amazon DynamoDB tables:** Seven preselected metrics at 5-minute intervals

You can also set up custom metrics to be monitored by CloudWatch. In this relatively straightforward process, you make a PUT API call with the metric to be monitored, and CloudWatch begins monitoring it for you.

CloudWatch stores its data for two weeks, making it possible to track metrics across an extended period. Of course, if you want to extend the period even further for tracking purposes, you can extract CloudWatch data via the API and store it elsewhere.

CloudWatch is enabled when you create an account. Thereafter, you simply select (or define) the metrics to track and then use the metrics that are generated as you choose. For example, you can

- ✔ Pull metric data via the CloudWatch API
- ✔ Pull metric data via the CloudWatch SDK

✔ Review metric data in the Management Console

✔ Notify someone (or something, as in an administrative process or a log) of the metric

✔ Set an alarm that then causes something to happen (terminate a nonresponsive instance and start another one, for example)

CloudWatch cost

CloudWatch provides a lot of monitoring for free. For example, for any EC2 instances you have, you get ten metrics at 5-minute intervals with no cost.

The following metrics impose no costs:

✔ Basic monitoring metrics (at 5-minute intervals) for Amazon EC2 instances are free, as are all metrics for Amazon EBS volumes, elastic load balancers, and Amazon RDS DB instances.

✔ New and existing customers also receive ten metrics (applicable to Detailed Monitoring for Amazon EC2 instances or Custom Metrics), ten alarms, and 1 million API requests per month for no additional charge.

Metrics beyond the free tier just described impose the following costs:

✔ **Amazon CloudWatch Detailed Monitoring for Amazon EC2 instances (at 1-minute intervals):** $3.50 per instance per month

✔ **Amazon CloudWatch Custom Metrics:** $0.50 per metric per month

✔ **Amazon CloudWatch Alarms:** $0.10 per alarm per month

✔ **Amazon CloudWatch API Requests:** $0.01 per 1,000 Get, List, or Put requests

A CloudWatch example

It's time for a concrete example of using CloudWatch, to see how it can work with EC2, the pay-as-you-go compute capacity area of AWS. In this example, I've started the launch process, and I want to enable CloudWatch for this particular instance. Figure 10-1 shows the second panel of the EC2 Launch Wizard; you can see that I've selected the Monitoring check box to enable CloudWatch for this instance. (For more detail on EC2 and the launching of instances, see Chapter 5.)

Figure 10-2 shows your options in the launch wizard for creating an alarm for a particular instance. I'll have CloudWatch trip an alarm any time the Status Check Failed metric is true — that is, whenever the EC2 instance status check reveals that something is wrong with the instance. Click the Create Alarm button in the bottom-right corner of the screen, and you've got yourself an alarm.

The Monitoring checkbox

Choose Status Check Failed (Any)
from the Whenever menu.

More often than not, one alarm isn't enough. Trust me: You'll want more. For example, I want an alarm sent whenever the instance CPU utilization increases to more than 80 percent. Figure 10-3 shows the CloudWatch Management Console alarm panel, showing all alarms for my EC2 instance. You can see both alarms listed.

Figure 10-3:
EC2
instance
CloudWatch
alarms.

The CloudWatch Management Console main page (accessed via the Management Console main page) provides a dashboard showing the health of the overall account resource. As you can see in Figure 10-4, the dashboard lists both of my alarms, and a graphical display of both. You look at the dashboard to gain a general sense of the health of your AWS resources.

For more comprehensive information or to create a more sophisticated display, leverage the CloudWatch API or SDK. As an example of how to pull the data associated with the metrics of my account CloudWatch, here's the API call:

```
http://monitoring.us-east-1.amazonaws.
           com/?Action=ListMetrics
&SignatureVersion=2
&SignatureMethod=HmacSHA256
&Timestamp=2010-11-17T05%3A13%3A00.000Z
&Signature=<URLEncode(Base64Encode(Signature))>
&Version=2010-08-01
&AWSAccessKeyId=<Your AWS Access Key Id>
```

If you want to understand the ins and outs of this API call, please see Chapter 2 — the one that covers the AWS API.

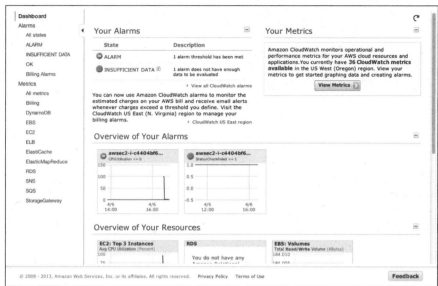

Figure 10-4:
The AWS
Management
Console
CloudWatch
dashboard.

The wonders of AWS Auto Scaling

The Auto Scaling AWS feature is designed to solve a big problem: how to have the correct number of EC2 instances available to support the load on an application at a given time.

You actually have a number of options to ensure that you have the correct number of instances running at any given time:

- ✔ **Wait for user complaints.** Performance issues often result from having insufficient resources, and squawking from unhappy users of your application can be an excellent way to identify a resource issue. Of course, you run the risk of users then refusing to interact with your application, which can be somewhat unfortunate if your company relies on the application to generate revenue.

- ✔ **Keep a hypervigilant system administrator on the payroll.** This person can then constantly monitor the application for acceptable performance. This expensive strategy, plus the natural human tendency to lose interest in infrequent though high-cost situations, is also unlikely to solve the problem.

✔ **Leverage monitoring of the application to notify you of performance issues.** You can either implement your own monitoring system or leverage AWS's CloudWatch service, as just described. Though this method resolves users' complaints and any shortcomings in the solutions of bored system administrators, it still leaves you in the position (after you've been informed of the problem) of having to execute a bunch of manual work to respond — all during a period when the application isn't working properly. Better, yes, but hardly optimal.

A far better solution is to have the application monitor itself and then, when additional EC2 instances are necessary, automatically start additional instances and have them join the computing pool immediately, all without requiring human intervention.

Guess what? Such a solution exists — AWS Auto Scaling. In a nutshell, *Auto Scaling* lets you define how your application should respond to changing load conditions. The idea is that, by starting (or stopping) instances at the right moments, you can ensure that only the correct number of instances are running to support the application load.

Auto Scaling works by adding instances to, or subtracting them from, a group of running instances based on a factor that you define. Auto Scaling takes care of all tasks associated with stopping or starting an instance, enabling it to automatically create the right instance configuration and add it to the pool.

Behind the simple concept of Auto Scaling lies a great deal of complexity. Fortunately, Amazon takes care of most of it, allowing you to efficiently manage your Auto Scaling configuration in a straightforward manner.

AWS uses the following elements to implement Auto Scaling:

✔ **Launch Configuration:** Your parameters here are what's required to start an instance properly. Think of this as the definition that's applied to a "blank" instance to make it into an instance that's appropriate for your application. Factors you'd define as part of a launch configuration include AMI ID; security key pair(s); security groups; and the EBS volume(s) to be attached to the instance.

✔ **Auto Scaling Group:** This definition gets applied to a collection of instances launched under a particular launch configuration. An Auto Scaling group defines items such as the minimum and maximum numbers of instances that the application should have. So you may always want two instances running to ensure availability, but you may never want to have more than five, so as to avoid excess cost.

✔ **Scaling Plan:** The scaling plan defines how the Auto Scaling group should respond to changing application workloads. The plan can be *dynamic* (executed in response to a metric such as instance load levels in the group) or *predictable,* which is appropriate if you want the group to scale according to a specific expected event (such as a predictable scaling plan designed to prepare the application to start three additional instances every Sunday, when the week's financial totals for the company are analyzed).

To achieve the best possible protection against application failure, let Auto Scaling use multiple availability zones and spread the group across them. This strategy ensures that even if an entire zone goes offline, your application continues running.

Here's an obvious question: If multiple instances are running within an application, how do you coordinate them? An Auto Scaling group can be associated with an AWS Elastic Load Balancer, which would then spread traffic across all instances in the group. As instances are stopped and started in response to the scaling plan, the Auto Scaling service coordinates the details of applying the launch configuration along with registering (or deregistering) the instances with the load balancer.

For Auto Scaling groups that aren't designed to manage instances that receive web traffic, another mechanism to spread the application load across all instances in the group must be used. For example, if a number of instances are processing photos uploaded by users who are submitting them, you may have all the image processing images read from a common queue; part of the instance Launch Configuration is the queue ID, which would allow all Auto Scaling Group members to know from where to read submitted images.

Actually using Auto Scaling

It's not possible (at this time, at least) to manage Auto Scaling via the AWS Management Console. You have to use the AWS API, SDK, or CLI instead. When you create any of the Auto Scaling elements via one of these mechanisms, AWS stores them in your account information and uses them to respond to the conditions you define in your Auto Scaling plan. (For more on the AWS API, see Chapter 2.)

The flow of interaction for creating and using one of these auto scaling elements is similar:

1. Use an Auto Scaling command to define the element. (Define an Auto Scaling group using the AWS API, for example.)

2. Receive the AWS response to the command, which includes the AWS identifier for the element.

3. Use the element to execute an Auto Scaling command. (Start an Auto Scaling group, for example.)

4. Confirm that your command was executed properly.

5. Sit back and enjoy as AWS manages your application!

Most of the work you do in Auto Scaling comes from planning and testing. Be sure that the launch configuration is correct — with the right keys, for example — because you won't be the one doing the instance launch — AWS Auto Scaling does it. So the Launch Configuration needs to be correctly defined (as do the Auto Scaling Groups and Scaling Plan) so that they operate properly in Hands-Off mode.

Be sure that all aspects of your Auto Scaling arrangement operate properly, and test it to ensure that it behaves as you wish. Run your application and load it up with traffic to observe how Auto Scaling responds.

Your Auto Scaling costs

This section is the simplest one in this book. Auto Scaling costs nothing. Of course, you'll incur a cost for the resources Auto Scaling manages, but you're smart enough to know that already, right?

An Auto Scaling example

Because Auto Scaling isn't supported by the AWS Management Console, I cannot offer any handy screen shots. However, here are some examples of the kinds of Auto Scaling API calls you'll use:

To create a Launch Configuration:

```
https://autoscaling.amazonaws.
          com/?LaunchConfigurationName=my-test-lc
&ImageId=ami-id
&InstanceType=m1.small
&Action=CreateLaunchConfiguration
&AUTHPARAMS
```

Note that you have assigned a configuration name: my-test-lc.

This example returns an XML document of this form:

```
<CreateLaunchConfigurationResponse xmlns="http://
          autoscaling.amazon
aws.com/doc/2011-01-01/">
<ResponseMetadata>
<RequestId>7c6e177f-f082-11e1-ac58-3714bEXAMPLE</RequestId>
</ResponseMetadata>
</CreateLaunchConfigurationResponse>
```

To create an Auto Scaling Group, you issue this API call:

```
https://autoscaling.amazonaws.
        com/?AutoScalingGroupName=my-test-asg
&AvailabilityZones.member.1=us-east-1a
&MinSize=1
&MaxSize=10
&DesiredCapacity=1
&LaunchConfigurationName=my-test-1c
&Action=CreateAutoScalingGroup
&AUTHPARAMS
```

This chunk of code returns (if it's successful, of course) an XML document of this form:

```
<CreateAutoScalingGroupResponse xmlns="http://autoscaling.
        amazonaws.com/doc/2011-
01-01/">
<ResponseMetadata>
<RequestId>8d798a29-f083-11e1-bdfb-cb223EXAMPLE</
        RequestId>
</ResponseMetadata>
</CreateAutoScalingGroupResponse>
```

This command starts the Auto Scaling Group, which in turn launches instances using the `my-test-1c` Launch Configuration.

Easy, eh?

Introducing AWS Elastic Beanstalk

In addition to low-level management services like CloudWatch and Auto Scaling, AWS offers several higher-level management services. The remainder of this chapter is devoted to these services, starting with a discussion of the (oddly named) Elastic Beanstalk.

The developer-oriented Elastic Beanstalk service is designed to let you move applications as easily as possible from the development environment to production in AWS — such as moving code from a laptop to AWS in the shortest possible time — and it's specifically oriented to integrate AWS with commonly used development environments.

Elastic Beanstalk supports container-based environments like .NET, Java, Python, PHP, Ruby, and Node.js. The basis of these languages is that your code isn't compiled into a standalone executable program that directly interacts with operating system resources; rather, your code is run by an executable program called a *container,* a *virtual machine,* or an *interpreter* (depending on the language you use) that interacts with system resources on your behalf. So, rather than make a call to an operating system file, your program makes a call to a storage function offered by your language that interacts in turn with the language virtual machine or interpreter, which interacts in turn with the operating system resources on your behalf.

The traditional drawback to these noncompiled languages (often referred to as *dynamic* or *interpreted* languages) is that their performance suffers in comparison to compiled languages, like COBOL or C. That's a fair assessment, but the improvement in server processing power and the flexibility of the languages have led to enormous growth in their use during the past decade. It's no exaggeration to say that dynamic languages are the dominant way programs are built today.

As an offering, Elastic Beanstalk is most directly comparable to the Platform as a Service (PaaS) development environment, like Heroku or CloudFoundry, in that it provides the ability to run code in a container that takes care of execution and resource management. Elastic Beanstalk is quite different from them, though: Other PaaS environments let you use their programming frameworks, and they handle details like managing storage, ensuring sufficient computing resources, and directing network traffic. However, most PaaS environments don't "play nice" when you need to do something outside their capabilities. In that case, you're in trouble. This type of platform generally provides no way to access functionality outside of the services it offers. Nor do you have a way to directly affect the management of the PaaS functionality itself; if your application isn't getting sufficient performance from the default PaaS configuration, well, you're going to have unhappy users.

Elastic Beanstalk, by contrast, does provide the appropriate language container and manages it on behalf of your application code. It also lets you access the full range of AWS services and manage the resources that Elastic Beanstalk uses to execute your application. For example, if it's suffering from poor performance, you can direct Elastic Beanstalk to use larger instance sizes to provide greater processing power. Moreover, you can interact with computing resources outside the Elastic Beanstalk environment; for example, you can interact with a relational database running on a separate instance in AWS.

Elastic Beanstalk, launched in early 2011, is widely used to run web-oriented applications. Just as AWS services, like its relational database service (RDS), are designed to reduce the workload associated with managing necessary computing resources, Elastic Beanstalk is designed to reduce the workload associated with managing the computing resources necessary to run dynamic language applications.

You may wonder why this service is named Elastic Beanstalk. (Well, you and me both.) In my opinion, it's the single worst name for any AWS service. The only explanation I can offer is that, when Elastic Beanstalk was first offered, it supported only one language: Java. Java is associated with beans (of the coffee variety), and the fable of *Jack and the Beanstalk* focuses on Jack's purchase of magic beans that grow to create an enormously tall beanstalk. Elastic Beanstalk, of course, helps your applications grow to enormous size. Frankly, it all seems like a stretch to me — a big stretch. Fortunately, its infelicitous (unfortunate) name doesn't get in the way of its excellent functionality, and people seem to have adopted it, so all's well that ends well, I guess!

In addition to the general capability of installing and running dynamic code, Elastic Beanstalk seamlessly supports other capabilities:

✔ It automatically registers your application with an Elastic Load Balancer to direct traffic to multiple instances running your code. In addition, Elastic Beanstalk automatically assigns an AWS URL to enable access to it.

✔ It supports the use of Auto Scaling to dynamically manage the resources used by your application.

✔ It supports application versioning by treating each new update to your application code as a fresh version. When you trigger an update, Elastic Beanstalk manages the installation of the new version on a set of AWS instances, terminates the existing instances, and switches the Elastic Load Balancer or AWS URL to the new instances. Elastic Beanstalk also supports rolling back your application to a previous version. In fact, Elastic Beanstalk can support running multiple versions of your application simultaneously, which can be useful for testing and support purposes.

Using Elastic Beanstalk

The specifics of moving code from a development environment to AWS vary, but these four steps show the general pattern for using Elastic Beanstalk:

1. Develop the application using your chosen local development environment.

   For .NET, it's Visual Studio. For Java, AWS supports the use of the Eclipse interactive development environment (IDE). For other languages, you can use the IDE of your choice.

2. Create the Elastic Beanstalk environment via the Management Console, AWS API, or AWS SDK.

3. Upload the application code to the Elastic Beanstalk environment.

   For .NET and Java, you can do it via the IDE. For the other languages, it's done via Git, a distributed source code management system. AWS provides instructions to configure Git to work with Elastic Beanstalk.

4. Manage your application, if you can't use the default Elastic Beanstalk configuration.

   For example, you may change the application's instance size or the Auto Scaling rules. Elastic Beanstalk is integrated with CloudWatch, so you can view important metrics or even set CloudWatch to alert you when those metrics trigger a specified condition.

Really, that's all there is to it. Elastic Beanstalk is the easiest way to manage applications built on dynamic code.

Elastic Beanstalk cost

There's no charge to use Elastic Beanstalk, though you incur charges, of course for the resources on which your application runs, like the EC2 instances used to run your code.

An Elastic Beanstalk example

Imagine creating a Tomcat-based application. Tomcat supports the Java language and is widely used (especially in enterprise environments) to create Internet applications that contain database-driven content — a parts catalog that displays part information based on user input, for example.

If you click on Elastic Beanstalk from the main page of the Management Console, you'll see that Elastic Beanstalk has a number of prepopulated language environments, including Tomcat 7, which is the environment I will choose. (See Figure 10-5.) This environment is a sample application that Amazon provides to show how Elastic Beanstalk operates. (**Note:** this example uses Tomcat code that has been uploaded to Elastic Beanstalk; most uses of Elastic Beanstalk begin with the upload set, in which you transfer the application from your development environment up to Elastic Beanstalk.)

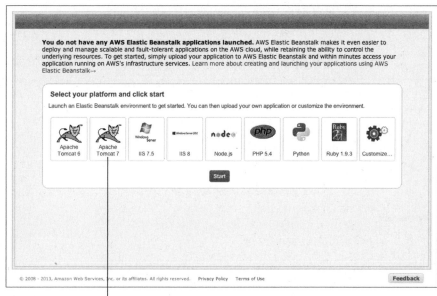

Figure 10-5:
Creating
the Tomcat
environment.

The Apache Tomcat 7
language environment

A few minutes after choosing the Tomcat 7 option, the Elastic Beanstalk environment is up and running, as shown in Figure 10-6. As you can see, about halfway down, Elastic Beanstalk presents several tabs; the one displayed in Figure 10-6 is the Overview tab.

To give you an idea of what the Elastic Beanstalk panel can potentially show you regarding the environment, check out the Monitoring tab in Figure 10-7. It shows a lot of CPU use and network traffic at instance start-up, which then rapidly falls off after the application is up and running.

At this point, the application is available for use (which is why, for this example, AWS puts up a big "Congratulations" page). Figure 10-8 shows what's displayed in the browser when you click the URL shown in Figure 10-6.

If a great deal of traffic were being sent to this application, Elastic Beanstalk would start new instances to handle the load. Also, if you decide at some point to modify the application, you can simply upload the new version to Elastic Beanstalk and notify it to start the new version and then terminate the older version. Not bad, right?

Your environment tabs

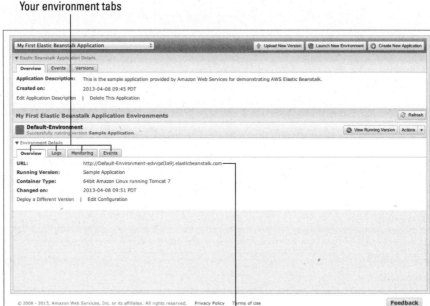

Figure 10-6:
The Elastic
Beanstalk
operating
environment.

Your Elastic Beanstalk URL

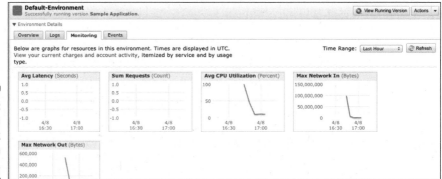

Figure 10-7:
Elastic
Beanstalk
application
monitoring.

To terminate the entire environment created via the API, use this command:

```
https://elasticbeanstalk.us-east-1.amazon.
          com/?EnvironmentId=e-icsgecu3wf
&EnvironmentName=SampleApp
&TerminateResources=true
&Operation=TerminateEnvironment
&AuthParams
```

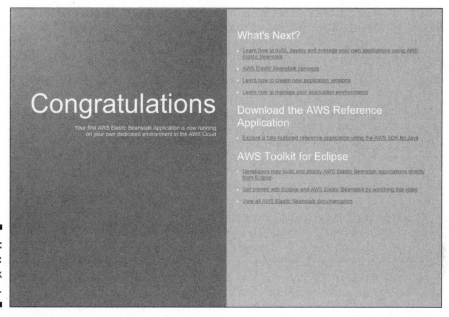

Congratulations

Your first AWS Elastic Beanstalk Application is now running
on your own dedicated environment in the AWS Cloud

What's Next?

- Learn how to build, deploy and manage your own applications using AWS Elastic Beanstalk
- AWS Elastic Beanstalk concepts
- Learn how to create new application versions
- Learn how to manage your application environments

Download the AWS Reference Application

- Explore a fully-featured reference application using the AWS SDK for Java

AWS Toolkit for Eclipse

- Developers may build and deploy AWS Elastic Beanstalk applications directly from Eclipse
- Get started with Eclipse and AWS Elastic Beanstalk by watching this video
- View all AWS Elastic Beanstalk documentation

Figure 10-8:
The Elastic
Beanstalk
application.

AWS CloudFormation

Elastic Beanstalk, is great for dynamic language applications that contain no more than a web tier and a database tier — but what if your application includes additional tiers to handle data caching and other application logic processes, or uses non-dynamic languages? For applications like these, CloudFormation is the right management solution.

Horizontally scaled refers to the use of multiple computing instances sharing the load in a single application tier. Horizontal scaling is a technique for applications to support load greater than a single instance can handle. A different approach to solving this problem is referred to as *vertical scaling* — using a higher-performance instance to support greater load. Vertical scaling is widely used, but it isn't the preferred solution for webscale applications, for multiple reasons, including the fact that a single (very large) instance exposes you to application failure instead of the redundancy that multiple smaller instances provide. Also, at a certain point, no larger instance size is available. (And then what do you do?) Consequently, horizontal scaling is the most commonly implemented application design in cloud computing environments.

Auto Scaling Groups (described in detail in the section "The wonders of AWS Auto Scaling," earlier in this chapter) are excellent solutions to address the requirements of horizontal scaling, but even Auto Scaling Groups need to be managed in the context of the entire application. For example, an Elastic Load Balancer needs to be created so that the Auto Scaling Group instances can register. You might say that Auto Scaling Groups are important components of a complex application management solution, but not the entire solution on their own.

Finally, of course, you face a final challenge in managing complex webscale applications: human ineptitude, where you can see the downside of human creativity and ingenuity. Humans excel at developing new creations, but they're terrible at repetitively executing complex tasks. They make mistakes. And webscale applications bring out the worst in people, with lots of complicated configuration settings, arcane installation instructions, and detailed monitoring output that must be responded to.

In short, webscale applications are increasingly difficult beasts to manage, and trying to do so via manual methods using the AWS Management Console — as useful as it is — is fraught with danger.

Fortunately, Amazon has recognized this issue and developed a management tool that converts the management of webscale applications from an ongoing challenge to a process that leverages a template defining the components of an application, coordinating their launch, and even managing its ongoing response to changing workloads. That solution is CloudFormation.

CloudFormation operation is based on a template — in this particular case, a JSON text document. The template, which is the key to CloudFormation, serves as the basis for service creation and operation. The following list describes the various sections in the template that you'll use to define your application:

- ✔ **Format:** *Format* refers to the CloudFormation template version (not the file format or any other obvious term). Amazon clearly envisions evolving the service and wants the flexibility to change the template format to incorporate future developments. The company is unlikely to deprecate existing templates, so don't worry that your carefully created template will become obsolete. (***Note:*** In CloudFormation terminology, the application is referred to as a *stack,* so keep this term in mind.)

- ✔ **Description:** Use this (text) section to describe the template and the application it manages. Think of it as a Comments section, where you can provide information for others as they use or modify your template.

- ✔ **Parameters:** These values, which are passed into CloudFormation at runtime, can be used to configure the application operated by the template. You may, for example, want to run CloudFormation templates in several Amazon regions; rather than create separate templates for each region, you can use one template and pass in a parameter to define in which region the template's application should run.

✔ **Mappings:** Here's where you declare conditional values. Think of this section as the one in which you set a variable used in the template to a particular value. For example, you may change the AMI ID that the template will launch, based on which region the "region" parameter is set to.

✔ **Resources:** This area describes the AWS resources used in the application and specifies the configuration settings. If you want the application to run all M1.Large instances, place that setting here. (For a description of the various instance types, please see Chapter 5.) Of course, you can adjust the setting based on parameters and mappings instead, if you so choose.

✔ **Outputs:** These values are the ones you want returned in the event of a request to describe the template. The output may return the name of a template's author or the date of creation, for example.

CloudFormation templates are simple . . . but not easy. It's always that way when you move from manual to automated administration. Organizing a template to support all the different values and variables that are needed to operate a complex application isn't easy. It requires lots of iterative creation and testing. The benefit is that when the template operates properly, you save enormous amounts of time thereafter.

Using CloudFormation

Probably the best way to describe how to use CloudFormation is to walk through an example. Fortunately, given the fact that it's not especially easy to create and test a template, AWS provides a number of templates to use as examples.

Actually, you should look at the AWS-sourced templates as more than just examples. In the time-honored method used by engineers everywhere, you can use a template as the foundation and hack it suit to your purposes.

Ready? Let's go:

1. **From the AWS Management Console page, click CloudFormation.**

   Doing so brings up the CloudFormation main page, as shown in Figure 10-9.

2. **Click the Create New Stack button.**

   The Template Wizard launches.

   AWS uses the term *stack* to refer to the application run by a CloudFormation template.

Figure 10-9:
The Cloud-
Formation
main page.

3. **Using the wizard's drop-down menu (see Figure 10-10), choose the template you want to use and then click Continue.**

   Now, AWS provides more than 20 templates. To make this example interesting, go ahead and choose the template for the multizone LAMP stack "Hello World" application. (You'll see it near the bottom of the list, above the Highly-Available, Multi-AZ section.)

   In case you're not familiar with the term *LAMP stack,* it's an acronym that stands for Linux, Apache, MySQL, PHP (though the *P* can also stand for Python or even Perl — other dynamic languages). LAMP is a commonly used collection of separate applications that, together, provide a complete and rich application operating environment.

4. **In the new wizard panel that appears, set parameters for the application and then click Continue.**

   Figure 10-11 shows that I have set the DBPassword and DBUsername values to enable the application tiers to communicate with each other. You will also need to specify a SSH keypair name to use for this application, so fill in the field with an existing keypair, or create a new keypair and use its name here. The other fields can be used to create a more failure-resistant application, but for this example, that's not necessary, so don't worry about them now.

   A summary panel appears (see Figure 10-12), displaying relevant information, along with the Create Stack button, near the bottom of the panel.

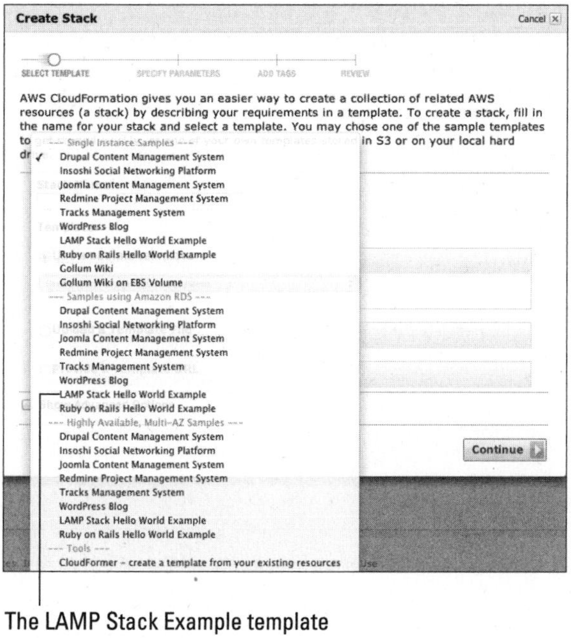

Create Stack   Cancel ⊠

SELECT TEMPLATE   SPECIFY PARAMETERS   ADD TAGS   REVIEW

AWS CloudFormation gives you an easier way to create a collection of related AWS
resources (a stack) by describing your requirements in a template. To create a stack, fill in
the name for your stack and select a template. You may chose one of the sample templates
to ... --- Single Instance Samples ---   in S3 or on your local hard
dr ✓ Drupal Content Management System
       Insoshi Social Networking Platform
       Joomla Content Management System
       Redmine Project Management System
       Tracks Management System
       WordPress Blog
       LAMP Stack Hello World Example
       Ruby on Rails Hello World Example
       Gollum Wiki
       Gollum Wiki on EBS Volume
       --- Samples using Amazon RDS ---
       Drupal Content Management System
       Insoshi Social Networking Platform
       Joomla Content Management System
       Redmine Project Management System
       Tracks Management System
       WordPress Blog
       LAMP Stack Hello World Example
       Ruby on Rails Hello World Example
       --- Highly Available, Multi-AZ Samples ---
       Drupal Content Management System
       Insoshi Social Networking Platform
       Joomla Content Management System
       Redmine Project Management System
       Tracks Management System
       WordPress Blog
       LAMP Stack Hello World Example
       Ruby on Rails Hello World Example
       --- Tools ---
       CloudFormer – create a template from your existing resources

                                                    Continue ▷

Figure 10-10:
The Cloud-
Formation
template
selection
panel.

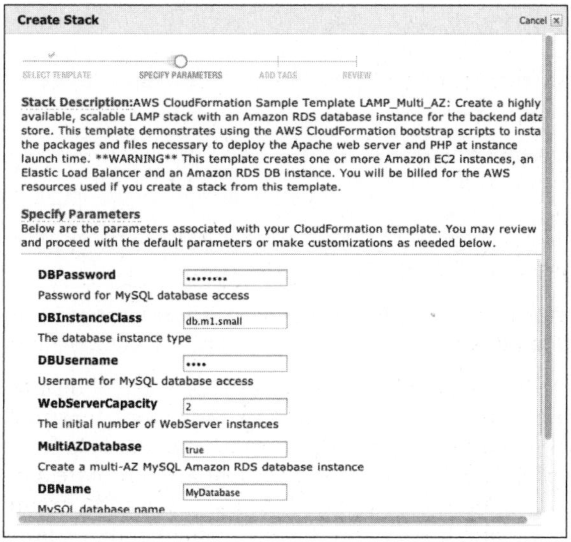

The LAMP Stack Example template

Create Stack   Cancel ⊠

SELECT TEMPLATE   SPECIFY PARAMETERS   ADD TAGS   REVIEW

Stack Description:AWS CloudFormation Sample Template LAMP_Multi_AZ: Create a highly
available, scalable LAMP stack with an Amazon RDS database instance for the backend data
store. This template demonstrates using the AWS CloudFormation bootstrap scripts to insta
the packages and files necessary to deploy the Apache web server and PHP at instance
launch time. **WARNING** This template creates one or more Amazon EC2 instances, an
Elastic Load Balancer and an Amazon RDS DB instance. You will be billed for the AWS
resources used if you create a stack from this template.

Specify Parameters
Below are the parameters associated with your CloudFormation template. You may review
and proceed with the default parameters or make customizations as needed below.

DBPassword   ••••••••
Password for MySQL database access

DBInstanceClass   db.m1.small
The database instance type

DBUsername   ••••
Username for MySQL database access

WebServerCapacity   2
The initial number of WebServer instances

MultiAZDatabase   true
Create a multi-AZ MySQL Amazon RDS database instance

DBName   MyDatabase
MySQL database name

Figure 10-11:
Setting the
Cloud-
Formation
template
parameters.

Figure 10-12:
The stack's
Summary
panel.

5. **Click Create Stack.**

   CloudFormation begins the process of creating and running the stack.

6. **On the new screen that appears, select the check box associated with the stack you created.**

   Doing so brings up a section devoted to information about the selected stack.

7. **Click the Resources tab.**

   A listing of all stack resources appears, as shown in Figure 10-13.

8. **Click to select the Outputs tab, and then cut and paste into a browser window the stack URL you find on the tab.**

   Doing so brings up the stack landing page shown in Figure 10-14. This page is equivalent to the instance page in EC2: It defines what you have running in your CloudFormation-managed application.

Name	Created	Status	Description
☑ AWSfDLampStack	2013-04-09 11:38:35 UTC-7	⚫ CREATE_COMPLETE	AWS CloudFormation Sample Te...

Stack: AWSfDLampStack

Description | Outputs | **Resources** | Events | Template | Parameters | Tags

Stack Resources   ⟳ Refresh

Logical ID	Physical ID	Type	Status
CfnUser	AWSfDLampStack-CfnUser-ZCO1IWKI5WW	AWS::IAM::User	⚫ CREATE_COMPLETE
ElasticLoadBalancer	AWSfDLamp-ElasticL-YLKLEHZDEKXM	AWS::ElasticLoadBalancing::LoadBalanc	⚫ CREATE_COMPLETE
WaitHandle	https://cloudformation-waitcondition-us-west-2.s3.amazonaws.com/arn%3Aaws%3Acl west-2%3A204956053165%3Astack%2FAWSfl a144-11e2-a34d-50ba157c60d2%2FWaitHandle?Expires=1365619147&AWSAccessKeyId=	AWS::CloudFormation::WaitConditionHa	⚫ CREATE_COMPLETE
WebServerSecurityGroup	AWSfDLampStack-WebServerSecurityGroup-1PYORWCYZWGNN	AWS::EC2::SecurityGroup	⚫ CREATE_COMPLETE
DBSecurityGroup	awsfdlampstack-dbsecuritygroup-z9jia3yzz23o	AWS::RDS::DBSecurityGroup	⚫ CREATE_COMPLETE
MySQLDatabase	am16fw899r431ec	AWS::RDS::DBInstance	⚫ CREATE_COMPLETE
LaunchConfig	AWSfDLampStack-LaunchConfig-MOYZNOA18PE7	AWS::AutoScaling::LaunchConfiguration	⚫ CREATE_COMPLETE

Figure 10-13:
The Resources tab in the Stack Resources panel.

Figure 10-14:
The Running Stack landing page.

Of course, the driver of all this activity is the template. A discussion of the Multi-AZ template is beyond the scope of this book (particularly because it's a more complex topology application), but Figure 10-15 shows a snippet of it, from the template Resources section. As you can see, the snippet shows the description of the WebServer tier, with the following information:

- ✔ **Type:** In this example, indicates that you're dealing with an Auto Scaling Group, with information to enable CloudFormation to set the execution conditions for the group.

- ✔ **Properties:** Lets you see the properties associated with the WebServerGroup. Four of the six properties use parameter or function substitution, precluding the need for hard-coding values here and thereby enabling more flexibility in use of the template. The `MinSize` and `MaxSize` parameters are defined in the Properties section, indicating the smallest and largest number of web servers that can be run in this group. These numbers probably shouldn't be hard-coded here, but passed in as parameters, making it easier to adjust deployment configurations.

Figure 10-15:
A template
snippet.

```
"WebServerGroup" : {
    "Type" : "AWS::AutoScaling::AutoScalingGroup",
    "Properties" : {
        "AvailabilityZones" : { "Fn::GetAZs" : "" },
        "LaunchConfigurationName" : { "Ref" : "LaunchConfig" },
        "MinSize" : "1",
        "MaxSize" : "5",
        "DesiredCapacity" : { "Ref" : "WebServerCapacity" },
        "LoadBalancerNames" : [ { "Ref" : "ElasticLoadBalancer" } ]
    }
},
```

Keep in mind that this snippet is only 11 lines, out of a total of nearly 200, so you can see the possible detail (and complexity) with CloudFormation. It seems complicated — and, to be fair, it *is* complicated — but in the context of running a complex multizone, multi-tier application that may be operated by numerous groups and in multiple simultaneous versions (development, testing, and production, in other words), the effort you spent in creating this complex template will be repaid many times over during the course of the application lifecycle.

To use the AWS API to manage CloudFormation, follow this example of a CloudFormation call to create a stack:

```
https://cloudformation.us-east-1.amazonaws.com/
?Action=CreateStack
&StackName=MyStack
&TemplateBody=[Template Document]
&NotificationARNs.member.1=arn:aws:sns:us-east-
          1:1234567890:my-topic
&Parameters.member.1.ParameterKey=AvailabilityZone
&Parameters.member.1.ParameterValue=us-east-1a
&Version=2010-05-15
&SignatureVersion=2
```

```
&Timestamp=2010-07-27T22%3A26%3A28.000Z
&AWSAccessKeyId=[AWS Access KeyID]
&Signature=[Signature]
```

The API call requires a template document to be "handed in" (note the variable Template Body=[Template Document] — this is where the template defining the specific application is moved into CloudFormation) and that this call is set up to use notifications to alert the application administrator of any important information raised during the stack creation process. Again, I'm illustrating that the power (and complexity) of CloudFormation lies in its templates, not in the API calls.

CloudFormation cost

As with Elastic Beanstalk, there's no cost to using CloudFormation. Amazon wants to make it easier to run large, complex applications, and free management tools are attractive to users. These tools also increase user satisfaction when users can avoid complicated, error-prone manual application administration.

AWS OpsWorks

OpsWorks is Amazon's latest addition to its management tool library, released in March 2013. Though you can reasonably ask why AWS needs *another* AWS-supplied management tool, I can think of three reasons:

- ✔ **AWS customers want better support for the complete application lifecycle.** They want it especially for incremental development and faster transitioning to production, both of which are now typical of applications. The other AWS management tools (Elastic Beanstalk and CloudFormation) tend to work on the assumption that the application code to be deployed is static and complete.

- ✔ **The demand for shorter application rollouts has developed a new IT set of practices and tools.** The practices are *DevOps,* a portmanteau (combination) word — or mash-up, if you prefer — that indicates the integration of development and operations in an effort to streamline the entire application lifecycle and shorten the time it takes to convert an application into a product. A couple open source products have become core parts of the DevOps movement, and one of them, Chef, is part of OpsWorks.

- ✔ **Though many technology employees are perfectly happy to work with text- and API-based tools, many would find complex tasks easier to implement with a visual tool.** Let's face it — JSON (particularly, complex JSON files like those required by CloudFormation) are challenging, to say the least.

In the hope of meeting these demands, Amazon released OpsWorks — a management tool designed to support complex, multi-tier applications throughout their deployment lifecycles (check!), integrate with Chef (check!), and provide a visual management interface (check — and done!).

OpsWorks terminology

Some of the terminology used by OpsWorks (stack, instance, application) may sound familiar to you, but OpsWorks often puts its own twist on a term's meaning. Here's a mini-dictionary of its terms:

✔ **Stack:** A complete application that spans multiple tiers and instances, which is consistent with CloudFormation terminology. Application-level elements, like instance blueprints (which are definitions of what software components are installed on a specific instance within a stack), user permissions, and AWS resources (S3 buckets and Elastic Load Balancers, for example) are defined at the stack level.

✔ **Layer:** Layer defines how to create and configure a set of instances and related resources, such as EBS volumes. Most people would refer to a layer as an application tier — like an application tier, a layer performs one well-defined set of functionality within the context of an application. For example, a layer may operate a PHP environment to run application logic. To reduce the development burden on AWS users, Amazon provides a number of preconfigured layers — such as Ruby, PHP, HAProxy (a load balancer), memcached, and MySQL — that you can either use as

is or extend to suit your particular needs. These layers can be combined to form a complete OpsWorks application.

✔ **Instance:** Instances become members of a layer and are configured to meet the needs of the layer in which they operate. Configuration includes setting its size and the location of the availability zone in which it operates. An instance can also be made part of an Auto Scaling Group to support erratic application workloads.

✔ **Applications:** The application-specific code that you write to perform the functionality you wish to implement. The other portions of OpsWorks exist to support you in deploying and running your application code. To place your application code on the instances within layers, you take advantage of the wonder that is Chef. (In fact, OpsWorks uses Chef to install its necessary software, which it does before it turns to installing your application code.)

✔ **Monitoring, logging:** To monitor the complex collection of instances, components, and configurations that is part of today's applications, OpsWorks implements CloudWatch, performs extensive logging, and also monitors application environments, using the open source tool Ganglia.

Chef is one of a new breed of tools used to automate code deployment and configuration. Instead of a human installing software and then setting configurations manually, Chef runs one or more scripts (known as *recipes* — clever, right?) to perform the same tasks a human would, only much faster and much more consistently. If you're configuring only a single instance, it may seem like too much work to set up Chef, but, believe me, if you're setting up hundreds of instances and doing it every time you deploy new code, all of a sudden Chef makes a ton of sense.

One great benefit of using Chef is that recipes are commonly shared — in fact, there's a public repository you can use, which increases your productivity. OpsWorks is set up to leverage the public repository and make it easier to operate complex applications.

You can operate OpsWorks via the Management Console, the API, or one of several SDKs: Java, .NET, PHP, Ruby, or Node.js., for example.

After you have created an OpsWorks application, you can bring it to life or, more prosaically, step it through its lifecycle:

- ✔ **Setup:** As each instance is booted, it needs to become ready to assume its role within the layer that it's part of and the application in which it operates. On instance boot, the operating system is brought up. If the layer definition requires system software (a MySQL database, for example), OpsWorks executes Chef's recipes to install and configure this software.

- ✔ **Deploy:** This lifecycle stage occurs when the application code is installed and configured on an instance that has completed the setup stage. OpsWorks runs the Chef recipes associated with your application code to ensure that the instance has all the code needed to perform its function.

- ✔ **Configure:** This stage occurs if the application environment changes during production. If, for example, an instance left an application layer because of an Auto Scaling event, the application configuration would need to be changed to deregister the instance from its load balancer, and so on.

- ✔ **Shutdown:** This stage is triggered when you shut down the OpsWorks application. In this stage, you may perform a database backup or write user state information out to a file. Shutdown executes Chef's recipes to perform these tasks before terminating the instance.

Using OpsWorks

The correct way to wrap your mind around OpsWorks is to approach it from the top down:

1. **Figure out the overall architecture of the application you want to implement and operate.**

   This "whiteboard design" stage presents a high-level overview of your application.

2. **Drill down to the layer level and assign specific responsibilities to each layer.**

   For example, make sure that your application's Memcached layer will be responsible for caching user information to reduce database reads. To do so, you define the functionality you'll need.

   Don't assume that you have to arrange for each layer and for all the code needed for that layer. You can leverage AWS functionality so that if you need, say, a key-value store as one layer in your application, you can use DynamoDB for it.

3. **Determine what functionality needs to reside in an instance to perform its role within the layer.**

   If part of your application transcodes images (transforms them from one digital format to another, in other words), you would want to incorporate a Chef recipe that defines and configures the appropriate instance resources and connects to the AWS Elastic Transcode service to perform the transcoding. You would also want to include a recipe to install your own code that manages receiving the images, submits them to Elastic Transcode, receives the bucket name in which the transcoded image is stored, and returns that information to the image submitter.

4. **Create the OpsWork stack by defining the different layers, the instance roles within the layers, and the necessary configuration for each type of instance.**

Just as CloudFormation requires a lot of iterative testing to evaluate whether the application definition is correct and operates properly, so too does OpsWorks. Recognize that getting an OpsWorks stack ready requires a fair amount of work, which is repaid over time as you repeatedly create the stack and run your application.

OpsWorks is so new that no one has a lot of experience with it "in the field," as they say, but I expect that most people will approach it like they approach CloudFormation: Walk through a design process as just outlined; and then use an existing AWS-supplied resource as a jumping-off point, and modify it to support the requirements of the design.

OpsWorks scope

OpsWorks has a curious scope: Because it's a *global* service, it operates without being tied to any particular region; but during stack creation, you're required to identify in which region you want your stack to operate — which seems to imply that Amazon operates the OpsWorks infrastructure globally, with service endpoints in each region to allow the lowest possible latency. This may represent the first step in Amazon's reducing its dependence on the regional partitioning of resources and operations; however, Amazon has not addressed this topic, so you'll have to wait and see!

OpsWorks cost

Like Amazon's other AWS management services, there's no charge for using OpsWorks. There is, of course, a charge for using any of the resources it manages — instances and EBS volumes, for example.

An OpsWorks example

Working with OpsWorks is similar to working with CloudFormation. Follow these steps:

1. **From the AWS Management Console page, click OpsWorks.**

   Doing so brings up the OpsWorks initial landing page, as shown in Figure 10-16.

The Add Your First Stack button

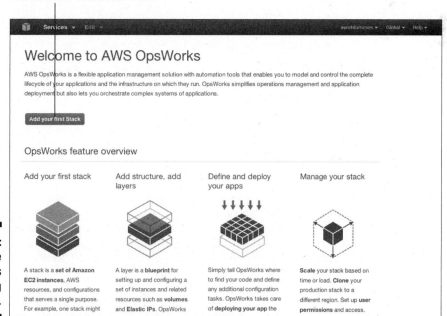

Figure 10-16:
The OpsWorks landing page.

2. Click the Add Your First Stack button.

Doing so brings up the Add Stack page, as shown in Figure 10-17.

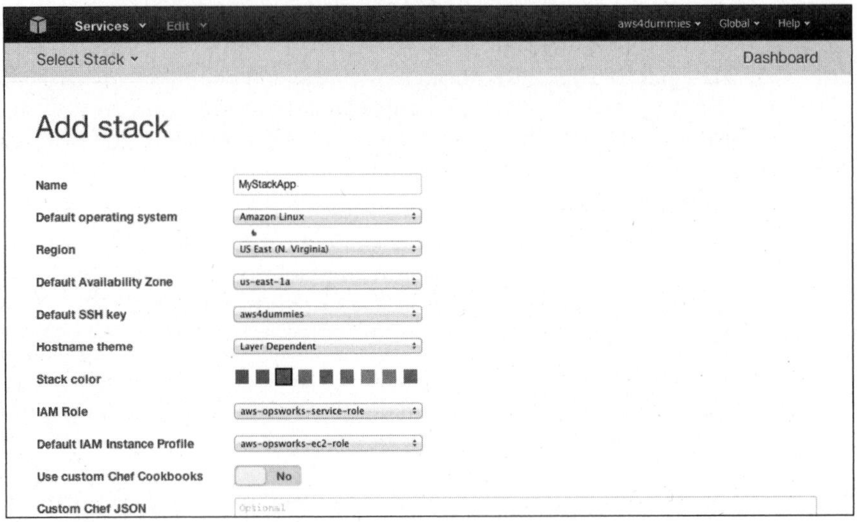

Figure 10-17:
The stack
configura-
tion page.

3. Enter the requested information into the fields of the Add Stack page.

The requested information is pretty much what you'd expect:

- *Name:* A name that you choose. I have decided to call my stack MyStackApp.

- *Default operating system:* Either Amazon Linux or Ubuntu, when you're using one of the sample AWS OpsWorks Stacks. I use Amazon Linux.

- *Region:* Where your stack runs. I run my stack in US East.

- *Default Availability Zone:* The zone in which your stack instances operate. AWS offers a single default zone, but if you choose, you can configure your layers to use multiple zones. I leave this one as is in this example.

- *Default SSH Key:* The SSH key that's used to access your stack instances for administrative purposes. Again, it can be overridden per instance, but I use a single SSH key, *aws4dummies,* in this example. (For more on SSH keys, see Chapters 2 and 12.)

- *Hostname Theme:* A way to identify resources associated with a given stack, because you may have multiple stacks running at a single time. I'm keeping the default — Layer Dependent.

- *Stack Color:* Associates a color with all the stack resources so that you can more easily identify what belongs where. I use the default color, which is blue.

4. After entering the required information, click the Add Stack button.

Your stack is added.

After my stack is created, I'm invited to define the resources associated with it, as shown in Figure 10-18. Well, as long as OpsWorks is asking nicely. . . .

Here's what I'd do:

1. Click the Add a Layer link on the MyStackApp page. (Refer to Figure 10-18.)

Doing so brings up the Add Layer page.

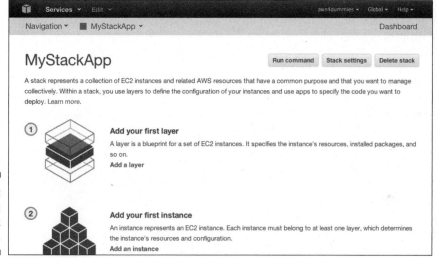

Figure 10-18:
Configuring
the stack
itself.

2. Choose a layer type from the Layer Type drop-down menu, and then click Add Layer.

OpsWorks provides a number of layer types; because I'm creating a PHP app, I chose the PHP App Server type, as shown in Figure 10-19.

3 Click the Add Layer button.

Doing so creates an instance to operate within the web server layer just created.

4. On the new page that appears, click the Add an Instance link.

5. When the (even newer) page displays. click the Advanced button to show all the necessary fields.

The page expands to reveal a new Add Instance section, as shown in Figure 10-20.

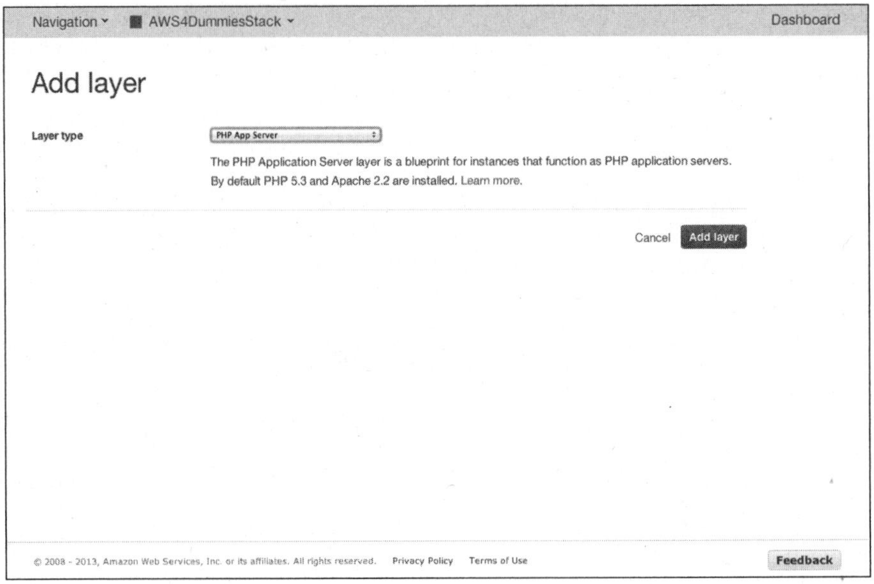

Navigation ∨ ■ AWS4DummiesStack ∨   Dashboard

Add layer

Layer type   [PHP App Server   ▼]

The PHP Application Server layer is a blueprint for instances that function as PHP application servers.
By default PHP 5.3 and Apache 2.2 are installed. Learn more.

                                                     Cancel   [Add layer]

© 2008 - 2013, Amazon Web Services, Inc. or its affiliates. All rights reserved.   Privacy Policy   Terms of Use   [Feedback]

Figure 10-19:
Creating a
stack layer.

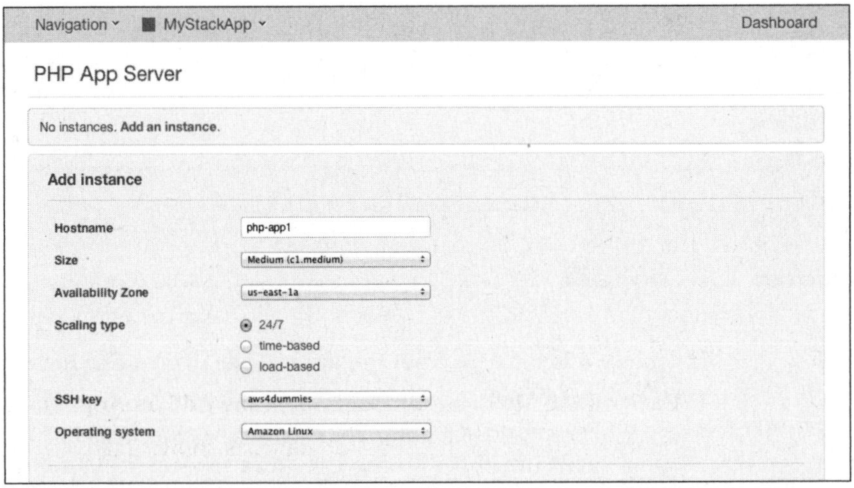

Navigation ∨ ■ MyStackApp ∨   Dashboard

PHP App Server

No instances. Add an instance.

Add instance

Hostname   [php-app1]
Size   [Medium (c1.medium)   ▼]
Availability Zone   [us-east-1a   ▼]
Scaling type   ◉ 24/7
                    ○ time-based
                    ○ load-based
SSH key   [aws4dummies   ▼]
Operating system   [Amazon Linux   ▼]

Figure 10-20:
Creating
a stack
instance.

Because I chose `layer dependent` as the hostname theme, OpsWorks
automatically assigns the name `php-app1` to my instance — 1 because
it's the first instance in the application. The wizard suggests `c1.medium`
as the instance type and sets 24/7 (24 hours a day, seven days a week)
as the Scaling type so that the instance runs immediately and is always
on. I will use the same ssh key as I defined for the overall stack, though I

could do instance-specific keys, if I wanted to. I stick with Amazon Linux as my operating system, and I'm ready to create the stack instance.

6. Click the Add an Instance link.

After you define the instance, you're invited to launch it, which I have done, as you can see in Figure 10-21. It shows the instance after it has started and OpsWorks has performed all its magic in connecting and configuring the instance as part of the layer. OpsWorks displays the status `Online` to indicate a successful instance start.

Figure 10-21: The stack instance as it's running.

Completing the previous step list prepares the underlying resources to begin running the actual application code; it's now time to deploy that code. To do that, I do the following:

1. Back on the MyStackApp page, click the Add an App button.

Doing so brings up the App New page, as shown in Figure 10-22.

2. Fill out the required fields with information that's appropriate for your application.

No surprises here — a simple name, the app type (again — PHP, in this case). Because I'm using a sample AWS application, I use the public AWS Git repository with the URL displayed in the Repository URL box. If you're following along, it's located at `git://github.com/amazon webservices/opsworks-demo-php-simple-app.git`.

This is the location of the repository, but I have to identify exactly which code base I want that's stored within the repository. I do so by typing `version1` in the Branch/Revision box.

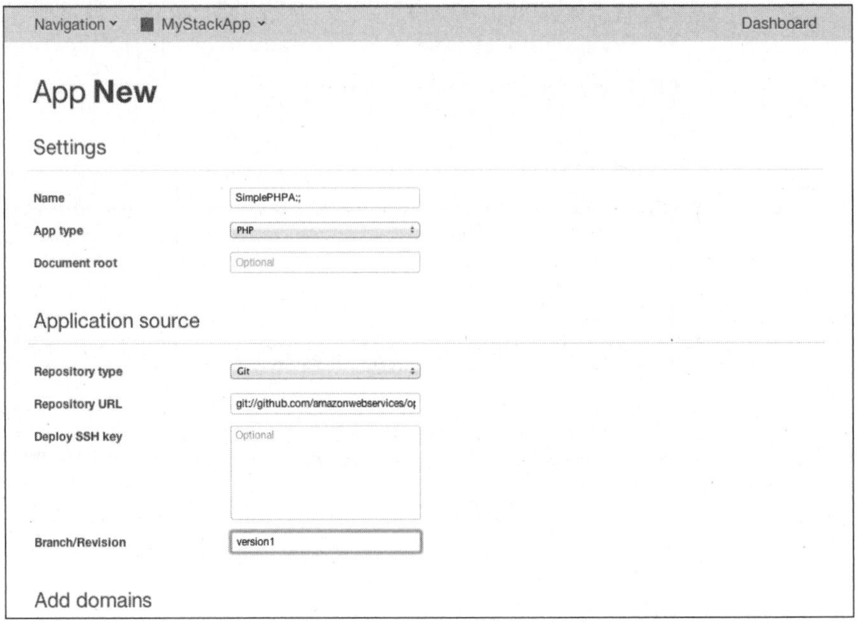

Navigation ˅   ■ MyStackApp ˅   Dashboard

App **New**

Settings

Name	SimplePHPA:;
App type	PHP ⇕
Document root	Optional

Application source

Repository type	Git ⇕
Repository URL	git://github.com/amazonwebservices/o
Deploy SSH key	Optional
Branch/Revision	version1

Add domains

Figure 10-22:
Adding the application code.

3. **Click the Continue button.**

   You then see a page inviting you to deploy the app code, as shown in Figure 10-23.

4. **Click Deploy.**

   OpsWorks has Chef download the application code and then install and configure it on the application's instance.

At this point, OpsWorks downloads the code repository from the Git location and installs it on the instance. In addition, OpsWorks executes any Chef recipes to configure the application code and begin running it. At the end of this process, an information screen appears and lets you know that the status of application deployment is now successful, as shown in Figure 10-24.

Of course, if the application code deployment failed, the status would be different. If you want to examine the details of the application deployment, you can examine the logs for the deployment phase by clicking the link on the right side of the hostname listing.

Naturally, you'll want to see this application operating, so you can go back to the instance page (refer to Figure 10-21) and click the IP address in the Hostname listing. When you do that, another browser window opens, and a connection is made to the OpsWorks PHP application. The window displays the message `Simple PHP App`, as shown in Figure 10-25, indicating that the application has been successfully installed and is operating normally.

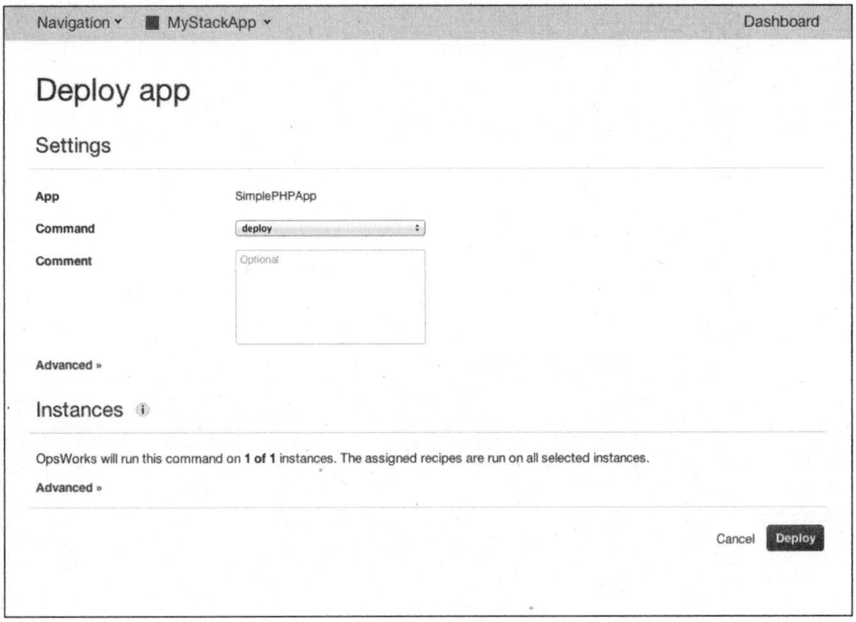

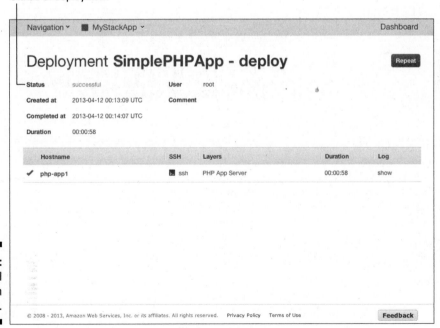

Figure 10-23: Deploying the application code.

Status of deployment

Figure 10-24: A successful application deployment.

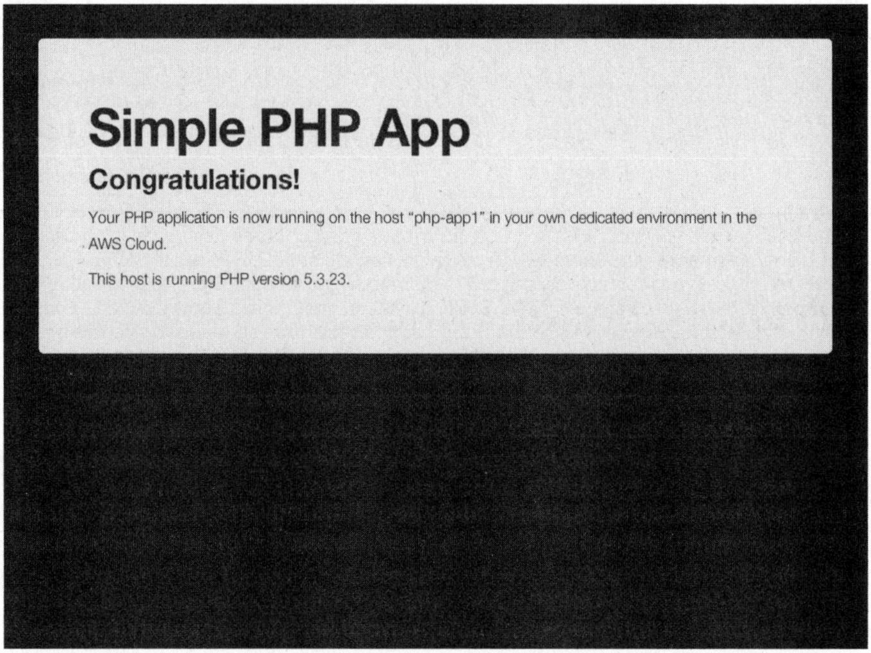

Simple PHP App
Congratulations!

Your PHP application is now running on the host "php-app1" in your own dedicated environment in the AWS Cloud.

This host is running PHP version 5.3.23.

Figure 10-25:
All
systems go.

Wooga runs on AWS

The European-based social gaming company Wooga offers Facebook-based games that run on browsers, mobile devices, and tablets. The very nature of its games produces very high traffic loads and highly variable traffic patterns.

Early in its life, Wooga selected AWS as its infrastructure, which removed concerns about infrastructure availability — important for a company whose games support more than 3 million players per day and more than 20,000 requests per second.

This high variability of load makes managing the application infrastructure challenging.

Launching and terminating instances when user loads change greatly over the course of a day or week is difficult, to say the least.

To address the manageability of its application infrastructure, Wooga has turned to OpsWorks, the AWS application management service. By defining its applications in an OpsWorks definition, Wooga can depend on AWS to manage deployment and resource management, with OpsWorks automatically adjusting the number of AWS instances to handle game traffic without running (and paying for) unused resources.

Don't let this simple application blind you to the power of OpsWorks. The combination of AWS, Chef, and an application management platform that auto-mates the installation and configuration process is extremely powerful; more-over, the more complex the application and the more frequently it's deployed, the more benefit you receive from using OpsWorks.

Which AWS Management Service Should 1 Use?

The fact that Amazon provides three application management solutions is, as the saying goes, a blessing and a curse. That Amazon provides applica-tion management solutions indicates that many of its users find it difficult to administer complex applications, but the availability of multiple solutions may make it difficult to decide which solution to use. Here are some guide-lines for you to use in choosing which management solution to adopt:

- ✔ **If your application is fairly simple and written in a dynamic language, choose Elastic Beanstalk.** By *fairly simple,* I refer to an application that runs in a single tier and, if the database isn't part of the application instance proper, you're at least using an AWS RDS service to manage persistent storage. If your application uses dynamic languages but has multiple tiers running software you have written, the application is too complex for Elastic Beanstalk.

- ✔ **If your application is fairly complex but uses Amazon Machine Images that contain both system resources (operating system and middleware, like databases or other servers) and application code, CloudFormation is a good choice.** It can manage multiple tiers and con-nect those tiers, even when Auto Scaling is involved. CloudFormation isn't designed to manage applications in which middleware and applica-tion code are dynamically installed on an instance. Of course, you have to be comfortable with working with fairly complicated JSON scripts to use CloudFormation, which may or may not be your cup of tea.

- ✔ **If you use a DevOps application lifecycle discipline or you prefer to dynamically install code on your application instances or you prefer a graphical interface to the joys of JSON, OpsWorks is a good option.** You should become familiar with Chef because it is OpsWorks' recom-mended method of managing code. OpsWorks hasn't been on the market long (at least not at the time this book was written), but I expect it to become a commonly used tool to manage complex application deployment.

Chapter 11

Managing AWS Costs

• •

In This Chapter

▶ Digging deeper into the complexities of AWS costs

▶ Keeping track of AWS costs and utilization

▶ Figuring out how to better manage your AWS costs

• •

*T*his chapter addresses two interrelated and vital issues for AWS users:

✔ How to ensure that your AWS applications operate efficiently and effectively

✔ How to best manage your AWS costs

Amazon is justly famous for its ability to run AWS at scale, its effective use of automation, and its track record in keeping costs extra low. However, Amazon's ability to run AWS efficiently and with low costs doesn't automatically mean that the resources *you* run in AWS are efficient and inexpensive.

In fact, using AWS inefficiently isn't difficult — because you can easily obtain AWS resources, there's a danger that you may end up using AWS less efficiently than on-premise computing resources. You may think, "Hey, it's easy to launch a server," believing that it costs only $.06 per hour and forgetting (or not bothering) to shut it down. Like a leaky tap, though, small amounts can add up to a gusher of wasted resources.

This wastefulness can be a true problem at scale, when an organization may have dozens of applications and hundreds of instances running in AWS. The growth of AWS services exacerbates this issue, given how many more services there are to keep track of.

Never fear, however: This chapter tells you about tools that are available to address the issues of efficiency and costs. I also throw in some general advice about how to keep your AWS usage both efficient and cost effective.

AWS Costs — It's Complicated

Wait a sec. How dare I say that AWS costs are complicated? Hasn't Amazon made a virtue of cost transparency? Hasn't it put the prices for each of its services right there on its website, available for all and sundry to view? Doesn't it provide reduced prices for increased volume? Hasn't it created new services to better and more efficiently support user workloads, thereby reducing their costs? Hasn't it created discount programs in the form of reserved resources that offer much lower costss in return for making a financial commitment upfront?

Yes, yes, yes, yes, and yes.

Amazon is completely transparent about charging for its services, unlike many of its competitors who post statements such as these on their websites: "For pricing, please contact a sales representative to review your requirements." (You'll never find out what *those* providers charge unless you subject yourself to a sales pitch.) Amazon is to be commended for breaking from those customer-unfriendly practices and making it easier to find accurate charges.

Amazon is also to be commended for its innovation in rolling out new services. Just during the writing of this book , it rolled out two new major services and a plethora of small improvements to its existing services. The company should be further commended for creating its EC2 reserved instances offering, which reduce the total cost of ownership (TCO). And, of course, Amazon deserves praise for offering price breaks for volume use.

The challenge in tracking Amazon costs results from all this commendable and praiseworthy behavior. Simply put, Amazon has rapidly developed such a variety of services and pricing structures that trying to understand all the costs that are being charged to your account is quite a challenge; it's even worse when you have complex applications that use many different AWS resources spread across multiple tiers — not to mention trying to understand how varying application load (which typically causes *resource scaling* — the temporary use of additional resources to ensure adequate application performance) affects costs.

Over its brief lifetime, AWS has evolved from a limited set of services offered with a limited set of options to a rich mélange of services and options that is much more difficult to track and that works against easy predictions of TCO. Obviously, you should fully understand your resource utilization, figure out its patterns, and analyze what you can do to ensure that your AWS costs are as low as possible; on the other hand, you don't want to reduce your costs to the point that your application's availability or performance suffers.

Feeling overwhelmed by this tug-of-war between costs and performance? Fortunately, help is at hand. Read on.

Taking Advantage of Cost and Utilization Tracking

How important is it to manage your AWS utilization and costs? It's very important. Cloudyn, one of the leading companies in the area of AWS utilization analysis, kindly shared some of its customer statistics in order to highlight common patterns of AWS use — and, of course, to profile the challenges that can arise when users don't manage their AWS use in a thoughtful manner.

Cloudyn sampled 400 customers and analyzed these companies' use of AWS in January 2013. In a discussion about its findings, the company noted that it had conducted a similar survey a year earlier and found similar results, so the January 2013 results can be considered representative of how many companies use (and misuse) AWS.

The companies primarily represent enterprise customers, which is to say that the survey population represents end users of IT, not vendors. Moreover, the companies tend to be larger, as opposed to small start-ups. (Cloudyn primarily serves the enterprise market, so it makes sense that this survey pool is composed primarily of mainstream companies.) Table 11-1 shows the breakdown (in terms of annual AWS expenditures) for the survey pool.

Table 11-1   AWS Annual Expenditure Survey Pool

Expenditure Amount	*Percentage of Survey Pool*	*Percentage of Total Survey Expenditure*
Less than $50,000	61 percent	4 percent
$50,000 to $100,000	11 percent	5 percent
$100,000 to $500,000	22 percent	30 percent
$500,000 to $1 million	2 percent	10 percent
More than $1 million	4 percent	52 percent

As you can see, a large percentage of the survey pool spends less than $50,000 per year, but of the total amount spent, this group represents only 4 percent. At the other end of the spectrum, only 4 percent of the survey pool spends more than $1 million per year on AWS, but those companies represent more than half of total AWS spending by the entire survey pool. Curiously, a greater percentage of the survey pool spends more than $1 million per year than the percentage that spends between $500,000 and $1 million.

I'll bet that this "more than $1 million per year spent on AWS" statistic grabbed your attention, right? It certainly grabbed mine. Any way you slice it, more than a million dollars per year is a healthy chunk of change. Clearly, the survey shows that a number of mainstream companies have adopted AWS as a platform for significant amounts of computing — in other words, AWS is a key part of their computing infrastructure. I hope you'll remember this statement the next time someone airily asserts, "AWS is mostly used by start-ups and for testing and development." It has moved way past that point.

To help you dig deeper into Cloudyn's survey results, Table 11-2 shows the breakdown of total spending on AWS services that the survey group uses.

Table 11-2	Distribution of Expenditure by AWS Service
Service	*Percentage of Spending*
S3	6 percent
RDS	7 percent
EBS	8 percent
Other	17 percent
EC2	62 percent

In this breakdown, network traffic falls into the Other category, which is why you don't see it identified specifically.

Frankly, these numbers surprised me. I would have expected more of the spending to be on S3, and I'm surprised that EC2 represents so much of the total amount. Nevertheless, you should draw two main lessons from this table:

- ✔ **EC2 will be a large proportion of your total spending.** Pay close attention to your use of EC2 to ensure that you use it in the most efficient fashion. I make some recommendations in this regard later in thing chapter.

- ✔ **Even though those AWS services listed as Other (SQS and SNS, for example) don't seem expensive, in sum they represent nearly 20 percent of total annual expenditure for the survey companies.** These services are likely to be more heavily used than generally recognized, and their use can add up to serious costs. Individually, the "Other" AWS services may not be expensive, but in aggregate they're significant.

Turning to how survey members purchase their EC2 instances, Table 11-3 shows the popularity of the various pricing models.

Table 11-3	Use of the EC2 Pricing Model
Pricing Model	*Percentage of Use*
On-demand instances	71 percent
Reserved instances	26 percent
Spot-priced instances	3 percent

Which pricing model you choose is much more important than it may seem at first glance. Many people believe that the hourly charge for a single on-demand EC2 instance is so low not to be worth the bother involved in ordering a reserved instance. Moreover, many people aren't sure how long they'll use a particular instance, so they shy away from reserved instances because they feel that they would be making a long-term commitment without knowing that it will be worthwhile.

These feelings are perfectly understandable. However, you should at least consider using reserved instances. Need convincing? Check out Figure 11-1, which Cloudyn prepared in order to illustrate the total cost trade-off between the EC2 pricing models.

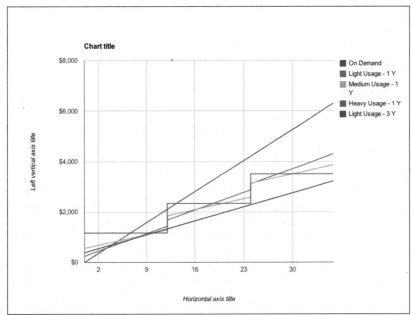

Figure 11-1:
Comparing the costs of the AWS pricing models.

The chart reflects total time on the horizontal axis, with months as the units, and a total time of three years (36 months). The vertical axis represents total cost in dollars. The chart compares these five pricing models:

- ✔ On-demand
- ✔ One-year light use reserved
- ✔ One-year medium use reserved
- ✔ One-year heavy use reserved
- ✔ Three-year heavy use

As Chapter 5 makes perfectly clear, understanding the ins and outs of the various benefits and commitments of the light, medium, and heavy use reserved instances can be difficult. However, if you're planning to use an instance for at least three months, you're better off doing so via a reserved instance, no matter which type of reserved instance you choose. (Refer to Figure 11-1.) Three months — that's all. In the section on managing AWS costs, I recommend how to apply reserved instances — the main point here is that you should consider using reserved instances if you plan any kind of significant AWS use.

If you're even more adventurous, evaluate using *spot instances*, where AWS lets you place bids on unused resources. The drawback to using spot instances is that you never can be sure whether you can obtain EC2 instances at your bid price. On the other hand, you can attempt a spot price launch, and if no instance is available at your bid price, go to an on-demand instance. Pinterest, the wildly successful and often quirky service that lets you "collect and organize the things you love," is a heavy user of spot instances as a strategy to reduce its total AWS spending. The site's commitment to spot instances is so strong that it's built into its application code. The application always tries to launch a spot instance first (via the AWS SDK), and if no spot instance is available, its code fails over to a second launch call for an on-demand instance. Cloudyn also analyzed how the survey pool used AWS resources and identified two other important findings:

- ✔ **Sixteen percent of Elastic Block Store volumes weren't attached to an instance.** The volumes were created but weren't in service at any point during the month-long survey period. Though it's possible that some of these volumes would be used at times other than during this period, the vast majority of them are likely formerly used, now-forgotten, abandoned volumes — even if they're not being used, though, the client is still being charged for them.

✔ **The average processor load across the entire pool of EC2 instances was only 19 percent.** In other words, more than 80 percent of the processing capacity was wasted. It makes sense to have some headroom for spiky load, but 80 percent represents an enormous amount of waste; again, even though the capacity isn't being used, it's still being charged for. That is, the AWS users are paying for something they're not using.

This list explains the main points of this extremely interesting survey:

✔ **AWS use is big.** Even if you're not a heavy user of AWS, you're likely to become one, especially if you follow what is, anecdotally, a common pattern: starting small, with an almost offhand use of AWS — perhaps a quick application prototype — and, after seeing how easy it is to obtain resources and be productive, rapidly increasing your use to a point where it's a fairly significant portion of total infrastructure use.

✔ **EC2 is likely to represent the vast majority of your expenditure.** Many organizations find that the easy availability of computing resources, especially compared with the protracted provisioning cycle of their on-premise infrastructure, makes EC2 almost seductively appealing. And don't forget that, for businesses under competitive pressure, the immediate EC2 provisioning process enables market agility, which is highly prized in today's global economy.

✔ **Despite EC2's prominence, other AWS services are sure to represent a significant portion of your total spending.** Pay attention to how you use any of the other AWS services. Just as important, work to understand them (using a valuable resource like this book) so that you can better evaluate how to use them to build better applications and further enable agility.

✔ **Watch your AWS use patterns to make sure that you're benefitting fully from what you're paying for and not wasting AWS resources.** Historically, given the difficulty in obtaining resources, many IT organizations would overprovision, believing that it was better to buy too much and avoid having to endure the tiresome process again rather than risk being caught short and having to repeat a miserable experience *again*. In the AWS world, where the overhead of obtaining (or releasing) computing resources is trivial, that "overbuying" behavior isn't necessary; worse, it imposes true costs given the fact that you pay for AWS all the time, even if you're not doing anything with the resources.

Pinterest runs on AWS

You're probably familiar with Pinterest, the wildly successful application that lets people share their interests via "pinning" theme-based images. From sewing to cooking to muscle cars, people are madly sharing items that they find compelling relating to their personal interests.

You might even be aware that Pinterest runs on AWS — lock, stock, and barrel. Its enormous community of users and all their images use AWS. But you likely aren't surprised that a hugely successful technical giant runs its entire business on AWS.

What you might be surprised about, however, is how cleverly Pinterest manages its AWS resources and how much it reduces its AWS spending by carefully choosing the kinds of EC2 instances it uses.

Like many online properties, Pinterest has wide variability in user load — much greater use in the evening than during working hours. When it originally started, it used (as do most other sites) on-demand EC2 instances, paying full rates for their use. This presents two kinds of wastefulness:

✔ **Not using reserved instances:** By simply prepaying for instances, Pinterest could save 30 percent or more in the hourly cost of an EC2 instance.

✔ **Variability of traffic:** It doesn't make sense to pay for an instance that is running but not being used, so an instance that's very busy at 8 p.m. might be idle most of the day while the level of Pinterest traffic is low.

To keep its costs low, Pinterest

✔ **Uses heavy reserved instances:** To help manage traffic at levels that are present at all hours (in other words, the minimum level of traffic that is always present no matter what time of day it is). By making the largest upfront payment, Pinterest receives the lowest possible hourly price.

✔ **Uses light reserved instances:** To manage traffic at levels that are predictably present during portions of the day. These receive less of a discount from the on-demand price but require less upfront payment.

✔ **Attempts to use spot priced instances, making low bids for idle instances:** To manage unpredictable spikes in traffic. The natural reaction would be to use on-demand instances for spike traffic that goes beyond what can be handled via reserved instances. After all, this is for short-lived instance use, and paying the full on-demand price would be acceptable for these short periods . Pinterest doesn't follow this approach, however. (Remember that much of its heavy traffic occurs during off-work hours, when AWS likely has idle resources, rather than use on-demand instances for its peak traffic.) This strategy enables it to save as much as 89 percent off the on-demand price for the same instance. Only if no spot instances are available during peak traffic conditions does Pinterest turn to standard on-demand instances.

By combining these techniques, Pinterest saves on the order of 60 percent off the cost of pure on-demand instances. It takes some clever planning, but achieving those kinds of financial results makes the work highly profitable.

Managing Your AWS Costs

Now that you know that AWS is a big deal, that you're likely to use a lot of it, and that it's challenging to manage it in a cost-effective manner, you probably want guidelines for ensuring that you're getting your money's worth from AWS.

You've come to the right place, because here are some best practice recommendations:

- **Design applications to be scalable — both up and down.** Use multiple smaller EC2 instances instead of a smaller number of larger instances. Doing so ensures that you more closely match your total computing capacity to application load so that you have just the right amount available at any given time.

- **Follow a "down and off" application management strategy.** This term, coined by Forrester analyst James Staten, means that you should seek to have only the right amount of computing resource available at any given point, and that you should aggressively reduce computing resources when the application load shrinks. The easy, immediate AWS provisioning capability supports this because, if the application load increases, you can easily add resources to your application. And if you followed the previous recommendation about making your application scalable, your application will easily accommodate a growing or shrinking resource pool.

- **Leverage Auto Scaling groups.** One challenge of following the "down and off" strategy (and the complementary "up and on" for responding to growing application load) is the operations burden. For every instance that needs to be launched or terminated, an operator has to perform some work: adding or subtracting the instance to a resource pool, connecting it to other instances, and, perhaps, adding a load balancer to the mix. To deal with this burden, use Auto Scaling groups, the AWS answer to this challenge. Configure your application up front, and then let Amazon take care of dynamically scaling your resource pool while you sit back with a cup of coffee. (For more on Auto Scaling groups, see Chapter 11.)

- **Leverage an AWS management tool from Amazon or a third party.** Auto Scaling groups are fantastic for managing EC2, but as the survey data indicates, you'll use plenty of other AWS resources. AWS management tools can reduce the operational overhead of managing those other resources, such as SQS and RDS. (That's less work and more coffee break time for you!)

- **Perform application load testing to help with your financial modeling.** By loading up your application with simulated traffic, you can see what resources it uses at higher volumes. Then you can see whether you're likely to expand your use of certain services enough to achieve price breaks based on volume. Conversely, it also shows if, at larger application loads, you use certain services wastefully and can redesign your application to reduce the use of those services and save money. Of course, I advocate performing load testing to ensure better application robustness; it's an additional benefit of load and performance testing.

A number of open source and commercial load/performance testing products and services are available. One I like is from the SOASTA (www.soasta.com), a company that offers the CloudTest service. It is, of course, an on-demand, cloud-based service that lets you use (and pay) for only what you need. SOASTA also offers the free product CloudTest Lite, which you can install on your local machine; it allows you to simulate as many as 100 simultaneous users. Frankly, given that it's free, and how important it is to design and test an application to be robust in the face of large and fluctuating load, you'd be foolish not to use CloudTest Lite.

✔ **Use analysis tools to ensure efficient, effective AWS use.** As you can see from the survey results at the beginning of this chapter, it's easy to use AWS. It's so easy, in fact, that you can easily lose track of what you're using — or, to be more precise, what you're provisioning, and paying for, but not using. Believe me: It's easy to forget all the resources you've provisioned. It's not a sign of forgetfulness or carelessness; it just happens. The important thing is what you should do to address this byproduct of AWS's easy provisioning.

Use an analysis tool like Cloudyn (www.cloudyn.com). Other third-party analysis tools are in the marketplace, and Amazon has recently launched the new service Trusted Advisor, which is free to use and performs some of the same kinds of analyses. Most of the third-party services also offer a free-use tier. Given the real cost of unused AWS resources, and the availability of free-use levels of tools such as Trusted Advisor and other, third-party tools, you should, at minimum, leverage an analysis tool to give you a reading on where you stand with respect to your AWS use. If the findings indicate some shortcomings in your use patterns (and they probably will — trust me), you can look at doing a more thorough analysis by moving to one of the paid options from third-party tools like Cloudyn.

Chapter 12

Bringing It All Together: An AWS Application

. . . .

In This Chapter

▶ Building a simple blogging site

▶ Partitioning the site to enhance performance

▶ Improving application robustness with geographical redundancy

. . . .

*T*his chapter presents a complete application that allows you to do some hands-on work with AWS. I present a step-by-step set of instructions for you to follow as you start from a simple EC2 application and incrementally increase its performance and robustness by taking advantage of additional AWS services to improve it. Along the way, I discuss the reasons for selecting these additional services and how they improve the application. If you follow along, by the time you finish working through the example, you'll be ready to take on AWS singlehandedly!

The example in this chapter focuses on AWS itself and on how to improve an application by layering on additional AWS services. The idea is *not* to come up with a whiz-bang application as well. That's why I'm presenting a simple, pre-packaged blogging application put out by WordPress. (Then you don't have to worry about writing any code. Big sigh of relief, eh?)

To get another confession out of the way, I do *not* discuss items critical to running this application in production mode, such as error checking and handling and version-control planning. Though they're important topics, I want you to experience the power of AWS and not get bogged down in unnecessary details.

Here's an outline of how to get the project up and running:

1. Create an AWS account.

2. Update the Default security group to accept network traffic on Ports 80 (HTTP) and 22 (SSH).

3. Locate and launch an appropriate WordPress Amazon Machine Image (AMI) to use as the basis of the hands-on examples.

4. Vertically partition your WordPress application by migrating its database to the AWS Relational Database Service (RDS), discussed in Chapter 8).

5. Create your own WordPress website AMI from your vertically partitioned WordPress application.

After you complete these five steps, you'll have converted a simple application into a highly robust one that's ready to handle significant loads.

Sound like fun? Good. Let's get started.

Putting the Pieces Together

The purpose of this section is to demonstrate how AWS is used in real-world settings. You'll start by launching a simple, pre-existing Wordpress AMI. This illustrates AWS ease of use and quick resource availability. You'll then incrementally improve the functionality and robustness of your Wordpress application, so you can see how additional AWS services can be used to build out applications. Along the way, you'll create a new Wordpress AMI, which will help you understand the power of the AWS infrastructure. Overall, at the end of this set of hands-on activities, you'll have developed some AWS skills; more importantly, you will (I hope) be convinced of the power of the AWS offering.

Creating your own AWS account

I describe the nuts-and-bolts of creating your own AWS account in Chapter 3, so you may want to review it now. To be honest, it's quite easy to create an account; all you need is an e-mail address, a credit card, and a phone. (You use the phone's keypad to enter a PIN number that AWS sends to you during the sign-up process.)

Setting up an account, which takes no more than 10 minutes, is covered in step-by-step detail in — you guessed it — Chapter 3, so if you don't already have an account, create one now. (Don't hurry. I'll go get a cup of tea while you're working through the process.)

Enabling access on your security group

In Chapter 7, where I discuss AWS security, I mention that one keystone of AWS security is the concept of a *security group,* which is, essentially, a software firewall that AWS installs on every AWS instance to control traffic to the instance. AWS supplies one security group — Default — to every account, and allows you to create additional security groups as necessary. For this exercise, you have to configure a security group to that traffic on two ports: 80 (for web HTTP traffic) and 22 (for SSH administrative access).

You can use the Default security group and open those ports on it for this exercise. Chapter 7 contains information on adding rules to security groups, so refer to that chapter in order to add ports 22 and 80 to the Default security group. Because these ports are commonly used, AWS provides them in a handy drop-down menu in the Create a New Rule selection box, so look for SSH and HTTP in the list and add them. Leave the Source box alone (at 0.0.0.0/0), to indicate that the instance accepts access from anywhere on the Internet.

Locating and launching an appropriate WordPress Amazon Machine Image (AMI)

I could have begun this chapter's exercise, of course, by having you write an application from scratch. But that would be hard work, and bo-o-o-oring to boot (in addition to asking you to do a lot of stuff before getting to the exciting part of using AWS).

A better way to start is from an existing software package, which requires much less work and allows you to focus on AWS itself, instead of on writing the entire application on your own. (Much better, don't you think?) Even this approach requires a fair amount of work: You'd need to install the software on a running EC2 instance, install the appropriate operating system and middleware packages, verify the proper configuration, and then create a new Amazon Machine Instance, or AMI. Whew! That's still a lot of work, right?

Fortunately, you can choose a better way — a much better way. One strength of AWS is its ability to leverage its ecosystem — the large number of users and commercial organizations that offer online services that run in and/or complement AWS itself. One way that the ecosystem helps people like you is to provide prebuilt AMIs. Depending on who offers the AMI, it may integrate a commercial software offering or open source software; if it's the former, you pay to use it; if it integrates open source, it's probably free to use, although the provider may provide additional commercial services, such as support or monitoring, as paid offerings. (Doesn't the free one sound like a good way to go?)

When following my instructions in this chapter, your best bet is to use an offering from one of the best of the breed: Bitnami. This company offers a range of prebuilt AMIs, all containing open source applications that are completely free for you to use. As you may expect, the company also offers support and services for them. Bitnami isn't limited to AWS, though — it offers similar capabilities and services for a number of other cloud computing environments. Your interest is AWS, of course, so I focus on Bitnami AWS AMIs.

Bitnami offers an amazing range of AMIs — ones that incorporate open source applications such as SugarCRM and Moodle (an educational app), technical configurations like the Java server Tomcat, and a selection of content management solutions (website management applications, in other words) such as Joomla, Plone, Alfresco, and WordPress. In this chapter, I've selected WordPress because it's an extremely popular content management system, and you may have worked with it. (It probably wouldn't surprise you to learn that my own website, www.bernardgolden.com, runs on WordPress.)

Go ahead and track down the Bitnami WordPress AMI. Start out by clicking on EC2 on the Management Console landing page to get to the EC2 AMI dashboard, but rather than sift through all the AMI offerings, take advantage of the Search capability on the page, as shown in Figure 12-1.

1. Using the Filter drop-down menus along the top of the page, narrow your search by selecting Public Images, EBS Images, and Ubuntu as the criteria for your search (see Figure 12-1).

Bitnami images are designed to be publicly accessible; if I didn't use Public Images as the image type, I wouldn't have been able to see Bitnami's WordPress image. I chose EBS Images because it simplifies making new AMIs based on this AMI; I chose Ubuntu because it's a convenient Linux version to use. I also used bitnami-wordpress as a search term within the AMI description because I wanted to select only from Bitnami-supplied WordPress images and not have to see the SugarCRM or Moodle (or whatever) images.

To understand why using EBS-backed images makes creating new AMIs easier, see Chapter 4.

Despite all the filters that are applied, notice that you still come up with quite a number of entries — so many that the one I want you to use isn't even listed on the initial page of entries.

Type in your search keywords here.

			Name	AMI Name	AMI ID	Source
	▸			bitnami-wordpress...	ami-e0d62389	979382823631/bitnami-wordpress-3.0.1-0-linux-ubuntu.
	▸			bitnami-wordpress...	ami-0ce61065	979382823631/bitnami-wordpress-3.0.2-0-linux-ubuntu.
	▸			bitnami-wordpress...	ami-3816e051	979382823631/bitnami-wordpress-3.0.3-0-linux-ubuntu.
	▸			bitnami-wordpress...	ami-ae7b8ac7	979382823631/bitnami-wordpress-3.0.4-0-linux-ubuntu.
	▸			bitnami-wordpress...	ami-76bb481f	979382823631/bitnami-wordpress-3.0.5-0-linux-ubuntu.
	▸			bitnami-wordpress...	ami-3c0af955	979382823631/bitnami-wordpress-3.1-0-linux-ubuntu-'
	▸			bitnami-wordpress...	ami-d2fc00bb	979382823631/bitnami-wordpress-3.1.1-0-linux-ubuntu.
	▸			bitnami-wordpress...	ami-04cd326d	979382823631/bitnami-wordpress-3.1.2-0-linux-ubuntu.
	▸			bitnami-wordpress...	ami-a29960cb	979382823631/bitnami-wordpress-3.1.3-0-linux-ubuntu.
	▸			bitnami-wordpress...	ami-58946f31	979382823631/bitnami-wordpress-3.1.3-0-linux-x64-ut
	▸			bitnami-wordpress...	ami-bed72cd7	979382823631/bitnami-wordpress-3.1.4-0-linux-ubuntu.
	▸			bitnami-wordpress...	ami-80d62de9	979382823631/bitnami-wordpress-3.1.4-0-linux-x64-ut
	▸			bitnami-wordpress...	ami-d653a8bf	979382823631/bitnami-wordpress-3.2-0-linux-ubuntu-'

EC2 Dashboard
Events
Tags

INSTANCES
Instances
Spot Requests
Reserved Instances

IMAGES
AMIs
Bundle Tasks

ELASTIC BLOCK STORE
Volumes
Snapshots

NETWORK & SECURITY
Security Groups
Elastic IPs
Placement Groups
Load Balancers
Key Pairs
Network Interfaces

Launch | Actions

Filter: Public Images | EBS Images | Ubuntu | Q bitnami-wordpr ✕

1 to 25 of 133 AMIs

© 2008 - 2013, Amazon Web Services, Inc. or its affiliates. All rights reserved.   Privacy Policy   Terms of Use   Feedback

Figure 12-1:
Searching
for a Bitnami
WordPress
AMI.

2. **Make your way to the third page to locate the AMI: a 64-bit 3.2.1-5 WordPress version, as shown in Figure 12-2.**

Note that the AMI I want you to use carries the ID `ami-1bbc7472`. However, I'm using AWS US East for this example. If you're using a different AWS region, you'll find that the Bitnami 64-bit Ubuntu EBS-backed WordPress 3.2.1-5 AMI carries a different AMI ID because of Amazon's AWS regional structure. Don't worry: The example still works the same — just find the right AMI in your chosen region or stick with the US-East region for your hands-on work to simplify your effort.

The next step is to launch the WordPress AMI. You can see that the EC2 Dashboard puts up a striking blue Launch button for exactly this situation (refer to Figure 12-1).

3. **After selecting the 64-bit 3.2.1-5 WordPress AMI to work with, click the Launch button.**

AWS starts the launch wizard, as you can see in Figure 12-3.

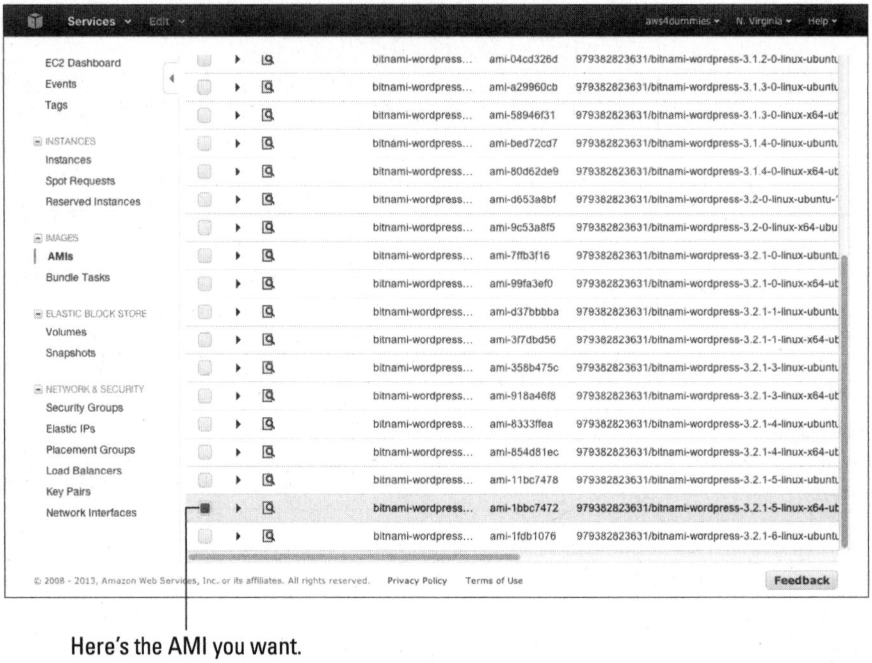

Figure 12-2:
The 64-bit
3.2.1-5
Ubuntu
WordPress
AMI.

Here's the AMI you want.

Figure 12-3:
The AWS
Launch
Wizard.

4. **Enter 1 in the Number of Instances field, and choose T1 Micro from the Instance Type drop-down menu.**

   To keep this example simple (and cheap), you start with only one instance and use the T1 Micro instance type, which provides as many as two EC2 compute units in Burst mode (but much less in normal operation) and only 613MB of memory. As small as it is, it's completely sufficient for this example; better yet, if you're using a new AWS account in this example, the T1 Micro instance is free for you to use.

5. **In the Launch Into section, keep the EC2-Classic radio button enabled (the default) and then click Continue.**

   AWS presents the next screen of the launch wizard, as shown in Figure 12-4, where you can choose to modify the instance's kernel modules or change its RAM disk, but in practice these options are rarely used, so leave them alone. Also leave monitoring turned off for now. The User Data box passes in information to the instance during the launch process; you don't have any launch information to communicate to the instance, so leave this one empty. Neither do you need to worry about termination protection in the example, and you aren't using IAM, so leave those options alone. (IAM, which refers to identity management services, is described in Chapter 8, if you want more information.)

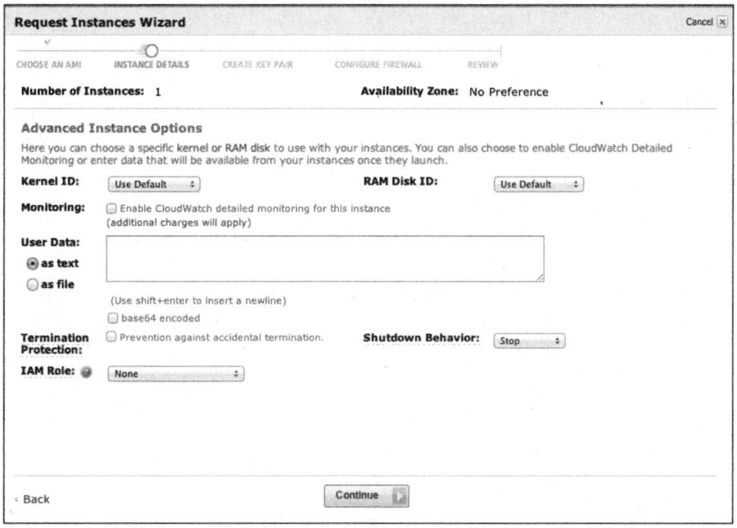

Figure 12-4: Setting advanced instance options — Kernel, User Data, and IAM Roles.

6. **After leaving everything as is on this screen, click Continue.**

   The next launch wizard screen appears, as shown in Figure 12-5, which you *can* use to identify additional EBS volumes that you might like to attach to this instance. The one listed in the Storage Device Configuration box is the EBS root volume for this instance, and it's necessary for it to operate.

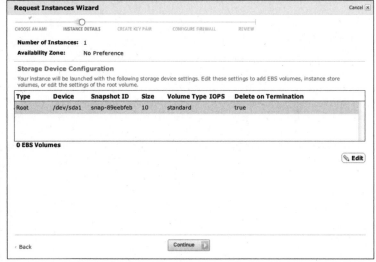

Request Instances Wizard · Cancel [x]

CHOOSE AN AMI · INSTANCE DETAILS · CREATE KEY PAIR · CONFIGURE FIREWALL · REVIEW

Number of Instances: 1
Availability Zone: No Preference

Storage Device Configuration

Your instance will be launched with the following storage device settings. Edit these settings to add EBS volumes, instance store volumes, or edit the settings of the root volume.

Type	Device	Snapshot ID	Size	Volume Type	IOPS	Delete on Termination
Root	/dev/sda1	snap-89eebfeb	10	standard		true

0 EBS Volumes

✎ Edit

‹ Back · Continue ▸

Figure 12-5:
Where to configure additional EBS volumes.

7. **You need no additional volumes in this example, so leave this screen unchanged and click Continue.**

   The new screen that appears, as shown in Figure 12-6, is used to enter any tags that you want to associate with the instance while it's running.

   Tags can be quite useful if you're running large numbers of instances, because you can search by tag and reduce the total number of instances you need to look at to find the specific instance you need.

8. **Because you're working with only a couple of instances in this example, just click Continue.**

   The next screen (see Figure 12-7) is one of the most important and, in my experience, challenging for new AWS users. Keep in mind that the method used to control administrative access to AWS Linux instances is Secure Shell, known as SSH. Rather than have to fuss with usernames and passwords, SSH uses cryptographic keys to control access to instances and to encrypt data that's transferred between an administrator's client machine and the instance being administered.

Request Instances Wizard   Cancel ⊠

CHOOSE AN AMI   INSTANCE DETAILS   CREATE KEY PAIR   CONFIGURE FIREWALL   REVIEW

Add tags to your instance to simplify the administration of your EC2 infrastructure. A form of metadata, tags consist of a case-sensitive key/value pair, are stored in the cloud and are private to your account. You can create user-friendly names that help you organize, search, and browse your resources. For example, you could define a tag with key = Name and value = Webserver. You can add up to 10 unique keys to each instance along with an optional value for each key. For more information, go to Tagging Your Amazon EC2 Resources in the *EC2 User Guide*.

Key (127 characters maximum)	Value (255 characters maximum)	Remove
Name		✖
		✖

Add another Tag.   (Maximum of 10)

‹ Back   Continue ▷

Figure 12-6:
Entering
tags, if you
so desire.

Request Instances Wizard   Cancel ⊠

CHOOSE AN AMI   INSTANCE DETAILS   CREATE KEY PAIR   CONFIGURE FIREWALL   REVIEW

Public/private key pairs allow you to securely connect to your instance after it launches. For Windows Server instances, a Key Pair is required to set and deliver a secure encrypted password. For Linux server instances, a key pair allows you to SSH into your instance. To create a key pair, enter a name and click **Create & Download Your Key Pair**. You will be prompted to save the private key to your computer. Note: You only need to generate a key pair once - not each time you want to deploy an Amazon EC2 instance.

◉ **Choose from your existing Key Pairs**

Your existing Key Pairs*:   [aws4dummies ⬍]

○ **Create a new Key Pair**
○ **Proceed without a Key Pair**

‹ Back   Continue ▷

Figure 12-7:
Creating
an SSH key
pair.

SSH uses a combination of a public key and a private key. The administrator holds the private key on the client machine. The remote resource
(the AWS instance, in this case) holds the public key. The client machine
makes an SSH connection and presents the private key. The remote
resource uses the private key and confirms that it matches the public
key and then, assuming that they match, allows SSH access to the
remote resource.

After you figure out how to use SSH, it's straightforward, but if you're not familiar with it, it can take some getting used to. Linux/Mac clients have an SSH client built in, accessible via the Terminal application. Windows machines don't have a native SSH client, but the free application Putty offers SSH support.

Showing you how to use SSH in all its infinite variety is beyond the scope of this book, but a number of good resources are available, including one at Bitnami's website: `http://wiki.bitnami.com/cloud/how_to_connect_to_your_amazon_instance`

In this example, I show you how to use SSH via a Terminal application, but Putty operates in much the same way.

9. **On the new screen that appears, select the Create a New Pair radio button.**

   This step is a bit tricky. AWS opens a screen offering to download the private part of the key pair — you must download it somewhere on your computer, and you can choose any location that's secure, robust, and convenient. On Linux or the Mac, a directory in your home directory — .ssh — is the traditional place to put a private key pair. In Windows, complete the key conversion process, as outlined on the Bitnami web page in Step 8.

10. **After downloading the private part of the key pair to your computer, click Continue.**

    On the next screen (see Figure 12-8), you choose one or more security groups to associate with your instance. If you followed the instructions at the beginning of this chapter, the Default security group should specify that ports 22 and 80 are open.

Figure 12-8: Specifying your security group.

11. **Select the Choose One or More of Your Existing Security Groups radio button, select the Default option from the list, and then click Continue.**

    That's it! The final confirmation screen lists all the choices you've made while completing the wizard, and, assuming that you click the Launch button on that screen, you see a confirmation panel like the one shown in Figure 12-9, indicating that your new EC2 instance is on its way!

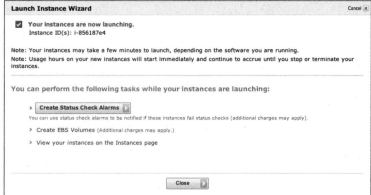

Figure 12-9:
Your EC2
instance is
launching.

Within a couple of minutes, if you click the Instances link (at the top of the Navigation pane on the left side of the EC2 dashboard) and then select the check box to the left of the running instance, you should see something like Figure 12-10.

Note several items on this screen:

- ✔ **An instance ID and the AMI ID you've been working with:** In my example, the AMI ID is `ami-1bbc7472`.

- ✔ **The instance state, which is listed as Running:** From AWS's perspective, everything is operating normally.

- ✔ **Information (below the gray bar) about your instance, including the full name of the AMI and the AWS DNS entry for this instance:** In this case, the DNS entry is `ec2-23-23-12-40.compute-1.amazonaws.com`.

- ✔ **Additional information on the Description tab:** Here you can find the zone the instance is operating within, the type of instance that's running, and the security group(s) associated with the instance.

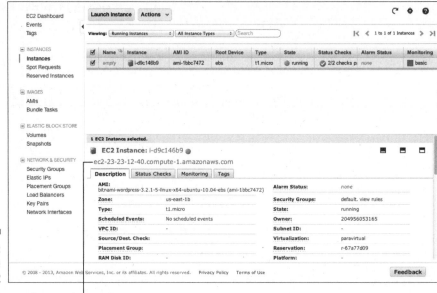

Figure 12-10:
The
running EC2
instance.

Your instance's URL

As I mention in this list, from the perspective of AWS, this instance is operating normally. But that doesn't mean the application code itself is also operating normally, so you have to check it. To do so, you need the instance's URL.

Look for the URL right above the Description tab. (In Figure 12-10, the instance URL is `ec2-23-23-12-40.compute-1.amazonaws.com`.) Copy the URL that's displayed in your browser in the same location as this example. Then open a blank browser tab so that you can enter your instance's URL. Paste the URL into the browser tab and press Return.

You then see something like Figure 12-11, which is the initial landing page of the Bitnami WordPress application.

When you click the Access My Application button, you should see the standard WordPress landing page, as shown in Figure 12-12.

The Access My Application button

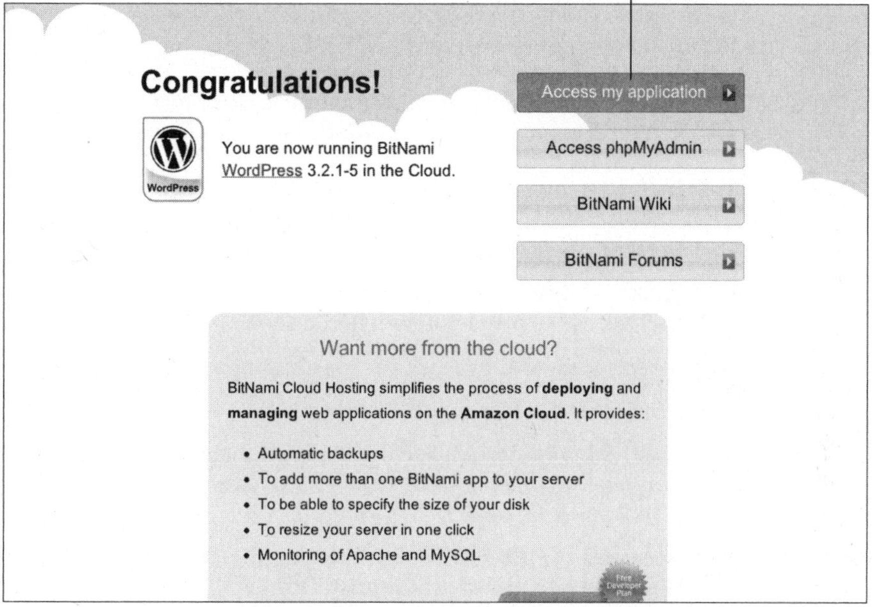

Figure 12-11:
The initial landing page in the Bitnami WordPress application.

Figure 12-12:
The WordPress landing page.

Bitnami provides full administrative access to the WordPress application, and you can access the WordPress administrative interface by clicking the Login link in the lower-right corner of the page. Doing so presents you with the login panel, as shown in Figure 12-13.

Enter **user** as the username and **bitnami** as the password, and you instantly see the WordPress administrative interface, as shown in Figure 12-14.

Take a step back and review what you've accomplished. You have

✔ **Created an AWS account**

✔ **Modified the default security group for your account to allow web and SSH access to any instance you launch**

✔ **Selected an AMI to work in this chapter's exercise**

✔ **Launched the Bitnami WordPress AMI**

This AMI contains a full WordPress application and allows you, for the purposes of this chapter, to focus on AWS itself and avoid having to install any software.

✔ **Accessed the Bitnami WordPress application and logged in to WordPress as the site administrator**

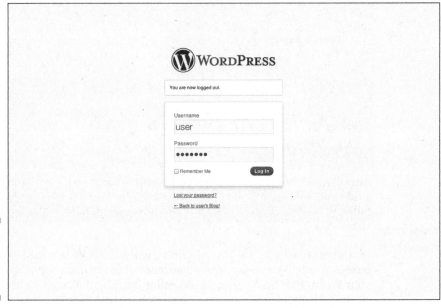

Figure 12-13:
The
WordPress
login panel.

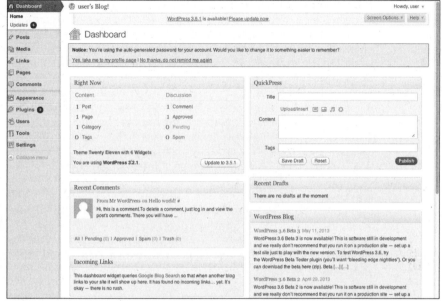

Figure 12-14:
The
WordPress
admin-
istrative
interface.

Well done! You've successfully used AWS to launch and run an application. I hope that, in completing this exercise, you've seen why AWS represents a revolution in computing. Even if you're a first-timer, you probably spent no more than 30 minutes moving from having no account to having a running application. As you gain experience, you may spend no more than 5 minutes — a far cry from the length of time that employees at many companies spend, where it can take 6 weeks to get a virtual machine from IT.

Vertically partitioning your WordPress application

After you've done all the work in the previous sections, you should have a fully functioning WordPress application. You can use it as the basis of a full-fledged website, leveraging all the power and plug-ins that WordPress is known for.

On the other hand, your site is running within a single instance, which would pose a problem if the site ever experiences heavy traffic — the throughput of your WordPress application could suffer because the instance has to manage all the web traffic while running the database that WordPress uses to store all its data — including the data that WordPress uses to create its webpages. In short, your WordPress application could suffer from performance overload.

Furthermore, running the database and the WordPress application on the same instance presents danger as well — if the application crashes (an occurrence that is, unfortunately, too common, typically caused by misbehaving plug-ins), any data entered in the database since the AMI was launched would be lost. In the case of the WordPress example, any changes you made to the base Bitnami AMI would disappear!

A common way to address this issue is to *vertically partition* the application — a fancy way of saying that you split the application, leaving the front end (the webpages part) on one instance and move the back end (the database part) to a separate instance. This strategy ensures that the two parts of the application don't contend for the single instance's processing resources.

However, vertical partitions don't address the issue of crashes. Though the likelihood of the database instance crashing is lower than if it were on the same instance as the running application, the potential still exists for the database instance to crash — your vertical partitioning would then be for naught, and you'd be back at Square One with your Bitnami WordPress application.

One way to address this whole crash business is to move the database from the database instance to a separate EBS volume, which wouldn't be affected by instance crashes. On the other hand, you would still need to manage the database instance and create snapshots and backups for data protection. In other words, you'd still be stuck with the work of running the database instance.

This situation is the type that Amazon's own RDS service is designed for. RDS operates and manages a database instance, taking care of creating snapshots and backing it up. To make everyone happy then, let me show you how to vertically partition your WordPress application by moving the database to the RDS service.

Doing this requires two steps:

1. Create the RDS service that will manage the WordPress application.

2. Modify the WordPress application to interact with the RDS database.

In the following section, I walk you through these steps.

Creating the RDS service to manage the WordPress application

Your database now resides on the single instance of the WordPress application. First, access that instance and use MySQL — a popular, open source RDBMS (relational database management system) — to download the information needed to create an RDS database that provides the same database and information that resides on the WordPress application. (Such downloads are commonly referred to as performing a *database dump*.) Start by accessing the WordPress application instance via the Secure Shell (SSH) network protocol. (For the sake of this example, remember that you use the Terminal application, which ships with both Mac and Linux operating systems.)

1. **Using Terminal, enter the correct** ssh **command for your system.**

   Figure 12-15 shows the ssh command I used to access the instance. Your ssh command will vary according to the name of your private key and the IP address of the instance. Note that you log on as user Bitnami, not root, as is common with SSH. Also note that I have used the IP address of the instance; be sure to use the IP address of your instance, which you can find at the bottom of the instance information page. (The IP address is contained in the DNS name of the instance — it's the four numbers in the middle of the DNS name.) You'll also need to change the permissions on the ssh key file for ssh to operate properly. The command to change permissions is:

   ```
   Chmod 700 aws4dummies.pem
   ```

   Of course, you'll need to substitute the name of your .pem file for aws-4dummies in the above example.

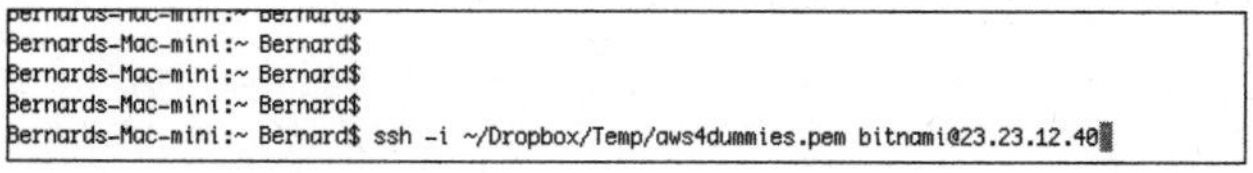

Figure 12-15:
The ssh
connection
command.

```
Bernards-Mac-mini:~ Bernard$
Bernards-Mac-mini:~ Bernard$
Bernards-Mac-mini:~ Bernard$
Bernards-Mac-mini:~ Bernard$
Bernards-Mac-mini:~ Bernard$ ssh -i ~/Dropbox/Temp/aws4dummies.pem bitnami@23.23.12.40
```

2. **During the connection process, you receive a message indicating that the host you're connecting to is unknown and asking whether you want to add it to the list of known hosts. Answer Yes.**

   Upon successful connection, you see the Bitnami instance terminal splash screen, as shown in Figure 12-16.

   To perform the database dump, you provide the database password, found in the WordPress configuration file.

3. **Go to the directory that contains the configuration file by typing this line into Terminal:**

   ```
   cd /opt/bitnami/apps/wordpress/htdocs/
   ```

   To obtain the password, you edit the file.

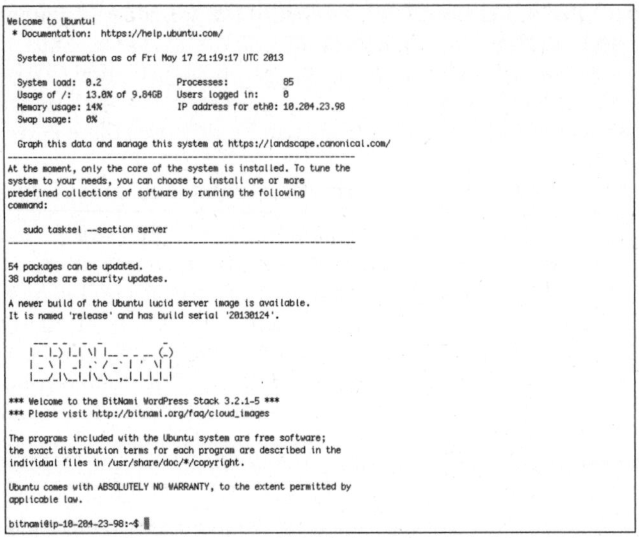

Figure 12-16:
The Bitnami
Instance
terminal
splash
screen.

```
Welcome to Ubuntu!
 * Documentation:  https://help.ubuntu.com/

  System information as of Fri May 17 21:19:17 UTC 2013

  System load:  0.2              Processes:           85
  Usage of /:   13.0% of 9.84GB  Users logged in:     0
  Memory usage: 14%              IP address for eth0: 10.204.23.98
  Swap usage:   0%

  Graph this data and manage this system at https://landscape.canonical.com/
----------------------------------------------------------------------
At the moment, only the core of the system is installed. To tune the
system to your needs, you can choose to install one or more
predefined collections of software by running the following
command:

   sudo tasksel --section server
----------------------------------------------------------------------
54 packages can be updated.
38 updates are security updates.

A newer build of the Ubuntu lucid server image is available.
It is named 'release' and has build serial '20130124'.

 _     _ _             (_)
| |__ (_) |_ _ __   __ _ _ __ ___ (_)
| '_ \| | __| '_ \ / _` | '_ ` _ \| |
|_.__/|_|\__|_| |_|\__,_|_| |_| |_|_|

*** Welcome to the BitNami WordPress Stack 3.2.1-5 ***
*** Please visit http://bitnami.org/faq/cloud_images

The programs included with the Ubuntu system are free software;
the exact distribution terms for each program are described in the
individual files in /usr/share/doc/*/copyright.

Ubuntu comes with ABSOLUTELY NO WARRANTY, to the extent permitted by
applicable law.

bitnami@ip-10-204-23-98:~$
```

4. **Type** sudo nano wp-config.php **into Terminal.**

   Doing so opens the WordPress configuration into the Nano text editor. Sudo indicates that you're executing the nano command as the administrator of the machine, superuser.

5. **After the configuration comes up, search it by moving the arrow key until you find the line containing MySQL database password, as shown in Figure 12-17.**

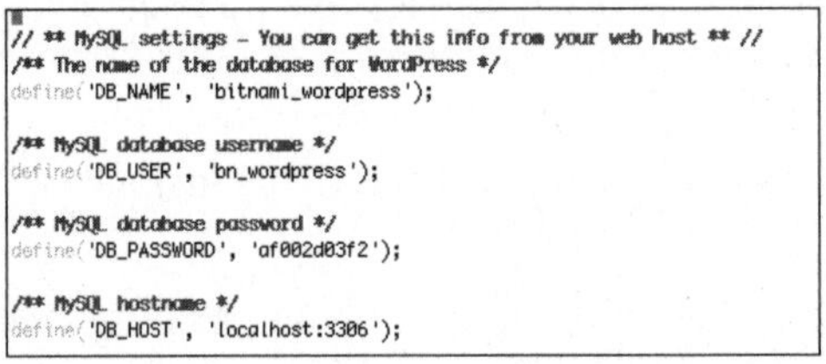

Figure 12-17:
The
WordPress
configura-
tion file
database
section.

```
// ** MySQL settings - You can get this info from your web host ** //
/** The name of the database for WordPress */
define('DB_NAME', 'bitnami_wordpress');

/** MySQL database username */
define('DB_USER', 'bn_wordpress');

/** MySQL database password */
define('DB_PASSWORD', 'af002d03f2');

/** MySQL hostname */
define('DB_HOST', 'localhost:3306');
```

6. **Write down the password associated with the database. Also write down the database name and username, which, as you can see in the figure, are listed in lines by the line that contains the password.**

   You need all this information when creating the RDS database.

7. **Close the Nano text editor by pressing control-x.**

8. **Perform the database dump by typing the following command into Terminal, as shown in Figure 12-18:**

```
mysqldump -u bn_wordpress -pyourpassword bitnami_
          wordpress > backup.sql
```

Substitute the database password you wrote down for `yourpassword` following the `-p` parameter shown in the preceding command.

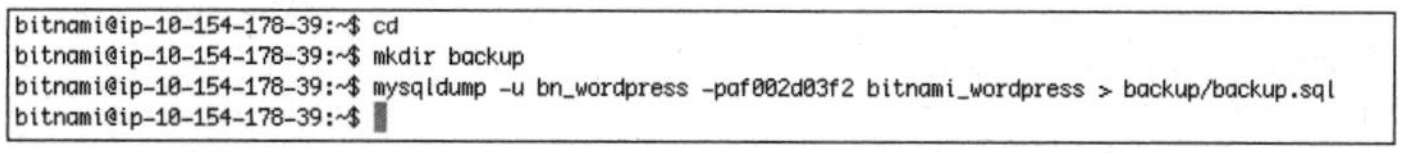

Figure 12-18:
The MySQL
database
dump
command.

```
bitnami@ip-10-154-178-39:~$ cd
bitnami@ip-10-154-178-39:~$ mkdir backup
bitnami@ip-10-154-178-39:~$ mysqldump -u bn_wordpress -paf002d03f2 bitnami_wordpress > backup/backup.sql
bitnami@ip-10-154-178-39:~$
```

Now you're ready to create the RDS database that WordPress will connect to. Follow these steps:

1. **Click the Management Console link to access the AWS Management Console.**

2. **Click the console's RDS link.**

   Doing so takes you to the main RDS page, which you can see in Figure 12-19.

The Launch a DB Instance button

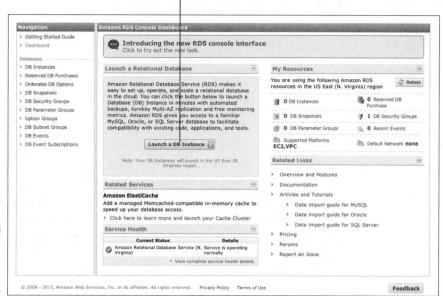

Figure 12-19:
The main
RDS page.

3. Click the Launch a DB Instance link.

The RDS wizard launches, as shown in Figure 12-20.

Launch DB Instance Wizard   Cancel ⊠

ENGINE SELECTION   DB INSTANCE DETAILS   ADDITIONAL CONFIGURATION   MANAGEMENT OPTIONS   REVIEW

To get started, choose the DB Instance details below and click **Continue**

MySQL.   **mysql**
                MySQL Community Edition   Select ▶

ORACLE   **oracle-se1**
                Oracle Database Standard Edition One   Select ▶

ORACLE   **oracle-se**
                Oracle Database Standard Edition   Select ▶

ORACLE   **oracle-ee**
                Oracle Database Enterprise Edition   Select ▶

                sqlserver-ex
SQL Server   Microsoft SQL Server Express Edition
                Note that SQL Server Express Edition limits the storage of per   Select ▶

Figure 12-20:
The first
panel of the
RDS wizard.

For your WordPress application, you will add a MySQL database, which, conveniently enough, is the first choice.

4. Click the Select button associated with the wizard's MySQL option.

5. On the next screen that appears (see Figure 12-21) leave the defaults in place for the options labeled DB Engine, DB Engine Version, and Auto Minor Version Upgrade, select a Micro Instance for DB Instance Class and No for Multi-AZ Deployment.

Doing so creates a micro instance type that's located in a single availability zone, with no provisioned IOPS.

In a production environment, consider using a large instance along with Provisioned IOPS option to guarantee high performance (but stick with the defaults in this example).

6. In the DB Instance Details section of the wizard panel (refer to Figure 12-21), create sufficient allocated storage for the instance by typing 5, which will create 5GB of storage, and fill in the DB Instance Identifier, Master Username, and Master Password fields.

You gathered all that information about the DB Instance Identifier, Master Username, and Master Password when you examined the `wp-config` file using the Nano text editor.

7. Click Continue.

The next screen, shown in Figure 12-22, holds even more information about the RDS DB instance configuration. On this panel, you can add a database name and leave everything else in place.

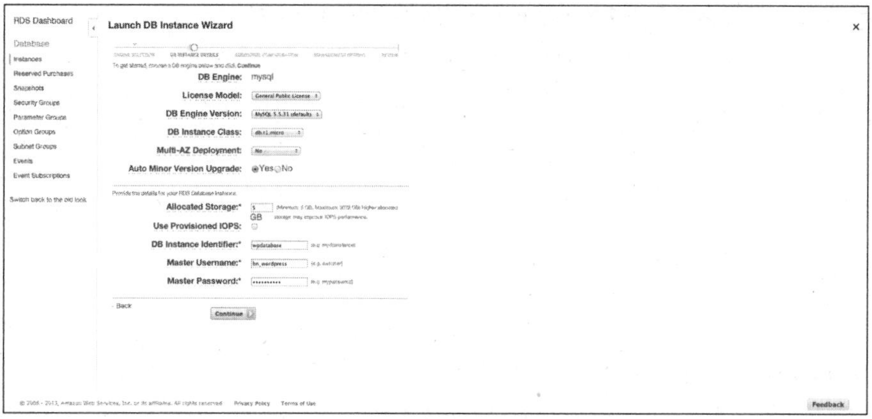

Figure 12-21:
The DB Instance Details panel in the wizard.

Figure 12-22:
Additional configuration information in the RDS wizard.

8. **Type the database name — bitnami_wordpress — into the Database Name field, be sure to select the same Availability Zone that your instance is running in, and then click Continue.**

   The next panel of the wizard, labeled Management Options (see Figure 12-23) lets you configure your database management information specifying whether you want to make automated backups and how long to retain them. By default, automated backups are enabled with a backup retention period of one day. In production systems, you may keep backups for a longer period, but leave the defaults in place for now.

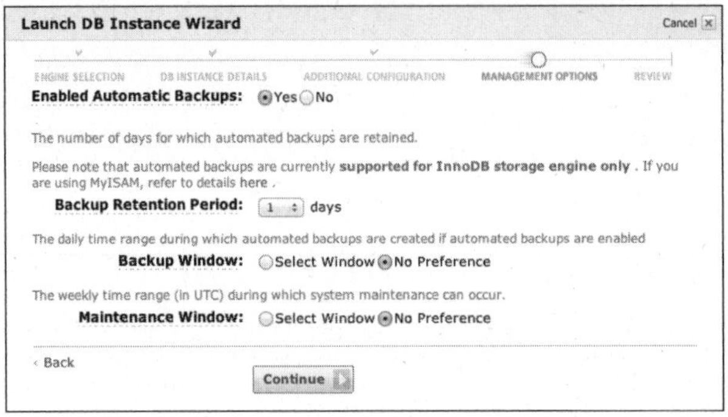

Figure 12-23:
The RDS
wizard
Management
Options
screen.

9. Leaving the defaults in place, click Continue.

Doing so brings up another wizard screen (see Figure 12-24), where
you're asked to confirm all the information you entered in the previous
panels.

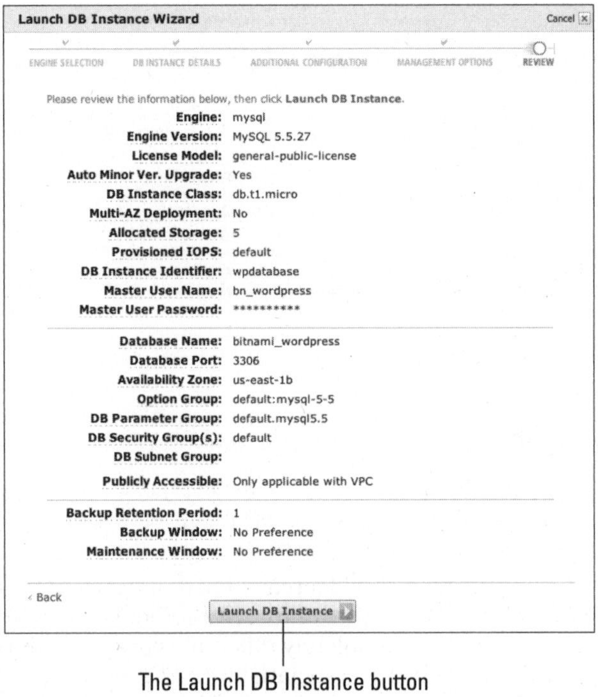

Figure 12-24:
The RDS
Wizard
Confirmation
screen.

The Launch DB Instance button

10. **After double-checking the displayed information, click the Launch DB Instance button.**

    Go ahead and grab a cup of coffee or tea while AWS creates the RDS instance. Eventually, the final wizard panel confirms that the instance is being created, as shown in Figure 12-25.

11. **Click Close.**

    Doing so brings you back to the main RDS panel.

12. **Click on the Instances link on the left hand side of the RDS main page.**

    This will take you to the RDS instances page, which, in a few minutes will show the new DB instance as Available, as shown in the status field in Figure 12-26.

In the final step, ensure that your RDS DB instance is ready to interact with your WordPress application: You must put your EC2 security group into the DB security group so that your EC2 instance can receive traffic from your RDS database.

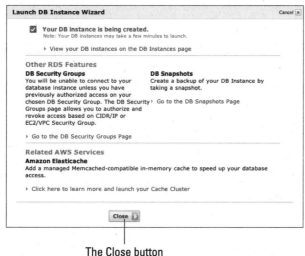

Figure 12-25: The final panel in the RDS wizard.

The Close button

This sounds a bit confusing — you'd already filled out a security group for RDS, so you may wonder why you need to add another security group to your instance. These are two completely different types of security groups — one associated with RDS and one associated with EC2 — and you need your EC2 instance associated so that traffic can flow between the two services.

Here's how to set up that association:

1. **In the main RDS panel, click the DB Security Groups link in the Navigation pane on the left.**

   Doing so brings up the RDS security groups.

2. **You have only the default RDS security group, so click on it.**

3. **Click on the small magnifying glass to the right of the DB Instance name.**

   A new screen appears, as shown in Figure 12-27. Note the area at the bottom of the list where you can configure information about the connection type that your RDS instance can support.

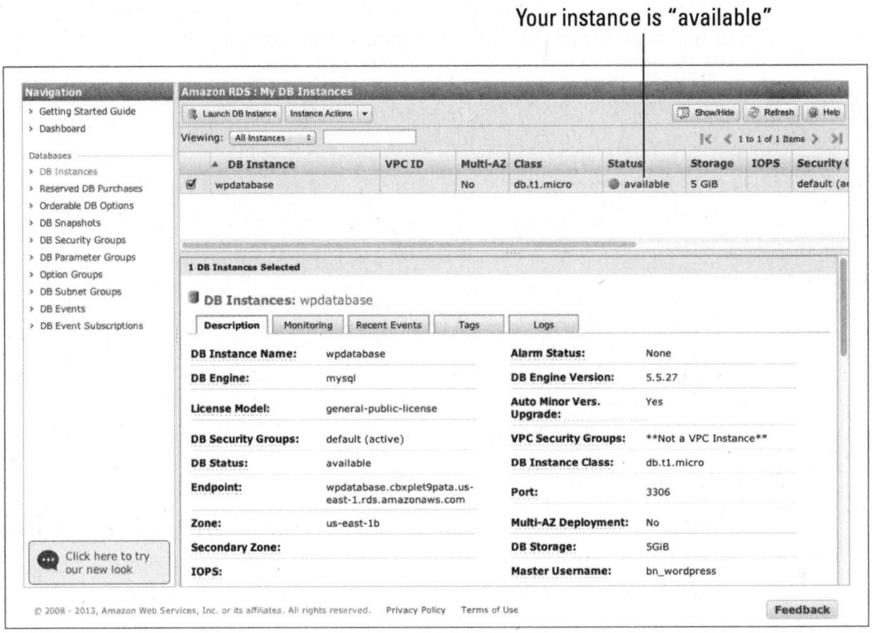

Your instance is "available"

Figure 12-26: Your RDS DB instance is available.

4. **Select EC2 Security Group from the Connection Type pull-down menu in the screen's configuration area.**

   You can leave the AWS Account ID unchanged. (This will list your account ID here; if you want to allow other accounts to access your RDS instance, you list them here.) Below the AWS account ID is the EC2 Security Group entry, where you select a security group that your RDS instance will include to allow traffic from any instance with that security group attached to it.

5. **Select the default EC2 security group from the EC2 Security Group pull-down menu.**

6. **Click the Add button on the right side of the configuration area to confirm your choice.**

   Your RDS instance can now send traffic to, and receive it from, your WordPress application instance.

The Connection Type pull-down menu

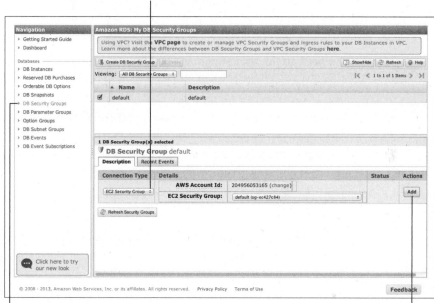

Figure 12-27:
RDS
security
groups.

The DB Security Groups link   The Add button

Modifying the WordPress application to interact with the RDS database

Creating the RDS database is only half the battle — you also have to modify your existing WordPress application so that it can communicate with it. Remember: The existing application is already up and running, with both the application and database co-located on the same instance. Given WordPress's architecture, that means even though it's a newly created application, the database already has information in it, such as which themes (the WordPress look and feel) that the application has installed, which user accounts are present (remember that the user account `user` has the password `bitnami` already installed), and any content you may have created. (My instructions don't direct you to create any new content, but, hey — WordPress makes it so easy to do that you may have gotten inspired and done something on your own!)

What this means is that you have to move the existing database from the WordPress application instance to the RDS database instance so that when

WordPress begins exchanging traffic with it, there's something to communicate to.

After you move the database into the RDS database, you need to modify WordPress so that it knows to talk to the RDS database rather than to the local one.

First, you transfer the existing database to your RDS database instance. Fortunately, that task is straightforward. You've already created the database dump, so it's only a matter of uploading it into the remote MySQL database, which requires only one command on the terminal:

1. Go back to the SSH terminal and enter the following command:

```
mysql -u bn_wordpress -pyourpassword --database=bitnami_wordpress
        --host=yourRDSdatabaseURL < backup.sql
```

Of course, you need to modify this command in two places:

- Replace `yourpassword` with the password for your WordPress application database — the same password you used when you created the database dump.

- Replace `yourRDSdatabaseURL` with the URL of your RDS database instance. You can cut and paste it from the RDS database instance detail.

This command tells MySQL to load the database dump into the database that can be contacted at the URL of the RDS database instance. (You can see in Figure 12-28 the version of the command that I executed.)

Now that the database is present on the RDS database instance, you need to modify your WordPress instance to talk to it, which involves going back into the `wp-config` file and changing the database location information so that WordPress connects to the RDS database instance rather than to the local instance.

Figure 12-28:
Creating
the RDS
database
instance
WordPress
database.

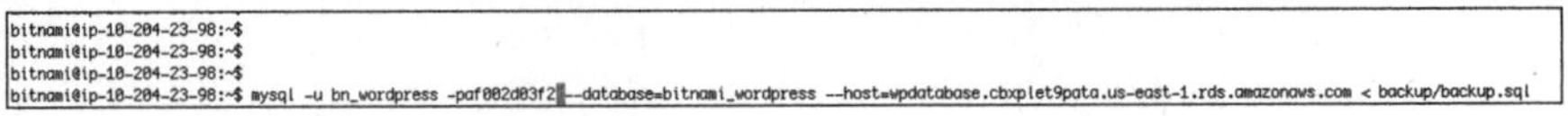

```
bitnami@ip-10-204-23-98:~$
bitnami@ip-10-204-23-98:~$
bitnami@ip-10-204-23-98:~$
bitnami@ip-10-204-23-98:~$ mysql -u bn_wordpress -paf002d83f2 --database=bitnami_wordpress --host=wpdatabase.cbxpiet9pata.us-east-1.rds.amazonaws.com < backup/backup.sql
```

2. Execute the same sudo nano **command that you executed in the previous section (**sudo nano wp-config.php**). Go to the same location within the configuration file, but scroll down until you see the MySQL hostname entry.**

3. **Change the location from localhost (which tells WordPress to connect to a database located on the same instance as WordPress itself) to the RDS database location.**

   Figure 12-29 shows you an example of how I changed my WordPress application configuration file. (Don't forget to save the file with crtl-x.)

Figure 12-29:
Modifying
the
WordPress
configura-
tion file.

```
// ** MySQL settings - You can get this info from your web host ** //
/** The name of the database for WordPress */
define('DB_NAME', 'bitnami_wordpress');

/** MySQL database username */
define('DB_USER', 'bn_wordpress');

/** MySQL database password */
define('DB_PASSWORD', 'af002d03f2');

/** MySQL hostname */
define('DB_HOST', 'wpdatabase.cbxpiet9pata.us-east-1.rds.amazonaws.com:3306');
```

Changing hostname

At this point, you've successfully modified your WordPress installation to talk to a remote database managed by AWS RDS — in other words, you've now vertically partitioned your application. Open a new browser window and connect to the WordPress instance URL. (Refer to Figure 12-10 if you're not sure how to find it.) You should see a screen like the shown in Figure 12-30.

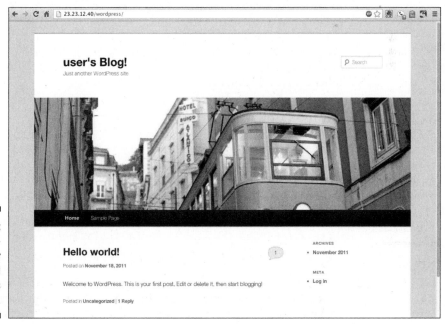

Figure 12-30:
The verti-
cally
partitioned
WordPress
application.

Creating a new Amazon Machine Image (AMI) from your WordPress application

If you've been making your way through this chapter step by step, by now you've already made some discernible progress with your WordPress application. However, you're still using a Bitnami public image, which isn't the ideal plan. You probably should create your own AMI from the modified Bitnami image. That way, any changes you make to the image will be persistent, and you're not dependent upon Bitnami's management of its public AMI.

Fortunately, it's quite easy to do. Follow these steps:

1. **In the EC2 Dashboard, select the check box for your running instance and then right-click the mouse button.**

   The drop-down menu that appears (see Figure 12-31) lists a number of options; choose Create Image (EBS AMI) — the fourth one down the list.

Figure 12-31: Starting the AMI creation process.

2. **Select Create Image (EBS AMI) from the contextual menu that appears.**

   Doing so brings up the AMI Create Image Wizard panel, as shown in Figure 12-32.

Figure 12-32:
Configuring
your AMI.

3. **Enter a name for your AMI in the Image Name field, and enter a description in the Image Description field.**

4. **(Optional) In the Volume Size field, modify the default size of the EBS volume used to store the root file system.**

5. **Click the Yes, Create button.**

   AWS puts up a confirmation panel, as shown in Figure 12-33, telling you that the image-creation process is under way, along with the ID of your new AMI (`ami-916f06f8`, in my case).

Figure 12-33:
The AMI
creation
confirmation
panel.

This process can take a number of minutes and causes the instance to reboot partway through the process, so don't be surprised if your application stops responding briefly while the new AMI is created.

Figure 12-34 shows the new AMI listed in the AMI section of the EC2 Dashboard. Note that the AMI is listed as a private image ("Owned by Me," in other words). I (or anyone using my account), therefore, am the only one authorized to perform any activities with this AMI.

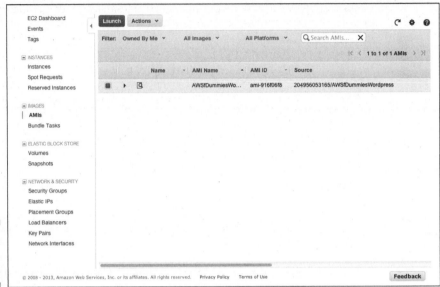

Figure 12-34:
The new,
private AMI.

Improving Application Robustness with Geographical Redundancy

If you're following along with all the steps in this chapter, let me summarize your progress: You've created a WordPress blogging site and then improved its performance by vertically partitioning it — which is a fancy way of saying that you moved the application database off the application instance. By separating the two parts of the application, you increase its total performance because two instances, rather than just one, now support the application's processing.

You also made the application more robust by using the AWS RDS service to manage the database instance. RDS takes care of managing the database and the instance it runs on, not to mention ensuring that backups and snapshots are performed.

However, both instances run in the same availability zone, which means that the application is exposed to failure if the entire zone is affected by a power outage or an Internet connectivity drop, for example.

Wouldn't it be great if you could make your application even more robust so that it isn't subject to an interruption even in the unlikely event of an availability zone outage?

Naturally, there's a fancy term for this: *Horizontal partitioning* refers to implementing redundancy at each tier of an application — in AWS terms, operating at least two instances of each application tier so that if one fails, the other stands ready to pick up the load and ensure that the application isn't interrupted. Horizontal partitioning can be taken a step further, with the redundant instances placed in different availability zones to avoid application failure caused by data center failure.

The good news is that not only is it possible to implement horizontal partitioning in AWS, Amazon makes it easy to do so. I show you how right now.

Three actions are necessary to implement horizontal partitioning for the WordPress application:

- ✔ Create a second instance of the RDS database and place it in a separate availability zone from the original instance.
- ✔ Launch a second WordPress application tier instance in a separate availability zone from the original instance.
- ✔ Create an Elastic Load Balancer and connect it to the two WordPress application instances so that it distributes traffic to them.

In the following section, I show you how to take on these tasks in order.

Horizontally partitioning the RDS database

AWS makes it ridiculously easy to place another instance of the RDS database in another availability zone:

1. **Click the RDS link on the main Management Console page.**

   The main RDS panel appears.

2. **Click Instance Actions along the top of the main RDS panel ((see Figure 12-35), and then choose Create Read Replica from the menu that appears.**

   RDS then displays the Create Read Replica DB Instance wizard panel, as shown in Figure 12-36.

The Instance Actions menu

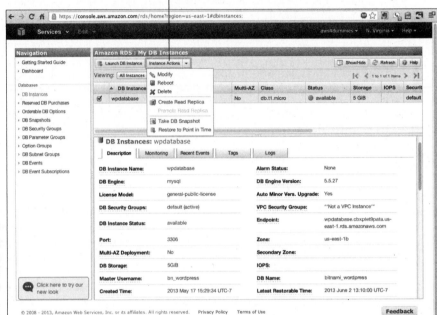

Figure 12-35:
The RDS
Instance
Actions
options.

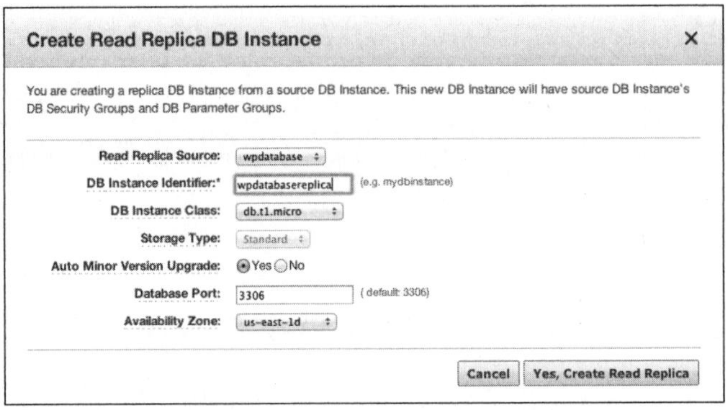

Figure 12-36:
The RDS
Read
Replica
panel in the
wizard.

3. **Select wpdatabase from the Read Replica Source drop-down menu.**

   It's the only RDS database I have, so it's the obvious choice. If I had more than one database, they would all be listed, and I could choose among them.

4. **Enter a name for your replica instance in the DB Instance Identifier field.**

   I went with wpdatabasereplica.

5. **Leave the rest of the fields unchanged from the wizard's suggestions, except for Availability Zone.**

   The wizard suggests us-east-1b, but that's where my main RDS database runs, and putting the replica there would defeat the purpose of creating this replica. Therefore, I chose another option and put the replica in us-east-1d.

6. **Click the Yes, Create Read Replica button.**

   After a few minutes, a second RDS instance is running; it will operate as a replica of the main RDS database, as shown in Figure 12-37.

This Read Replica instance is designed to provide robustness for the RDS database. Any changes to the main database are replicated to it, but it's used only in the event of main database unavailability, which can occur as a result of a technical problem (the availability zone is, well, unavailable for some reason) or because of regular RDS maintenance. The Read Replica instance doesn't act as a secondary query resource for the application. It's possible to set up MySQL to spread reads across a master database and one or more replicas, but RDS doesn't provide that functionality. If you want that capability, you have to manage MySQL directly. If you experience the need for higher read performance than can be handled by a master MySQL instance, my recommendation is to set up an intervening cache server via ElastiCache.

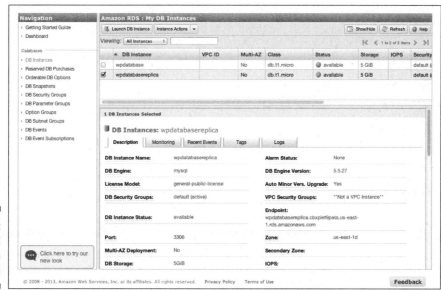

Figure 12-37:
RDS Read Replica Up and Running

That's it — you now have a horizontally scaled database tier. It took just a few clicks and no more than 10 minutes to set up (not bad for a few minutes' work).

Launching a second WordPress application tier instance in a separate availability zone

Placing an instance of your RDS database in another availability zone is the first step, but you still have to be able to launch a WordPress instance linked to that database. Luckily for you, the launching part is just as easy as the placing part. Essentially, you have to perform only the same steps you did when you first launched the WordPress application, being sure to launch the new AMI you created in the previous section of this chapter. Before starting the launch process of your new instance, be sure to click on your currently running instance in the Instance panel of the EC2 Management Console and note the Availability Zone this instance is running in.

I describe the launch process earlier in the chapter; use that section as a guide to perform this launch process.

Be sure to use the new AMI you created in the previous section of this chapter, because it contains the database configuration information to connect to your RDS instance. If you use the *original* AMI, it will attempt to do a new install and use a local database, which isn't at all what you want.

Also, choose an availability zone for your new instance that's different from the one used by your current WordPress instance. Otherwise, you get a horizontally partitioned application, but you won't have it spread across multiple availability zones, thereby losing the full level of application robustness you want. This means that when you come to the second panel of the launch wizard (as shown in Figure 12-2), you must choose an availability zone different from the one you noted by looking at the current instance's information.

After you launch the second instance, you'll have two instances, each running in a separate Availability Zone, as shown in Figure 12-38. From the figure you can see I have two instances running, each with its own instance ID, but both share a common AMI ID. They're operating in different availability zones; that's not indicated in the figure, but — trust me — they are.

A common ID

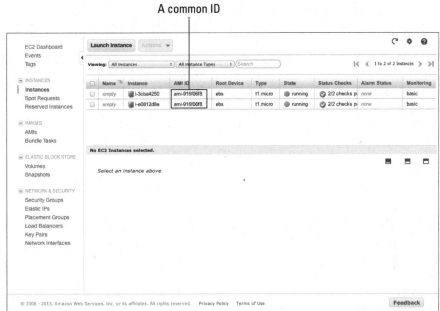

Figure 12-38:
Multiple
WordPress
instances.

Creating an Elastic Load Balancer

After you have two instances of the application running, you should spread traffic among them, using a mechanism that will ensure that, in case one of the instances becomes unavailable, all traffic is sent to the instance that is still operating properly.

The AWS Elastic Load Balancer is perfect for this task. It's easy to set up, and it performs health checks on the instances it's connected to; if one becomes unresponsive, the ELB discontinues sending traffic to it.

Setting up ELB is straightforward:

1. **Starting from the EC2 Dashboard, click the Load Balancers link near the bottom of the Navigation pane on the lower-left side.**

   Doing so brings up the ELB landing page, which you can see in Figure 12-39.

   Because I have no existing ELB instances, the page invites me to create a new load balancer.

The Create Load Balance button

Figure 12-39:
The Elastic
Load
Balancer
main page.

2. **Click the Create Load Balancer button.**

   The first screen of the ELB wizard opens, as shown in Figure 12-40.

Figure 12-40:
Naming
your Elastic
Load
Balancer.

3. **Enter a name for your load balancer in the Load Balancer Name field, and leave the other defaults as is.**

   AWS4DummiesLB is a good name. (It's the one I went with.)

   To support additional load balancer protocols (port 443 to support SSL, for example), you can select them from the Listener Configuration pull-down menu or define your own, if you want to use a nonstandard port.

4. **Click Continue.**

   Doing so brings you to the second screen of the ELB wizard, as shown in Figure 12-41. On this screen, you configure the health-check information, which defines how ELB assesses whether the instances attached to it are operational. Leave the default settings in place in this example.

5. **Click Continue on the new screen.**

   On the new screen that appears, you define which instances to attach to the new load balancer. The wizard lists all instances you have running and allows you to choose which ones you want to be managed by this load balancer.

6. **Because you want to attach both instances to the load balancer, keep both check boxes selected, as shown in Figure 12-42, and then click Continue.**

Create a New Load Balancer   Cancel ⊠

> DEFINE LOAD BALANCER • CONFIGURE HEALTH CHECK • ADD EC2 INSTANCES • REVIEW

Your load balancer will automatically perform health checks on your EC2 instances and only route traffic to instances that pass the health check. If an instance fails the health check, it is automatically removed from the load balancer. Customize the health check to meet your specific needs.

Configuration Options:

Ping Protocol: [HTTP ÷]

Ping Port: [80]

Ping Path: [/index.html]

Advanced Options:

Response Timeout: [5] Seconds — Time to wait when receiving a response from the health check (2 sec - 60 sec).

Health Check Interval: [0.5] Minutes — Amount of time between health checks (0.1 min - 5 min)

Unhealthy Threshold: ⊘ 2 3 4 5 6 7 8 9 10 — Number of consecutive health check failures before declaring an EC2 instance unhealthy.

Healthy Threshold: 2 3 4 5 6 7 8 9 **10** — Number of consecutive health check successes before declaring an EC2 instance healthy.

‹ Back   [Continue ▸]

Figure 12-41: Setting the health-check criteria.

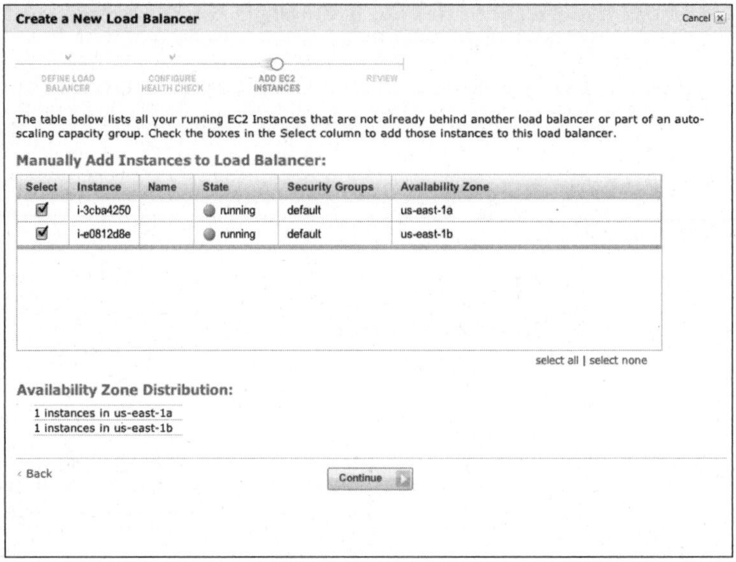

Create a New Load Balancer   Cancel ⊠

DEFINE LOAD   CONFIGURE   ADD EC2   REVIEW
BALANCER   HEALTH CHECK   INSTANCES

The table below lists all your running EC2 Instances that are not already behind another load balancer or part of an auto-scaling capacity group. Check the boxes in the Select column to add those instances to this load balancer.

Manually Add Instances to Load Balancer:

Select	Instance	Name	State	Security Groups	Availability Zone
☑	i-3cba4250		● running	default	us-east-1a
☑	i-e0812d8e		● running	default	us-east-1b

select all | select none

Availability Zone Distribution:

1 instances in us-east-1a
1 instances in us-east-1b

‹ Back   Continue ▸

Figure 12-42:
Manually
adding
instances
to your
Elastic Load
Balancer.

The wizard displays a review panel (see Figure 12-43) identifying all the information entered on the previous screens and invites you to create the Elastic Load Balancer.

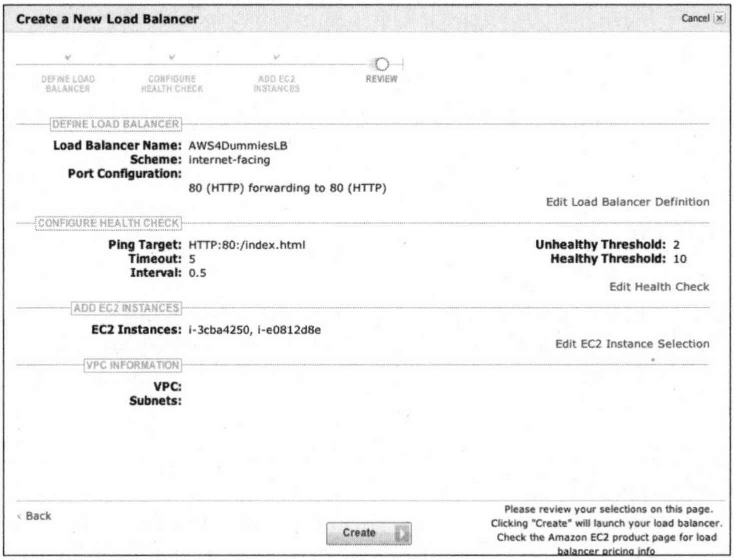

Create a New Load Balancer   Cancel ⊠

DEFINE LOAD   CONFIGURE   ADD EC2   REVIEW
BALANCER   HEALTH CHECK   INSTANCES

DEFINE LOAD BALANCER

Load Balancer Name: AWS4DummiesLB
Scheme: internet-facing
Port Configuration:
80 (HTTP) forwarding to 80 (HTTP)

Edit Load Balancer Definition

CONFIGURE HEALTH CHECK

Ping Target: HTTP:80:/index.html   **Unhealthy Threshold:** 2
Timeout: 5   **Healthy Threshold:** 10
Interval: 0.5

Edit Health Check

ADD EC2 INSTANCES

EC2 Instances: i-3cba4250, i-e0812d8e

Edit EC2 Instance Selection

VPC INFORMATION

VPC:
Subnets:

Figure 12-43:
The wizard's
Summary
panel.

‹ Back   Create ▸   Please review your selections on this page.
                                  Clicking "Create" will launch your load balancer.
                                  Check the Amazon EC2 product page for load
                                  balancer pricing info.

7. Click Create and let ELB do its magic.

It usually takes a few minutes (in this example, fewer than ten) for AWS to set up the ELB, attach the running instances, and make the ELB available. However, after a bit you should see the screen shown in Figure 12-44, which shows that the ELB is now operational. If you look at the Status line near the bottom of Figure 12-44, you can see that it shows 2 of 2 instances in service — two instances are attached to the ELB and are responding properly to the ELB health check.

The DNS name for your ELB

Figure 12-44: The operational Elastic Load Balancer.

The status line

The ELB has a DNS name that can be used to connect to it. Copy the top line in the Summary panel's DNS Name section and paste it into a new browser window. This should show you the Bitnami WordPress landing page, as illustrated in Figure 12-45.

What's happening, however, is quite different from the previous time you saw this landing page. With the ELB in place, it receives all traffic from the Internet and the ELB distributes each request according to the availability of WordPress instances to receive the traffic. The distribution rule for this ELB is "round robin," which means that each instance receives $1/n$ of the traffic, distributed sequentially, where n is the number of operational instances connected to the ELB. In this example, because of the round robin rule, each instance receives 1/2 of all traffic and receives every other traffic request.

That's it. With just a few configuration tweaks and a little typing, you've changed your application from one with little resilience to one that's both horizontally scaled and geographically distributed — one that is robust up to and including complete failure of the availability zone.

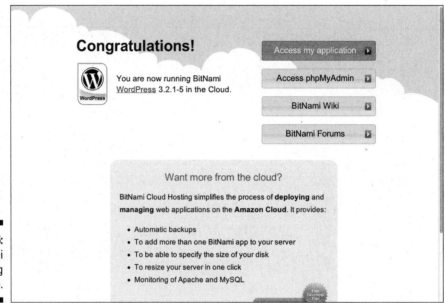

Part IV
The Part of Tens

Enjoy an additional AWS Part of Tens chapter online at www.dummies.com/extras/amazonwebservices.

In this part . . .

✔ Check out my ten reasons to use Amazon Web Services.

✔ See the ten design principles to use when you create your AWS applications so that they'll be more scalable, robust, secure, and cost-effective.

✔ Enjoy an additional AWS Part of Tens chapter online at www.dummies.com/extras/amazonwebservices.

Chapter 13

Ten Reasons to Use Amazon Web Services

● ●

*T*here are many users of AWS who struggle to describe why they adopted it. Still others are interested in AWS, but aren't sure about exactly what it is. And others who know what it is, and why they adopted it, but get tongue-tied when asked to justify their decision by higher management. To solve all those problems in one fell swoop, here is a list of the ten best reasons to use AWS.

AWS Provides IT Agility

IT has a reputation as the "Department of No." Though it's true that some IT organizations seem to revel in a *Dilbert*-like obstinacy, where innumerable and inexplicable roadblocks are placed in the way of anyone seeking access to the wizardry of "infrastructure," others are frustrated by the sheer complexity of coordinating many different resources, each with its own interface and configuration rules, all of which must be successfully stitched together to provide access to computing resources. Most of these multidepartment, manual, time-consuming efforts are the result of the years-long build-up of established processes executed in serial fashion, resulting in IT provisioning cycles that commonly require weeks to months to deliver computing resources. The result of all this: It's slower than molasses and widely despised.

Amazon, as is its wont, rethought the provisioning process as though it were being designed from scratch and implemented it as an integrated and automated service. Because every part of the infrastructure is managed via an API, no human interaction is necessary for the installation or configuration of resources. And, because the services are offered in a fine-grained fashion (IP addresses are managed separately from storage, as one example), resources can be defined and started in parallel, rather than having to be done one step at a time. The result: IT resources are available in minutes, not in weeks or months.

Consequently, AWS enables the presence of *IT agility* — the ability of IT organizations to respond rapidly to resource requirements — and allows it to stop being thought of as the "Department of No."

AWS Provides Business Agility

Guess what? If you're a business unit within a company — sales or human resources, for example — *you're* the one who calls IT the "Department of No." And being faced with a slow-moving IT organization today isn't only inconvenient — it's also dangerous to your business.

This danger results from the changing nature of IT applications. In the past, IT applications primarily automated internal company processes @— payroll, invoicing, document management — commonly referred to as *systems of record* because they, well, recorded information. Applications are now far more likely to be used to interact with customers or, indeed, to enable customers to "self-service" their needs. These applications are often called *systems of engagement* because they foster engagement with parties outside the organization. And the rise of smartphones, tablets, and sophisticated websites raises the bar on customer expectations. When I realize that a company I use offers me a way to check the status of my orders online, I quickly expect the other companies I use to offer the same capability. And if those other companies don't provide it, I'm likely to look for other providers that do.

In other words, to satisfy today's customers, businesses have to roll out new applications quickly — to be *agile,* in other words. And AWS enables business agility enormously. It's no secret that a significant part of the AWS user base is made up of business units that adopt AWS as a way around IT and its protracted provisioning processes. This business unit adoption is sometimes called *shadow IT* or, even more pejoratively, *rogue IT.* No matter what you call it, this adoption occurs because business units feel the need to roll out new applications quickly in order to respond to market demands — and AWS helps businesses quicken their response time by being more agile.

AWS Offers a Rich Services Ecosystem

One drawback to other cloud service providers is how much work users have to do to build applications using functionality like queues, administrative alerting, dynamic scaling in response to user load, and the like. Though those other services capably provide virtual machines on demand, the building out of applications with software components and outside services is left as an exercise to the student, so to speak.

Building an application can take a long time, therefore, because the developer needs to install and configure the software components, all of which takes time. For components that require commercial licensing, you have to arrange for payment — which can take a long time, given the complexities of budget approval and contract negotiation. Online services (a tax calculation service, for example) may not be available on the chosen cloud service provider, thereby requiring a call across the Internet to access the service at another online location, which imposes network latency and hinders application performance.

Amazon makes application development faster and less difficult with a rich services ecosystem capable of offering your favorite search engine benefits:

✔ **A range of services as part of its AWS offering:** These services range from foundation building blocks, such as object and volume storage, to platform services, such as queues and e-mail, all the way to full applications, such as Elastic MapReduce and Redshift.

✔ **Services hosted on AWS by many third-party companies:** For example, both Informatica and Dell Boomi offer application integration services within AWS. AWS users can integrate applications running in AWS via these services and never have network traffic exit AWS, causing lower network latency and better application performance.

✔ **All home-grown (and most third-party) AWS services are offered with the same pricing model as AWS:** Pricing is standardized with simplified contracts that can be executed online. The result is that users can avoid protracted contract negotiations and large upfront payments in favor of on-demand payment, which aligns with the user of AWS itself.

The rich AWS ecosystem is one of the least trumpeted but most valuable aspects of AWS. Quickness of response (agility, in other words) is critical today, for business in general *and* IT in particular. The rich AWS ecosystem fosters agility, and it's an important reason to use AWS.

AWS Simplifies IT Operations

IT operations are thankless — and endless — tasks. In fact, the term *Sisyphean* may have been coined to describe the eternal job of administering IT resources. Earlier in this chapter, I outline how AWS makes resource provisioning easier, but AWS also makes ongoing operations simpler.

First, because AWS takes responsibility for much of the traditional IT infrastructure — buildings, power, network, and physical servers, for example — a huge amount of work is taken off the IT plate, and the burden for IT operations shrinks immediately.

"But wait," as the infomercials say, "there's more!" Beyond taking responsibility for the physical infrastructure, AWS also takes on much of the IT administrative burden associated with systems operations. For example, the relational database service (RDS) takes on responsibility for running databases, backing them up, and restarting failed instances to ensure necessary uptime. All these tasks are important, and all of them occupy people's time and attention.

By simplifying IT operations, AWS allows its users to focus on the truly important part of IT: applications. In effect, AWS allows a user to devote more of the IT budget to the qualities that differentiate the business while letting users reduce investment in the important, but nondifferentiating tasks associated with "keeping the lights on."

AWS Spans the Globe

AWS is organized into regions, and Amazon has regions throughout the world: the United States, Europe, South America, and a number of locations in the Asia Pacific region.

Because AWS is a global service, users can take advantage of a service located nearby, which results in lower network latency and better application performance. The global nature of AWS also leads to local services ecosystems, in the form of native consultancies and system integrators, making it easy for users to obtain help delivered in native languages and with local expertise.

Amazon continues to roll out new regional locations, so you're likely to have access to a nearby service location as well as to the rich AWS ecosystem.

AWS Is the Leading Cloud-Computing Service Provider

Yogi Berra, the Hall of Fame baseball catcher, is a font of wisdom, expressed by malaprops, in seemingly confused fashion. Once, when invited to a popular restaurant, he politely declined, saying, "Nobody goes there any more — it's too crowded." His insight, pithily stated, is based on the fact that most services, once they gain popularity, inevitably decline based on overwhelmed staff, resource shortages, and competition between users.

AWS, on the other hand, is incredibly popular, but its popularity has the effect of making the service better. Today, Amazon has a reinforcing cycle occurring:

✔ Having more users creates a greater volume of use, which increases the amount of hardware Amazon buys, which reduces its costs via economies of scale, which are passed on to users in the form of lower prices.

✔ Because of the large number of users, companies that offer complementary services (online application integration, for example) decide to place their services in AWS first, which makes the overall service better, which attracts more users.

✔ As more people and companies use AWS, more knowledge is made available in the form of human capital and other resources (like this book!). This knowledge makes it easier for new users to get started and to be productive quickly, making AWS more attractive.

So, unlike Yogi, you should embrace AWS's popularity and recognize that its status as the largest cloud service provider brings enormous benefits to you and that, moreover, those benefits will continue to grow as the service expands. It's another gift that keeps on giving.

AWS Enables Innovation

Everywhere you turn, the word *innovation* is a hot topic. People recognize that innovation makes life better and that it can improve the future for generations to come. It probably won't surprise you, given my excitement about AWS, to know that I am firmly convinced that cloud computing wouldn't exist without the presence of Amazon. All of the incumbent technology market leaders had no incentive to change the way they did business. It took an outsider like Amazon, which had no legacy business to protect, to rethink the way technology is delivered.

AWS has transformed how technology is offered to customers and, as a result, has enabled an explosion of innovation. The innovation and low cost associated with AWS allow small and large companies alike to launch new offerings quickly and inexpensively. As one innovation consultant put it: "AWS has reduced the cost of failure. AWS lets you easily try out a new product to see whether it "gets traction." Moreover, if a new offering gets traction and starts to accelerate, AWS lets you easily scale it up. On the other hand, if the service doesn't achieve adoption, that's no problem — the ease of shutting down AWS resources means that not much is lost if a potential innovative offering doesn't pan out."

The kinds of things that AWS enables range from the useful-but-not-life-changing (Netflix video streaming) to, well, life-changing (enhanced drug discovery via genetic analysis from companies like Eli Lilly).

I predict that even more innovation will occur as more people and companies become familiar with AWS and its capabilities. AWS will be to the information age what Henry Ford's mass production was to the industrial age — and we all know how that turned out!

AWS Is Cost Effective

Commenters who analyze Silicon Valley trends note that the cost of starting an Internet business is now less than 10 percent of what it cost a mere decade ago. Much of that cost reduction is due to AWS: its on-demand low pricing and easy termination with no penalties make it possible to use and pay for exactly as much computing capacity as you need, when you need it.

The cost effectiveness of AWS isn't limited to start-ups, though. Every company can benefit from access to inexpensive computing that doesn't require a lengthy commitment. It's a sign of the powerful benefits of AWS that much of the existing vendor community is terrified of what will happen when their customers begin to demand AWS-like prices and convenience from *them*.

Amazon is a unique company. Unlike many companies that strive for efficiency to raise their own profit margins, Amazon passes on the benefits of efficiency in the form of lower prices. There's no reason to expect that this approach will change.

If you're a part of any company small or large, Amazon can make your IT dollars go further. It's significantly more cost effective than the traditional mode of obtaining IT resources: large up-front payments with little certainty about whether the amount provisioned is too small (or too much).

AWS Aligns Your Organization with the Future of Technology

Every 10 to 15 years, the IT industry is profoundly disrupted by the emergence of a new platform — a new form of computing that changes the way applications are built and used. In the 1980s, the rise of networked PCs (the client-server architecture) transformed mainframes into a legacy environment — and led to Microsoft becoming the dominant player in the software industry. Likewise, in the 1990s the Internet made the web (and the HTTP protocol) the de facto architecture for all applications — and led to the dominance of companies such as Google and, yes, Amazon.

Cloud computing is the next-generation platform for computing. Its characteristics of highly scalable, on-demand computing services that are available within minutes and carrying no requirement for long-term commitment will become the foundation for all future applications. As the saying goes, resistance is futile.

Amazon Web Services, by far the leading cloud computing provider in the industry, is growing at rates of more than 100 percent. Its record of innovation and price competitiveness is unmatched in the industry. I predict that, ten years from now, AWS will be the Microsoft or Google of its era. Your organization *must* become familiar with AWS and figure out how to use it effectively — otherwise, it may find itself the IT equivalent of a buggy whip manufacturer after Henry Ford invented the assembly line.

AWS Is Good for Your Career

Great careers are built on being the right person in the right place at the right time. Being the right person is all about you — your capacity for hard work, productive work relationships, and intelligence, for example. These characteristics will help you be successful no matter which field or role you work in.

But being in the right place at the right time — that has a lot to do with insight about where a new market, made possible by some type of innovation, is emerging and planting your flag there. People who moved into the automobile industry in the 1920s or into the television business in the 1950s or into the Internet in the 1990s all encountered enormous opportunities as a new market searched for expertise to enable great companies to be built.

Technology innovation creates huge skills gaps in the industry and makes those with knowledge and experience invaluable. If you believe that AWS is the next-generation platform, it too can represent "the right place at the right time" for you.

Chapter 14

Ten Design Principles for Cloud Applications

· ·

*T*hose in the know will tell you that you have to use the right tool for the job. For the new generation of webscale applications like Pinterest, AWS is the right tool. Overlooked in that truism is the undeniable fact that using a tool effectively requires having the right skills. With respect to AWS, the right skills involve aligning your application design with AWS's operational characteristics. It's critical to get the application design right — so here are ten design principles to help you get your alignment straight.

Everything Fails All the Time

The truism "Everything fails all the time" is adapted from Werner Vogels, the chief technology officer of Amazon. IT departments have traditionally attempted to render both infrastructure and applications impervious to failure: A hardware resource or an application component that "fell down on the job" increased the urgency of the search for perfection in order to banish failure. Unfortunately, that search was never successful — the failure of resources and applications has been part of the IT world from the beginning.

Amazon starts from a different perspective, borne of its experience as the world's largest online retailer and as one of *the* largest webscale companies worldwide. When you run data centers containing thousands of servers and tens of thousands of disk drives, resource failure is a daily occurrence. And when a hardware resource fails, the software or data residing on that resource suddenly stops working or becomes unavailable.

Neither can you count on the smooth and continuous functioning of software components or external services — they fail, too. An element of a software package configuration or an unforeseen program execution path or an excessive load on an external service means that, even if hardware continues operating properly, portions of an application can fail.

Therefore, the single most important cloud application design principle is to acknowledge that the perfect system doesn't exist — that failure is a constant companion. Rather than become frustrated by this state of affairs, you should recognize this principle and embrace it. Having recognized that failure is inevitable, be sure to adopt cloud application measures to mitigate circumstances and insulate yourself from failure. The rest of this chapter is all about insulating yourself from failure — so read on!

Redundancy Protects Against Resource Failure

If you can't count on individual resources to always work properly, what can you do? The best insurance against resource failure is to use redundant resources, managed in such a way that if a single resource fails, the remaining resource (or resources — you can have more than one additional resource in a redundant design) can seamlessly pick up the workload and continue operating with no interruption.

Amazon has adopted this principle in its AWS offering. Many of its services use redundant resources. For example, every S3 object has three copies, each stored on a single machine. Likewise, the AWS Queue service spreads user queues across multiple machines, using redundancy to maintain availability.

Design your applications to operate with two (or more!) instances at each tier in the application. Every tier should be cross-connected to all instances in any adjacent tier. In this way, if a resource (either hardware or software) becomes unavailable, the remaining resources can accept all of the application traffic and maintain application availability.

Of course, if resource failure brings your application to a state in which only a single resource is still operating at a given tier, redundancy is no longer protecting you — launch a new resource to ensure that redundancy is retained. I address this state of affairs later in this chapter.

Geographic Distribution Protects Against Infrastructure Failure

Okay, you recognize the need to protect yourself against resource failure, whether it's hardware or software, and you resolve to use multiple instances to avoid application failure in the event of a server crash, disk breakdown, or even software or service unresponsiveness. But that still doesn't help if a problem occurs at a higher level, such as the entire data center that your application runs going dark from a power outage or natural disaster.

Well, just as you use redundancy at the individual-component level, you use redundancy at the data-center level to avoid this problem. Rather than run your application on multiple instances within a single data center, you run those instances in *different* data centers. Fortunately, Amazon makes it easy with its Regional Availability Zone architecture. Every region has at least two availability zones, which are essentially separate data centers, to provide higher-level redundancy for applications.

Availability zones are located far enough apart to be resistant to natural disasters, so even if one is knocked off the air by a storm or an earthquake, another one remains operating so that you can continue to run your application. And availability zones are connected by high-speed network connections to ensure that your application's performance doesn't suffer if it spans multiple availability zones.

Monitoring Prevents Problems

Redundancy is good, and it's important to avoid a situation in which your application, once neat and tidy with redundant resources, becomes nonredundant through the failure of a redundant resource. The question then is, how to *know* when the formerly neat-and-tidy redundant application is no longer so because of failure?

The answer is that you keep an eye on the application to determine when resource failure occurs. Now, one way to do this is to station someone at the AWS Management Console to click a mouse button continually in order to refresh the display. Of course, this method has two drawbacks:

- ✔ The button clicker will become incredibly bored.
- ✔ It's a huge waste of money because you'll pay an experienced (and expensive) operations person to mindlessly click mouse buttons.

A much more efficient mode of operation is to have the system *itself* tell you when something fails — a process known as *monitoring*. You set up an automated resource to take the place of a human, and whenever something important happens, it notifies you (*alerts* you, in other words). Automated monitoring has two virtues:

- ✔ Computers don't get bored, so watching over systems endlessly doesn't faze them in the least.
- ✔ It's cheap! You don't pay salaries to computers.

Fortunately, AWS offers two excellent services to support automated monitoring:

- ✔ **CloudWatch:** You can set it up to monitor many AWS resources, including EC2 instances, EBS volumes, SQS queues, and more. CloudWatch is free for certain capabilities, and it's inexpensive for additional capabilities. (For more on CloudWatch, see Chapter 10.)

- ✔ **Simple Notification Service (SNS):** It can deliver alerts to you via e-mail, SMS, and even HTTP so that you can publish alerts to a web page. You can easily wire CloudWatch into SNS so that alerts from CloudWatch are automatically and immediately delivered to you, thereby enabling you to take quick action to resolve system deficiencies, including resource failure resulting in a lack of redundancy. (For more on SNS, see Chapter 8.)

Monitoring is a critical companion to redundant application design, and I encourage you to integrate it into your application from the get-go.

Utilization Review Prevents Waste

It's an unfortunate fact that many, many AWS users fail to keep track of the resources they use, which can lead to underused, or even *unused,* resources running in AWS.

This problem is significant because AWS resources continue to run up charges, even if the resources aren't performing useful work. An entire chapter of this book (Chapter 11) is devoted to discussing this problem and providing guidance about how to avoid it. Here's the short version of my advice:

- ✔ Use the AWS Trusted Advisor service or a commercial utilization and cost tracking services like Cloudyn (which kindly provided the fascinating utilization information discussed in Chapter 11).

- ✔ Design your application so that it can have individual resources added or subtracted so that resource utilization rates stay high and resources don't sit around idle or lightly utilized.

- ✔ Use AWS EC2 reserved instances to reduce the cost of the computing side of your application.

- ✔ Regularly review your AWS bills to see if there are resources or applications being used that you don't know about — and then go find out about them!

Again, for a more in depth look at how to effectively manage your resources, check out Chapter 11.

Application Management Automates Administration

In the earlier section "Monitoring Prevents Problems," I point out that, rather than dedicate a person's efforts to monitoring an application 24/7, monitoring and alerts allow the *system* to track an application's behavior and then notify a human that intervention is required.

The drawback to this setup is that you still need a human to implement the intervention.

Wouldn't it be cool if no human was required in order to take action, based on the specific situation? The good news is that AWS management systems have this capability. Amazon offers three: CloudWatch, Auto Scaling, and Elastic Beanstalk, all discussed in Chapter 10. And commercial offerings have management capability that extends beyond the type that Amazon itself offers.

Common to all these management systems is a set of monitoring capabilities, along with the ability to execute AWS instructions to perform tasks such as restarting resources when failure occurs or starting and adding resources to an application when the user load increases to the extent of requiring more computing capacity.

As applications become more complex, sophisticated management systems are practically a prerequisite. Trying to track and respond to application issues thrown up by a six- or seven-tiered application that uses a number of AWS services is quite challenging. It makes sense to seek out tools to help reduce the burden.

Security Design Prevents Breaches and Data Loss

The number-one concern expressed about cloud computing in general, and AWS in particular, is security. This area of concern focuses on AWS itself, with common questions raised about how well Amazon manages its data center security measures or to what extent Amazon can prevent its personnel from improperly accessing user systems. (Answers: very well, probably better than most IT organizations can do themselves, and nothing can prevent someone from improperly using her administrative permissions, although Amazon has measures in place to monitor improper access.)

Unfortunately, the focus on Amazon's security is misplaced. First, as just noted, Amazon does a good job of securing its offering, at least as well as the best in the industry and certainly better than most. Second (and this point is crucial), users retain significant responsibility for their application's security when using AWS, and *user security shortcomings account for by far the largest percentage of security issues within the AWS environment.*

You *must* recognize your security responsibility and take measures to implement and support it. Your application design can help prevent security breaches and potential access to critical data. Though Chapter 7 covers these issues quite thoroughly (and I encourage you to read it at your earliest opportunity), here are some guidelines, boiled down to the basics:

✔ **Use multiple security groups to partition your application.** Doing so ensures that malicious actors cannot gain direct access to application logic and data. Methods to implement partitioned security groups are discussed in Chapter 7, so look there for details.

✔ **Use Amazon Virtual Private Cloud (VPC) to shield EC2 instances that don't require external access from the Internet.** VPC is an outstanding way to increase application security and will become the default operating environment for AWS, so learn how to use it.

✔ **Implement the specific application security measures outlined in Chapter 7.** Patch software packages quickly, implement intrusion-prevention software, and manage security keys carefully.

Encryption Ensures Privacy

One concern that potential users of AWS often raise centers around what can be done to prevent inappropriate data access by AWS personnel. The answer is "nothing." The best-designed security systems in the world have too often fallen vulnerable to malicious insiders. Amazon screens its employees, and methodically tracks all employee access to AWS infrastructure, but the simple truth is that it would always be possible — at least theoretically — for an Amazon employee to access your data, whether on disk or during transit across the AWS network.

Does this information imply that someone with a clear need to avoid even a theoretically possible access breach is out of luck when it comes to using AWS? No, not at all.

Rather than attempt to prevent access to the resources on which your important data is stored or transmitted, follow this approach: Recognize the potential for such access, and make it useless if it occurs. The way to do this is to make the data itself useless via encryption. With data privately encrypted by the user and available only to those with the private key associated with the data encryption, it doesn't matter whether Amazon personnel attempt to access the data — it looks like meaningless gobbledygook from the perspective of the intruder.

This approach to security — data encryption — can be applied in two ways to protect data security:

- ✔ **Encrypt network traffic.** Network traffic — often referred to as "data in transit" — can easily be encrypted using the Secure Sockets Layer (SSL). SSL ensures that no one can gain useful information from accessing network traffic. This approach can also be used for network traffic across the Internet, preventing outside intruders from accessing network traffic.

- ✔ **Encrypt data residing on storage.** Data residing on storage is commonly called *data at rest* — it refers to data that's written to and read from disk storage in encrypted fashion. The private keys to access disk data can be held secure on your own premises, preventing access to your data by any Amazon personnel.

With these two measures, along with the security-design measures mentioned in the previous section, you can make your application as secure as possible, and certainly as secure as it will be running in your own data center.

Tier-Based Design Increases Efficiency

I mention multi-tier application design several times throughout this book, noting, for example, that a tiered design makes it possible to improve security by partitioning security groups.

It may not be as obvious that using a tier-based application design, particularly one that uses redundant, *scalable* tiers (tiers that can grow and shrink by the addition or subtraction of instances to the tier) can also improve the efficiency of your application.

The reason is that tiered, scalable applications can adjust the number of computing resources assigned to an application, growing and shrinking dynamically in response to user load. This approach ensures that all running resources are being used to support user traffic and not sitting idle. The idea is that these resources should be available for use in case the application load grows sufficiently to require the processing of the idle instance.

Moreover, partitioning your application into tiers allows you to work on improving one portion of it while leaving the rest undisturbed. You can improve the efficiency of the entire application while methodically moving through the tiers, improving performance and reducing resource consumption one tier at a time.

Even if your application begins life as a single instance, with all software packages contained in a single, integrated code base, you should design it so that it may have portions removed and moved to other tiers. This approach supports incremental, gradual improvement to ensure that high resource consumption is reduced over time.

Good Application Architecture Prevents Technical Debt

Technical debt refers to a concept in computer science in which software code, having been implemented earlier in a project's lifespan, ends up poorly written and not efficient. Technical debt, like its financial counterpart, imposes a cost and hampers efficiency.

The obvious way to reduce technical debt is to periodically revisit and rethink application design and implementation, with an eye toward updating the design and reimplementing important portions of the code.

The most effective method for completing this task is to have all portions of the application designed with an input-and-output interface that defines how an application portion (or package) is called by others and how it calls on other application portions to fulfill their responsibilities. When you use this design approach, different components or portions of an application can be updated or replaced without disturbing the other portions of the application or the overall application itself — as long as the interface "contracts" are adhered to (in other words, the interface operates as advertised).

Updating the functionality of an application as needed is easier when the section that the functionality resides in can be easily modified without disturbing other portions of the application. Without this approach, an application that consists of a large, mingled code base is nearly impossible to modify, if for no other reason than no single software engineer is likely to be able to understand all the different portions of the application design or code.

So when you move forward with your AWS applications (inspired and guided by this book, I hope), concentrate on partitioning the application into tiers and ensure that each partition has good input and output interfaces defined to enable you to avoid the dreaded technical debt.

Index

• *L* •